DAILY LIGHT
on the
DAILY PATH

DAILY LIGHT
ON THE
DAILY PATH
NEW KING JAMES VERSION

THOMAS NELSON PUBLISHERS
Nashville · Camden · New York

Second printing

Copyright © 1983 by Thomas Nelson Publishers

Published in Nashville, Tennessee, by Thomas Nelson,
Inc., and distributed in Canada by Lawson Falle, Ltd.,
Cambridge, Ontario.

Printed in the United States of America.

Scripture Quotations are from the New King James Version.
Copyright © 1979, 1980, 1982, Thomas Nelson, Inc., Publishers.

ISBN 0-8407-5278-4

Your word is a lamp to my feet
And a light to my path (Ps. 119:105).

DAILY LIGHT
on the
DAILY PATH

MORNING

> **But one thing I do, forgetting those things which are behind and reaching forward to those things which are ahead, . . . I press toward the goal for the prize of the upward call of God in Christ Jesus.**

Father, I desire that they . . . whom You gave Me may be with Me where I am, that they may behold My glory which You have given Me. ◊ I know whom I have believed and am persuaded that He is able to keep what I have committed to Him until that Day. ◊ He who has begun a good work in you will complete it until the day of Jesus Christ.

Do you not know that those who run in a race all run, but one receives the prize? Run in such a way that you may obtain it. ◊ Lay aside every weight, and the sin which so easily ensnares us, and let us run with endurance the race that is set before us, . . . looking unto Jesus.

PHIL 3:13-14. JOHN 17:24. 2 TIM 1:12. PHIL 1:6. 1 COR 9:24-25. HEB 12:1-2

EVENING

> **The Lord, He is the one who goes before you. He will be with you, He will not leave you nor forsake you.**

If Your Presence does not go with us, do not bring us up from here. ◊ O Lord, I know the way of man is not in himself; it is not in man who walks to direct his own steps.

The steps of a good man are ordered by the Lord, and He delights in his way. Though he fall, he shall not be utterly cast down; for the Lord upholds him with His hand.

I am continually with You; You hold me by my right hand. You will guide me with Your counsel, and afterward receive me to glory. ◊ For I am persuaded that neither death nor life, nor angels nor principalities nor powers, nor things present nor things to come, . . . nor height nor depth, nor any other created thing, shall be able to separate us from the love of God which is in Christ Jesus our Lord.

DEUT 31:8. EX 33:15. JER 10:23. PS 37:23-24. PS 73:23-24. ROM 8:38-39

JANUARY 2

MORNING

Sing to the Lord a new song.

Sing aloud to God our strength; make a joyful shout to the God of Jacob. Raise a song and strike the timbrel, the pleasant harp with the lute. ◊ He has put a new song in my mouth—praise to our God; many will see it and fear, and will trust in the Lord.

Be strong and of good courage; do not be afraid, nor be dismayed, for the Lord your God is with you wherever you go. ◊ The joy of the Lord is your strength. ◊ Paul . . . thanked God and took courage.

The night is far spent, the day is at hand. Therefore let us cast off the works of darkness, and let us put on the armor of light. Let us walk properly, as in the day, not in revelry and drunkenness, not in licentiousness and lewdness, not in strife and envy. But put on the Lord Jesus Christ, and make no provision for the flesh, to fulfill its lusts.

IS 42:10. PS 81:1-2. PS 40:3. JOSH 1:9. NEH 8:10. ACTS 28:15. ROM 13:12-14

EVENING

Let my prayer be set before You as incense, the lifting up of my hands as the evening sacrifice.

You shall make an altar to burn incense on; you shall make it of acacia wood. ◊ And you shall put it before the veil that is before the ark of the Testimony, before the mercy seat that is over the Testimony, where I will meet with you. Aaron shall burn on it sweet incense every morning; when he tends the lamps, he shall burn incense on it. And when Aaron lights the lamps at twilight, he shall burn incense on it, a perpetual incense before the Lord throughout your generations.

Therefore [Jesus] is also able to save to the uttermost those who come to God through Him, since He ever lives to make intercession for them. ◊ The smoke of the incense, with the prayers of the saints, ascended before God from the angel's hand.

You also, as living stones, are being built up a spiritual house, a holy priesthood, to offer up spiritual sacrifices acceptable to God through Jesus Christ. ◊ Pray without ceasing.

PS 141:2. EX 30:1. EX 30:6-8. HEB 7:25. REV 8:4. 1 PET 2:5. 1 THESS 5:17

MORNING

**He led them forth by the right way, that they might
go to a city for habitation.**

In the wasteland, a howling wilderness, He encircled him, He instructed him, He kept him as the apple of His eye. As an eagle stirs up its nest, hovers over its young, spreading out its wings, taking them up, carrying them on its wings, . . . so the Lord alone led him. ◊ Even to your old age, I am He, and even to gray hairs I will carry you! I have made, and I will bear; even I will carry, and will deliver you.

He restores my soul; He leads me in the paths of righteousness for His name's sake. Yea, though I walk through the valley of the shadow of death, I will fear no evil; for You are with me; Your rod and Your staff, they comfort me.

The Lord will guide you continually, and satisfy your soul in drought, and strengthen your bones; you shall be like a watered garden, and like a spring of water, whose waters do not fail. ◊ For this is God, our God forever and ever; He will be our guide even to death. ◊ Who teaches like Him?

PS 107:7. DEUT 32:10-12. IS 46:4. PS 23:3-4. IS 58:11. PS 48:14. JOB 36:22

EVENING

**"What do you want Me to do for you?" And he said,
"Lord, that I may receive my sight."**

Open my eyes, that I may see wondrous things from Your law.

And He opened their understanding, that they might comprehend the Scriptures. ◊ But the Helper, the Holy Spirit, whom the Father will send in My name, He will teach you all things, and bring to your remembrance all things that I said to you. ◊ Every good gift and every perfect gift is from above, and comes down from the Father of lights, with whom there is no variation or shadow of turning.

God of our Lord Jesus Christ, the Father of glory, . . . give to you the spirit of wisdom and revelation in the knowledge of Him, the eyes of your understanding being enlightened; that you may know what is the hope of His calling, what are the riches of the glory of His inheritance in the saints, and what is the exceeding greatness of His power toward us who believe, according to the working of His mighty power which He worked in Christ when He raised Him from the dead and seated Him at His right hand in the heavenly places.

LUKE 18:41. PS 119:18. LUKE 24:45. JOHN 14:26. JAMES 1:17. EPH 1:17-20

MORNING

For as yet you have not come to the rest and the inheritance which the Lord your God is giving you.

This is not your rest. ◊ There remains therefore a rest for the people of God. ◊ Behind the veil, where the forerunner has entered for us, even Jesus.

In My Father's house are many mansions; if it were not so, I would have told you. I go to prepare a place for you. And if I go and prepare a place for you, I will come again and receive you to Myself; that where I am, there you may be also. ◊ With Christ, which is far better.

God will wipe away every tear from their eyes; there shall be no more death, nor sorrow, nor crying; and there shall be no more pain, for the former things have passed away. ◊ There the wicked cease from troubling, and there the weary are at rest.

Lay up for yourselves treasures in heaven, . . . for where your treasure is, there your heart will be also. ◊ Set your mind on things above, not on things on the earth.

DEUT 12:9.MIC 2:10.HEB 4:9.HEB 6:19-20.JOHN 14:2-3.PHIL 1:23.REV 21:4.JOB 3:17.MATT 6:20-21.COL 3:2

EVENING

O Death, where is your sting?
O Hades, where is your victory?

The sting of death is sin. ◊ Now, once at the end of the ages, He has appeared to put away sin by the sacrifice of Himself. And as it is appointed for men to die once, but after this the judgment, so Christ was offered once to bear the sins of many. To those who eagerly wait for Him He will appear a second time, apart from sin, for salvation.

Inasmuch then as the children have partaken of flesh and blood, He Himself likewise shared in the same, that through death He might destroy him who had the power of death, that is, the devil, and release those who through fear of death were all their lifetime subject to bondage.

The time of my departure is at hand. I have fought the good fight, I have finished the race, I have kept the faith. Finally, there is laid up for me the crown of righteousness.

1 COR 15:55.1 COR 15:56.HEB 9:26-28.HEB 2:14-15.2 TIM 4:6-8

MORNING

We who have believed do enter that rest.

They . . . weary themselves to commit iniquity. ◊ I see another law in my members, warring against the law of my mind, and bringing me into captivity to the law of sin which is in my members. O wretched man that I am! Who will deliver me from this body of death?

Come to Me, all you who labor and are heavy laden, and I will give you rest. ◊ Having been justified by faith, we have peace with God through our Lord Jesus Christ, through whom also we have access by faith into this grace in which we stand, and rejoice in hope of the glory of God.

He who has entered His rest has himself also ceased from his works. ◊ Not having my own righteousness, which is from the law, but that which is through faith in Christ, the righteousness which is from God by faith. ◊ This is the rest with which you may cause the weary to rest, and, this is the refreshing.

HEB 4:3.JER 9:5.ROM 7:23-24.MATT 11:28.ROM 5:1-2.HEB 4:10.PHIL
3:9.IS 28:12

EVENING

**Set a guard, O Lord, over my mouth; keep watch over
the door of my lips.**

If You, Lord, should mark iniquities, O Lord, who could stand? ◊ Not what goes into the mouth defiles a man; but what comes out of the mouth, this defiles a man.

A whisperer separates the best of friends. ◊ There is one who speaks like the piercings of a sword, but the tongue of the wise promotes health. ◊ The truthful lip shall be established forever, but a lying tongue is but for a moment. ◊ No man can tame the tongue. It is an unruly evil, full of deadly poison. ◊ Out of the same mouth proceed blessing and cursing. My brethren, these things ought not to be so.

Now you must also put off all these: anger, wrath, malice, blasphemy, filthy language. . . . Do not lie to one another, since you have put off the old man with his deeds. ◊ For this is the will of God, your sanctification. ◊ A wholesome tongue is a tree of life.

PS 141:3.PS 130:3.MATT 15:11.PROV 16:28.PROV 12:18.PROV
12:19.JAMES 3:8.JAMES 3:10.COL 3:8-9.1 THESS 4:3.PROV 15:4

JANUARY 6

MORNING⸻

Let the beauty of the Lord our God be upon us, and establish the work of our hands for us.

"Your beauty, . . . was perfect through My splendor which I had bestowed on you," says the Lord God. ◇ We all, with unveiled face, beholding as in a mirror the glory of the Lord, are being transformed into the same image from glory to glory, just as by the Spirit of the Lord.

Blessed is every one who fears the Lord, who walks in His ways. When you eat the labor of your hands, you shall be happy, and it shall be well with you. ◇ Commit your works to the Lord, and your thoughts will be established.

Work out your own salvation with fear and trembling; for it is God who works in you both to will and to do for His good pleasure. ◇ Our Lord Jesus Christ Himself, and our God and Father, who has loved us and given us everlasting consolation and good hope by grace, comfort your hearts and establish you in every good word and work.

PS 90:17.EZEK 16:14.2 COR 3:18.PS 128:1-2.PROV 16:3.PHIL 2:12-13.
2 THESS 2:16-17

EVENING⸻

The apostles gathered to Jesus and told Him all . . . they had done.

The Lord spoke to Moses face to face, as a man speaks to his friend. ◇ You are My friends if you do whatever I command you. No longer do I call you servants, for a servant does not know what his master is doing; but I have called you friends, for all things that I heard from My Father I have made known to you.

So likewise you, when you have done all those things which you are commanded, say, "We are unprofitable servants. We have done what was our duty to do."

For you did not receive the spirit of bondage again to fear, but you received the Spirit of adoption by whom we cry out, "Abba, Father." ◇ And because you are sons, God has sent forth the Spirit of His Son into your hearts, crying out, "Abba, Father!" Therefore you are no longer a slave but a son, and if a son, then an heir of God through Christ.

Be anxious for nothing, but in everything by prayer and supplication, with thanksgiving, let your requests be made known to God. ◇ The prayer of the upright is His delight.

MARK 6:30.EX 33:11.JOHN 15:14-15.LUKE 17:10.ROM 8:15.GAL
4:6-7.PHIL 4:6.PROV 15:8

MORNING

Remember me, my God, for good.

Thus says the Lord: "I remember you, the kindness of your youth, the love of your betrothal, when you went after Me in the wilderness." ◊ I will remember My covenant with you in the days of your youth, and I will establish an everlasting covenant with you. ◊ I will visit you and perform My good word toward you, . . . For I know the thoughts that I think toward you, says the Lord, thoughts of peace and not of evil, to give you a future and a hope.

As the heavens are higher than the earth, so are My ways higher than your ways, and My thoughts than your thoughts. ◊ I would seek God, and to God I would commit my cause—who does great things, and unsearchable, marvelous things without number. ◊ Many, O Lord my God, are Your wonderful works which You have done; and Your thoughts which are toward us cannot be recounted to You in order; if I would declare and speak of them, they are more than can be numbered.

NEH 5:19.JER 2:2.EZEK 16:60.JER 29:10-11.IS 55:9.JOB 5:8-9.PS 40:5

EVENING

I will not leave you nor forsake you.

Not a word failed of any good thing which the Lord had spoken to the house of Israel. All came to pass.

God is not a man, that He should lie, nor a son of man, that He should repent. Has He said, and will He not do it? Or has He spoken, and will He not make it good?

Therefore know that the Lord your God, He is God, the faithful God who keeps covenant and mercy for a thousand generations with those who love Him and keep His commandments. ◊ He will ever be mindful of His covenant. ◊ Do not worry about tomorrow, for tomorrow will worry about its own things. Sufficient for the day is its own trouble.

Can a woman forget her nursing child, and not have compassion on the son of her womb? Surely they may forget, yet I will not forget you. See, I have inscribed you on the palms of My hands.

The Lord your God in your midst, the Mighty One, will save; He will rejoice over you with gladness, He will quiet you in His love, He will rejoice over you with singing.

JOSH 1:5.JOSH 21:45.NUM 23:19.DEUT 7:9.PS 111:5.MATT 6:34.IS 49:15-16.ZEPH 3:17

JANUARY 8

MORNING

**Those who know Your name will put their trust in
You; for You, Lord, have not forsaken
those who seek You.**

The name of the Lord is a strong tower; the righteous run to it and are safe. ◊ I will trust and not be afraid; for YAH, the Lord, is my strength and my song; He also has become my salvation.

I have been young, and now am old; yet I have not seen the righteous forsaken, nor his descendants begging bread. ◊ For the Lord loves justice, and does not forsake His saints; they are preserved forever, but the descendants of the wicked shall be cut off. ◊ The Lord will not forsake His people, for His great name's sake, because it has pleased the Lord to make you His people. ◊ [He] delivered us from so great a death, and does deliver us; in whom we trust that He will still deliver us.

Be content with such things as you have. For He Himself has said, "I will never leave you nor forsake you." So we may boldly say: "The Lord is my helper; I will not fear. What can man do to me?"

PS 9:10.PROV 18:10.IS 12:2.PS 37:25.PS 37:28.1 SAM 12:22.2 COR
1:10.HEB 13:5-6

EVENING

**In their mouth was found no guile, for they are
without fault.**

The iniquity of Israel shall be sought, but there shall be none; and the sins of Judah, but they shall not be found; for I will pardon those whom I preserve. ◊ Who is a God like You, pardoning iniquity and passing over the transgression of the remnant of His heritage? He does not retain His anger forever, because He delights in mercy. He will again have compassion on us, and will subdue our iniquities. You will cast all our sins into the depths of the sea.

He has made us accepted in the Beloved. ◊ He has reconciled in the body of His flesh through death, to present you holy, and blameless, and irreproachable in His sight—if indeed you continue in the faith, grounded and steadfast, and are not moved away from the hope of the gospel which you heard.

Now to Him who is able to keep you from stumbling, and to present you faultless before the presence of His glory with exceeding joy, to God our Savior, who alone is wise, be glory and majesty, dominion and power, both now and forever. Amen.

REV 14:5.JER 50:20.MIC 7:18-19.EPH 1:6.COL 1:21-23.JUDE 1:24-25

MORNING

**You have given a banner to those who fear You, that
it may be displayed because of the truth.**

The-Lord-Is-My-Banner. ◊ When the enemy comes in like a flood, the Spirit of the Lord will lift up a standard against him.

We will rejoice in your salvation, and in the name of our God we will set up our banners! ◊ The Lord has revealed our righteousness. Come and let us declare in Zion the work of the Lord our God. ◊ We are more than conquerors through Him who loved us. ◊ Thanks be to God, who gives us the victory through our Lord Jesus Christ.

My brethren, be strong in the Lord and in the power of His might. ◊ [Be] valiant for the truth. ◊ Fight the Lord's battles. ◊ "Be strong, all you people of the land," says the Lord, "and work; . . . do not fear!" ◊ Lift up your eyes and look at the fields, for they are already white for harvest! ◊ For yet a little while, and He who is coming will come and will not tarry.

PS 60:4.EX 17:15.IS 59:19.PS 20:5.JER 51:10.ROM 8:37.1 COR 15:57.EPH
6:10.JER 9:3.1 SAM 18:17.HAG 2:4-5.JOHN 4:35.HEB 10:37

EVENING

But one thing is needed.

There are many who say, "Who will show us any good?" Lord, lift up the light of Your countenance upon us. You have put gladness in my heart, more than in the season that their grain and wine increased.

As the deer pants for the water brooks, so pants my soul for You, O God. My soul thirsts for God, for the living God. ◊ O God, You are my God; early will I seek You; my soul thirsts for You; my flesh longs for You in a dry and thirsty land where there is no water.

I am the bread of life. He who comes to Me shall never hunger, and he who believes in Me shall never thirst. ◊ Lord, give us this bread always. ◊ Mary . . . sat at Jesus' feet and heard His word. ◊ One thing I have desired of the Lord, that will I seek: that I may dwell in the house of the Lord all the days of my life, to behold the beauty of the Lord, and to inquire in His temple. ◊ Surely goodness and mercy shall follow me all the days of my life; and I will dwell in the house of the Lord forever.

LUKE 10:42.PS 4:6-7.PS 42:1,2.PS 63:1.JOHN 6:35.JOHN 6:34.LUKE
10:39.PS 27:4.PS 23:6

MORNING

**May your whole spirit, soul, and body be preserved
blameless at the coming of our Lord Jesus Christ.**

Christ . . . loved the church and gave Himself for it, . . . that He might present it to Himself a glorious church, not having spot or wrinkle or any such thing, but that it should be holy and without blemish. ◊ Him we preach, warning every man and teaching every man in all wisdom, that we may present every man perfect in Christ Jesus.

The peace of God . . . surpasses all understanding. ◊ Let the peace of God rule in your hearts, to which also you were called in one body.

May our Lord Jesus Christ Himself, and our God and Father, who has loved us and given us everlasting consolation and good hope by grace, comfort your hearts and establish you in every good word and work. ◊ [God] will also confirm you to the end, that you may be blameless in the day of our Lord Jesus Christ.

> 1 THESS 5:23.EPH 5:25,27.COL 1:28.PHIL 4:7.COL 3:15.2 THESS
> 2:16-17.1 COR 1:8

EVENING

Will God indeed dwell with men on the earth?

Let them make Me a sanctuary, that I may dwell among them. ◊ I will meet with the children of Israel, and the tabernacle shall be sanctified by My glory. ◊ I will dwell among the children of Israel and will be their God. ◊ I will bring them back, and they shall dwell in the midst of Jerusalem. They shall be My people and I will be their God, in truth and righteousness.

You have ascended on high, You have led captivity captive; You have received gifts among men, even among the rebellious, that the Lord God might dwell there. ◊ Christ [is] a Son over His own house, whose house we are if we hold fast the confidence and the rejoicing of the hope firm to the end.

You are the temple of the living God. As God has said: "I will dwell in them and walk among them. I will be their God, and they shall be My people." ◊ Your body is the temple of the Holy Spirit who is in you, whom you have from God. ◊ You also are being built together for a habitation of God in the Spirit.

Immanuel, . . . "God with us."

> 2 CHR 6:18.EX 25:8.EX 29:43.EX 29:45.ZECH 8:8.PS 68:18.HEB 3:6.
> 2 COR 6:16.1 COR 6:19.EPH 2:22.MATT 1:23

MORNING

Praise is awaiting You, O God, in Zion.

For us there is only one God, the Father, of whom are all things, and we for Him; and one Lord Jesus Christ. ◊ All should honor the Son just as they honor the Father. He who does not honor the Son does not honor the Father who sent Him. ◊ Therefore by Him let us continually offer the sacrifice of praise to God, that is, the fruit of our lips, giving thanks to His name. ◊ Whoever offers praise glorifies Me; and to him who orders his conduct aright I will show the salvation of God.

I looked, and behold, a great multitude which no one could number, of all nations, tribes, peoples, and tongues, standing before the throne and before the Lamb, clothed with white robes, with palm branches in their hands, and crying out with a loud voice, saying, "Salvation belongs to our God who sits on the throne, and to the Lamb!" ◊ Amen! Blessing and glory and wisdom, thanksgiving and honor and power and might, be to our God forever and ever. Amen.

PS 65:1.1 COR 8:6.JOHN 5:23.HEB 13:15.PS 50:23.REV 7:9-10.REV 7:12

EVENING

Who redeems your life from destruction.

Their Redeemer is strong; the Lord of hosts is His name. ◊ I will ransom them from the power of the grave; I will redeem them from death. O Death, I will be your plagues! O Grave, I will be your destruction!

Inasmuch then as the children have partaken of flesh and blood, He Himself likewise shared in the same, that through death He might destroy him who had the power of death, that is, the devil; and release those who through fear of death were all their lifetime subject to bondage.

He who believes in the Son has everlasting life; and he who does not believe the Son shall not see life, but the wrath of God abides on him.

For you died, and your life is hidden with Christ in God. When Christ who is our life appears, then you also will appear with Him in glory. ◊ When He comes, in that Day, to be glorified in His saints and to be admired among all those who believe, because our testimony among you was believed.

PS 103:4.JER 50:34.HOS 13:14.HEB 2:14-15.JOHN 3:36.COL 3:3-4.
2 THESS 1:10

JANUARY 12

MORNING

To God our Savior, who alone is wise.

[You] are in Christ Jesus, who became for us wisdom from God—and righteousness and sanctification and redemption. ◊ Can you search out the deep things of God? Can you find out the limits of the Almighty? . . . They are higher than heaven—what can you do? Deeper than Sheol—what can you know?

We speak the wisdom of God in a mystery, the hidden wisdom which God ordained before the ages for our glory. ◊ The mystery, which from the beginning of the ages has been hidden in God who created all things through Jesus Christ; . . . to the intent that now the manifold wisdom of God might be made known by the church to the principalities and powers in the heavenly places.

If any of you lacks wisdom, let him ask of God, who gives to all liberally and without reproach, and it will be given to him. ◊ The wisdom that is from above is first pure, then peaceable, gentle, willing to yield, full of mercy and good fruits, without partiality and without hypocrisy.

JUDE 1:25.1 COR 1:30.JOB 11:7-8.1 COR 2:7.EPH 3:9-10.JAMES 1:5.JAMES 3:17

EVENING

When I lie down, I say, "When shall I arise, and the night be ended?" For I have had my fill of tossing till dawn.

"Watchman, what of the night?" The watchman said, "The morning comes."

He who is coming will come and will not tarry. ◊ He shall be like the light of the morning when the sun rises, a morning without clouds, like the tender grass springing out of the earth.

In My Father's house are many mansions; if it were not so, I would have told you. I go to prepare a place for you. And . . . I will come again and receive you to Myself; that where I am, there you may be also. Peace I leave with you, My peace I give to you; not as the world gives do I give to you. Let not your heart be troubled, neither let it be afraid. You have heard Me say to you, "I am going away and coming back to you."

Set your mind on things above, not on things on the earth. For you died, and your life is hidden with Christ in God. When Christ who is our life appears, then you also will appear with Him in glory.

JOB 7:4.IS 21:11-12.HEB 10:37.2 SAM 23:4.JOHN 14:2-3.JOHN 14:27-28.COL 3:2-4

MORNING

**You will keep him in perfect peace, whose mind is
stayed on You, because he trusts in You.**

Cast your burden on the Lord, and He shall sustain you; He shall never permit the righteous to be moved. ◊ I will trust and not be afraid; for YAH, the Lord, is my strength and my song; He also has become my salvation.

Why are you fearful, O you of little faith? ◊ Be anxious for nothing, but in everything by prayer and supplication, with thanksgiving, let your requests be made known to God; and the peace of God, which surpasses all understanding, will guard your hearts and minds through Christ Jesus. ◊ In quietness and confidence shall be your strength.

The work of righteousness will be peace, and the effect of righteousness, quietness and assurance forever. ◊ Peace I leave with you, My peace I give to you; not as the world gives do I give to you. Let not your heart be troubled, neither let it be afraid. ◊ Peace from Him who is and who was and who is to come.

IS 26:3.PS 55:22.IS 12:2.MATT 8:26.PHIL 4:6-7.IS 30:15.IS 32:17.JOHN
14:27.REV 1:4

EVENING

Do not let the sun go down on your wrath.

If your brother sins against you, go and tell him his fault between you and him alone. If he hears you, you have gained your brother. ◊ "Lord, how often shall my brother sin against me, and I forgive him? Up to seven times?" Jesus said to him, "I do not say to you, up to seven times, but up to seventy times seven."

And whenever you stand praying, if you have anything against anyone, forgive him, that your Father in heaven may also forgive you your trespasses.

Therefore, as the elect of God, holy and beloved, put on tender mercies, kindness, humbleness of mind, meekness, longsuffering; bearing with one another, and forgiving one another, if anyone has a complaint against another; even as Christ forgave you, so you also must do. ◊ Be kind to one another, tenderhearted, forgiving one another, just as God in Christ also forgave you.

EPH 4:26.MATT 18:15.MATT 18:21-22.MARK 11:25.COL 3:12-13.EPH
4:32

MORNING

My Father is greater than I.

When you pray, say: Our Father in heaven. ◊ My Father and your Father, and . . . My God and your God.

As the Father gave Me commandment, so I do. ◊ The words that I speak to you I do not speak on My own authority; but the Father who dwells in Me does the works.

The Father loves the Son, and has given all things into His hand. ◊ You have given Him authority over all flesh, that He should give eternal life to as many as You have given Him.

"Lord, show us the Father, and it is sufficient for us." Jesus said to him, "Have I been with you so long, and yet you have not known Me, Philip? He who has seen Me has seen the Father; so how can you say, 'Show us the Father'?" ◊ I and My Father are one. ◊ As the Father loved Me, I also have loved you; abide in My love. If you keep My commandments, you will abide in My love, just as I have kept My Father's commandments and abide in His love.

JOHN 14:28.LUKE 11:2.JOHN 20:17.JOHN 14:31.JOHN 14:10.JOHN 3:35.JOHN 17:2.JOHN 14:8-9.JOHN 10:30.JOHN 15:9-10

EVENING

He shall bruise your head, and you shall bruise His heel.

His visage was marred more than any man. ◊ But He was wounded for our transgressions, He was bruised for our iniquities; the chastisement for our peace was upon Him, and by His stripes we are healed.

This is your hour, and the power of darkness. ◊ You could have no power at all against Me unless it had been given you from above.

Inasmuch then as the children have partaken of flesh and blood, He Himself likewise shared in the same, that through death He might destroy him who had the power of death, that is, the devil. ◊ The Son of God was manifested, that He might destroy the works of the devil. ◊ [Jesus] . . . cast out many demons; and He did not allow the demons to speak, because they knew Him.

All authority has been given to Me in heaven and on earth. ◊ Those who believe: In My name they will cast out demons.

The God of peace will crush Satan under your feet shortly.

GEN 3:15.IS 52:14.IS 53:5.LUKE 22:53.JOHN 19:11.HEB 2:14.1 JOHN 3:8.MARK 1:34.MATT 28:18.MARK 16:17.ROM 16:20

MORNING

**My soul clings to the dust; revive me according to
Your word.**

If then you were raised with Christ, seek those things which are above, where Christ is, sitting at the right hand of God. Set your mind on things above, not on things on the earth. For . . . your life is hidden with Christ in God. ◊ For our citizenship is in heaven, from which we also eagerly wait for the Savior, the Lord Jesus Christ, who will transform our lowly body that it may be conformed to His glorious body, according to the working by which He is able even to subdue all things to Himself.

The flesh lusts against the Spirit, and the Spirit against the flesh; and these are contrary to one another, so that you do not do the things that you wish. ◊ Brethren, we are debtors—not to the flesh, to live according to the flesh. For if you live according to the flesh you will die; but if by the Spirit you put to death the deeds of the body, you will live. ◊ Beloved, I beg you as sojourners and pilgrims, abstain from fleshly lusts which war against the soul.

PS 119:25.COL 3:1-3.PHIL 3:20-21.GAL 5:17.ROM 8:12-13.1 PET 2:11

EVENING

God has dealt to each one a measure of faith.

Receive one who is weak in the faith. ◊ He did not waver at the promise of God through unbelief, but was strengthened in faith, giving glory to God. ◊ O you of little faith, why did you doubt? ◊ Great is your faith! Let it be to you as you desire.

"Do you believe that I am able to do this?" They said to Him, "Yes, Lord." . . . "According to your faith let it be to you."

Increase our faith. ◊ [Build] yourselves up on your most holy faith. ◊ Rooted and built up in Him and established in the faith, as you have been taught, abounding in it with thanksgiving. ◊ He who establishes us with you in Christ and has anointed us is God. ◊ The God of all grace, who called us to His eternal glory by Christ Jesus, after you have suffered a while, perfect, establish, strengthen, and settle you.

We then who are strong ought to bear with the scruples of the weak, and not to please ourselves. ◊ Let us not judge one another anymore, but rather resolve this, not to put a stumbling block or a cause to fall in our brother's way.

ROM 12:3.ROM 14:1.ROM 4:20.MATT 14:31.MATT 15:28.MATT 9:28-
29.LUKE 17:5.JUDE 1:20.COL 2:7.2 COR 1:21.1 PET 5:10.ROM
15:1.ROM 14:13

JANUARY 16

MORNING

**It pleased the Father that in Him all the fullness
should dwell.**

The Father loves the Son, and has given all things into His hand. ◊
God also has highly exalted Him and given Him the name which is above
every name, that at the name of Jesus every knee should bow, . . . and
that every tongue should confess that Jesus Christ is Lord, to the glory of
God the Father. ◊ [He is] far above all principality and power and might
and dominion, and every name that is named, not only in this age but
also in that which is to come. ◊ By Him all things were created that are in
heaven and that are on earth, visible and invisible, whether thrones or
dominions or principalities or powers. All things were created through
Him and for Him.

Christ died and rose and lived again, that He might be Lord of both the
dead and the living. ◊ And you are complete in Him, who is the head of
all principality and power. ◊ Of His fullness we have all received.

COL 1:19.JOHN 3:35.PHIL 2:9-11.EPH 1:21.COL 1:16.ROM 14:9.COL
2:10.JOHN 1:16

EVENING

**Write the things which you have seen, and the things
which are, and the things which will take place
after this.**

Holy men of God spoke as they were moved by the Holy Spirit. ◊ The
Spirit of Christ who was in them was indicating when He testified
beforehand the sufferings of Christ and the glories that would follow. ◊
That which we have seen and heard we declare to you, that you also may
have fellowship with us; and truly our fellowship is with the Father and
with His Son Jesus Christ.

"Behold My hands and My feet, that it is I Myself. Handle Me and see,
for a spirit does not have flesh and bones as you see I have." When He
had said this, He showed them His hands and His feet. ◊ He who has
seen has testified, and his testimony is true; and he knows that he is
telling the truth, so that you may believe.

We did not follow cunningly devised fables when we made known to
you the power and coming of our Lord Jesus Christ, but were
eyewitnesses of His majesty. ◊ Your faith should not be in the wisdom
of men but in the power of God.

REV 1:19.2 PET 1:21.1 PET 1:11.1 JOHN 1:3.LUKE 24:39-40.JOHN
19:35.2 PET 1:16.1 COR 2:5

MORNING

But You have lovingly delivered my soul from the pit of corruption.

God has sent His only begotten Son into the world, that we might live through Him. In this is love, not that we loved God, but that He loved us and sent His Son to be the propitiation for our sins.

Who is a God like You, pardoning iniquity and passing over the transgression of the remnant of His heritage? He does not retain His anger forever, because He delights in mercy. He will again have compassion on us, and will subdue our iniquities. You will cast all our sins into the depths of the sea. ◊ O Lord my God, I cried out to You, and You have healed me. O Lord, You have brought my soul up from the grave; You have kept me alive, that I should not go down to the pit. ◊ When my soul fainted within me, I remembered the Lord; and my prayer went up to You, into Your holy temple. ◊ I waited patiently for the Lord. . . . He . . . brought me up out of a horrible pit, out of the miry clay, and set my feet upon a rock, and established my steps.

IS 38:17.1 JOHN 4:9-10.MIC 7:18-19.PS 30:2-3.JON 2:7.PS 40:1-2

EVENING

Write the things which you have seen.

For now we see in a mirror, dimly, but then face to face. Now I know in part, but then I shall know just as I also am known.

We also have the prophetic word made more sure, which you do well to heed as a light that shines in a dark place, until the day dawns and the morning star rises in your hearts. ◊ Your word is a lamp to my feet and a light to my path.

Beloved, remember the words which were spoken before by the apostles of our Lord Jesus Christ: how they told you that there would be mockers. ◊ The Spirit expressly says that in latter times some will depart from the faith, giving heed to deceiving spirits and doctrines of demons.

Little children, it is the last hour. ◊ The night is far spent, the day is at hand. . . . Let us put on the armor of light.

REV 1:19.1 COR 13:12.2 PET 1:19.PS 119:105.JUDE 1:17-18.1 TIM 4:1.
1 JOHN 2:18.ROM 13:12

JANUARY 18

[Christ] was to come.

Jesus . . . was made a little lower than the angels, for the suffering of death . . . that He, by the grace of God, might taste death for everyone. ◊ One died for all. ◊ As by one man's disobedience many were made sinners, so also by one Man's obedience many will be made righteous.

The first man Adam became a living being. The last Adam became a life-giving spirit. However, the spiritual is not first, but the natural, and afterward the spiritual. ◊ God said, "Let Us make man in Our image, according to Our likeness." . . . So God created man in His own image; in the image of God He created him. ◊ God . . . has in these last days spoken to us by His Son, . . . the brightness of His glory and the express image of His person. ◊ You have given Him authority over all flesh.

The first man was of the earth, made of dust; the second Man is the Lord from heaven. As was the man of dust, so also are those who are made of dust; and as is the heavenly Man, so also are those who are heavenly.

ROM 5:14.HEB 2:9.2 COR 5:14.ROM 5:19.1 COR 15:45-46.GEN
1:26-27.HEB 1:1-3.JOHN 17:2.1 COR 15:47-48

EVENING

The things which will take place after this.

It is written: "Eye has not seen, nor ear heard, nor have entered into the heart of man the things which God has prepared for those who love Him." But God has revealed them to us through His Spirit.

Behold, He is coming with clouds, and every eye will see Him, and they also who pierced Him. And all the tribes of the earth will mourn because of Him. Even so, Amen.

But I do not want you to be ignorant, brethren, concerning those who have fallen asleep, lest you sorrow as others who have no hope. For if we believe that Jesus died and rose again, even so God will bring with Him those who sleep in Jesus. . . . For the Lord Himself will descend from heaven with a shout, with the voice of an archangel, and with the trumpet of God. And the dead in Christ will rise first. Then we who are alive and remain shall be caught up together with them in the clouds to meet the Lord in the air. And thus we shall always be with the Lord.

REV 1:19.1 COR 2:9-10.REV 1:7.1 THESS 4:13-14,16-17

MORNING

Serve the Lord with all humility.

Whoever desires to become great among you, let him be your servant. And whoever desires to be first among you, let him be your slave—just as the Son of Man did not come to be served, but to serve, and to give His life a ransom for many.

If anyone thinks himself to be something, when he is nothing, he deceives himself. ◊ I say, through the grace given to me, to everyone, . . . not to think of himself more highly than he ought to think, but to think soberly, as God has dealt to each one a measure of faith. ◊ When you have done all those things which you are commanded, say, "We are unprofitable servants. We have done what was our duty to do."

Our boasting is this: . . . we conducted ourselves in the world in simplicity and godly sincerity, not with fleshly wisdom but by the grace of God. ◊ We have this treasure in earthen vessels, that the excellence of the power may be of God and not of us.

ACTS 20:19.MATT 20:26-28.GAL 6:3.ROM 12:3.LUKE 17:10.2 COR 1:12.2 COR 4:7

EVENING

We like sheep have gone astray.

Noah . . . planted a vineyard. Then he drank of the wine and was drunk. ◊ [Abram] said to Sarai his wife, . . . "Please say you are my sister, that it may be well with me." ◊ Isaac . . . said, "The voice is Jacob's voice, but the hands are the hands of Esau. Are you really my son Esau?" And [Jacob] said, "I am." ◊ They angered Him . . . so that it went ill with Moses . . . so that he spoke rashly. ◊ The men of Israel . . . did not ask counsel of the Lord. Joshua . . . made a covenant with them. ◊ David did what was right in the eyes of the Lord, . . . all the days of his life, except in the matter of Uriah the Hittite.

All these . . . obtained a good testimony through faith. ◊ Truly if they had called to mind that country from which they had come out, they would have had opportunity to return. But . . . they desire . . . a heavenly country. ◊ [All are] justified freely by His grace through the redemption that is in Christ Jesus. ◊ The Lord has laid on Him the iniquity of us all.

Be ashamed and confounded for your own ways.

IS 53:6.GEN 9:20-21.GEN 12:11,13.GEN 27:22,24.PS 106:32-33.JOSH 9:14-15.1 KIN 15:5.HEB 11:39.HEB 11:15-16.ROM 3:24.IS 53:6.EZEK 36:32

JANUARY 20

MORNING

His name will be called Wonderful.

The Word became flesh and dwelt among us, and we beheld His glory, the glory as of the only begotten of the Father, full of grace and truth. ◊ For You have magnified Your word above all Your name.

They shall call His name Immanuel, which is translated, "God with us." ◊ Call His name JESUS, for He will save His people from their sins.

All should honor the Son just as they honor the Father. ◊ God . . . has highly exalted Him and given Him the name which is above every name. ◊ Far above all principality and power and might and dominion, and every name that is named, not only in this age but also in that which is to come. And He put all things under His feet. ◊ He has . . . a name written: KING OF KINGS AND LORD OF LORDS.

As for the Almighty, we cannot find Him. ◊ What is His name, and what is His Son's name, if you know?

IS 9:6.JOHN 1:14.PS 138:2.MATT 1:23.MATT 1:21.JOHN 5:23.PHIL 2:9.EPH 1:21-22.REV 19:16.JOB 37:23.PROV 30:4

EVENING

The Lord's portion is His people.

You are Christ's, and Christ is God's. ◊ I am my beloved's, and his desire is toward me. ◊ I am his. ◊ The Son of God . . . loved me and gave Himself for me.

Your body is . . . not your own. For you were bought at a price; therefore glorify God in your body and in your spirit, which are God's. ◊ The Lord has taken you and brought you out of the iron furnace, . . . to be His people, His inheritance, as you are this day.

You are God's field, you are God's building. ◊ But Christ [is] a Son over His own house, whose house we are if we hold fast the confidence and the rejoicing of the hope firm to the end. ◊ You also as living stones, are . . . a holy priesthood.

"They shall be Mine," says the Lord of hosts, "on the day that I make them My jewels." ◊ And all Mine are Yours, and Yours are Mine, and I am glorified in them.

DEUT 32:9.1 COR 3:23.SONG 7:10.SONG 2:16.GAL 2:20.1 COR 6:19-20.DEUT 4:20.1 COR 3:9.HEB 3:6.1 PET 2:5.MAL 3:17.JOHN 17:10

MORNING

**Every branch in Me that does not bear fruit
He takes away.**

He is like a refiner's fire and like fuller's soap. He will sit as a refiner and a purifier of silver; He will purify the sons of Levi, and purge them as gold and silver, that they may offer to the Lord an offering in righteousness.

We . . . glory in tribulations, knowing that tribulation produces perseverance; and perseverance, character; and character, hope. Hope does not disappoint, because the love of God has been poured out in our hearts by the Holy Spirit who was given to us. ◊ If you endure chastening, God deals with you as with sons; for what son is there whom a father does not chasten? But if you are without chastening, of which all have become partakers, then you are illegitimate and not sons. ◊ Now no chastening seems to be joyful for the present, but grievous; nevertheless, afterward it yields the peaceable fruit of righteousness to those who have been trained by it. Therefore strengthen the hands which hang down, and the feeble knees.

JOHN 15:2.MAL 3:2-3.ROM 5:3-5.HEB 12:7-8.HEB 12:11-12

EVENING

The proud . . . will be stubble.

Thus says the High and Lofty One who inhabits eternity, whose name is Holy: "I dwell in the high and holy place, with him who has a contrite and humble spirit, to revive the spirit of the humble, and to revive the heart of the contrite ones."

Better to be of a humble spirit with the lowly, than to divide the spoil with the proud. ◊ Blessed are the poor in spirit, for theirs is the kingdom of heaven.

These six things the Lord hates, yes, seven are an abomination to Him. ◊ Everyone who is proud in heart is an abomination to the Lord.

Search me, O God, and know my heart; try me, and know my anxieties; and see if there is any wicked way in me, and lead me in the way everlasting.

Grace to you and peace from God our Father and the Lord Jesus Christ. ◊ I thank my God upon every remembrance of you.

Blessed are the meek, for they shall inherit the earth.

MAL 4:1.IS 57:15.PROV 16:19.MATT 5:3.PROV 6:16.PROV 16:5.PS 139:23-24.PHIL 1:2-3.MATT 5:5

JANUARY 22

MORNING

For this is God, our God forever and ever; He will be our guide even to death.

O Lord, You are my God. I will exalt You, I will praise Your name, for You have done wonderful things; Your counsels of old are faithfulness and truth. ◊ You, O Lord, are the portion of my inheritance and my cup.

He restores my soul; He leads me in the paths of righteousness for His name's sake. Yea, though I walk through the valley of the shadow of death, I will fear no evil; for You are with me; Your rod and Your staff, they comfort me. ◊ You hold me by my right hand. You will guide me with Your counsel, and afterward receive me to glory. Whom have I in heaven but You? And there is none upon earth that I desire besides You. My flesh and my heart fail; but God is the strength of my heart and my portion forever. ◊ Our heart shall rejoice in Him, because we have trusted in His holy name. ◊ The Lord will perfect that which concerns me; Your mercy, O Lord, endures forever; do not forsake the works of Your hands.

PS 48:14.IS 25:1.PS 16:5.PS 23:3-4.PS 73:23-26.PS 33:21.PS 138:8

EVENING

In the multitude of my anxieties within me, Your comforts delight my soul.

When my heart is overwhelmed; lead me to the rock that is higher than I. ◊ O Lord, I am oppressed; undertake for me! ◊ Cast your burden on the Lord, and He shall sustain you; He shall never permit the righteous to be moved.

I am a little child; I do not know how to go out or come in. ◊ If any of you lacks wisdom, let him ask of God, who gives to all liberally and without reproach, and it will be given to him.

I know that in me (that is, in my flesh) nothing good dwells. ◊ My grace is sufficient for you, for My strength is made perfect in weakness.

Son, be of good cheer; your sins are forgiven you. ◊ Be of good cheer, daughter; your faith has made you well.

My soul shall be satisfied as with marrow and fatness, and my mouth shall praise You with joyful lips. When I remember You on my bed, I meditate on You in the night watches. Because You have been my help, therefore in the shadow of Your wings I will rejoice. My soul follows close behind You; Your right hand upholds me.

PS 94:19.PS 61:2.IS 38:14.PS 55:22.1 KIN 3:7.JAMES 1:5.ROM 7:18.2 COR 12:9.MATT 9:2.MATT 9:22.PS 63:5-8

MORNING

Hope does not disappoint.

They shall not be ashamed who wait for Me. ◊ Blessed is the man who trusts in the Lord, and whose hope is the Lord. ◊ You will keep him in perfect peace, whose mind is stayed on You, because he trusts in You. Trust in the Lord forever, for in YAH, the Lord, is everlasting strength. ◊ My soul, wait silently for God alone, for my expectation is from Him. He only is my rock and my salvation; He is my defense; I shall not be moved. ◊ I am not ashamed, for I know whom I have believed.

God, determining to show more abundantly to the heirs of promise the immutability of His counsel, confirmed it by an oath, that by two immutable things, in which it is impossible for God to lie, we might have strong consolation, who have fled for refuge to lay hold of the hope set before us. This hope we have as an anchor of the soul, both sure and steadfast, and which enters the Presence behind the veil, where the forerunner has entered for us, even Jesus.

ROM 5:5.IS 49:23.JER 17:7.IS 26:3-4.PS 62:5-6.2 TIM 1:12.HEB 6:17-20

EVENING

Brethren, if I still preach circumcision, why do I still suffer persecution? Then the offense of the cross has ceased.

If anyone desires to come after Me, let him deny himself, and take up his cross, and follow Me.

Do you not know that friendship with the world is enmity with God? Whoever therefore wants to be a friend of the world makes himself an enemy of God. ◊ We must through many tribulations enter the kingdom of God.

Whoever believes on Him will not be put to shame. ◊ To you who believe, He is precious.

God forbid that I should glory except in the cross of our Lord Jesus Christ, by whom the world has been crucified to me, and I to the world. ◊ I have been crucified with Christ. ◊ Those who are Christ's have crucified the flesh with its passions and desires.

If we endure, we shall also reign with Him. If we deny Him, He also will deny us.

GAL 5:11.MATT 16:24.JAMES 4:4.ACTS 14:22.ROM 9:33.1 PET 2:7.GAL 6:14.GAL 2:20.GAL 5:24.2 TIM 2:12

JANUARY 24

MORNING

The Lord is at hand.

The Lord Himself will descend from heaven with a shout, with the voice of an archangel, and with the trumpet of God. And the dead in Christ will rise first. We who are alive and remain shall be caught up together with them in the clouds to meet the Lord in the air. And thus we shall always be with the Lord. Therefore comfort one another with these words. ◊ He who testifies to these things says, "Surely I am coming quickly." Amen. Even so, come, Lord Jesus!

Therefore, beloved, looking forward to these things, be diligent to be found by Him in peace, without spot and blameless. ◊ Abstain from every form of evil. May the God of peace Himself sanctify you completely; and may your whole spirit, soul, and body be preserved blameless at the coming of our Lord Jesus Christ. He who calls you is faithful, who also will do it.

You also be patient. Establish your hearts, for the coming of the Lord is at hand.

PHIL 4:5.1 THESS 4:16-18.REV 22:20.2 PET 3:14.1 THESS 5:22-24.JAMES 5:8

EVENING

The choice vine.

Now let me sing to my Well-beloved a song of my Beloved regarding His vineyard: my Well-beloved has a vineyard on a very fruitful hill. He dug it up and cleared out its stones, and planted it with the choicest vine. . . . He expected it to bring forth good grapes, but it brought forth wild grapes. ◊ Yet I had planted you a noble vine, a seed of highest quality. How then have you turned before Me into the degenerate plant of an alien vine?

Now the works of the flesh are evident, which are: adultery, fornication, uncleanness, licentiousness, envy, murders, drunkenness, revelries. . . . But the fruit of the Spirit is love, joy, peace, longsuffering, kindness, goodness, faithfulness, gentleness, self-control.

I am the true vine, and My Father is the vinedresser. Every branch in Me that does not bear fruit He takes away; and every branch that bears fruit He prunes, that it may bear more fruit. ◊ Abide in Me, and I in you. ◊ By this My Father is glorified, that you bear much fruit; so you will be My disciples.

GEN 49:11.IS 5:1-2.JER 2:21.GAL 5:19,21-23.JOHN 15:1-2.JOHN 15:4.JOHN 15:8

MORNING

Let us search out and examine our ways, and turn back to the Lord.

Examine me, O Lord, and prove me; try my mind and my heart. ◊ Behold, You desire truth in the inward parts, and in the hidden part You will make me to know wisdom. ◊ I thought about my ways, and turned my feet to Your testimonies. ◊ I made haste, and did not delay to keep Your commandments. ◊ Let a man examine himself, and so let him eat of that bread and drink of that cup. ◊ If we confess our sins, He is faithful and just to forgive us our sins and to cleanse us from all unrighteousness. ◊ We have an Advocate with the Father, Jesus Christ the righteous. ◊ Therefore, brethren, having boldness to enter the Holiest by the blood of Jesus, by a new and living way which He consecrated for us, through the veil, that is, His flesh, and having a High Priest over the house of God, let us draw near with a true heart in full assurance of faith, having our hearts sprinkled from an evil conscience and our bodies washed with pure water.

LAM 3:40. PS 26:2. PS 51:6. PS 119:59-60. 1 COR 11:28. 1 JOHN 1:9. 1 JOHN 2:1. HEB 10:19-22

EVENING

There was a rainbow around the throne, in appearance like an emerald.

This is the sign of the covenant which I make between Me and you, and every living creature that is with you, for perpetual generations: I set My rainbow in the cloud, and it shall be for the sign of the covenant between Me and the earth. ◊ I will . . . remember the everlasting covenant. ◊ [It is] ordered in all things and secure. ◊ God . . . confirmed it by an oath, that by two immutable things, in which it is impossible for God to lie, we might have strong consolation, who have fled for refuge to lay hold of the hope set before us.

This hope we have as an anchor of the soul, both sure and steadfast, and which enters the Presence behind the veil, where the forerunner has entered for us, even Jesus, having become High Priest forever according to the order of Melchizedek. ◊ Through this Man is preached to you the forgiveness of sins; and by Him everyone who believes is justified from all things.

Jesus Christ is the same yesterday, today, and forever.

REV 4:3. GEN 9:12-13. GEN 9:16. 2 SAM 23:5. HEB 6:17-18. HEB 6:19-20. ACTS 13:38-39. HEB 13:8

FEBRUARY 27

MORNING

Reckon yourselves to be dead indeed to sin, but alive to God in Christ Jesus our Lord.

He who hears My word and believes in Him who sent Me has everlasting life, and shall not come into judgment, but has passed from death into life. ◊ For I through the law died to the law that I might live to God. I have been crucified with Christ; it is no longer I who live, but Christ lives in me; and the life which I now live in the flesh I live by faith in the Son of God, who loved me and gave Himself for me.

Because I live, you will live also. ◊ And I give them eternal life, and they shall never perish; neither shall anyone snatch them out of My hand. My Father, who has given them to Me, is greater than all; and no one is able to snatch them out of My Father's hand. I and My Father are one.

If then you were raised with Christ, seek those things which are above, where Christ is, sitting at the right hand of God. . . . For you died, and your life is hidden with Christ in God.

ROM 6:11.JOHN 5:24.GAL 2:19-20.JOHN 14:19.JOHN 10:28-30.COL 3:1-3

EVENING

Ask of God, who gives to all liberally.

Jesus . . . said to her, . . . "Where are those accusers of yours? Has no one condemned you?" . . . She said, "No one, Lord." And Jesus said to her, "Neither do I condemn you; go and sin no more."

But the free gift is not like the offense. For if by the one man's offense many died, much more the grace of God and the gift by the grace of the one Man, Jesus Christ, abounded to many. For the judgment which came from one offense resulted in condemnation, but the free gift which came from many offenses resulted in justification.

God, who is rich in mercy, because of His great love with which He loved us, even when we were dead in trespasses, made us alive together with Christ (by grace you have been saved), and raised us up together, and made us sit together in the heavenly places in Christ Jesus, that in the ages to come He might show the exceeding riches of His grace in His kindness toward us in Christ Jesus.

He who did not spare His own Son, but delivered Him up for us all, how shall He not with Him also freely give us all things?

JAMES 1:5.JOHN 8:10-11.ROM 5:15-16.EPH 2:4-7.ROM 8:32

MORNING

**For God so loved the world that He gave His only
begotten Son, that whoever believes in Him should
not perish but have everlasting life.**

God, . . . has reconciled us to Himself through Jesus Christ, and has given us the ministry of reconciliation, that is, that God was in Christ reconciling the world to Himself, not imputing their trespasses to them, and has committed to us the word of reconciliation. Therefore we are ambassadors for Christ, as though God were pleading through us: we implore you on Christ's behalf, be reconciled to God. For He made Him who knew no sin to be sin for us, that we might become the righteousness of God in Him. ◊ God is love. In this the love of God was manifested toward us, that God has sent His only begotten Son into the world, that we might live through Him. In this is love, not that we loved God, but that He loved us and sent His Son to be the propitiation for our sins. Beloved, if God so loved us, we also ought to love one another.

JOHN 3:16.2 COR 5:18-21.1 JOHN 4:8-11

EVENING

**The spirit of a man is the lamp of the Lord, searching
all the inner depths of his heart.**

"He who is without sin among you, let him throw a stone at her first." . . . Then those who heard it, being convicted by their conscience, went out one by one, beginning with the oldest.

Who told you that you were naked? Have you eaten from the tree of which I commanded you that you should not eat?

Therefore, to him who knows to do good and does not do it, to him it is sin. ◊ For everyone practicing evil hates the light and does not come to the light, lest his deeds should be exposed. But he who does the truth comes to the light, that his deeds may be clearly seen, that they have been done in God. ◊ Do not destroy the work of God for the sake of food. All things indeed are pure, but it is evil for the man who eats with offense. ◊ Happy is he who does not condemn himself in what he approves.

Search me, O God, and know my heart; try me, and know my anxieties; and see if there is any wicked way in me, and lead me in the way everlasting.

PROV 20:27.JOHN 8:7,9.GEN 3:11.JAMES 4:17.JOHN 3:20-21.ROM
14:20.ROM 14:22.PS 139:23-24

FEBRUARY 29

MORNING

**Do not boast about tomorrow, for you do not know
what a day may bring forth.**

Behold, now is the accepted time; behold, now is the day of salvation. ◊ A little while longer the light is with you. Walk while you have the light, lest darkness overtake you; he who walks in darkness does not know where he is going. While you have the light, believe in the light, that you may become sons of light.

Whatever your hand finds to do, do it with your might; for there is no work or device or knowledge or wisdom in the grave where you are going.

"Soul, you have many goods laid up for many years; take your ease; eat, drink, and be merry." . . . You fool! This night your soul will be required of you; then whose will those things be which you have provided? So is he who lays up treasure for himself, and is not rich toward God.

The world is passing away, and the lust of it; but he who does the will of God abides forever.

PROV 27:1.2 COR 6:2. JOHN 12:35-36. ECCL 9:10. LUKE 12:19-21.1 JOHN
2:17

EVENING

You are the same, and Your years will have no end.

Before the mountains were brought forth, or ever You had formed the earth and the world, even from everlasting to everlasting, You are God.

I am the Lord, I do not change; therefore you are not consumed. ◊ Jesus Christ is the same yesterday, today, and forever.

Every good gift and every perfect gift is from above, and comes down from the Father of lights, with whom there is no variation or shadow of turning. ◊ For the gifts and the calling of God are irrevocable.

God is not a man, that He should lie, nor a son of man, that He should repent. ◊ Through the Lord's mercies we are not consumed, because His compassions fail not.

But He, because He continues forever, has an unchangeable priesthood. Therefore He is also able to save to the uttermost those who come to God through Him, since He ever lives to make intercession for them. ◊ Do not be afraid; I am the First and the Last.

PS 102:27.PS 90:2.MAL 3:6.HEB 13:8.JAMES 1:17.ROM 11:29.NUM
23:19.LAM 3:22.HEB 7:24-25.REV 1:17

MORNING

The fruit of the Spirit is love.

God is love, and he who abides in love abides in God, and God in him. ◊ The love of God has been poured out in our hearts by the Holy Spirit who was given to us. ◊ To you who believe, He is precious. ◊ We love Him because He first loved us. ◊ The love of Christ constrains us, because we judge thus: that if One died for all, then all died; and He died for all, that those who live should live no longer for themselves, but for Him who died for them and rose again.

You yourselves are taught by God to love one another. ◊ This is My commandment, that you love one another as I have loved you. ◊ Above all things have fervent love for one another, for love will cover a multitude of sins. ◊ Walk in love, as Christ also has loved us and given Himself for us, an offering and a sacrifice to God for a sweet-smelling aroma.

GAL 5:22.1 JOHN 4:16.ROM 5:5.1 PET 2:7.1 JOHN 4:19.2 COR 5:14-15.
1 THESS 4:9.JOHN 15:12.1 PET 4:8.EPH 5:2

EVENING

The-Lord-Is-My-Banner.

If God is for us, who can be against us? ◊ The Lord is on my side; I will not fear. What can man do to me?

You have given a banner to those who fear You, that it may be displayed because of the truth.

The Lord is my light and my salvation; whom shall I fear? . . . Though an army should encamp against me, my heart shall not fear; though war should rise against me, in this I will be confident. ◊ God Himself is with us as our head. ◊ The Lord of hosts is with us; the God of Jacob is our refuge.

These will make war with the Lamb, and the Lamb will overcome them. ◊ Why do the nations rage, and the people plot a vain thing?

He who sits in the heavens shall laugh; the Lord shall hold them in derision. ◊ Take counsel together, but it will come to nothing; speak the word, but it will not stand, for God is with us.

EX 17:15.ROM 8:31.PS 118:6.PS 60:4.PS 27:1-3.2 CHR 13:12.PS 46:7.REV
17:14.PS 2:1.PS 2:4.IS 8:10

MORNING

God has caused me to be fruitful in the land of my affliction.

Blessed be the God and Father of our Lord Jesus Christ, the Father of mercies and God of all comfort, who comforts us in all our tribulation, that we may be able to comfort those who are in any trouble, with the comfort with which we ourselves are comforted by God. For as the sufferings of Christ abound in us, so our consolation also abounds through Christ.

He will sit as a refiner and a purifier of silver; He will purify the sons of Levi. ◊ Now for a little while, if need be, you have been grieved by various trials, that the genuineness of your faith, being much more precious than gold that perishes, though it is tested by fire, may be found to praise, honor, and glory at the revelation of Jesus Christ. ◊ The Lord stood with me and strengthened me.

Let those who suffer according to the will of God commit their souls to Him in doing good, as to a faithful Creator.

GEN 41:52.2 COR 1:3-5.MAL 3:3.1 PET 1:6-7.2 TIM 4:17.1 PET 4:19

EVENING

There remains therefore a rest for the people of God.

Blessed are the dead who die in the Lord from now on . . . that they may rest from their labors, and their works follow them.

We who are in this tent groan. ◊ We also who have the firstfruits of the Spirit, even we ourselves groan within ourselves, eagerly waiting for the adoption, the redemption of our body. ◊ The sufferings of this present time are not worthy to be compared with the glory which shall be revealed in us.

Therefore we are always confident, knowing that while we are at home in the body we are absent from the Lord. For we walk by faith, not by sight. We are confident, yes, well pleased rather to be absent from the body and to be present with the Lord.

I . . . desire to depart and be with Christ.

HEB 4:9.REV 14:13.2 COR 5:4.ROM 8:23.ROM 8:18.2 COR 5:6-8.PHIL 1:23

MORNING

**Trust in the Lord with all your heart, and lean not on
your own understanding; in all your ways
acknowledge Him, and He shall direct your paths.**

Trust in Him at all times, you people; pour out your heart before Him;
God is a refuge for us.

O our God, will You not judge them? For we have no power against
this great multitude that is coming against us; nor do we know what to
do, but our eyes are upon You. ◊ I will lift up my eyes to the hills—from
whence comes my help? My help comes from the Lord, who made
heaven and earth. ◊ But my eyes are upon You, O God the Lord; in You
I take refuge; do not leave my soul destitute.

If Your Presence does not go with us, do not bring us up from here. For
how then will it be known that Your people and I have found grace in
Your sight, except You go with us? So we shall be separate, Your people
and I, from all the people who are upon the face of the earth.

PROV 3:5-6.PS 62:8.2 CHR 20:12.PS 121:1-2.PS 141:8.EX 33:15-16

EVENING

The prize of the upward call of God in Christ Jesus.

You will have treasure in heaven; . . . come, follow Me. ◊ I am . . . your
exceedingly great reward.

His lord said to him, "Well done, good and faithful servant; you were
faithful over a few things, I will make you ruler over many things. Enter
into the joy of your lord." ◊ They shall reign forever and ever.

You will receive the crown of glory that does not fade away. ◊ The
crown of life. ◊ There is laid up for me the crown. ◊ An imperishable
crown.

Father, I desire that they also whom You gave Me may be with Me
where I am, that they may behold My glory which You have given Me;
for You loved Me before the foundation of the world. ◊ We shall always
be with the Lord.

The sufferings of this present time are not worthy to be compared with
the glory which shall be revealed in us. ◊ Eye has not seen, nor ear
heard, nor have entered into the heart of man the things which God has
prepared for those who love Him. But God has revealed them to us
through His Spirit.

PHIL 3:14.MATT 19:21.GEN 15:1.MATT 25:21.REV 22:5.1 PET
5:4.JAMES 1:12.2 TIM 4:8.1 COR 9:25.JOHN 17:24.1 THESS 4:17.ROM
8:18.1 COR 2:9-10

MARCH 4

_____

Set your mind on things above,
not on things on the earth.

Do not love the world or the things in the world. If anyone loves the world, the love of the Father is not in him. ◊ Do not lay up for yourselves treasures on earth, where moth and rust destroy and where thieves break in and steal; but lay up for yourselves treasures in heaven, where neither moth nor rust destroys and where thieves do not break in and steal. For where your treasure is, there your heart will be also.

We walk by faith, not by sight. ◊ We do not lose heart. Even though our outward man is perishing, yet the inward man is being renewed day by day. For our light affliction, which is but for a moment, is working for us a far more exceeding and eternal weight of glory, while we do not look at the things which are seen, but at the things which are not seen. For the things which are seen are temporary, but the things which are not seen are eternal. ◊ An inheritance incorruptible and undefiled and that does not fade away [is] reserved in heaven for you.

COL 3:2.1 JOHN 2:15.MATT 6:19-21.2 COR 5:7.2 COR 4:16-18.1 PET 1:4

EVENING_____

He bowed his shoulder to bear a burden.

Take the prophets, who spoke in the name of the Lord, as an example of suffering and patience. ◊ All these things happened to them as examples, and they were written for our admonition, on whom the ends of the ages have come.

Shall we indeed accept good from God, and shall we not accept adversity? ◊ You have heard of the perseverance of Job and seen the end intended by the Lord that the Lord is very compassionate and merciful. ◊ It is the Lord. Let Him do what seems good to Him.

Cast your burden on the Lord, and He shall sustain you; He shall never permit the righteous to be moved. ◊ He has borne our griefs and carried our sorrows; yet we esteemed Him stricken, smitten by God, and afflicted.

Come to Me, all you who labor and are heavy laden, and I will give you rest. Take My yoke upon you and learn from Me, for I am gentle and lowly in heart, and you will find rest for your souls. For My yoke is easy and My burden is light.

GEN 49:15.JAMES 5:10.1 COR 10:11.JOB 2:10.JAMES 5:11.1 SAM
3:18.PS 55:22.IS 53:4.MATT 11:28-30

MORNING

O Lord, I am oppressed; undertake for me!

Unto You I lift up my eyes, O You who dwell in the heavens. Behold, as the eyes of servants look to the hand of their masters, as the eyes of a maid to the hand of her mistress, so our eyes look to the Lord our God. ◊ Hear my cry, O God; attend to my prayer. From the end of the earth I will cry to You, when my heart is overwhelmed; lead me to the rock that is higher than I. For You have been a shelter for me, and a strong tower from the enemy. I will abide in Your tabernacle forever; I will trust in the shelter of Your wings. ◊ You have been a strength to the poor, a strength to the needy in his distress, a refuge from the storm.

Christ . . . suffered for us, leaving us an example, that you should follow His steps: who committed no sin, nor was guile found in His mouth; who, when He was reviled, did not revile in return; when He suffered, He did not threaten, but committed Himself to Him who judges righteously.

IS 38:14.PS 123:1-2.PS 61:1-4.IS 25:4.1 PET 2:21-23

EVENING

Fight the good fight of faith.

We were troubled on every side. Outside were conflicts, inside were fears. ◊ Do not fear, for those who are with us are more than those who are with them. ◊ Be strong in the Lord and in the power of His might. You come to me with a sword, with a spear, and with a javelin. But I come to you in the name of the Lord of hosts, the God of the armies of Israel, whom you have defied. ◊ God is my strength and power. . . . He teaches my hands to make war, so that my arms can bend a bow of bronze. ◊ Our sufficiency is from God.

The angel of the Lord encamps all around those who fear Him, and delivers them. ◊ Elisha prayed, . . . "Lord, I pray, open his eyes that he may see." Then the Lord opened the eyes of the young man, and he saw. And behold, the mountain was full of horses and chariots of fire all around Elisha.

What more shall I say? For the time would fail me to tell of [those] who through faith subdued kingdoms, worked righteousness, . . . out of weakness were made strong, became valiant in battle, turned to flight the armies of the aliens.

1 TIM 6:12.2 COR 7:5.2 KIN 6:16.EPH 6:10.1 SAM 17:45.2 SAM 22:33,35.
2 COR 3:5.PS 34:7.2 KIN 6:17.HEB 11:32-34

MORNING

He . . . preserves the way of His saints.

The Lord your God, . . . went in the way before you to search out a place for you to pitch your tents, to show you the way you should go, in the fire by night and in the cloud by day. ◊ As an eagle stirs up its nest, hovers over its young, spreading out its wings, taking them up, carrying them on its wings, so the Lord alone led him. ◊ The steps of a good man are ordered by the Lord, and He delights in his way. Though he fall, he shall not be utterly cast down; for the Lord upholds him with His hand. ◊ Many are the afflictions of the righteous, but the Lord delivers him out of them all. ◊ For the Lord knows the way of the righteous, but the way of the ungodly shall perish. ◊ We know that all things work together for good to those who love God, to those who are the called according to His purpose. ◊ With us is the Lord our God, to help us and to fight our battles.

The Lord your God in your midst, the Mighty One, will save; He will rejoice over you with gladness.

PROV 2:8.DEUT 1:32-33.DEUT 32:11-12.PS 37:23-24.PS 34:19.PS 1:6.ROM 8:28.2 CHR 32:8.ZEPH 3:17

EVENING

My God, My God, why have You forsaken Me?

He was wounded for our transgressions, He was bruised for our iniquities; the chastisement for our peace was upon Him, and by His stripes we are healed. All we like sheep have gone astray . . . and the Lord has laid on Him the iniquity of us all. . . . He was taken from prison and from judgment, . . . He was cut off from the land of the living; for the transgressions of My people He was stricken.

[He] was delivered up because of our offenses. ◊ Christ also suffered once for sins, the just for the unjust, that He might bring us to God. ◊ [He] Himself bore our sins in His own body on the tree, that we, having died to sins, might live for righteousness—by whose stripes you were healed.

He made Him who knew no sin to be sin for us, that we might become the righteousness of God in Him.

Christ has redeemed us from the curse of the law, having become a curse for us (for it is written, "Cursed is everyone who hangs on a tree").

MATT 27:46.IS 53:5-6,8.ROM 4:25.1 PET 3:18.1 PET 2:24.2 COR 5:21.GAL 3:13

MORNING

Your Maker is your husband, the Lord of hosts
is His name.

This is a great mystery, but I speak concerning Christ and the church. You shall no longer be termed Forsaken, . . . but you shall be called Hephzibah [My Delight in Her], . . . for the Lord delights in you. . . . As the bridegroom rejoices over the bride, so shall your God rejoice over you. ◊ He has sent Me . . . to comfort all who mourn, . . . to console those who mourn in Zion, to give them beauty for ashes, the oil of joy for mourning, the garment of praise for the spirit of heaviness.

I will greatly rejoice in the Lord, my soul shall be joyful in my God; for He has clothed me with the garments of salvation, He has covered me with the robe of righteousness, as a bridegroom decks himself with ornaments, and as a bride adorns herself with her jewels.

I will betroth you to Me forever; yes, I will betroth you to Me in righteousness and justice, in lovingkindness and mercy.

Who shall separate us from the love of Christ?

IS 54:5.EPH 5:32.IS 62:4-5.IS 61:1-3.IS 61:10.HOS 2:19.ROM 8:35

EVENING

My times are in Your hand.

His saints are in Your hand. ◊ The word of the Lord came to [Elijah], saying, "Get away from here and turn eastward, and hide by the Brook Cherith, which flows into the Jordan. Drink from the brook, and I have commanded the ravens to feed you there." . . . Then the word of the Lord came to him, saying, "Arise, go to Zarephath, which belongs to Sidon, and dwell there. See, I have commanded a widow there to provide for you."

Do not worry about your life, what you will eat or what you will drink; nor about your body, what you will put on. Is not life more than food and the body more than clothing? . . . Your heavenly Father knows that you need all these things.

Seek first the kingdom of God and His righteousness, and all these things shall be added to you. . . . Do not worry about tomorrow, for tomorrow will worry about its own things. Sufficient for the day is its own trouble. ◊ Trust in the Lord with all your heart, and lean not on your own understanding. In all your ways acknowledge Him, and He shall direct your paths. ◊ [Cast] all your care upon Him, for He cares for you.

PS 31:15.DEUT 33:3.1 KIN 17:2-4,8-9.MATT 6:25,32.MATT 6:33-34.
PROV 3:5-6.1 PET 5:7

MARCH 8

MORNING_____

You have cast all my sins behind Your back.

Who is a God like You, pardoning iniquity and passing over the transgression of the remnant of His heritage? He does not retain His anger forever, because He delights in mercy. He will again have compassion on us, and will subdue our iniquities. You will cast all our sins into the depths of the sea.

I will forgive their iniquity, and their sin I will remember no more. ◊ "For a mere moment I have forsaken you, but with great mercies I will gather you. With a little wrath I hid My face from you for a moment; but with everlasting kindness I will have mercy on you," says the Lord, your Redeemer.

Blessed is he whose transgression is forgiven, whose sin is covered. Blessed is the man to whom the Lord does not impute iniquity, and in whose spirit there is no guile. ◊ The blood of Jesus Christ His Son cleanses us from all sin.

IS 38:17.MIC 7:18-19.JER 31:34.IS 54:7-8.PS 32:1-2.1 JOHN 1:7

EVENING_____

**I know whom I have believed and am persuaded that
He is able to keep what I have committed to Him
until that Day.**

[He] is able to do exceedingly abundantly above all that we ask or think.

God is able to make all grace abound toward you, that you, always having all sufficiency in all things, have an abundance for every good work.

He is able to aid those who are tempted.

He is also able to save to the uttermost those who come to God through Him, since He ever lives to make intercession for them.

[He] is able to keep you from stumbling, and to present you faultless before the presence of His glory with exceeding joy.

He is able to keep what I have committed to Him until that Day. ◊ [He] will transform our lowly body that it may be conformed to His glorious body, according to the working by which He is able even to subdue all things to Himself.

"Do you believe that I am able to do this?" They said to Him, "Yes, Lord." . . . "According to your faith let it be to you."

2 TIM 1:12.EPH 3:20.2 COR 9:8.HEB 2:18.HEB 7:25.JUDE 1:24.2 TIM
1:12.PHIL 3:21.MATT 9:28-29

MORNING

**The living God, who gives us richly
all things to enjoy.**

Beware that you do not forget the Lord your God by not keeping His commandments, His judgments, and His statutes which I command you today, lest—when you have eaten and are full, and have built beautiful houses and dwell in them; . . . when your heart is lifted up, and you forget the Lord your God. . . . For it is He who gives you power to get wealth.

Unless the Lord builds the house, they labor in vain who build it; unless the Lord guards the city, the watchman stays awake in vain. It is vain for you to rise up early, to sit up late, to eat the bread of sorrows; for so He gives His beloved sleep. ◊ They did not gain possession of the land by their own sword, nor did their own arm save them; but it was Your right hand, Your arm, and the light of Your countenance, because You favored them. ◊ There are many who say, "Who will show us any good?" Lord, lift up the light of Your countenance upon us.

1 TIM 6:17.DEUT 8:11-12,14,18.PS 127:1-2.PS 44:3.PS 4:6

EVENING

They sang as it were a new song.

Enter the Holiest by a new and living way which He consecrated for us. ◊ Not by works of righteousness which we have done, but according to His mercy He saved us, through the washing of regeneration and renewing of the Holy Spirit, whom He poured out on us abundantly through Jesus Christ our Savior. ◊ For by grace you have been saved through faith, and that not of yourselves; it is the gift of God, not of works, lest anyone should boast.

To Your name give glory, because of Your mercy, and because of Your truth. ◊ To Him who loved us and washed us from our sins in His own blood, and has made us kings and priests to His God and Father, to Him be glory and dominion forever and ever. Amen. ◊ You were slain, and have redeemed us to God by Your blood out of every tribe and tongue and people and nation. ◊ I looked, and behold, a great multitude which no one could number, . . . crying out with a loud voice, saying, "Salvation belongs to our God who sits on the throne, and to the Lamb!"

REV 14:3.HEB 10:20.TITUS 3:5-6.EPH 2:8-9.PS 115:1.REV 1:5-6.REV 5:9.REV 7:9-10

MARCH 10

MORNING

The-Lord-Will-Provide.

God will provide for Himself the lamb for a burnt offering.

Behold, the Lord's hand is not shortened, that it cannot save; nor His ear heavy, that it cannot hear. ◊ The Deliverer will come out of Zion, and He will turn away ungodliness from Jacob.

Happy is he who has the God of Jacob for his help, whose hope is in the Lord his God. ◊ Behold, the eye of the Lord is on those who fear Him, on those who hope in His mercy, to deliver their soul from death.

My God shall supply all your need according to His riches in glory by Christ Jesus. ◊ He Himself has said, "I will never leave you nor forsake you." So we may boldly say: "The Lord is my helper; I will not fear. What can man do to me?" ◊ The Lord is my strength and my shield; my heart trusted in Him, and I am helped; therefore my heart greatly rejoices, and with my song I will praise Him.

GEN 22:14.GEN 22:8.IS 59:1.ROM 11:26.PS 146:5.PS 33:18-19.PHIL 4:19.HEB 13:5-6.PS 28:7

EVENING

I am my beloved's, and my beloved is mine. He feeds his flock among the lilies.

Where two or three are gathered together in My name, I am there in the midst of them. ◊ If anyone loves Me, he will keep My word; and My Father will love him, and We will come to him and make Our home with him.

If you keep My commandments, you will abide in My love, just as I have kept My Father's commandments and abide in His love.

Let my beloved come to his garden and eat its pleasant fruits. ◊ I have come to my garden, my sister, my spouse; I have gathered my myrrh with my spice; I have eaten my honeycomb with my honey. ◊ The fruit of the Spirit is love, joy, peace, longsuffering, kindness, goodness, faithfulness, gentleness, self-control.

By this My Father is glorified, that you bear much fruit; so you will be My disciples. ◊ Every branch in Me that does not bear fruit He takes away; and every branch that bears fruit He prunes, that it may bear more fruit. ◊ [Be] filled with the fruits of righteousness which are by Jesus Christ, to the glory and praise of God.

SONG 6:3.MATT 18:20.JOHN 14:23.JOHN 15:10.SONG 4:16.SONG 5:1.GAL 5:22-23.JOHN 15:8.JOHN 15:2.PHIL 1:11

MORNING

The Lord bless you and keep you.

The blessing of the Lord makes one rich, and He adds no sorrow with it. ◊ You, O Lord, will bless the righteous; with favor You will surround him as with a shield.

He will not allow your foot to be moved; He who keeps you will not slumber. Behold, He who keeps Israel shall neither slumber nor sleep. The Lord is your keeper; the Lord is your shade at your right hand. . . . The Lord shall preserve you from all evil; He shall preserve your soul. The Lord shall preserve your going out and your coming in from this time forth, and even forevermore. ◊ I, the Lord, keep it, I water it every moment; lest any hurt it, I keep it night and day.

Holy Father, keep through Your name those whom You have given Me. . . . While I was with them in the world, I kept them in Your name. ◊ Those whom You gave Me I have kept.

The Lord will deliver me from every evil work and preserve me for His heavenly kingdom. To Him be glory forever and ever. Amen!

NUM 6:24.PROV 10:22.PS 5:12.PS 121:3-5.PS 121:7-8.IS 27:3.JOHN 17:11-12.2 TIM 4:18

EVENING

Jesus wept.

A man of sorrows and acquainted with grief. ◊ We do not have a High Priest who cannot sympathize with our weaknesses, but was in all points tempted as we are, yet without sin. ◊ It was fitting for Him, for whom are all things and by whom are all things, in bringing many sons to glory, to make the author of their salvation perfect through sufferings. ◊ Though He was a Son, yet He learned obedience by the things which He suffered.

I was not rebellious, nor did I turn away. I gave My back to those who struck Me, and My cheeks to those who plucked out the beard; I did not hide My face from shame and spitting.

How He loved him! ◊ He does not give aid to angels, but He does give aid to the seed of Abraham. Therefore, in all things He had to be made like His brethren, that He might be a merciful and faithful High Priest in things pertaining to God, to make propitiation for the sins of the people.

JOHN 11:35.IS 53:3.HEB 4:15.HEB 2:10.HEB 5:8.IS 50:5-6.JOHN 11:36.HEB 2:16-17

MORNING

The Lord make His face shine upon you, and be gracious to you; the Lord lift up His countenance upon you, and give you peace.

No one has seen God at any time. The only begotten Son, who is in the bosom of the Father, He has declared Him. ◊ [Jesus is] the brightness of His glory and the express image of His person. ◊ The god of this age has blinded [their minds], who do not believe, lest the light of the gospel of the glory of Christ, who is the image of God, should shine on them.

Make Your face shine upon Your servant; save me for Your mercies' sake. Do not let me be ashamed, O Lord, for I have called upon You. ◊ Lord, by Your favor You have made my mountain stand strong; You hid Your face, and I was troubled. ◊ Blessed are the people who know the joyful sound! They walk, O Lord, in the light of Your countenance.

The Lord will give strength to His people; the Lord will bless His people with peace. ◊ Be of good cheer! It is I; do not be afraid.

NUM 6:25-26.JOHN 1:18.HEB 1:3.2 COR 4:4.PS 31:16-17.PS 30:7.PS 89:15.PS 29:11.MATT 14:27

EVENING

Do those things that are pleasing in His sight.

Without faith it is impossible to please Him, for he who comes to God must believe that He is, and that He is a rewarder of those who diligently seek Him. ◊ Those who are in the flesh cannot please God. ◊ The Lord takes pleasure in His people; He will beautify the humble with salvation.

For this is commendable, if because of conscience toward God one endures grief, suffering wrongfully. For what credit is it if, when you are beaten for your faults, you take it patiently? But when you do good and suffer for it, if you take it patiently, this is commendable before God. ◊ Let it be the hidden person of the heart, with the incorruptible ornament of a gentle and quiet spirit, which is very precious in the sight of God.

Whoever offers praise glorifies Me; and to him who orders his conduct aright I will show the salvation of God. ◊ I will praise the name of God with a song, and will magnify Him with thanksgiving. This also shall please the Lord better than an ox or bull.

I beseech you . . . brethren, by the mercies of God, that you present your bodies a living sacrifice, holy, acceptable to God, which is your reasonable service.

1 JOHN 3:22.HEB 11:6.ROM 8:8.PS 149:4.1 PET 2:19-20.1 PET 3:4.PS 50:23.PS 69:30-31.ROM 12:1

MORNING

For there is one God and one Mediator between God and men, the Man Christ Jesus.

Inasmuch . . . as the children have partaken of flesh and blood, He Himself likewise shared in the same.

Look to Me, and be saved, all you ends of the earth! For I am God, and there is no other.

We have an Advocate with the Father, Jesus Christ the righteous. ◊ In Christ Jesus you who once were far off have been made near by the blood of Christ. For He Himself is our peace.

With His own blood He entered the Most Holy Place once for all, having obtained eternal redemption. . . . And for this reason He is the Mediator of the new covenant, by means of death, for the redemption of the transgressions under the first covenant, that those who are called may receive the promise of the eternal inheritance. ◊ He is also able to save to the uttermost those who come to God through Him, since He ever lives to make intercession for them.

1 TIM 2:5.HEB 2:14.IS 45:22.1 JOHN 2:1.EPH 2:13-14.HEB 9:12,15.HEB 7:25

EVENING

My soul is cast down within me.

You will keep him in perfect peace, whose mind is stayed on You, because he trusts in You. Trust in the Lord forever, for in YAH, the Lord, is everlasting strength.

Cast your burden on the Lord, and He shall sustain you; He shall never permit the righteous to be moved. ◊ For He has not despised nor abhorred the affliction of the afflicted; nor has He hidden His face from Him; but when He cried to Him, He heard. ◊ Is anyone among you suffering? Let him pray.

Let not your heart be troubled, neither let it be afraid. ◊ Do not worry about your life. . . . Is not life more than food and the body more than clothing? Look at the birds of the air, for they neither sow nor reap nor gather into barns; yet your heavenly Father feeds them. Are you not of more value than they? . . . Consider the lilies of the field, . . . even Solomon in all his glory was not arrayed like one of these. Now if God so clothes the grass of the field, which today is, and tomorrow is thrown into the oven, will He not much more clothe you, O you of little faith? ◊ Do not be unbelieving, but believing. ◊ I am with you always.

PS 42:6.IS 26:3-4.PS 55:22.PS 22:24.JAMES 5:13.JOHN 14:27.MATT 6:25-30.JOHN 20:27.MATT 28:20

MORNING

Adorn the doctrine of God our Savior in all things.

Let your conduct be worthy of the gospel of Christ. ◊ If you are reproached for the name of Christ, blessed are you. . . . But let none of you suffer as a murderer, a thief, an evildoer, or as a busybody in other people's matters. ◊ Become blameless and harmless, children of God without fault in the midst of a crooked and perverse generation, among whom you shine as lights in the world. ◊ Let your light so shine before men, that they may see your good works and glorify your Father in heaven.

Bind [mercy and truth] around your neck, write them on the tablet of your heart, and so find favor and high esteem in the sight of God and man. ◊ Whatever things are true, whatever things are noble, whatever things are just, whatever things are pure, whatever things are lovely, whatever things are of good report, if there is any virtue and if there is anything praiseworthy meditate on these things.

TITUS 2:10.PHIL 1:27.1 PET 4:14-15.PHIL 2:15.MATT 5:16.PROV 3:3-4.
PHIL 4:8

EVENING

The words that I speak to you are spirit,
and they are life.

Of His own will He brought us forth by the word of truth, that we might be a kind of firstfruits of His creatures. ◊ [God] also made us sufficient as ministers of the new covenant, not of the letter but of the Spirit; for the letter kills, but the Spirit gives life.

Christ also loved the church and gave Himself for it, that He might sanctify and cleanse it with the washing of water by the word, that He might present it to Himself a glorious church, not having spot or wrinkle or any such thing, but that it should be holy and without blemish.

How can a young man cleanse his way? By taking heed according to Your word. ◊ This is my comfort in my affliction, for Your word has given me life. ◊ Your word I have hidden in my heart, that I might not sin against You. ◊ The law of Your mouth is better to me than thousands of shekels of gold and silver. ◊ I will never forget Your precepts, for by them You have given me life. ◊ How sweet are Your words to my taste, sweeter than honey to my mouth! Through Your precepts I get understanding; therefore I hate every false way.

JOHN 6:63.JAMES 1:18.2 COR 3:6.EPH 5:25-27.PS 119:9.PS 119:50.PS
119:11.PS 119:72.PS 119:93.PS 119:103-104

MORNING

Perfect through sufferings.

"My soul is exceedingly sorrowful, even to death. Stay here and watch with Me." He went a little farther and fell on His face, and prayed, saying, "O My Father, if it is possible, let this cup pass from Me; nevertheless, not as I will, but as You will." ◊ And being in agony, He prayed more earnestly. And His sweat became like great drops of blood falling down to the ground.

The pains of death encompassed me, and the pangs of Sheol laid hold of me; I found trouble and sorrow. ◊ Reproach has broken my heart, and I am full of heaviness; I looked for someone to take pity, but there was none; and for comforters, but I found none. ◊ Look on my right hand and see, for there is no one who acknowledges me; refuge has failed me; no one cares for my soul.

He is despised and rejected by men, a man of sorrows and acquainted with grief. And we hid, as it were, our faces from Him; He was despised, and we did not esteem Him.

HEB 2:10.MATT 26:38-39.LUKE 22:44.PS 116:3.PS 69:20.PS 142:4.IS 53:3

EVENING

The Lord made the heavens and the earth, the sea, and all that is in them.

The heavens declare the glory of God; and the firmament shows His handiwork. ◊ By the word of the Lord the heavens were made, and all the host of them by the breath of His mouth. He gathers the waters of the sea together as a heap; He lays up the deep in storehouses. . . . For He spoke, and it was done; He commanded, and it stood fast. ◊ Behold, the nations are as a drop in a bucket, and are counted as the small dust on the balance; look, He lifts up the isles as a very little thing. ◊ Who has measured the waters in the hollow of his hand, measured heaven with a span and calculated the dust of the earth in a measure? Weighed the mountains in scales and the hills in a balance?

By faith we understand that the worlds were framed by the word of God, so that the things which are seen were not made of things which are visible.

When I consider Your heavens, the work of Your fingers, the moon and the stars, which You have ordained, what is man that You are mindful of him, and the son of man that You visit him?

EX 20:11.PS 19:1.PS 33:6-7,9.IS 40:15.IS 40:12.HEB 11:3.PS 8:3-4

MARCH 16

MORNING———————————————————

**What is your life? It is even a vapor that appears for a
little time and then vanishes away.**

Now my days are swifter than a runner; they flee away, they see no
good. They pass by like swift ships, like an eagle swooping on its prey. ◊
You carry them away like a flood; they are like a sleep. In the morning
they are like grass which grows up: in the morning it flourishes and
grows up; in the evening it is cut down and withers. ◊ Man who is born
of woman is of few days and full of trouble. He comes forth like a flower
and fades away.

The world is passing away, and the lust of it; but he who does the will
of God abides forever. ◊ They will perish, but You will endure; yes, all of
them will grow old like a garment; like a cloak You will change them, and
they will be changed. But You are the same, and Your years will have no
end. ◊ Jesus Christ is the same yesterday, today, and forever.

JAMES 4:14.JOB 9:25-26.PS 90:5-6.JOB 14:1-2.1 JOHN 2:17.PS 102:26-
27.HEB 13:8

EVENING———————————————————————

**I will sing with the spirit, and I will also sing with
the understanding.**

Be filled with the Spirit, speaking to one another in psalms and hymns
and spiritual songs, singing and making melody in your heart to the
Lord. ◊ Let the word of Christ dwell in you richly in all wisdom,
teaching and admonishing one another in psalms and hymns and
spiritual songs, singing with grace in your hearts to the Lord.

My mouth shall speak the praise of the Lord, and all flesh shall bless
His holy name forever and ever.

Praise the Lord! For it is good to sing praises to our God; for it is
pleasant, and praise is beautiful. . . . For God is the King of all the earth;
sing praises with understanding.

And I heard a voice from heaven, like the voice of many waters, and
like the voice of loud thunder. And I heard the sound of harpists playing
their harps. ◊ I saw another sign in heaven, great and marvelous: seven
angels . . . having harps of God. And they sing the song of Moses, the
servant of God, and the song of the Lamb, saying: "Great and marvelous
are Your works, Lord God Almighty! Just and true are Your ways, O
King of the saints!"

1 COR 14:15.EPH 5:18-19.COL 3:16.PS 145:21.PS 147:1,7.REV 14:2.REV
15:1-3

MORNING

He shall put his hand on the head of the burnt offering, and it will be accepted on his behalf to make atonement for him.

You were not redeemed with corruptible things, like silver or gold, . . . but with the precious blood of Christ, as of a lamb without blemish and without spot. ◊ [He] Himself bore our sins in His own body. ◊ He has made us accepted in the Beloved.

You also, as living stones, are being built up a spiritual house, a holy priesthood, to offer up spiritual sacrifices acceptable to God through Jesus Christ. ◊ I beseech you therefore, brethren, by the mercies of God, that you present your bodies a living sacrifice, holy, acceptable to God, which is your reasonable service.

Now to Him who is able to keep you from stumbling, and to present you faultless before the presence of His glory with exceeding joy, to God our Savior, who alone is wise, be glory and majesty, dominion and power, both now and forever.

LEV 1:4.1 PET 1:18-19.1 PET 2:24.EPH 1:6.1 PET 2:5.ROM 12:1.JUDE 1:24-25

EVENING

For we do not have a High Priest who cannot sympathize with our weaknesses, but was in all points tempted as we are, yet without sin.

So when the woman saw that the tree was good for food, that it was pleasant to the eyes, and a tree desirable to make one wise, she took of its fruit and ate. She also gave to her husband with her, and he ate.

When the tempter came to Him, he said, "If You are the Son of God, command that these stones become bread." But He answered and said, "It is written, 'Man shall not live by bread alone, but by every word that proceeds from the mouth of God.'" . . . Again, the devil took Him up on an exceedingly high mountain, and showed Him all the kingdoms of the world and their glory. And he said to Him, "All these things I will give You if You will fall down and worship me." Then Jesus said to him, "Away with you, Satan!" ◊ For all that is in the world is not of the Father.

In that He Himself has suffered, being tempted, He is able to aid those who are tempted. ◊ Blessed is the man who endures temptation.

HEB 4:15.GEN 3:6.MATT 4:3-4,8-10.1 JOHN 2:16.HEB 2:18.JAMES 1:12

MORNING

My eyes fail from looking upward.

Have mercy on me, O Lord, for I am weak; O Lord, heal me, for my bones are troubled. My soul also is greatly troubled; but You, O Lord—how long? Return, O Lord, deliver me! Oh, save me for Your mercies' sake! ◊ Fearfulness and trembling have come upon me, and horror has overwhelmed me. And I said, "Oh, that I had wings like a dove! For then I would fly away and be at rest."

You have need of endurance.

While they looked steadfastly toward heaven as He went up, behold, two men stood by them in white apparel, who also said, "Men of Galilee, why do you stand gazing up into heaven? This same Jesus, who was taken up from you into heaven, will so come in like manner as you saw Him go into heaven." ◊ Our citizenship is in heaven, from which we also eagerly wait for the Savior, the Lord Jesus Christ. ◊ We should . . . [be] looking for the blessed hope and glorious appearing of our great God and Savior Jesus Christ.

IS 38:14.PS 6:2-4.PS 55:5-6.HEB 10:36.ACTS 1:10-11.PHIL 3:20.TITUS 2:12-13

EVENING

His name shall be on their foreheads.

I am the good shepherd; and I know My sheep. ◊ Nevertheless the solid foundation of God stands, having this seal: "The Lord knows those who are His."

The Lord is good, a stronghold in the day of trouble; and He knows those who trust in Him.

You heard the word of truth, the gospel of your salvation; in whom also, having believed, you were sealed with the Holy Spirit of promise, who is the guarantee of our inheritance until the redemption of the purchased possession, to the praise of His glory. ◊ Now He who establishes us with you in Christ and has anointed us is God, who also has sealed us and given us the Spirit in our hearts as a deposit.

I will write on him the name of My God and the name of the city of My God, the New Jerusalem, which comes down out of heaven from My God. And I will write on him My new name.

This is the name by which she will be called: THE LORD OUR RIGHTEOUSNESS.

REV 22:4.JOHN 10:14.2 TIM 2:19.NAH 1:7.EPH 1:13-14.2 COR 1:21-22.REV 3:12.JER 33:16

MORNING

God, having raised up His Servant Jesus, sent Him to bless you, in turning away every one of you from your iniquities.

Blessed be the God and Father of our Lord Jesus Christ, who according to His abundant mercy has begotten us again to a living hope through the resurrection of Jesus Christ from the dead.

Our great God and Savior Jesus Christ, . . . gave Himself for us, that He might redeem us from every lawless deed and purify for Himself His own special people, zealous for good works. ◊ But as He who called you is holy, you also be holy in all your conduct, because it is written, "Be holy, for I am holy."

The God and Father of our Lord Jesus Christ, . . . has blessed us with every spiritual blessing in the heavenly places in Christ. ◊ In Him dwells all the fullness of the Godhead bodily; and you are complete in Him. ◊ Of His fullness we have all received, and grace for grace.

He who did not spare His own Son, but delivered Him up for us all, how shall He not with Him also freely give us all things?

ACTS 3:26.1 PET 1:3.TITUS 2:13-14.1 PET 1:15-16.EPH 1:3.COL 2:9-10.JOHN 1:16.ROM 8:32

EVENING

Strengthen me according to Your word.

Remember the word to Your servant, upon which You have caused me to hope. ◊ O Lord, I am oppressed; undertake for me!

Heaven and earth will pass away, but My words will by no means pass away. ◊ You know in all your hearts and in all your souls that not one thing has failed of all the good things which the Lord your God spoke concerning you.

Fear not, for I am with you; be not dismayed, for I am your God. ◊ "Be strong, . . . and work; for I am with you," says the Lord of hosts. ◊ "Not by might nor by power, but by My Spirit," says the Lord of hosts. ◊ Meditate in [This Book of the Law] day and night, that you may observe to do according to all that is written in it. For then you will make your way prosperous, and then you will have good success. . . . Be strong and of good courage; do not be afraid, nor be dismayed, for the Lord your God is with you wherever you go. ◊ Be strong in the Lord and in the power of His might.

PS 119:28.PS 119:49.IS 38:14.LUKE 21:33.JOSH 23:14.IS 41:10.HAG 2:4.ZECH 4:6.JOSH 1:8-9.EPH 6:10

MARCH 20

——————————————————

The entrance of Your words gives light.

This is the message which we have heard from Him and declare to you, that God is light and in Him is no darkness at all. ◊ God who commanded light to shine out of darkness who has shone in our hearts to give the light of the knowledge of the glory of God in the face of Jesus Christ. ◊ The Word was with God. ◊ In Him was life, and the life was the light of men. ◊ If we walk in the light as He is in the light, we have fellowship with one another, and the blood of Jesus Christ His Son cleanses us from all sin.

Your word I have hidden in my heart, that I might not sin against You. ◊ You are already clean because of the word which I have spoken to you.

You were once darkness, but now you are light in the Lord. Walk as children of light. ◊ You are a chosen generation, a royal priesthood, a holy nation, His own special people, that you may proclaim the praises of Him who called you out of darkness into His marvelous light.

PS 119:130.1 JOHN 1:5.2 COR 4:6.JOHN 1:1.JOHN 1:4.1 JOHN 1:7.PS 119:11.JOHN 15:3.EPH 5:8.1 PET 2:9

EVENING——————————————————

Noah . . . was a just man, perfect in his generations.

But that no one is justified by the law in the sight of God is evident, for "The just shall live by faith." ◊ Noah built an altar to the Lord, and took of every clean animal and of every clean bird, and offered burnt offerings on the altar. And the Lord smelled a soothing aroma.

Therefore by the deeds of the law no flesh will be justified in His sight, for by the law is the knowledge of sin. But now the righteousness of God apart from the law is revealed, . . . even the righteousness of God which is through faith in Jesus Christ to all and on all who believe. For there is no difference.

We also rejoice in God through our Lord Jesus Christ, through whom we have now received the reconciliation. ◊ Whom He predestined, these He also called; whom He called, these He also justified; and whom He justified, these He also glorified.

GEN 6:8-9.GAL 3:11.GEN 8:20-21.ROM 3:20-22.ROM 5:11.ROM 8:30

MORNING

**Be watchful, and strengthen the things which remain,
that are ready to die.**

The end of all things is at hand; therefore be serious and watchful in your prayers. ◇ Be sober, be vigilant; because your adversary the devil walks about like a roaring lion, seeking whom he may devour. ◇ Take heed to yourself, and diligently keep yourself, lest you forget the things your eyes have seen, and lest they depart from your heart all the days of your life. ◇ The just shall live by faith; but if anyone draws back, my soul has no pleasure in him. But we are not of those who draw back to perdition, but of those who believe to the saving of the soul.

What I say to you, I say to all: Watch!

Fear not, for I am with you; be not dismayed, for I am your God. I will strengthen you, yes, I will help you, I will uphold you with My righteous right hand. . . . I, the Lord your God, will hold your right hand.

REV 3:2.1 PET 4:7.1 PET 5:8.DEUT 4:9.HEB 10:38-39.MARK 13:37.IS 41:10,13

EVENING

Has His mercy ceased forever?

[He] remembered us in our lowly state, for His mercy endures forever. ◇ The Lord is longsuffering and abundant in mercy, forgiving iniquity and transgression. ◇ Who is a God like You, pardoning iniquity and passing over the transgression of the remnant of His heritage? He does not retain His anger forever, because He delights in mercy. He will again have compassion on us, and will subdue our iniquities. You will cast all our sins into the depths of the sea. ◇ Not by works of righteousness which we have done, but according to His mercy He saved us, through the washing of regeneration and renewing of the Holy Spirit.

Blessed be the God and Father of our Lord Jesus Christ, the Father of mercies and God of all comfort, who comforts us in all our tribulation.

In all things He had to be made like His brethren, that He might be a merciful and faithful High Priest in things pertaining to God, to make propitiation for the sins of the people. For in that He Himself has suffered, being tempted, He is able to aid those who are tempted.

PS 77:8.PS 136:23.NUM 14:18.MIC 7:18-19.TITUS 3:5.2 COR 1:3-4.HEB 2:17-18

MARCH 22

MORNING_____

**Lot lifted his eyes and saw all the plain of Jordan,
that it was well watered everywhere . . . like the
garden of the Lord. . . . Then Lot chose for himself all
the plain of Jordan.**

Righteous Lot, . . . dwelling among them, tormented his righteous soul . . . by seeing and hearing their lawless deeds.

Do not be deceived, God is not mocked; for whatever a man sows, that he will also reap. ◊ Remember Lot's wife.

Do not be unequally yoked together with unbelievers. For what fellowship has righteousness with lawlessness? And what communion has light with darkness? ◊ Therefore "Come out from among them and be separate," says the Lord. "Do not touch what is unclean." ◊ Do not be partakers with them. For you were once darkness, but now you are light in the Lord. Walk as children of light . . . proving what is acceptable to the Lord. And have no fellowship with the unfruitful works of darkness, but rather expose them.

GEN 13:10-11.2 PET 2:7-8.GAL 6:7.LUKE 17:32.2 COR 6:14.2 COR
6:17.EPH 5:7-8,10-11

EVENING_____

**It may be that the Lord will be with me, and I shall
be able to drive them out.**

He Himself has said, "I will never leave you nor forsake you." So we may boldly say: "The Lord is my helper; I will not fear. What can man do to me?" ◊ I will go in the strength of the Lord God; I will make mention of Your righteousness, of Yours only.

The work of righteousness will be peace, and the effect of righteousness, quietness and assurance forever.

Stand therefore, having girded your waist with truth, having put on the breastplate of righteousness, . . . taking the shield of faith with which you will be able to quench all the fiery darts of the wicked one. And take the helmet of salvation, and the sword of the Spirit, which is the word of God. ◊ For we do not wrestle against flesh and blood, but against principalities, against powers, against the rulers of the darkness of this age, against spiritual hosts of wickedness in the heavenly places. Therefore take up the whole armor of God, that you may be able to withstand in the evil day, and having done all, to stand. ◊ The Lord is with you, you mighty man of valor! ◊ Go. . . . Have I not sent you?

JOSH 14:12.HEB 13:5-6.PS 71:16.IS 32:17.EPH 6:14,16-17.EPH 6:12-
13.JUDG 6:12.JUDG 6:14

MORNING

Holy, holy, holy, Lord God Almighty.

But You are holy, who inhabit the praises of Israel. ◊ [God] said, "Do not draw near this place. Take your sandals off your feet, for the place where you stand is holy ground." Moreover He said, "I am the God of your father—the God of Abraham, the God of Isaac, and the God of Jacob." And Moses hid his face, for he was afraid to look upon God. ◊ "To whom then will you liken Me, or to whom shall I be equal?" says the Holy One. ◊ I am the Lord your God, the Holy One of Israel, your Savior. ◊ I, even I, am the Lord, and besides Me there is no savior.

As He who called you is holy, you also be holy in all your conduct, because it is written, "Be holy, for I am holy." ◊ Do you not know that your body is the temple of the Holy Spirit who is in you, whom you have from God, and you are not your own? ◊ You are the temple of the living God. As God has said: "I will dwell in them and walk among them. I will be their God, and they shall be My people." ◊ Can two walk together, unless they are agreed?

REV 4:8.PS 22:3.EX 3:5-6.IS 40:25.IS 43:3.IS 43:11.1 PET 1:15-16.1 COR 6:19.2 COR 6:16.AMOS 3:3

EVENING

Do not hide Your face from me.

Behold, I stand at the door and knock. If anyone hears My voice and opens the door, I will come in to him and dine with him, and he with Me. ◊ Tell me, O you whom I love, where you feed your flock, where you make it rest at noon. For why should I be as one who veils herself by the flocks of your companions? ◊ I found the one I love. I held him and would not let him go.

Let my beloved come to his garden and eat its pleasant fruits. ◊ I have come to my garden. ◊ I did not say to the seed of Jacob, "Seek Me in vain"; I, the Lord, speak righteousness, I declare things that are right.

I am with you always, even to the end of the age. ◊ I will never leave you nor forsake you. ◊ For where two or three are gathered together in My name, I am there in the midst of them. ◊ The world will see Me no more, but you will see Me. ◊ You are complete in Him.

PS 27:9.REV 3:20.SONG 1:7.SONG 3:4.SONG 4:16.SONG 5:1.IS 45:19.MATT 28:20.HEB 13:5.MATT 18:20.JOHN 14:19.COL 2:10

MARCH 24

MORNING

He believed in the Lord, and He accounted it to him for righteousness.

He did not waver at the promise of God through unbelief, but was strengthened in faith, giving glory to God, and being fully convinced that what He had promised He was also able to perform. And therefore "it was accounted to him for righteousness." Now it was not written for his sake alone that it was imputed to him, but also for us. It shall be imputed to us who believe in Him who raised up Jesus our Lord from the dead.

The promise that he would be the heir of the world was not to Abraham or to his seed through the law, but through the righteousness of faith. ◊ The just shall live by faith. ◊ Let us hold fast the confession of our hope without wavering, for He who promised is faithful. ◊ Our God is in heaven; He does whatever He pleases. ◊ With God nothing will be impossible. ◊ Blessed is she who believed, for there will be a fulfillment of those things which were told her from the Lord.

GEN 15:6.ROM 4:20-24.ROM 4:13.ROM 1:17.HEB 10:23.PS 115:3.LUKE 1:37.LUKE 1:45

EVENING

God who calls you into His own kingdom and glory.

Jesus answered, "My kingdom is not of this world. If My kingdom were of this world, My servants would fight, so that I should not be delivered to the Jews; but now My kingdom is not from here."

The kingdoms of this world have become the kingdoms of our Lord and of His Christ, and He shall reign forever and ever! ◊ You have made us kings and priests to our God; and we shall reign on the earth. ◊ I saw thrones, and they sat on them, and judgment was committed to them. . . . And they lived and reigned with Christ for a thousand years.

Father, I desire that they also whom You gave Me may be with Me where I am, that they may behold My glory which You have given Me; for You loved Me before the foundation of the world. ◊ Then the righteous will shine forth as the sun in the kingdom of their Father. ◊ Do not fear, little flock, for it is your Father's good pleasure to give you the kingdom.

The glory of God illuminated it, and the Lamb is its light. And the nations of those who are saved shall walk in its light. . . . They shall bring the glory and the honor of the nations into it. ◊ Your kingdom come.

1 THESS 2:12.JOHN 18:36.REV 11:15.REV 5:10.REV 20:4.JOHN 17:24.MATT 13:43.LUKE 12:32.REV 21:23-24,26.MATT 6:10

MORNING

I will never leave you nor forsake you.

So we may boldly say: "The Lord is my helper; I will not fear. What can man do to me?"

Behold, I am with you and will keep you wherever you go, and will bring you back to this land; for I will not leave you until I have done what I have spoken to you. ◊ Be strong and of good courage, do not fear nor be afraid of them; for the Lord your God, He is the One who goes with you. He will not leave you nor forsake you.

Demas has forsaken me, having loved this present world. . . . At my first defense no one stood with me, but all forsook me. . . . But the Lord stood with me and strengthened me. ◊ When my father and my mother forsake me, then the Lord will take care of me.

Lo, I am with you always, even to the end of the age. ◊ I am He who lives, and was dead, and behold, I am alive forevermore. ◊ I will not leave you orphans; I will come to you.

HEB 13:5.HEB 13:6.GEN 28:15.DEUT 31:6.2 TIM 4:10,16-17.PS
27:10.MATT 28:20.REV 1:18.JOHN 14:18

EVENING

Master, we have toiled all night and caught nothing; nevertheless at Your word I will let down the net.

All authority has been given to Me in heaven and on earth. Go therefore and make disciples of all the nations, baptizing them in the name of the Father and of the Son and of the Holy Spirit, and lo, I am with you always, even to the end of the age.

The kingdom of heaven is like a dragnet that was cast into the sea.

For if I preach the gospel, I have nothing to boast of, for necessity is laid upon me; yes, woe is me if I do not preach the gospel! ◊ To the weak I became as weak, that I might win the weak. I have become all things to all men, that I might by all means save some.

Let us not grow weary while doing good, for in due season we shall reap if we do not lose heart. ◊ My word . . . shall accomplish what I please, and it shall prosper in the thing for which I sent it. ◊ Neither he who plants is anything, nor he who waters, but God who gives the increase. ◊ I . . . appointed you that you should go and bear fruit, and that your fruit should remain.

LUKE 5:5.MATT 28:18-20.MATT 13:47.1 COR 9:16.1 COR 9:22.GAL
6:9.IS 55:11.1 COR 3:7.JOHN 15:16

MARCH 26

The kingdom of heaven is like a man traveling to a far country, who called his own servants and delivered his goods to them. . . . He gave . . . to each according to his own ability.

Do you not know that to whom you present yourselves slaves to obey, you are that one's slaves whom you obey?

One and the same Spirit works all these things, distributing to each one individually as He wills. ◊ The manifestation of the Spirit is given to each one for the profit of all. ◊ As each one has received a gift, minister it to one another, as good stewards of the manifold grace of God. ◊ It is required in stewards that one be found faithful. ◊ For everyone to whom much is given, from him much will be required; and to whom much has been committed, of him they will ask the more.

Who is sufficient for these things? ◊ I can do all things through Christ who strengthens me.

MATT 25:14-15.ROM 6:16.1 COR 12:11.1 COR 12:7.1 PET 4:10.
1 COR.4:2.LUKE 12:48.2 COR 2:16.PHIL 4:13

Distributing to the needs of the saints, given to hospitality.

David said, "Is there still anyone who is left of the house of Saul, that I may show him kindness for Jonathan's sake?"

Come, you blessed of My Father, inherit the kingdom prepared for you from the foundation of the world: for I was hungry and you gave Me food; I was thirsty and you gave Me drink; I was a stranger and you took Me in; I was naked and you clothed Me; I was sick and you visited Me; I was in prison and you came to Me. . . . Inasmuch as you did it to one of the least of these My brethren, you did it to Me. ◊ Whoever gives one of these little ones only a cup of cold water in the name of a disciple, assuredly, I say to you, he shall by no means lose his reward.

Do not forget to do good and to share, for with such sacrifices God is well pleased. ◊ For God is not unjust to forget your work and labor of love which you have shown toward His name, in that you have ministered to the saints, and do minister. And we desire that each one of you show the same diligence to the full assurance of hope until the end.

ROM 12:13.2 SAM 9:1.MATT 25:34-36,40.MATT 10:42.HEB 13:16.HEB
6:10-11

MORNING

To him who sows righteousness will be a sure reward.

After a long time the lord of those servants came and settled accounts with them. So he who had received five talents came and brought five other talents, saying, "Lord, you delivered to me five talents; look, I have gained five more talents besides them." His lord said to him, "Well done, good and faithful servant; you were faithful over a few things, I will make you ruler over many things. Enter into the joy of your lord."

We must all appear before the judgment seat of Christ, that each one may receive the things done in the body, according to what he has done, whether good or bad.

I have fought the good fight, I have finished the race, I have kept the faith. Finally, there is laid up for me the crown of righteousness, which the Lord, the righteous Judge, will give to me on that Day.

Behold, I come quickly! Hold fast what you have, that no one may take your crown.

PROV 11:18.MATT 25:19-21.2 COR 5:10.2 TIM 4:7-8.REV 3:11

EVENING

God is faithful.

God is not a man, that He should lie, nor a son of man, that He should repent. Has He said, and will He not do it? ◇ The Lord has sworn and will not relent.

God, determining to show more abundantly to the heirs of promise the immutability of His counsel, confirmed it by an oath, that by two immutable things, in which it is impossible for God to lie, we might have strong consolation, who have fled for refuge to lay hold of the hope set before us. ◇ Therefore let those who suffer according to the will of God commit their souls to Him in doing good, as to a faithful Creator.

I know whom I have believed and am persuaded that He is able to keep what I have committed to Him until that Day. ◇ He who calls you is faithful, who also will do it. ◇ All the promises of God in Him are Yes, and in Him Amen, to the glory of God through us.

1 COR 10:13.NUM 23:19.HEB 7:21.HEB 6:17-18.1 PET 4:19.2 TIM 1:12.
1 THESS 5:24.2 COR 1:20

MARCH 28

Be strong and of good courage.

The Lord is my light and my salvation; whom shall I fear? The Lord is the strength of my life; of whom shall I be afraid? ◇ He gives power to the weak, and to those who have no might He increases strength. Even the youths shall faint and be weary, and the young men shall utterly fall, but those who wait on the Lord shall renew their strength; they shall mount up with wings like eagles, they shall run and not be weary, they shall walk and not faint. ◇ My flesh and my heart fail; but God is the strength of my heart and my portion forever.

If God is for us, who can be against us? ◇ The Lord is on my side; I will not fear. What can man do to me? ◇ Through You we will push down our enemies; through Your name we will trample those who rise up against us. ◇ We are more than conquerors through Him who loved us.

Arise and begin working, and the Lord be with you.

JOSH 1:18. PS 27:1. IS 40:29-31. PS 73:26. ROM 8:31. PS 118:6. PS 44:5. ROM 8:37. 1 CHR 22:16

Our friend Lazarus sleeps.

I do not want you to be ignorant, brethren, concerning those who have fallen asleep, lest you sorrow as others who have no hope. For if we believe that Jesus died and rose again, even so God will bring with Him those who sleep in Jesus.

For if the dead do not rise, then Christ is not risen. And if Christ is not risen, your faith is futile; you are still in your sins! Then also those who have fallen asleep in Christ have perished. . . . But now Christ is risen from the dead, and has become the firstfruits of those who have fallen asleep.

When all the people had completely crossed over the Jordan, . . . the Lord spoke to Joshua, saying: "Take for yourselves twelve men from the people, one man from every tribe, and command them, saying, 'Take for yourselves twelve stones from here, out of the midst of the Jordan, from the place where the priests' feet stood firm. You shall carry them over with you and leave them.' . . . These stones shall be for a memorial to the children of Israel forever." ◇ This Jesus God has raised up, of which we are all witnesses. ◇ Witnesses chosen before by God, . . . ate and drank with Him after He arose from the dead.

JOHN 11:11. 1 THESS 4:13-14. 1 COR 15:16-18,20. JOSH 4:1-3,7. ACTS 2:32. ACTS 10:41

MORNING

Come, you blessed of My Father, inherit the kingdom prepared for you from the foundation of the world.

Do not fear, little flock, for it is your Father's good pleasure to give you the kingdom. ◊ Has God not chosen the poor of this world to be rich in faith and heirs of the kingdom which He promised to those who love Him? ◊ Heirs of God and joint heirs with Christ, if indeed we suffer with Him, that we may also be glorified together.

The Father Himself loves you, because you have loved Me. ◊ God is not ashamed to be called their God, for He has prepared a city for them.

He who overcomes shall inherit all things, and I will be his God and he shall be My son. ◊ There is laid up for me the crown of righteousness, which the Lord, the righteous Judge, will give to me on that Day, and not to me only but also to all who have loved His appearing. ◊ He who has begun a good work in you will complete it until the day of Jesus Christ.

MATT 25:34.LUKE 12:32.JAMES 2:5.ROM 8:17.JOHN 16:27.HEB
11:16.REV 21:7.2 TIM 4:8.PHIL 1:6

EVENING

Riches are not forever, nor does a crown endure to all generations.

Every man walks about like a shadow; surely they busy themselves in vain; he heaps up riches, and does not know who will gather them. ◊ Set your mind on things above, not on things on the earth. ◊ Do not lay up for yourselves treasures on earth, where moth and rust destroy and where thieves break in and steal; but lay up for yourselves treasures in heaven. . . . For where your treasure is, there your heart will be also.

Everyone who competes for the prize is temperate in all things. Now they do it to obtain a perishable crown, but we for an imperishable crown. ◊ We do not look at the things which are seen, but at the things which are not seen. For the things which are seen are temporary, but the things which are not seen are eternal. ◊ To him who sows righteousness will be a sure reward. ◊ There is laid up for me the crown of righteousness, which the Lord, the righteous Judge, will give to me on that Day, and not to me only but also to all who have loved His appearing. ◊ You will receive the crown of glory that does not fade away.

PROV 27:24.PS 39:6.COL 3:2.MATT 6:19-21.1 COR 9:25.2 COR
4:18.PROV 11:18.2 TIM 4:8.1 PET 5:4

MARCH 30

MORNING

Isaac went out to meditate in the field in the evening.

Let the words of my mouth and the meditation of my heart be acceptable in Your sight, O Lord, my strength and my redeemer.

When I consider Your heavens, the work of Your fingers, the moon and the stars, which You have ordained, what is man that You are mindful of him, and the son of man that You visit him? ◊ The works of the Lord are great, studied by all who have pleasure in them.

Blessed is the man who walks not in the counsel of the ungodly, nor stands in the path of sinners, nor sits in the seat of the scornful; but his delight is in the law of the Lord, and in His law he meditates day and night. ◊ This Book of the Law shall not depart from your mouth, but you shall meditate in it day and night. ◊ My soul shall be satisfied as with marrow and fatness, and my mouth shall praise You with joyful lips. When I remember You on my bed, I meditate on You in the night watches.

GEN 24:63.PS 19:14.PS 8:3-4.PS 111:2.PS 1:1-2.JOSH 1:8.PS 63:5-6

EVENING

How long, O Lord? Will You forget me forever? How long will You hide Your face from me?

Every good gift and every perfect gift is from above, and comes down from the Father of lights, with whom there is no variation or shadow of turning. ◊ But Zion said, "The Lord has forsaken me, and my Lord has forgotten me." Can a woman forget her nursing child, and not have compassion on the son of her womb? Surely they may forget, yet I will not forget you.

You will not be forgotten by Me! I have blotted out, like a thick cloud, your transgressions, and like a cloud, your sins.

Now Jesus loved Martha and her sister and Lazarus. So, when He heard that he was sick, He stayed two more days in the place where He was. ◊ A woman of Canaan came from that region and cried out to Him, saying, "Have mercy on me, O Lord. . . ." But He answered her not a word.

The genuineness of your faith, being much more precious than gold that perishes, though it is tested by fire, may be found to praise, honor, and glory at the revelation of Jesus Christ.

PS 13:1.JAMES 1:17.IS 49:14-15.IS 44:21-22.JOHN 11:5-6.MATT 15:22-23.1 PET 1:7

MORNING———————————————————

My God shall supply all your need according to his riches in glory by Christ Jesus.

Seek first the kingdom of God and His righteousness, and all . . . things shall be added to you. ◊ He who did not spare His own Son, but delivered Him up for us all, how shall He not with Him also freely give us all things? ◊ All things are yours: whether Paul or Apollos or Cephas, or the world or life or death, or things present or things to come—all are yours. And you are Christ's, and Christ is God's. ◊ We commend ourselves as ministers of God: . . . as having nothing, and yet possessing all things.

The Lord is my shepherd; I shall not want. ◊ The Lord God is a sun and shield; the Lord will give grace and glory; no good thing will He withhold from those who walk uprightly. ◊ The living God . . . gives us richly all things to enjoy. ◊ God is able to make all grace abound toward you, that you, always having all sufficiency in all things, have an abundance for every good work.

PHIL 4:19.MATT 6:33.ROM 8:32.1 COR 3:21-23.2 COR 6:4,10.PS 23:1.PS 84:11.1 TIM 6:17.2 COR 9:8.

EVENING———————————————————

What fellowship has righteousness with lawlessness?

Men loved darkness rather than light, because their deeds were evil. ◊ You are all sons of light and sons of the day. We are not of the night nor of darkness.

Darkness has blinded his eyes. ◊ Your word is a lamp to my feet and a light to my path.

The dark places of the earth are full of the habitations of cruelty. ◊ Love is of God; and everyone who loves is born of God and knows God. He who does not love does not know God, for God is love.

The way of the wicked is like darkness; they do not know what makes them stumble. ◊ But the path of the just is like the shining sun, that shines ever brighter unto the perfect day.

I have come as a light into the world, that whoever believes in Me should not abide in darkness. ◊ You were once darkness, but now you are light in the Lord. Walk as children of light (for the fruit of the Spirit is in all goodness, righteousness, and truth), proving what is acceptable to the Lord.

2 COR 6:14.JOHN 3:19.1 THESS 5:5.1 JOHN 2:11.PS 119:105.PS 74:20. 1 JOHN 4:7-8.PROV 4:19.PROV 4:18.JOHN 12:46.EPH 5:8-10

APRIL 1

The fruit of the Spirit is . . . joy.

The kingdom of God is . . . joy in the Holy Spirit. ◊ Believing, you rejoice with joy inexpressible and full of glory.

We commend ourselves . . . as sorrowful, yet always rejoicing. ◊ I am exceedingly joyful in all our tribulation.

Jesus, the author and finisher of our faith, . . . for the joy that was set before Him endured the cross, despising the shame. ◊ These things I have spoken to you, that My joy may remain in you, and that your joy may be full. ◊ As the sufferings of Christ abound in us, so our consolation also abounds through Christ.

Rejoice in the Lord always. Again I will say, rejoice! ◊ The joy of the Lord is your strength.

In Your presence is fullness of joy; at Your right hand are pleasures forevermore. ◊ For the Lamb who is in the midst of the throne will shepherd them and lead them to living fountains of waters. And God will wipe away every tear from their eyes.

GAL 5:22.ROM 14:17.1 PET 1:8.2 COR 6:4,10.2 COR 7:4.HEB 12:2.JOHN 15:11.2 COR 1:5.PHIL 4:4.NEH 8:10.PS 16:11.REV 7:17

Gideon built an altar there to the Lord, and called it The-Lord-Shalom.

Behold, a son shall be born to you, who shall be a man of rest; and I will give him rest from all his enemies all around. His name shall be Solomon [peaceful], for I will give peace and quietness to Israel in his days.

A greater than Solomon is here. ◊ For unto us a Child is born, unto us a Son is given; and the government will be upon His shoulder. And His name will be called Wonderful, Counselor, Mighty God, Everlasting Father, Prince of Peace. ◊ My people will dwell in a peaceful habitation, in secure dwellings, and in quiet resting places, though hail comes down on the forest, and the city is brought low in humiliation.

He Himself is our peace. ◊ This One shall be peace. ◊ You will keep him in perfect peace, whose mind is stayed on You, because he trusts in You.

Peace I leave with you, My peace I give to you; not as the world gives do I give to you. ◊ The peace of God, which surpasses all understanding, will guard your hearts and minds through Christ Jesus.

JUDG 6:24.1 CHR 22:9.MATT 12:42.IS 9:6.IS 32:18-19.EPH 2:14.MIC 5:5.IS 26:3.JOHN 14:27.PHIL 4:7

MORNING

If you return to the Lord with all your hearts, then put away the foreign gods and the Ashtoreths from among you, and prepare your hearts for the Lord, and serve Him only.

Little children, keep yourselves from idols. ◊ Therefore "Come out from among them and be separate, says the Lord. Do not touch what is unclean, and I will receive you. I will be a Father to you, and you shall be My sons and daughters, says the Lord Almighty." ◊ You cannot serve God and mammon.

You shall worship no other god, for the Lord, whose name is Jealous, is a jealous God. ◊ Serve Him with a loyal heart and with a willing mind; for the Lord searches all hearts and understands all the intent of the thoughts.

For man looks at the outward appearance, but the Lord looks at the heart. ◊ Beloved, if our heart does not condemn us, we have confidence toward God.

1 SAM 7:3.1 JOHN 5:21.2 COR 6:17-18.MATT 6:24.EX 34:14.1 CHR 28:9.
1 SAM 16:7.1 JOHN 3:21

EVENING

When the Son of Man comes, will He really find faith on the earth?

He came to His own, and His own did not receive Him. ◊ The Spirit expressly says that in latter times some will depart from the faith. ◊ Preach the word! Be ready in season and out of season. Convince, rebuke, exhort, with all longsuffering and teaching. For the time will come when they will not endure sound doctrine, but according to their own desires, because they have itching ears, they will heap up for themselves teachers; and they will turn their ears away from the truth, and be turned aside to fables.

Of that day and hour no one knows, neither the angels in heaven, nor the Son, but only the Father. Take heed, watch and pray; for you do not know when the time is. ◊ Blessed are those servants whom the master, when he comes, will find watching. ◊ [Look] for the blessed hope and glorious appearing of our great God and Savior Jesus Christ.

LUKE 18:8.JOHN 1:11.1 TIM 4:1.2 TIM 4:2-4.MARK 13:32-33.LUKE
12:37.TITUS 2:13

APRIL 3

Beloved, do not forget this one thing, that with the Lord one day is as a thousand years, and a thousand years as one day. The Lord is not slack concerning His promise, as some count slackness.

"For My thoughts are not your thoughts, nor are your ways My ways," says the Lord. "For as the heavens are higher than the earth, so are My ways higher than your ways, and My thoughts than your thoughts. For as the rain comes down, and the snow from heaven, and do not return there, but water the earth, . . . so shall My word be that goes forth from My mouth; it shall not return to Me void, but it shall accomplish what I please, and it shall prosper in the thing for which I sent it."

For God has committed them all to disobedience, that He might have mercy on all. Oh, the depth of the riches both of the wisdom and knowledge of God! How unsearchable are His judgments and His ways past finding out!

2 PET 3:8-9.IS 55:8-11.ROM 11:32-33

I overthrew some of you, . . . you were like a firebrand plucked from the burning.

The sinners in Zion are afraid; fearfulness has seized the hypocrites: . . . who among us shall dwell with everlasting burnings? ◊ We had the sentence of death in ourselves, that we should not trust in ourselves but in God who raises the dead, who delivered us from so great a death, and does deliver us; in whom we trust that He will still deliver us. ◊ The wages of sin is death, but the gift of God is eternal life in Christ Jesus our Lord.

It is a fearful thing to fall into the hands of the living God. ◊ Knowing, therefore, the terror of the Lord, we persuade men.

Preach the word! Be ready in season and out of season. ◊ Others save with fear, pulling them out of the fire.

"Not by might nor by power, but by My Spirit," says the Lord of hosts. ◊ [He] desires all men to be saved and to come to the knowledge of the truth.

AMOS 4:11.IS 33:14.2 COR 1:9-10.ROM 6:23.HEB 10:31.2 COR 5:11.
2 TIM 4:2.JUDE 1:23.ZECH 4:6.1 TIM 2:4

MORNING

Do not be afraid; I am the First and the Last.

You have not come to the mountain that may be touched and that burned with fire, and to blackness and darkness and tempest, . . . but you have come to Mount Zion to God the Judge of all, to the spirits of just men made perfect, . . . to Jesus the Mediator of the new covenant. ◊ Jesus, the author and finisher of our faith. ◊ We do not have a High Priest who cannot sympathize with our weaknesses, but was in all points tempted as we are, yet without sin. Let us therefore come boldly to the throne of grace, that we may obtain mercy and find grace to help in time of need.

Thus says the Lord, the King of Israel, and his Redeemer, the Lord of hosts: "I am the First and I am the Last; besides Me there is no God." ◊ Mighty God, Everlasting Father, Prince of Peace.

Are You not from everlasting, O Lord my God, my Holy One? ◊ Who is God, except the Lord? And who is a rock, except our God?

REV 1:17.HEB 12:18,22-24.HEB 12:2.HEB 4:15-16.IS 44:6.IS 9:6.HAB 1:12.2 SAM 22:32

EVENING

Lead me to the rock that is higher than I.

Be anxious for nothing, but in everything by prayer and supplication, with thanksgiving, let your requests be made known to God; and the peace of God, which surpasses all understanding, will guard your hearts and minds through Christ Jesus.

When my spirit was overwhelmed within me, then You knew my path. ◊ He knows the way that I take; when He has tested me, I shall come forth as gold. ◊ Lord, You have been our dwelling place in all generations. ◊ You have been . . . to the poor . . . a refuge from the storm, a shade from the heat.

For who is God, except the Lord? And who is a rock, except our God? ◊ They shall never perish; neither shall anyone snatch them out of My hand. ◊ Uphold me according to Your word, that I may live; and do not let me be ashamed of my hope. ◊ This hope we have as an anchor of the soul, both sure and steadfast, and which enters the Presence behind the veil.

PS 61:2.PHIL 4:6-7.PS 142:3.JOB 23:10.PS 90:1.IS 25:4.PS 18:31.JOHN 10:28.PS 119:116.HEB 6:19

MORNING

I will not let You go unless You bless me!

Or let him take hold of My strength, that he may make peace with Me; and he shall make peace with Me.

O woman, great is your faith! Let it be to you as you desire. ◊ According to your faith let it be to you. ◊ Let him ask in faith, with no doubting, for he who doubts is like a wave of the sea driven and tossed by the wind. For let not that man suppose that he will receive anything from the Lord.

They drew near to the village where they were going, and He indicated that He would have gone farther. But they constrained Him, saying, "Abide with us." . . . He vanished from their sight. And they said to one another, "Did not our heart burn within us while He talked with us on the road, and while He opened the Scriptures to us?" ◊ I pray, if I have found grace in Your sight, show me now Your way, that I may know You and that I may find grace in Your sight. ◊ My Presence will go with you, and I will give you rest.

GEN 32:26.IS 27:5.MATT 15:28.MATT 9:29.JAMES 1:6-7.LUKE 24:28-29,31-32.EX 33:13-14

EVENING

Jesus, the author and finisher of our faith.

"I am the Alpha and the Omega, the Beginning and the End," says the Lord, "who is and who was and who is to come, the Almighty." ◊ Who has performed and done it, calling the generations from the beginning? I, the Lord, am the first; and with the last I am He.

Abide in Me, and I in you. ◊ May the God of peace Himself sanctify you completely; and may your whole spirit, soul, and body be preserved blameless at the coming of our Lord Jesus Christ. ◊ He who has begun a good work in you will complete it until the day of Jesus Christ. ◊ Are you so foolish? Having begun in the Spirit, are you now being made perfect by the flesh? ◊ The Lord will perfect that which concerns me.

It is God who works in you both to will and to do for His good pleasure.

HEB 12:2.REV 1:8.IS 41:4.JOHN 15:4.1 THESS 5:23.PHIL 1:6.GAL 3:3.PS 138:8.PHIL 2:13

MORNING

He ever lives to make intercession.

Who is he who condemns? It is Christ who died, . . . who also makes intercession for us. ◇ Christ has not entered the holy places made with hands, which are copies of the true, but into heaven itself, now to appear in the presence of God for us.

If anyone sins, we have an Advocate with the Father, Jesus Christ the righteous. ◇ There is one God and one Mediator between God and men, the Man Christ Jesus.

Let us hold fast our confession. For we do not have a High Priest who cannot sympathize with our weaknesses, but was in all points tempted as we are, yet without sin. Let us therefore come boldly to the throne of grace, that we may obtain mercy and find grace to help in time of need.

Through Him we . . . have access by one Spirit to the Father.

Heb 7:25.ROM 8:34.HEB 9:24.1 JOHN 2:1.1 TIM 2:5.HEB 4:14-16.EPH 2:18.

EVENING

Those who know Your name will put their trust in You.

This is His name by which He will be called: THE LORD OUR RIGHTEOUSNESS. ◇ I will go in the strength of the Lord God; I will make mention of Your righteousness, of Yours only.

His name will be called Wonderful, Counselor. ◇ O Lord, I know the way of man is not in himself; it is not in man who walks to direct his own steps.

Mighty God, Everlasting Father. ◇ I know whom I have believed and am persuaded that He is able to keep what I have committed to Him until that Day.

Prince of Peace. ◇ He Himself is our peace. ◇ Therefore, having been justified by faith, we have peace with God through our Lord Jesus Christ.

The name of the Lord is a strong tower; the righteous run to it and are safe. ◇ Woe to those who go down to Egypt for help, and rely on horses, who trust in chariots because they are many, and in horsemen because they are very strong, but who do not look to the Holy One of Israel, nor seek the Lord! ◇ There is no one like the God of Jeshurun, who rides the heavens to help you, and in His excellency on the clouds. The eternal God is your refuge, and underneath are the everlasting arms.

PS 9:10.JER 23:6.PS 71:16.IS 9:6.JER 10:23.IS 9:6.2 TIM 1:12.IS 9:6.EPH 2:14.ROM 5:1.PROV 18:10.IS 31:1.DEUT 33:26-27

APRIL 7

**We commend ourselves . . . as sorrowful, yet always
rejoicing; as poor, yet making many rich; as having
nothing, and yet possessing all things.**

We . . . rejoice in hope of the glory of God. And not only that, but we also
glory in tribulations. ◊ Believing, you rejoice with joy inexpressible.

In a great trial of affliction the abundance of their joy and their deep
poverty abounded in the riches of their liberality. ◊ To me, who am less
than the least of all the saints, this grace was given, that I should preach
among the Gentiles the unsearchable riches of Christ, and to make all
people see what is the fellowship of the mystery, which from the
beginning of the ages has been hidden in God who created all things
through Jesus Christ.

Has God not chosen the poor of this world to be rich in faith and heirs
of the kingdom which He promised to those who love Him? ◊ God is
able to make all grace abound toward you, that you, always having all
sufficiency in all things, have an abundance for every good work.

2 COR 6:4,10.ROM 5:2-3.2 COR 7:4.1 PET 1:8.2 COR 8:2.EPH
3:8-9.JAMES 2:5.2 COR 9:8

**The Lord will strengthen him on his bed of illness;
You will sustain him on his sickbed.**

In all their affliction He was afflicted, and the Angel of His Presence
saved them; in His love and in His pity He redeemed them; and He bore
them and carried them all the days of old. ◊ Lord, behold, he whom You
love is sick. ◊ My grace is sufficient for you, for My strength is made
perfect in weakness.

Most gladly I will rather boast in my infirmities, that the power of
Christ may rest upon me. ◊ I can do all things through Christ who
strengthens me.

Though our outward man is perishing, yet the inward man is being
renewed day by day.

For in Him we live and move and have our being. ◊ He gives power to
the weak, and to those who have no might He increases strength. Even
the youths shall faint and be weary, and the young men shall utterly fall,
but those who wait on the Lord shall renew their strength. ◊ The eternal
God is your refuge, and underneath are the everlasting arms.

PS 41:3.IS 63:9.JOHN 11:3.2 COR 12:9.PHIL 4:13.2 COR 4:16.ACTS
17:28.IS 40:29-31.DEUT 33:27

MORNING

You were enriched in everything by Him.

When we were still without strength, in due time Christ died for the ungodly. ◊ He who did not spare His own Son, but delivered Him up for us all, how shall He not with Him also freely give us all things?

For in Him dwells all the fullness of the Godhead bodily; and you are complete in Him, who is the head of all principality and power.

Abide in Me, and I in you. As the branch cannot bear fruit of itself, unless it abides in the vine, neither can you, unless you abide in Me. I am the vine, you are the branches. He who abides in Me, and I in him, bears much fruit; for without Me you can do nothing. ◊ To will is present with me, but how to perform what is good I do not find. ◊ To each one of us grace was given according to the measure of Christ's gift.

If you abide in Me, and My words abide in you, you will ask what you desire, and it shall be done for you. ◊ Let the word of Christ dwell in you richly in all wisdom.

1 COR 1:5.ROM 5:6.ROM 8:32.COL 2:9-10.JOHN 15:4-5.ROM 7:18.EPH 4:7.JOHN 15:7.COL 3:16

EVENING

They shall see His face.

Moses said, "Please, show me Your glory." . . . But [God] said, "You cannot see My face; for no man shall see Me, and live." ◊ No one has seen God at any time. The only begotten Son, who is in the bosom of the Father, He has declared Him.

Every eye will see Him, and they also who pierced Him. And all the tribes of the earth will mourn because of Him. ◊ Now we see in a mirror, dimly.

I know that my Redeemer lives, and He shall stand at last on the earth; and after my skin is destroyed, this I know, that in my flesh I shall see God. ◊ I will see Your face in righteousness; I shall be satisfied when I awake in Your likeness. ◊ We shall be like Him, for we shall see Him as He is. ◊ For the Lord Himself will descend from heaven. . . . And the dead in Christ will rise first. Then we who are alive and remain shall be caught up together with them in the clouds to meet the Lord in the air. And thus we shall always be with the Lord.

REV 22:4.EX 33:18,20.JOHN 1:18.REV 1:7.1 COR 13:12.JOB 19:25-26.PS 17:15.1 JOHN 3:2.1 THESS 4:16-17

MORNING

Fear not, for I have redeemed you.

Do not fear, for you will not be ashamed; nor be disgraced, for you will not be put to shame; for you will forget the shame of your youth, and will not remember the reproach of your widowhood anymore. For your Maker is your husband, the Lord of hosts is His name; and your Redeemer is the Holy One of Israel; He is called the God of the whole earth. ◊ I have blotted out, like a thick cloud, your transgressions, and like a cloud, your sins. Return to Me, for I have redeemed you. ◊ You were . . . redeemed . . . with the precious blood of Christ, as of a lamb without blemish and without spot.

Their Redeemer is strong; the Lord of hosts is His name. He will thoroughly plead their case. ◊ My Father, who has given them to Me, is greater than all; and no one is able to snatch them out of My Father's hand.

Grace to you and peace from God the Father and our Lord Jesus Christ, who gave Himself for our sins, that He might deliver us from this present evil age, according to the will of our God and Father, to whom be glory forever and ever. Amen.

IS 43:1.IS 54:4-5.IS 44:22.1 PET 1:18-19.JER 50:34.JOHN 10:29.GAL 1:3-5

EVENING

I will mention the lovingkindnesses of the Lord and the praises of the Lord, according to all that the Lord has bestowed on us.

He also brought me up out of a horrible pit, out of the miry clay, and set my feet upon a rock, and established my steps. ◊ The Son of God, . . . loved me and gave Himself for me. ◊ He who did not spare His own Son, but delivered Him up for us all, how shall He not with Him also freely give us all things? ◊ God demonstrates His own love toward us, in that while we were still sinners, Christ died for us.

Who also has sealed us and given us the Spirit in our hearts as a deposit. ◊ Who is the guarantee of our inheritance until the redemption of the purchased possession, to the praise of His glory.

God, who is rich in mercy, because of His great love with which He loved us, even when we were dead in trespasses, made us alive together with Christ (by grace you have been saved), and raised us up together, and made us sit together in the heavenly places in Christ Jesus.

IS 63:7.PS 40:2.GAL 2:20.ROM 8:32.ROM 5:8.2 COR 1:22.EPH 1:14.EPH 2:4-6

MORNING

I am dark, but lovely.

Behold, I was brought forth in iniquity, and in sin my mother conceived me. ◊ "Your fame went out among the nations because of your beauty, for it was perfect through My splendor which I had bestowed on you," says the Lord God.

I am a sinful man, O Lord! ◊ Behold, you are fair, my love! Behold, you are fair!

I abhor myself, and repent in dust and ashes." ◊ You are all fair, my love, and there is no spot in you.

I find then a law, that evil is present with me, the one who wills to do good. ◊ Be of good cheer; your sins are forgiven you.

I know that in me (that is, in my flesh) nothing good dwells. ◊ You are complete in Him. ◊ Perfect in Christ Jesus.

You were washed, . . . you were sanctified, . . . you were justified in the name of the Lord Jesus and by the Spirit of our God. ◊ Proclaim the praises of Him who called you out of darkness into His marvelous light.

SONG 1:5.PS 51:5.EZEK 16:14.LUKE 5:8.SONG 4:1.JOB 42:6.SONG 4:7.ROM 7:21.MATT 9:2.ROM 7:18.COL 2:10.COL 1:28.1 COR 6:11. 1 PET 2:9

EVENING

Yes, and all who desire to live godly in Christ Jesus will suffer persecution.

I have come to set a man against his father, a daughter against her mother, and a daughter-in-law against her mother-in-law. . . . A man's foes will be those of his own household.

Whoever therefore wants to be a friend of the world makes himself an enemy of God. ◊ Do not love the world or the things in the world. If anyone loves the world, the love of the Father is not in him. For all that is in the world—the lust of the flesh, the lust of the eyes, and the pride of life—is not of the Father but is of the world.

If the world hates you, you know that it hated Me before it hated you. . . . Remember the word that I said to you, "A servant is not greater than his master." ◊ I have given them Your word; and the world has hated them because they are not of the world, just as I am not of the world. ◊ The world is passing away, . . . but he who does the will of God abides forever.

2 TIM 3:12.MATT 10:35-36.JAMES 4:4.1 JOHN 2:15-16.JOHN 15:18-20.JOHN 17:14.1 JOHN 2:17

MORNING

In the multitude of words sin is not lacking, but he who restrains his lips is wise.

My beloved brethren, let every man be swift to hear, slow to speak, slow to wrath. ◇ He who is slow to anger is better than the mighty, and he who rules his spirit than he who takes a city. ◇ If anyone does not stumble in word, he is a perfect man, able also to bridle the whole body. ◇ For by your words you will be justified, and by your words you will be condemned. ◇ Set a guard, O Lord, over my mouth; keep watch over the door of my lips.

Christ . . . suffered for us, leaving us an example, that you should follow His steps: who committed no sin, nor was guile found in His mouth; who, when He was reviled, did not revile in return; when He suffered, He did not threaten, but committed Himself to Him who judges righteously. ◇ Consider Him who endured such hostility from sinners against Himself, lest you become weary and discouraged in your souls.

In their mouth was found no guile, for they are without fault before the throne of God.

PROV 10:19.JAMES 1:19.PROV 16:32.JAMES 3:2.MATT 12:37.PS 141:3.
1 PET 2:21-23.HEB 12:3.REV 14:5

EVENING

Teach me Your way, O Lord.

I will instruct you and teach you in the way you should go; I will guide you with My eye. ◇ Good and upright is the Lord; therefore He teaches sinners in the way. The humble He guides in justice, and the humble He teaches His way.

I am the door. If anyone enters by Me, he will be saved, and will go in and out and find pasture.

Jesus said to him, "I am the way, the truth, and the life. No one comes to the Father except through Me." ◇ Having boldness to enter the Holiest by the blood of Jesus, by a new and living way which He consecrated for us, through the veil, that is, His flesh, and having a High Priest over the house of God, let us draw near with a true heart in full assurance of faith.

Let us know, let us pursue the knowledge of the Lord. ◇ All the paths of the Lord are mercy and truth, to such as keep His covenant and His testimonies.

PS 27:11.PS 32:8.PS 25:8-9.JOHN 10:9.JOHN 14:6.HEB 10:19-22.HOS
6:3.PS 25:10

MORNING

**What the law could not do in that it was weak
through the flesh, God did by sending His own Son
in the likeness of sinful flesh, on account of sin: He
condemned sin in the flesh.**

The law, having a shadow of the good things to come, and not the very image of the things, can never with these same sacrifices, which they offer continually year by year, make those who approach perfect. For then would they not have ceased to be offered? ◇ By Him everyone who believes is justified from all things from which you could not be justified by the law of Moses.

Inasmuch . . . as the children have partaken of flesh and blood, He Himself likewise shared in the same, that through death He might destroy him who had the power of death, that is, the devil, and release those who through fear of death were all their lifetime subject to bondage. For indeed He does not give aid to angels, but He does give aid to the seed of Abraham. Therefore, in all things He had to be made like His brethren.

ROM 8:3.HEB 10:1-2.ACTS 13:39.HEB 2:14-17

EVENING

All have sinned and fall short of the glory of God.

There is none righteous, no, not one. . . . There is none who does good, no, not one. ◇ There is not a just man on earth who does good and does not sin. ◇ How then can man be righteous before God? Or how can he be pure who is born of a woman?

Therefore, since a promise remains of entering His rest, let us fear lest any of you seem to have come short of it. ◇ For I acknowledge my transgressions, and my sin is ever before me. . . . Behold, I was brought forth in iniquity, and in sin my mother conceived me.

The Lord also has put away your sin; you shall not die. ◇ He called, . . . and whom He justified, these He also glorified. ◇ We all, with unveiled face, beholding as in a mirror the glory of the Lord, are being transformed into the same image from glory to glory, just as by the Spirit of the Lord. ◇ Indeed you continue in the faith, grounded and steadfast, and are not moved away from the hope of the gospel which you heard, which was preached to every creature under heaven.

ROM 3:23.ROM 3:10,12.ECCL 7:20.JOB 25:4.HEB 4:1.PS 51:3,5.2 SAM
12:13.ROM 8:30.2 COR 3:18.COL 1:23

MORNING

Honor the Lord with your possessions, and with the firstfruits of all your increase.

He who sows sparingly will also reap sparingly, and he who sows bountifully will also reap bountifully. ◊ On the first day of the week let each one of you lay something aside, storing up as he may prosper.

God is not unjust to forget your work and labor of love which you have shown toward His name, in that you have ministered to the saints, and do minister.

I beseech you . . . brethren, by the mercies of God, that you present your bodies a living sacrifice, holy, acceptable to God, which is your reasonable service. ◊ The love of Christ constrains us, because we judge thus: that if One died for all, then all died; and He died for all, that those who live should live no longer for themselves, but for Him who died for them and rose again. ◊ Whether you eat or drink, or whatever you do, do all to the glory of God.

PROV 3:9.2 COR 9:6.1 COR 16:2.HEB 6:10.ROM 12:1.2 COR 5:14-15.
1 COR 10:31

EVENING

There shall be no night.

The Lord will be your everlasting light, and the days of your mourning shall be ended. ◊ The city had no need of the sun or of the moon to shine in it, for the glory of God illuminated it, and the Lamb is its light. ◊ There shall be no night there: they need no lamp nor light of the sun, for the Lord God gives them light.

You are a chosen generation, a royal priesthood, a holy nation, His own special people, that you may proclaim the praises of Him who called you out of darkness into His marvelous light. ◊ [Give] thanks to the Father who has qualified us to be partakers of the inheritance of the saints in the light. He has delivered us from the power of darkness and translated us into the kingdom of the Son of His love. ◊ For you were once darkness, but now you are light in the Lord. Walk as children of light.

We are not of the night nor of darkness. ◊ The path of the just is like the shining sun, that shines ever brighter unto the perfect day. The way of the wicked is like darkness; they do not know what makes them stumble.

REV 21:25.IS 60:20.REV 21:23.REV 22:5.1 PET 2:9.COL 1:12-13.EPH 5:8.
1 THESS 5:5.PROV 4:18-19

MORNING

My soul shall be satisfied as with marrow and fatness, and my mouth shall praise You with joyful lips. When I remember You on my bed, I meditate on You in the night watches.

How precious . . . are Your thoughts to me, O God! How great is the sum of them! If I should count them, they would be more in number than the sand; when I awake, I am still with You. ◊ How sweet are Your words to my taste, sweeter than honey to my mouth! ◊ Whom have I in heaven but You? And there is none upon earth that I desire besides You.

Like an apple tree among the trees of the woods, so is my beloved among the sons. I sat down in his shade with great delight, and his fruit was sweet to my taste. He brought me to the banqueting house, and his banner over me was love. ◊ His countenance is like Lebanon, excellent as the cedars. His mouth is most sweet, yes, he is altogether lovely. This is my beloved, and this is my friend.

PS 63:5-6.PS 139:17-18.PS 119:103.PS 73:25.SONG 2:3-4.SONG 5:15-16

EVENING

Restore to me the joy of Your salvation.

I have seen his ways, and will heal him; I will also lead him, and restore comforts to him and to his mourners.

"Come now, and let us reason together," says the Lord, "though your sins are like scarlet, they shall be as white as snow; though they are red like crimson, they shall be as wool." ◊ "Return, you backsliding children, and I will heal your backslidings." Indeed we do come to You, for You are the Lord our God. ◊ I will hear what God the Lord will speak, for He will speak peace to His people and to His saints; but let them not turn back to folly.

Bless the Lord, O my soul, and forget not all His benefits: who forgives all your iniquities, who heals all your diseases. ◊ He restores my soul. ◊ O Lord, I will praise You; though You were angry with me, Your anger is turned away, and You comfort me.

Hold me up, and I shall be safe.

I, even I, am He who blots out your transgressions for My own sake; and I will not remember your sins.

PS 51:12.IS 57:18.IS 1:18.JER 3:22.PS 85:8.PS 103:2-3.PS 23:3.IS 12:1.PS 119:117.IS 43:25

APRIL 15

Their Redeemer is strong.

For I know your manifold transgressions and your mighty sins. ◊ I have given help to one who is mighty. ◊ I, the Lord, am your Savior, and your Redeemer, the Mighty One of Jacob. ◊ I [am] mighty to save. ◊ [He] is able to keep you from stumbling. ◊ Where sin abounded, grace abounded much more.

He who believes in Him is not condemned; but he who does not believe is condemned already, because he has not believed in the name of the only begotten Son of God. ◊ He is also able to save to the uttermost those who come to God through Him.

Is My hand shortened at all that it cannot redeem?

Who shall separate us from the love of Christ? . . . For I am persuaded that neither death nor life, nor angels nor principalities nor powers, nor things present nor things to come, nor height nor depth, nor any other created thing, shall be able to separate us from the love of God which is in Christ Jesus our Lord.

JER 50:34.AMOS 5:12.PS 89:19.IS 49:26.IS 63:1.JUDE 1:24.ROM 5:20.JOHN 3:18.HEB 7:25.IS 50:2.ROM 8:35,38-39

Do you seek great things for yourself?
Do not seek them.

Take My yoke upon you and learn from Me, for I am gentle and lowly in heart, and you will find rest for your souls. ◊ Let this mind be in you which was also in Christ Jesus, who, being in the form of God, did not consider it robbery to be equal with God, but made Himself of no reputation, taking the form of a servant, and coming in the likeness of men. And being found in appearance as a man, He humbled Himself and became obedient to the point of death, even the death of the cross.

He who does not take his cross and follow after Me is not worthy of Me. ◊ Christ also suffered for us, leaving us an example, that you should follow His steps. ◊ Many who are first will be last, and the last first.

Godliness with contentment is great gain. For we brought nothing into this world, and it is certain we can carry nothing out. And having food and clothing, with these we shall be content. ◊ I have learned in whatever state I am, to be content.

JER 45:5.MATT 11:29.PHIL 2:5-8.MATT 10:38.1 PET 2:21.MATT 19:30. 1 TIM 6:6-8.PHIL 4:11

MORNING

I said in my haste, "I am cut off from before Your eyes"; nevertheless You heard the voice of my supplications when I cried out to You.

I sink in deep mire, where there is no standing; I have come into deep waters, where the floods overflow me. ◊ Waters flowed over my head; I said, "I am cut off!" I called on Your name, O Lord, from the lowest pit. You have heard my voice: "Do not hide Your ear from my sighing, from my cry for help." You drew near on the day I called on You, and said, "Do not fear!"

Will the Lord cast off forever? And will He be favorable no more? Has His mercy ceased forever? Has His promise failed forevermore? Has God forgotten to be gracious? . . . And I said, "This is my anguish; but I will remember the years of the right hand of the Most High." I will remember the works of the Lord; surely I will remember Your wonders of old. ◊ I would have lost heart, unless I had believed that I would see the goodness of the Lord in the land of the living.

PS 31:22.PS 69:2.LAM 3:54-57.PS 77:7-11.PS 27:13

EVENING

He shall call upon Me, and I will answer him; I will be with him in trouble; I will deliver him.

Jabez called on the God of Israel saying, "Oh, that You would bless me indeed, and enlarge my territory, that Your hand would be with me, and that You would keep me from evil, that I may not cause pain!" So God granted him what he requested. ◊ God appeared to Solomon, and said to him, "Ask! What shall I give you?" And Solomon said to God: . . . "Now give me wisdom and knowledge, that I may go out and come in before this people; for who can judge this great people of Yours?" ◊ God gave Solomon wisdom and exceedingly great understanding. . . . Solomon's wisdom excelled the wisdom of all the men of the East.

Asa went out against [Ethiopia]. . . . And Asa cried out to the Lord his God, and said, "Lord, it is nothing for You to help, whether with many or with those who have no power; help us, O Lord our God, for we rest on You, and in Your name we go against this multitude. O Lord, You are our God; do not let man prevail against You!" So the Lord struck the Ethiopians before Asa and Judah, and the Ethiopians fled.

O You who hear prayer, to You all flesh will come.

PS 91:15.1 CHR 4:9-10.2 CHR 1:7-8,10.1 KIN 4:29-30.2 CHR 14:10-12.PS 65:2

MORNING

Whoever offers praise glorifies Me.

Let the word of Christ dwell in you richly in all wisdom, teaching and admonishing one another in psalms and hymns and spiritual songs, singing with grace in your hearts to the Lord. And whatever you do in word or deed, do all in the name of the Lord Jesus, giving thanks to God the Father through Him. ◊ Glorify God in your body and in your spirit, which are God's.

You are . . . a royal priesthood, . . . that you may proclaim the praises of Him who called you out of darkness into His marvelous light. ◊ You . . . as living stones, are being built up a spiritual house, a holy priesthood, to offer up spiritual sacrifices acceptable to God through Jesus Christ. ◊ By Him let us continually offer the sacrifice of praise to God.

My soul shall make its boast in the Lord; the humble shall hear of it and be glad. Oh, magnify the Lord with me, and let us exalt His name together.

PS 50:23.COL 3:16-17.1 COR 6:20.1 PET 2:9.1 PET 2:5.HEB 13:15.PS
34:2-3

EVENING

Lead me away!

The Lord has appeared of old to me, saying: "Yes, I have loved you with an everlasting love; therefore with lovingkindness I have drawn you." ◊ I drew them with gentle cords, with bands of love. ◊ And I, if I am lifted up from the earth, will draw all peoples to Myself. ◊ Behold, the Lamb of God! ◊ And as Moses lifted up the serpent in the wilderness, even so must the Son of Man be lifted up, that whoever believes in Him should not perish but have eternal life.

Whom have I in heaven but You? And there is none upon earth that I desire besides You. ◊ We love Him because He first loved us.

My beloved spoke, and said to me: "Rise up, my love, my fair one, and come away. For lo, the winter is past, the rain is over and gone. The flowers appear on the earth; the time of singing has come, and the voice of the turtledove is heard in our land. The fig tree puts forth her green figs, and the vines with the tender grapes give a good smell. Rise up, my love, my fair one, and come away!"

Keep yourselves in the love of God, looking for the mercy of our Lord Jesus Christ unto eternal life.

SONG 1:4.JER 31:3.HOS 11:4.JOHN 12:32.JOHN 1:36.JOHN 3:14-15.PS
73:25.1 JOHN 4:19.SONG 2:10-13.JUDE 1:21

MORNING

I will raise up for them a Prophet like you from among their brethren.

I [Moses] stood between the Lord and you at that time, to declare to you the word of the Lord; for you were afraid. ◊ There is one God and one Mediator between God and men, the Man Christ Jesus. ◊ (Now the man Moses was very humble, more than all men who were on the face of the earth.) ◊ Take My yoke upon you and learn from Me, for I am gentle and lowly in heart, and you will find rest for your souls. ◊ Christ Jesus, . . . being in the form of God, did not consider it robbery to be equal with God, but made Himself of no reputation, taking the form of a servant, and coming in the likeness of men.

Moses indeed was faithful in all His house as a servant, for a testimony of those things which would be spoken afterward, but Christ as a Son over His own house, whose house we are if we hold fast the confidence and the rejoicing of the hope firm to the end.

DEUT 18:18.DEUT 5:5.1 TIM 2:5.NUM 12:3.MATT 11:29.PHIL 2:5-7.HEB 3:5-6

EVENING

Our God and Father . . . has loved us and given us everlasting consolation.

I will remember My covenant with you in the days of your youth, and I will establish an everlasting covenant with you.

By . . . one offering He has perfected forever those who are being sanctified. ◊ He is also able to save to the uttermost those who come to God through Him, since He ever lives to make intercession for them. ◊ I know whom I have believed and am persuaded that He is able to keep what I have committed to Him until that Day.

The gifts and the calling of God are irrevocable. ◊ Who shall separate us from the love of Christ? ◊ The Lamb who is in the midst of the throne will shepherd them and lead them to living fountains of waters. And God will wipe away every tear from their eyes. ◊ We . . . shall be caught up . . . to meet the Lord. . . . And thus we shall always be with the Lord. Therefore comfort one another with these words.

I am hard pressed between the two, having a desire to depart and be with Christ, which is far better. ◊ For here we have no continuing city, but we seek the one to come.

2 THESS 2:16.EZEK 16:60.HEB 10:14.HEB 7:25.2 TIM 1:12.ROM 11:29.ROM 8:35.REV 7:17.1 THESS 4:17-18.PHIL 1:23.HEB 13:14

APRIL 19

Most assuredly, I say to you, I am the door
of the sheep.

The veil of the temple was torn in two from top to bottom. ◊ Christ also suffered once for sins, the just for the unjust, that He might bring us to God. ◊ The Holy Spirit indicating this, that the way into the Holiest of All was not yet made manifest while the first tabernacle was still standing.

I am the door. If anyone enters by Me, he will be saved, and will go in and out and find pasture. ◊ No one comes to the Father except through Me. ◊ Through Him we . . . have access by one Spirit to the Father. Now, therefore, you are no longer strangers and foreigners, but fellow citizens with the saints and members of the household of God. ◊ [Have] boldness to enter the Holiest by the blood of Jesus, by a new and living way which He consecrated for us, through the veil, that is, His flesh. ◊ We have peace with God through our Lord Jesus Christ, through whom also we have access by faith into this grace in which we stand.

JOHN 10:7.MATT 27:51.1 PET 3:18.HEB 9:8.JOHN 10:9.JOHN 14:6.EPH 2:18-19.HEB 10:19-20.ROM 5:1-2

EVENING

His word was in my heart like a burning fire shut up
in my bones; I was weary of holding it back, and I
could not.

For if I preach the gospel . . . willingly, I have a reward; but if against my will, I have been entrusted with a stewardship. What is my reward then? That when I preach the gospel, I may present the gospel of Christ without charge. ◊ They . . . commanded them not to speak at all nor teach in the name of Jesus. But Peter and John answered and said, . . . "We cannot but speak the things which we have seen and heard."

"I was afraid, and went and hid your talent in the ground. Look, there you have what is yours." . . . "You wicked and lazy servant, . . . you ought to have deposited my money with the bankers, and at my coming I would have received back my own with interest. . . . For to everyone who has, more will be given, and he will have abundance; but from him who does not have, even what he has will be taken away."

Go home to your friends, and tell them what great things the Lord has done for you. ◊ Woe is me if I do not preach the gospel!

JER 20:9.1 COR 9:16-18.ACTS 4:18-20.MATT 25:25-27,29.MARK 5:19.
1 COR 9:16

MORNING

None of the accursed things shall remain in your hand.

Come out from among them and be separate, says the Lord. Do not touch what is unclean. ◇ Beloved, I beg you as sojourners and pilgrims, abstain from fleshly lusts which war against the soul. ◇ [Hate] even the garment defiled by the flesh.

Beloved, now we are children of God; and it has not yet been revealed what we shall be, but we know that when He is revealed, we shall be like Him, for we shall see Him as He is. And everyone who has this hope in Him purifies himself, just as He is pure. ◇ For the grace of God that brings salvation has appeared to all men, teaching us that, denying ungodliness and worldly lusts, we should live soberly, righteously, and godly in the present age, looking for the blessed hope and glorious appearing of our great God and Savior Jesus Christ, who gave Himself for us, that He might redeem us from every lawless deed and purify for Himself His own special people, zealous for good works.

DEUT 13:17.2 COR 6:17.1 PET 2:11.JUDE 1:23.1 JOHN 3:2-3.TITUS 2:11-14

EVENING

"Who are You, Lord?" And He said, "I am Jesus."

Do not be afraid. ◇ When you pass through the waters, I will be with you; and through the rivers, they shall not overflow you. When you walk through the fire, you shall not be burned, nor shall the flame scorch you. For I am the Lord your God, the Holy One of Israel, your Savior.

Yea, though I walk through the valley of the shadow of death, I will fear no evil; for You are with me; Your rod and Your staff, they comfort me. ◇ Immanuel, . . . "God with us."

You shall call His name Jesus, for He will save His people from their sins. ◇ If anyone sins, we have an Advocate with the Father, Jesus Christ the righteous. ◇ Who is he who condemns? It is Christ who died, and furthermore is also risen, who is even at the right hand of God, who also makes intercession for us. Who shall separate us from the love of Christ? Shall tribulation, or distress, or persecution, or famine, or nakedness, or peril, or sword?

ACTS 26:15.MATT 14:27.IS 43:2-3.PS 23:4.MATT 1:23.MATT 1:21. 1 JOHN 2:1.ROM 8:34-35

MORNING

Stand fast in the Lord.

My foot has held fast to His steps; I have kept His way and not turned aside.

The Lord loves justice, and does not forsake His saints; they are preserved forever. ◊ The Lord shall preserve you from all evil; He shall preserve your soul.

The just shall live by faith; but if anyone draws back, my soul has no pleasure in him. But we are not of those who draw back to perdition, but of those who believe to the saving of the soul. ◊ They went out from us, but they were not of us; for if they had been of us, they would have continued with us; but they went out that they might be made manifest, that none of them were of us.

If you abide in My word, you are My disciples indeed. ◊ He who endures to the end shall be saved. ◊ Watch, stand fast in the faith, be brave, be strong. ◊ Hold fast what you have, that no one may take your crown. ◊ He who overcomes shall be clothed in white garments, and I will not blot out his name from the Book of Life.

PHIL 4:1.JOB 23:11.PS 37:28.PS 121:7.HEB 10:38-39.1 JOHN 2:19.JOHN 8:31.MATT 24:13.1 COR 16:13.REV 3:11.REV 3:5

EVENING

Enoch walked with God.

Can two walk together, unless they are agreed?

[He] made peace through the blood of His cross. And you . . . once were alienated and enemies in your mind by wicked works, yet now He has reconciled in the body of His flesh through death, to present you holy, and blameless, and irreproachable in His sight.

Now in Christ Jesus you who once were far off have been made near by the blood of Christ. ◊ We were reconciled to God through the death of His Son, . . . and not only that, but we also rejoice in God through our Lord Jesus Christ, through whom we have now received the reconciliation.

Our fellowship is with the Father and with His Son Jesus Christ.

The grace of the Lord Jesus Christ, and the love of God, and the communion of the Holy Spirit be with you all.

GEN 5:22.AMOS 3:3.COL 1:20-22.EPH 2:13.ROM 5:10-11.1 JOHN 1:3.
2 COR 13:14

MORNING

> **If his offering is a burnt sacrifice of the herd, let him offer a male without blemish; he shall offer it of his own free will. . . . Then he shall put his hand on the head of the burnt offering, and it will be accepted on his behalf to make atonement for him.**

God will provide for Himself the lamb for a burnt offering. ◇ Behold! The Lamb of God who takes away the sin of the world! ◇ We have been sanctified through the offering of the body of Jesus Christ once for all. ◇ The Son of Man . . . [gave] his life, a ransom for many.

No one takes it from Me, but I lay it down of Myself. I have power to lay it down, and I have power to take it again. ◇ I will love them freely. ◇ The Son of God . . . loved me and gave Himself for me.

He made Him who knew no sin to be sin for us, that we might become the righteousness of God in Him. ◇ He has made us accepted in the Beloved.

LEV 1:3-4.GEN 22:8.JOHN 1:29.HEB 10:10.MATT 20:28.JOHN 10:18.HOS 14:4.GAL 2:20.2 COR 5:21.EPH 1:6

EVENING

> **Great is Your mercy toward me, and You have delivered my soul from the depths of Sheol.**

Fear not, for I have redeemed you; I have called you by your name; you are Mine. ◇ I, even I, am the Lord, and besides Me there is no savior. . . . I, even I, am He who blots out your transgressions for My own sake; and I will not remember your sins. ◇ Those who trust in their wealth and boast in the multitude of their riches, none of them can by any means redeem his brother, nor give to God a ransom for him—for the redemption of their souls is costly.

I have found a ransom. ◇ God, who is rich in mercy, because of His great love with which He loved us, even when we were dead in trespasses, made us alive together with Christ (by grace you have been saved).

Nor is there salvation in any other, for there is no other name under heaven given among men by which we must be saved.

PS 86:13.IS 43:1.IS 43:11,25.PS 49:6-8.JOB 33:24.EPH 2:4-5.ACTS 4:12

MORNING

The Lord was my support.

Truly, in vain is salvation hoped for from the hills, and from the multitude of mountains; truly, in the Lord our God is the salvation of Israel. ◊ The Lord is my rock and my fortress and my deliverer; my God, my strength, in whom I will trust; my shield and the horn of my salvation, my stronghold. ◊ Cry out and shout, O inhabitant of Zion, for great is the Holy One of Israel in your midst!

The angel of the Lord encamps all around those who fear Him, and delivers them. . . . The righteous cry out, and the Lord hears, and delivers them out of all their troubles. ◊ The eternal God is your refuge, and underneath are the everlasting arms. ◊ So we may boldly say: "The Lord is my helper; I will not fear. What can man do to me?" ◊ For who is God, except the Lord? And who is a rock, except our God? It is God who arms me with strength, and makes my way perfect.

By the grace of God I am what I am.

PS 18:18.JER 3:23.PS 18:2.IS 12:6.PS 34:7,17.DEUT 33:27.HEB 13:6.PS
18:31-32.1 COR 15:10

EVENING

We like sheep have gone astray.

If we say that we have no sin, we deceive ourselves, and the truth is not in us. ◊ There is none righteous, no, not one; there is none who understands; there is none who seeks after God. They have all gone out of the way; they have together become unprofitable; there is none who does good, no, not one.

You were like sheep going astray, but have now returned to the Shepherd and Overseer of your souls. ◊ I have gone astray like a lost sheep; seek Your servant, for I do not forget Your commandments.

He restores my soul; He leads me in the paths of righteousness for His name's sake.

My sheep hear My voice, and I know them, and they follow Me. I give them eternal life, and they shall never perish; neither shall anyone snatch them out of My hand. ◊ What man of you, having a hundred sheep, if he loses one of them, does not leave the ninety-nine in the wilderness, and go after the one which is lost until he finds it?

IS 53:6.1 JOHN 1:8.ROM 3:10-12.1 PET 2:25.PS 119:176.PS 23:3.JOHN
10:27-28.LUKE 15:4

MORNING

**The Lord visited Sarah as He had said, and the Lord
did for Sarah as He had spoken.**

Trust in Him at all times, you people; pour out your heart before Him;
God is a refuge for us. ◊ David strengthened himself in the Lord his
God. ◊ God will surely visit you, and bring you out of this land to the
land of which He swore to Abraham, to Isaac, and to Jacob. ◊ "I have
certainly seen the oppression of my people who are in Egypt; I have
heard their groaning and have come down to deliver them." . . . He
brought them out, after he had shown wonders and signs in the land of
Egypt, and in the Red Sea, and in the wilderness forty years. ◊ Not a
word failed of any good thing which the Lord had spoken. . . . All came to
pass.

He who promised is faithful. ◊ Has He said, and will He not do it? Or
has He spoken, and will He not make it good? ◊ Heaven and earth will
pass away, but My words will by no means pass away. ◊ The grass
withers, the flower fades, but the word of our God stands forever.

GEN 21:1.PS 62:8.1 SAM 30:6.GEN 50:24.ACTS 7:34,36.JOSH 21:45.HEB
10:23.NUM 23:19.MATT 24:35.IS 40:8

EVENING

The eyes of all look expectantly to You.

He gives to all life, breath, and all things. ◊ The Lord is good to all, and
His tender mercies are over all His works. ◊ Look at the birds of the air,
for they neither sow nor reap nor gather into barns; yet your heavenly
Father feeds them.

The same Lord over all is rich to all who call upon Him.

My help comes from the Lord, who made heaven and earth. ◊ Behold,
as the eyes of servants look to the hand of their masters, as the eyes of a
maid to the hand of her mistress, so our eyes look to the Lord our God,
until He has mercy on us.

The Lord is a God of justice; blessed are all those who wait for Him. ◊
It will be said in that day: "Behold, this is our God; we have waited for
Him, and He will save us. This is the Lord; we have waited for Him; we
will be glad and rejoice in His salvation." ◊ If we hope for what we do
not see, then we eagerly wait for it with perseverance. Likewise the Spirit
also helps in our weaknesses. The Spirit Himself makes intercession for
us.

PS 145:15.ACTS 17:25.PS 145:9.MATT 6:26.ROM 10:12.PS 121:2.PS
123:2.IS 30:18.IS 25:9.ROM 8:25-26

MORNING

You shall call His name Jesus, for He will save His people from their sins.

You know that He was manifested to take away our sins. ◊ That we, having died to sins, might live for righteousness. ◊ He is also able to save to the uttermost those who come to God through Him.

He was wounded for our transgressions, He was bruised for our iniquities; the chastisement for our peace was upon Him, and by His stripes we are healed. The Lord has laid on Him the iniquity of us all. ◊ Thus it was necessary for the Christ to suffer . . . that repentance and remission of sins should be preached in His name to all nations. ◊ He has appeared to put away sin by the sacrifice of Himself.

Him God has exalted to His right hand to be Prince and Savior, to give repentance. ◊ Through this Man is preached to you the forgiveness of sins; and by Him everyone who believes is justified from all things from which you could not be justified by the law of Moses. ◊ Your sins are forgiven you for His name's sake.

MATT 1:21.1 JOHN 3:5.1 PET 2:24.HEB 7:25.IS 53:5-6.LUKE 24:46-47.HEB 9:26.ACTS 5:31.ACTS 13:38-39.1 JOHN 2:12

EVENING

Our Lord Jesus Christ, . . . though He was rich, yet for your sakes . . . became poor, that you through His poverty might become rich.

For it pleased the Father that in Him all the fullness should dwell. ◊ Who being the brightness of His glory and the express image of His person, and upholding all things by the word of His power, when He had by Himself purged our sins, sat down at the right hand of the Majesty on high, having become so much better than the angels, as He has by inheritance obtained a more excellent name than they. ◊ Who, being in the form of God, did not consider it robbery to be equal with God, but made Himself of no reputation, taking the form of a servant, and coming in the likeness of men.

Foxes have holes and birds of the air have nests, but the Son of Man has nowhere to lay His head.

All things are yours: whether . . . the world or life or death, or things present or things to come—all are yours. And you are Christ's, and Christ is God's.

2 COR 8:9.COL 1:19.HEB 1:3-4.PHIL 2:6-7.MATT 8:20.1 COR 3:21-23

MORNING

His left hand is under my head, and his right hand embraces me.

Underneath are the everlasting arms. ◊ When he saw that the wind was boisterous, he was afraid; and beginning to sink he cried out, saying, "Lord, save me!" And immediately Jesus stretched out His hand and caught him, and said to him, "O you of little faith, why did you doubt?" ◊ The steps of a good man are ordered by the Lord, and He delights in his way. Though he fall, he shall not be utterly cast down; for the Lord upholds him with His hand.

The beloved of the Lord shall dwell in safety by Him, who shelters him all the day long; and he shall dwell between His shoulders. ◊ [Cast] all your care upon Him, for He cares for you. ◊ He who touches you touches the apple of His eye.

They shall never perish; neither shall anyone snatch them out of My hand. My Father, who has given them to Me, is greater than all.

SONG 2:6.DEUT 33:27.MATT 14:30,31.PS 37:23-24.DEUT 33:12 .1 PET 5:7.ZECH 2:8.JOHN 10:28-29

EVENING

Who is she who looks forth as the morning, fair as the moon, clear as the sun, awesome as an army with banners?

The church of God . . . He purchased with His own blood.

Christ also loved the church and gave Himself for it, that He might sanctify and cleanse it with the washing of water by the word, that He might present it to Himself a glorious church, not having spot or wrinkle or any such thing, but that it should be holy and without blemish.

A great sign appeared in heaven: a woman clothed with the sun, with the moon under her feet, and on her head a garland of twelve stars. ◊ Let us be glad and rejoice and give Him glory, for the marriage of the Lamb has come, and His wife has made herself ready. And to her it was granted to be arrayed in fine linen, clean and bright, for the fine linen is the righteous acts of the saints. ◊ The righteousness of God which is through faith in Jesus Christ to all and on all who believe.

The glory which You gave Me I have given them, that they may be one just as We are one.

SONG 6:10.ACTS 20:28.EPH 5:25-27.REV 12:1.REV 19:7-8.ROM 3:22.JOHN 17:22

MORNING

Brethren, the time is short.

Man who is born of woman is of few days and full of trouble. He comes forth like a flower and fades away; he flees like a shadow and does not continue. ◊ The world is passing away, and the lust of it; but he who does the will of God abides forever. ◊ As in Adam all die, even so in Christ all shall be made alive. . . . Death is swallowed up in victory. ◊ For if we live, we live to the Lord; and if we die, we die to the Lord. Therefore, whether we live or die, we are the Lord's. ◊ To live is Christ, and to die is gain.

Do not cast away your confidence, which has great reward. For you have need of endurance, so that after you have done the will of God, you may receive the promise. . . . "For yet a little while, and He who is coming will come and will not tarry." ◊ The night is far spent, the day is at hand. Therefore let us cast off the works of darkness, and let us put on the armor of light. ◊ The end of all things is at hand; therefore be serious and watchful in your prayers.

1 COR 7:29.JOB 14:1-2.1 JOHN 2:17.1 COR 15:22,54.ROM 14:8.PHIL 1:21.HEB 10:35-37.ROM 13:12.1 PET 4:7

EVENING

I will give him a new name.

The disciples were first called Christians in Antioch. ◊ Let everyone who names the name of Christ depart from iniquity. ◊ Those who are Christ's have crucified the flesh with its passions and desires. ◊ You were bought at a price; therefore glorify God in your body and in your spirit, which are God's.

God forbid that I should glory except in the cross of our Lord Jesus Christ, by whom the world has been crucified to me, and I to the world. For in Christ Jesus neither circumcision nor uncircumcision avails anything, but a new creation.

Be followers of God as dear children. Walk in love, as Christ also has loved us and given Himself for us, an offering and a sacrifice to God for a sweet-smelling aroma. . . . For you were once darkness, but now you are light in the Lord. Walk as children of light.

REV 2:17.ACTS 11:26.2 TIM 2:19.GAL 5:24.1 COR 6:20.GAL 6:14-15.EPH 5:1-2.8

MORNING

Behold! The Lamb of God.

It is not possible that the blood of bulls and goats could take away sins. Therefore, when He came into the world, He said: "Sacrifice and offering You did not desire, but a body You have prepared for Me. In burnt offerings and sacrifices for sin you had no pleasure. Then I said, 'Behold, I have come—in the volume of the book it is written of Me—to do Your will, O God.'" ◇ He was oppressed and He was afflicted, yet He opened not His mouth; He was led as a lamb to the slaughter, and as a sheep before its shearers is silent, so He opened not his mouth.

You were not redeemed with corruptible things, like silver or gold, . . . but with the precious blood of Christ, as of a lamb without blemish and without spot. He indeed was . . . manifest in these last times for you who through Him believe in God, . . . that your faith and hope are in God.

Worthy is the Lamb who was slain to receive power and riches and wisdom, and strength and honor and glory and blessing!

JOHN 1:29.HEB 10:4-7.IS 53:7.1 PET 1:18-21.REV 5:12

EVENING

I will hope continually.

Not that I . . . am already perfected; but I press on. ◇ Leaving the discussion of the elementary principles of Christ, let us go on to perfection, not laying again the foundation of repentance from dead works and of faith toward God. ◇ The path of the just is like the shining sun, that shines ever brighter unto the perfect day.

I love the Lord, because He has heard My voice and my supplications. Because He has inclined His ear to me, therefore I will call upon Him as long as I live. ◇ I will bless the Lord at all times; His praise shall continually be in my mouth.

Praise is awaiting You, O God, in Zion. ◇ They do not rest day or night, saying: "Holy, holy, holy, Lord God Almighty." ◇ Whoever offers praise glorifies Me. ◇ Rejoice always, pray without ceasing, in everything give thanks; for this is the will of God in Christ Jesus for you. ◇ Rejoice in the Lord always. Again I will say, rejoice!

PS 71:14.PHIL 3:12.HEB 6:1.PROV 4:18.PS 116:1-2.PS 34:1.PS 65:1.REV 4:8.PS 50:23.1 THESS 5:16-18.PHIL 4:4

APRIL 29

_____

Consider what great things He has done for you.

You shall remember that the Lord your God led you all the way these forty years in the wilderness, to humble you and test you, to know what was in your heart, whether you would keep His commandments or not. . . . So you should know in your heart that as a man chastens his son, so the Lord your God chastens you.

I know, O Lord, that Your judgments are right, and that in faithfulness You have afflicted me. ◊ It is good for me that I have been afflicted, that I may learn Your statutes. ◊ Before I was afflicted I went astray, but now I keep Your word. ◊ The Lord has chastened me severely, but He has not given me over to death. ◊ He has not dealt with us according to our sins, nor punished us according to our iniquities. For as the heavens are high above the earth, so great is His mercy toward those who fear Him. . . . He knows our frame; He remembers that we are dust.

1 SAM 12:24.DEUT 8:2,5.PS 119:75.PS 119:71.PS 119:67.PS 118:18.PS 103:10-11,14

EVENING_____

Looking for the blessed hope and glorious appearing of our great God and Savior Jesus Christ.

This hope we have as an anchor of the soul, both sure and steadfast, and which enters the Presence behind the veil, where the forerunner has entered for us. ◊ Heaven must receive [Him] until the times of restoration of all things. ◊ When He comes, in that Day, to be glorified in His saints and to be admired among all those who believe.

We know that the whole creation groans and labors with birth pangs together until now. And not only they, but we also who have the firstfruits of the Spirit, even we ourselves groan within ourselves, eagerly waiting for the adoption, the redemption of our body. ◊ Beloved, now we are children of God; and it has not yet been revealed what we shall be, but we know that when He is revealed, we shall be like Him, for we shall see Him as He is. ◊ When Christ who is our life appears, then you also will appear with Him in glory. ◊ "I am coming quickly." Amen. Even so, come, Lord Jesus!

TITUS 2:13.HEB 6:19-20.ACTS 3:21.2 THESS 1:10.ROM 8:22-23.1 JOHN 3:2.COL 3:4.REV 22:20

MORNING

Whoever keeps His word, truly the love of God is perfected in him.

The God of peace who brought up our Lord Jesus from the dead, that great Shepherd of the sheep, through the blood of the everlasting covenant, make you complete in every good work to do His will, working in you what is well pleasing in His sight, through Jesus Christ, to whom be glory forever and ever. Amen.

Now by this we know that we know Him, if we keep His commandments. ◊ If anyone loves Me, he will keep My word; and My Father will love him, and We will come to him and make Our home with him. ◊ Whoever abides in Him does not sin. Whoever sins has neither seen Him nor known Him. Little children, let no one deceive you. He who practices righteousness is righteous, just as He is righteous. ◊ Love has been perfected among us in this: that we may have boldness in the day of judgment; because as He is, so are we in this world.

1 JOHN 2:5. HEB 13:20-21. 1 JOHN 2:3. JOHN 14:23. 1 JOHN 3:6-7. 1 JOHN 4:17

EVENING

He who is slow to wrath has great understanding.

The Lord passed before him and proclaimed, "The Lord, the Lord God, merciful and gracious, longsuffering, and abounding in goodness and truth."

Be followers of God as dear children. . . . The fruit of the Spirit is love, joy, peace, longsuffering, kindness, goodness, faithfulness, gentleness, self-control. ◊ This is commendable, if because of conscience toward God one endures grief, suffering wrongfully. For what credit is it if, when you are beaten for your faults, you take it patiently? But when you do good and suffer for it, if you take it patiently, this is commendable before God. For to this you were called, because Christ also suffered for us, leaving us an example, that you should follow His steps: "Who committed no sin, nor was guile found in His mouth"; who, when He was reviled, did not revile in return; when He suffered, He did not threaten, but committed Himself to Him who judges righteously.

"Be angry, and do not sin": do not let the sun go down on your wrath.

PROV 14:29. EX 34:6. EPH 5:1. GAL 5:22-23. 1 PET 2:19-23. EPH 4:26

MORNING_____

The fruit of the Spirit is . . . peace.

To be spiritually minded is life and peace. ◊ God has called us to peace. ◊ Peace I leave with you, My peace I give to you; not as the world gives do I give to you. Let not your heart be troubled, neither let it be afraid. ◊ The God of hope fill you with all joy and peace in believing.

I know whom I have believed and am persuaded that He is able to keep what I have committed to Him until that Day. ◊ You will keep him in perfect peace, whose mind is stayed on You, because he trusts in You.

The work of righteousness will be peace, and the effect of righteousness, quietness and assurance forever. My people will dwell in a peaceful habitation, in secure dwellings, and in quiet resting places. ◊ Whoever listens to me will dwell safely, and will be secure, without fear of evil. ◊ Great peace have those who love Your law.

GAL 5:22.ROM 8:6.1 COR 7:15.JOHN 14:27.ROM 15:13.2 TIM 1:12.IS 26:3.IS 32:17-18.PROV 1:33.PS 119:165

EVENING_____

The name of the city from that day shall be: The Lord Is There.

The tabernacle of God is with men, and He will dwell with them, and they shall be His people, and God Himself will be with them.

I saw no temple in it, for the Lord God Almighty and the Lamb are its temple. And the city had no need of the sun or of the moon to shine in it, for the glory of God illuminated it, and the Lamb is its light.

The nations of those who are saved shall walk in its light, and the kings of the earth bring their glory and honor into it. I will see Your face in righteousness; I shall be satisfied when I awake in Your likeness. ◊ Whom have I in heaven but You? And there is none upon earth that I desire besides You.

Judah shall abide forever, and Jerusalem from generation to generation. For I will acquit them of bloodguilt, whom I had not acquitted; for the Lord dwells in Zion. ◊ "Sing and rejoice, O daughter of Zion! For behold, I am coming and I will dwell in your midst," says the Lord. ◊ There shall be no more curse, but the throne of God and of the Lamb shall be in it, and His servants shall serve Him.

EZEK 48:35.REV 21:3.REV 21:22-24.PS 17:15.PS 73:25.JOEL 3:20-21.ZECH 2:10.REV 22:3

MORNING

Surely the Lord is in this place,
and I did not know it.

Where two or three are gathered together in My name, I am there in the midst of them. ◊ Lo, I am with you always, even to the end of the age. ◊ My Presence will go with you, and I will give you rest.

Where can I go from Your Spirit? Or where can I flee from Your presence? If I ascend into heaven, You are there; if I make my bed in hell, behold, You are there. ◊ "Am I a God near at hand," says the Lord, "and not a God afar off? Can anyone hide himself in secret places, so I shall not see him?" says the Lord; "do I not fill heaven and earth?" says the Lord.

Behold, heaven and the heaven of heavens cannot contain You. How much less this temple which I have built! ◊ Thus says the High and Lofty One who inhabits eternity, whose name is Holy: "I dwell in the high and holy place, with him who has a contrite and humble spirit, to revive the spirit of the humble, and to revive the heart of the contrite ones."

GEN 28:16.MATT 18:10.MATT 28:20.EX 33:14.PS 139:7-8.JER 23:23-24.
1 KIN 8:27.IS 57:15

EVENING

Keep yourselves from idols.

My son, give me your heart. ◊ Set your mind on things above, not on things on the earth.

Son of man, these men have set up their idols in their hearts. . . . Should I let Myself be inquired of at all by them? ◊ Therefore put to death your members which are on the earth: fornication, uncleanness, passion, evil desire, and covetousness, which is idolatry. ◊ Those who desire to be rich fall into temptation and a snare, and into many foolish and harmful lusts which drown men in destruction and perdition. For the love of money is a root of all kinds of evil, for which some have strayed from the faith in their greediness, and pierced themselves through with many sorrows. You, O man of God, flee these things and pursue righteousness, godliness, faith, love, patience, gentleness.

Do not trust in oppression, nor vainly hope in robbery. ◊ My fruit is better than gold, yes, than fine gold, and my revenue than choice silver.

For where your treasure is, there your heart will be also. ◊ The Lord does not see as man sees; . . . the Lord looks at the heart.

1 JOHN 5:21.PROV 23:26.COL 3:2.EZEK 14:3.COL 3:5.1 TIM 6:9-11.PS
62:10.PROV 8:19.MATT 6:21.1 SAM 16:7

MORNING

You shall be perfect, just as your Father in heaven is perfect.

I am Almighty God; walk before Me and be blameless. ◊ You shall be holy to Me, for I the Lord am holy, and have separated you from the peoples, that you should be Mine. ◊ You were bought at a price; therefore glorify God in your body and in your spirit, which are God's.

You are complete in Him, who is the head of all principality and power. ◊ Who gave Himself for us, that He might redeem us from every lawless deed. ◊ Be diligent to be found by Him in peace, without spot and blameless.

Blessed are the undefiled in the way, who walk in the law of the Lord! ◊ He who looks into the perfect law of liberty and continues in it, and is not a forgetful hearer but a doer of the work, this one will be blessed in what he does. ◊ Search me, O God, and know my heart; try me, and know my anxieties; and see if there is any wicked way in me, and lead me in the way everlasting.

MATT 5:48.GEN 17:1.LEV 20:26.1 COR 6:20.COL 2:10.TITUS 2:14.2 PET 3:14.PS 119:1.JAMES 1:25.PS 139:23-24

EVENING

Let us cleanse ourselves . . . perfecting holiness in the fear of God.

Let us cleanse ourselves from all filthiness of the flesh and spirit.

You desire truth in the inward parts, and in the hidden part You will make me to know wisdom. ◊ Teaching us that, denying ungodliness and worldly lusts, we should live soberly, righteously, and godly in the present age. ◊ Let your light so shine before men, that they may see your good works and glorify your Father in heaven. ◊ Not that I have already attained, or am already perfected; but I press on.

We know that when He is revealed, we shall be like Him, for we shall see Him as He is. And everyone who has this hope in Him purifies himself, just as He is pure.

He who has prepared us for this very thing is God, who also has given us the Spirit as a guarantee. ◊ For the equipping of the saints for the work of ministry, for the edifying of the body of Christ, till we all come to the unity of the faith and the knowledge of the Son of God, to a perfect man, to the measure of the stature of the fullness of Christ.

2 COR 7:1.2 COR 7:1.PS 51:6.TITUS 2:12.MATT 5:15,16.PHIL 3:12. 1 JOHN 3:2-3.2 COR 5:5.EPH 4:12-13

MORNING

Behold, the Lord's hand is not shortened, that it cannot save; nor His ear heavy, that it cannot hear.

In the day when I cried out, You answered me, and made me bold with strength in my soul. ◇ While I was speaking in prayer, the man Gabriel, whom I had seen in the vision at the beginning, being caused to fly swiftly, reached me about the time of the evening offering.

Do not hide Your face from me; do not turn Your servant away in anger; You have been my help; do not leave me nor forsake me, O God of my salvation. ◇ But You, O Lord, do not be far from Me; O My Strength, hasten to help Me!

Ah, Lord God! Behold, You have made the heavens and the earth by Your great power and outstretched arm. There is nothing too hard for You. ◇ [He] delivered us from so great a death, and does deliver us; in whom we trust that He will still deliver us. ◇ Shall God not avenge His own elect who cry out day and night to Him, though He bears long with them? I tell you that He will avenge them speedily.

IS 59:1.PS 138:3.DAN 9:21.PS 27:9.PS 22:19.JER 32:17.2 COR 1:10.LUKE 18:7-8

EVENING

I have glorified You on the earth.

My food is to do the will of Him who sent Me, and to finish His work. ◇ I must work the works of Him who sent Me while it is day; the night is coming when no one can work.

"Did you not know that I must be about My Father's business?" But they did not understand the statement which He spoke to them. ◇ Jesus . . . said, "This sickness is not unto death, but for the glory of God, that the Son of God may be glorified through it. . . . Did I not say to you that if you would believe you would see the glory of God?"

Jesus increased in wisdom and stature, and in favor with God and men. ◇ "You are My beloved Son; in You I am well pleased." ◇ All bore witness to Him, and marveled at the gracious words which proceeded out of His mouth.

You are worthy . . . for You were slain, and have redeemed us to God by Your blood out of every tribe and tongue and people and nation, and have made us kings and priests to our God; and we shall reign on the earth.

JOHN 17:4.JOHN 4:34.JOHN 9:4.LUKE 2:49-50.JOHN 11:4,40.LUKE 2:52.LUKE 3:22.LUKE 4:22.REV 5:9-10

MAY 5

MORNING

**Therefore do not worry, saying, "What shall we eat?"
or "What shall we drink?" or "What shall we wear?"
For your heavenly Father knows that you need all
these things.**

Oh, fear the Lord, you His saints! There is no want to those who fear Him. The young lions lack and suffer hunger; but those who seek the Lord shall not lack any good thing. ◊ No good thing will He withhold from those who walk uprightly. O Lord of hosts, blessed is the man who trusts in You!

I want you to be without care. ◊ Be anxious for nothing, but in everything by prayer and supplication, with thanksgiving, let your requests be made known to God.

Are not two sparrows sold for a copper coin? And not one of them falls to the ground apart from your Father's will. But the very hairs of your head are all numbered. Do not fear therefore; you are of more value than many sparrows. ◊ Why are you so fearful? How is it that you have no faith? ◊ Have faith in God.

MATT 6:31-32.PS 34:9-10.PS 84:11-12.1 COR 7:32.PHIL 4:6.MATT 10:29-31.MARK 4:40.MARK 11:22

EVENING

**He spread a cloud for a covering, and fire to give light
in the night.**

As a father pities his children, so the Lord pities those who fear Him. For He knows . . . we are dust.

The sun shall not strike you by day, nor the moon by night. ◊ There will be a tabernacle for shade in the daytime from the heat, for a place of refuge, and for a shelter from storm and rain.

The Lord is your keeper; the Lord is your shade at your right hand. . . . The Lord shall preserve your going out and your coming in from this time forth, and even forevermore. ◊ He found him in . . . a howling wilderness; . . . He kept him as the apple of His eye. ◊ In Your manifold mercies You did not forsake them in the wilderness. The pillar of the cloud did not depart from them by day . . . nor the pillar of fire by night. . . . Forty years You sustained them in the wilderness, so that they lacked nothing; their clothes did not wear out and their feet did not swell. ◊ You in Your mercy have led forth the people whom You have redeemed; you have guided them in Your strength to Your holy habitation.

Jesus Christ is the same yesterday, today, and forever.

PS 105:39.PS 103:13-14.PS 121:6.IS 4:6.PS 121:5.PS 121:8.DEUT 32:10.NEH 9:19-21.EX 15:13.HEB 13:8

MORNING

**Mercy and truth have met together; righteousness and
peace have kissed each other.**

[I am] a just God and a Savior.

The Lord is well pleased for His righteousness' sake; He will magnify
the law and make it honorable.

God was in Christ reconciling the world to Himself, not imputing their
trespasses to them. ◊ God set [Him] forth to be a propitiation by His
blood, through faith, to demonstrate His righteousness, because in His
forbearance God had passed over the sins that were previously
committed, to demonstrate at the present time His righteousness, that
He might be just and the justifier of the one who has faith in Jesus. ◊ He
was wounded for our transgressions, He was bruised for our iniquities;
the chastisement for our peace was upon Him, and by His stripes we are
healed. ◊ Who shall bring a charge against God's elect? It is God who
justifies. ◊ To him who does not work but believes on Him who justifies
the ungodly, his faith is accounted for righteousness.

PS 85:10.IS 45:21.IS 42:21.2 COR 5:19.ROM 3:25-26.IS 53:5.ROM
8:33.ROM 4:5

EVENING

**How are the dead raised up? And with what body do
they come?**

Beloved, now we are children of God; and it has not yet been revealed
what we shall be, but we know that when He is revealed, we shall be like
Him, for we shall see Him as He is. ◊ As we have borne the image of the
man of dust, we shall also bear the image of the heavenly Man.

Our citizenship is in heaven, from which we also eagerly wait for the
Savior, the Lord Jesus Christ, who will transform our lowly body that it
may be conformed to His glorious body, according to the working by
which He is able even to subdue all things to Himself.

Jesus Himself stood in the midst of them. . . . But they were terrified
and frightened, and supposed they had seen a spirit. ◊ He was seen by
Cephas, then by the twelve. After that He was seen by over five hundred
brethren at once.

If the Spirit of Him who raised Jesus from the dead dwells in you, He
who raised Christ from the dead will also give life to your mortal bodies
through His Spirit who dwells in you.

1 COR 15:35.1 JOHN 3:2.1 COR 15:49.PHIL 3:20-21.LUKE 24:36-
37.1COR 15:5-6.ROM 8:11

MORNING

You will hear of wars and rumors of wars. See that you are not troubled.

God is our refuge and strength, a very present help in trouble. Therefore we will not fear, though the earth be removed, and though the mountains be carried into the midst of the sea. ◊ Come, my people, enter your chambers, and shut your doors behind you; hide yourself, as it were, for a little moment, until the indignation is past. For behold, the Lord comes out of His place to punish the inhabitants of the earth for their iniquity. ◊ In the shadow of Your wings I will make my refuge, until these calamities have passed by. ◊ Your life is hidden with Christ in God.

He will not be afraid of evil tidings; his heart is steadfast, trusting in the Lord.

These things I have spoken to you, that in Me you may have peace. In the world you will have tribulation; but be of good cheer, I have overcome the world.

MATT 24:6.PS 46:1-2.IS 26:20-21.PS 57:1.COL 3:3.PS 112:7.JOHN 16:33

EVENING

They persecute him whom You have struck.

It is impossible that no offenses should come, but woe to him through whom they do come! ◊ [Jesus], being delivered by the determined counsel and foreknowledge of God, you have taken by lawless hands, have crucified, and put to death. ◊ Then they spat in His face and beat Him, . . . saying, "Prophesy to us, Christ! Who is the one who struck You?" ◊ Likewise the chief priests, also mocking with the scribes and elders, said, "He saved others; Himself He cannot save." ◊ For truly against Your holy Servant Jesus, whom You anointed, both Herod and Pontius Pilate, with the Gentiles and the people of Israel, were gathered together to do whatever Your hand and Your purpose determined before to be done. ◊ The kings of the earth took their stand, and the rulers were gathered together against the Lord and against His Christ.

Surely He has borne our griefs and carried our sorrows; yet we esteemed Him stricken, smitten by God, and afflicted. He was wounded for our transgressions, He was bruised for our iniquities; the chastisement for our peace was upon Him, and by His stripes we are healed.

PS 69:26.LUKE 17:1.ACTS 2:23.MATT 26:67-68.MATT 27:41-42.ACTS
4:27-28.ACTS 4:26.IS 53:4-5

MORNING

It pleased the Lord to bruise Him;
He has put Him to grief.

"Now My soul is troubled, and what shall I say? 'Father, save Me from this hour'? But for this purpose I came to this hour. Father, glorify Your name." Then a voice came from heaven, saying, "I have both glorified it and will glorify it again." ◊ "Father, if it is Your will, remove this cup from Me; nevertheless not My will, but Yours, be done." Then an angel appeared to Him from heaven, strengthening Him.

Being found in appearance as a man, He humbled Himself and became obedient to the point of death, even the death of the cross. ◊ Therefore My Father loves Me, because I lay down My life that I may take it again. ◊ For I have come down from heaven, not to do My own will, but the will of Him who sent Me. ◊ Shall I not drink the cup which My Father has given Me?

The Father has not left Me alone, for I always do those things that please Him. ◊ This is My beloved Son, in whom I am well pleased.

IS 53:10.JOHN 12:27-28.LUKE 22:42-43.PHIL 2:8.JOHN 10:17.JOHN 6:38.JOHN 18:11.JOHN 8:29.MATT 3:17

EVENING

I have set watchmen on your walls, O Jerusalem, who
shall never hold their peace day or night.

[You] have made us kings and priests to our God; and we shall reign on the earth. ◊ The priests, shall blow the trumpets; and these shall be to you as an ordinance forever throughout your generations. When you go to war in your land against the enemy who oppresses you, then you shall sound an alarm with the trumpets, and you will be remembered before the Lord your God, and you will be saved from your enemies.

I did not say to the seed of Jacob, "Seek Me in vain." ◊ Their voice was heard; and their prayer came up to His holy dwelling place, to heaven. ◊ The eyes of the Lord are on the righteous, and His ears are open to their cry. ◊ Pray for one another. . . . The effective, fervent prayer of a righteous man avails much.

Come, Lord Jesus! ◊ You are my . . . deliverer. ◊ The day of the Lord will come as a thief in the night. ◊ Looking for and hastening the coming of the day of God, . . . we, according to His promise, look for new heavens and a new earth in which righteousness dwells.

IS 62:6.REV 5:10.NUM 10:8-9.IS 45:19.2 CHR 30:27.PS 34:15.JAMES 5:16.REV 22:20.PS 40:17.2 PET 3:10.2 PET 3:12-13

MAY 9

MORNING

**Faith is the substance of things hoped for, the
evidence of things not seen.**

If in this life only we have hope in Christ, we are of all men the most pitiable.

Eye has not seen, nor ear heard, nor have entered into the heart of man the things which God has prepared for those who love Him. But God has revealed them to us through His Spirit. ◊ After you . . . believed, you were sealed with the Holy Spirit of promise, who is the guarantee of our inheritance until the redemption of the purchased possession.

Jesus said to him, "Thomas, because you have seen Me, you have believed. Blessed are those who have not seen and yet have believed." ◊ Jesus Christ whom having not seen you love. Though now you do not see Him, yet believing, you rejoice with joy inexpressible and full of glory, receiving the end of your faith—the salvation of your souls.

We walk by faith, not by sight. ◊ Do not cast away your confidence, which has great reward.

HEB 11:1.1 COR 15:19.1 COR 2:9-10.EPH 1:13-14.JOHN 20:29.1 PET
1:7-9.2 COR 5:7.HEB 10:35

EVENING

He said to them, " . . . do not be afraid."

When I saw Him, I fell at His feet as dead. But He laid His right hand on me, saying to me, "Do not be afraid; I am the First and the Last. I am He who lives, and was dead, and behold, I am alive forevermore. Amen. And I have the keys of Hades and of Death." ◊ I, even I, am He who blots out your transgressions for My own sake; and I will not remember your sins.

"Woe is me, for I am undone! Because I am a man of unclean lips, . . . my eyes have seen the King, the Lord of hosts." Then one of the seraphim flew to me, having in his hand a live coal which he had taken with the tongs from the altar. And he touched my mouth with it, and said: "Behold, this has touched your lips; your iniquity is taken away, and your sin purged." ◊ I have blotted out, like a thick cloud, your transgressions, and like a cloud, your sins. Return to Me, for I have redeemed you.

If anyone sins, we have an Advocate with the Father, Jesus Christ the righteous. He Himself is the propitiation for our sins, and not for ours only but also for the whole world.

JOHN 6:20.REV 1:17-18.IS 43:25.IS 6:5-7.IS 44:22.1 JOHN 2:1-2

MORNING

**For this purpose the Son of God was manifested, that
He might destroy the works of the devil.**

For we do not wrestle against flesh and blood, but against principalities, against powers, against the rulers of the darkness of this age, against spiritual hosts of wickedness in the heavenly places. ◊ Inasmuch . . . as the children have partaken of flesh and blood, He Himself likewise shared in the same, that through death He might destroy him who had the power of death, that is, the devil. ◊ Having disarmed principalities and powers, He made a public spectacle of them, triumphing over them in it. ◊ I heard a loud voice saying in heaven, "Now salvation, and strength, and the kingdom of our God, and the power of His Christ have come, for the accuser of our brethren, who accused them before our God day and night, has been cast down. And they overcame him by the blood of the Lamb and by the word of their testimony and they did not love their lives to the death."

Thanks be to God, who gives us the victory through our Lord Jesus Christ.

1 JOHN 3:8.EPH 6:12.HEB 2:14.COL 2:15.REV 12:10-11.1 COR 15:57

EVENING

Vanity of vanities, all is vanity.

All our days have passed away in Your wrath; we finish our years like a sigh. The days of our lives are seventy years; and if by reason of strength they are eighty years, yet their boast is only labor and sorrow; for it is soon cut off, and we fly away.

If in this life only we have hope in Christ, we are of all men the most pitiable. ◊ For here we have no continuing city, but we seek the one to come. ◊ I am the Lord, I do not change. ◊ For our citizenship is in heaven, from which we also eagerly wait for the Savior, the Lord Jesus Christ, who will transform our lowly body that it may be conformed to His glorious body, according to the working by which He is able even to subdue all things to Himself. ◊ Looking for and hastening the coming of the day of God, . . . look for . . . righteousness. For the creation was subjected to futility, not willingly, but because of Him who subjected it in hope.

Jesus Christ is the same yesterday, today, and forever. ◊ Holy, holy, holy, Lord God Almighty, who was and is and is to come!

ECCL 1:2.PS 90:9-10.1 COR 15:19.HEB 13:14.MAL 3:6.PHIL 3:20-21.
2 PET 3:12-13.ROM 8:20.HEB 13:8.REV 4:8

MORNING_____

Awake to righteousness, and do not sin.

You are all sons of light and sons of the day. Therefore let us not sleep, as others do, but let us watch and be sober.

It is high time to awake out of sleep; for now our salvation is nearer than when we first believed. The night is far spent, the day is at hand. Therefore let us cast off the works of darkness, and let us put on the armor of light. ◊ Therefore take up the whole armor of God, that you may be able to withstand in the evil day, and having done all, to stand. ◊ Cast away from you all the transgressions which you have committed, and get yourselves a new heart and a new spirit. ◊ Lay aside all filthiness and overflow of wickedness, and receive with meekness the implanted word, which is able to save your souls. ◊ Little children, abide in Him, that when He appears, we may have confidence and not be ashamed before Him at His coming. If you know that He is righteous, you know that everyone who practices righteousness is born of Him.

1 COR 15:34.1 THESS 5:5-6.ROM 13:11-12.EPH 6:13.EZEK 18:31.JAMES 1:21.1 JOHN 2:28-29

EVENING_____

My sheep hear My voice.

Behold, I stand at the door and knock. If anyone hears My voice and opens the door, I will come in to him and dine with him, and he with Me.

I sleep, but my heart is awake; it is the voice of my beloved! He knocks, saying, "Open for me, my sister, my love, my dove, my perfect one; for my head is covered with dew, my locks with the drops of the night." . . . I opened for my beloved, but my beloved had turned away and was gone. My heart went out to him when he spoke. I sought him, but I could not find him; I called him, but he gave me no answer.

My people shall know My name; therefore they shall know in that day that I am He who speaks: "Behold, it is I." ◊ When Jesus came to the place, He looked up and saw him, and said to him, "Zacchaeus, make haste and come down, for today I must stay at your house." So he made haste and came down, and received Him joyfully. ◊ I will hear what God the Lord will speak, for He will speak peace to His people and to His saints.

JOHN 10:27.REV 3:20.SONG 5:2,6.IS 52:6.LUKE 19:5-6.PS 85:8

MORNING

**Beloved, let us love one another, for love is of God;
and everyone who loves is born of God
and knows God.**

The love of God has been poured out in our hearts by the Holy Spirit who was given to us. ◊ You did not receive the spirit of bondage again to fear, but you received the Spirit of adoption by whom we cry out, "Abba, Father." The Spirit Himself bears witness with our spirit that we are children of God. ◊ He who believes in the Son of God has the witness in himself.

In this the love of God was manifested toward us, that God has sent His only begotten Son into the world, that we might live through Him. ◊ In Him we have redemption through His blood, the forgiveness of sins, according to the riches of His grace. ◊ That in the ages to come He might show the exceeding riches of His grace in His kindness toward us in Christ Jesus.

Beloved, if God so loved us, we also ought to love one another.

1 JOHN 4:7.ROM 5:5.ROM 8:15-16.1 JOHN 5:10.1 JOHN 4:9.EPH 1:7.EPH 2:7.1 JOHN 4:11

EVENING

Reproach has broken my heart.

"Is this not the carpenter's son?" ◊ "Can anything good come out of Nazareth?" ◊ "He casts out demons by the ruler of the demons." ◊ "We know that this Man is a sinner." ◊ "He deceives the people." ◊ "This Man blasphemes!" ◊ The Son of Man came eating and drinking, and they say, "Look, a gluttonous man and a winebibber, a friend of tax collectors and sinners!"

It is enough for a disciple that he be like his teacher, and a servant like his master. ◊ For this is commendable, if because of conscience toward God one endures grief, suffering wrongfully. For what credit is it if, when you are beaten for your faults, you take it patiently? But when you do good and suffer for it, if you take it patiently, this is commendable before God. Christ also suffered for us, leaving us an example, that you should follow His steps: "Who committed no sin, nor was guile found in His mouth"; who, when He was reviled, did not revile in return; when He suffered, He did not threaten, but committed Himself to Him who judges righteously. ◊ If you are reproached for the name of Christ, blessed are you.

PS 69:20.MATT 13:55.JOHN 1:46.MATT 9:34.JOHN 9:24.JOHN 7:12.MATT 9:3.MATT 11:19.MATT 10:25.1 PET 2:19-23.1 PET 4:14

MORNING———————————————————————

Pray everywhere, lifting up holy hands, without wrath and doubting.

The true worshipers will worship the Father in spirit and truth; for the Father is seeking such to worship Him. God is Spirit, and those who worship Him must worship in spirit and truth. ◊ Then you shall call, and the Lord will answer; you shall cry, and He will say, "Here I am." ◊ Whenever you stand praying, if you have anything against anyone, forgive him.

Without faith it is impossible to please Him, for he who comes to God must believe that He is, and that He is a rewarder of those who diligently seek Him. ◊ Let him ask in faith, with no doubting, for he who doubts is like a wave of the sea driven and tossed by the wind. For let not that man suppose that he will receive anything from the Lord.

If I regard iniquity in my heart, the Lord will not hear. ◊ My little children, these things I write to you, that you may not sin. And if anyone sins, we have an Advocate with the Father, Jesus Christ the righteous.

1 TIM 2:8.JOHN 4:23-24.IS 58:9.MARK 11:25.HEB 11:6.JAMES 1:6-7.PS 66:18.1 JOHN 2:1

EVENING———————————————————————

My heart pants, my strength fails me.

Hear my cry, O God; attend to my prayer. From the end of the earth I will cry to You, when my heart is overwhelmed; lead me to the rock that is higher than I.

He said to me, "My grace is sufficient for you, for My strength is made perfect in weakness." Therefore most gladly I will rather boast in my infirmities, that the power of Christ may rest upon me. When I am weak, then I am strong.

When [Peter] saw that the wind was boisterous, he was afraid; and beginning to sink he cried out, saying, "Lord, save me!" And immediately Jesus stretched out His hand and caught him, and said to him, "O you of little faith, why did you doubt?" ◊ If you faint in the day of adversity, your strength is small. ◊ He gives power to the weak, and to those who have no might He increases strength. ◊ The eternal God is your refuge, and underneath are the everlasting arms. ◊ Be strengthened with all might, according to His glorious power, for all patience and longsuffering with joy.

PS 38:10.PS 61:1-2.2 COR 12:9-10.MATT 14:30-31.PROV 24:10.IS 40:29.DEUT 33:27.COL 1:11

MORNING

I may know Him and . . . the fellowship of His sufferings.

It is enough for a disciple that he be like his teacher, and a servant like his master.

He is despised and rejected by men, a man of sorrows and acquainted with grief. And we hid, as it were, our faces from Him; He was despised, and we did not esteem Him. ◊ Because you are not of the world, but I chose you out of the world, therefore the world hates you.

I looked for someone to take pity, but there was none. ◊ At my first defense no one stood with me, but all forsook me.

Foxes have holes and birds of the air have nests, but the Son of Man has nowhere to lay His head. ◊ Here we have no continuing city, but we seek the one to come.

Let us run with endurance the race that is set before us, looking unto Jesus, the author and finisher of our faith, who for the joy that was set before Him endured the cross, despising the shame, and has sat down at the right hand of the throne of God.

PHIL 3:10.MATT 10:25.IS 53:3.JOHN 15:19.PS 69:20.2 TIM 4:16.MATT 8:20.HEB 13:14.HEB 12:1-2

EVENING

Thanks be to God, who gives us the victory through our Lord Jesus Christ.

Who shall bring a charge against God's elect? It is God who justifies. Who is he who condemns? It is Christ who died, and . . . who also makes intercession for us. ◊ The life of the flesh is in the blood, . . . that makes atonement for the soul. ◊ I am the Lord. The blood shall be a sign for you on the houses where you are. And when I see the blood, I will pass over you. ◊ There is . . . no condemnation to those who are in Christ Jesus.

Who are these arrayed in white robes, and where did they come from? These are the ones who come out of the great tribulation, and washed their robes and made them white in the blood of the Lamb. Therefore they are before the throne of God, and serve Him day and night in His temple. They shall neither hunger anymore nor thirst anymore.

To Him who loved us and washed us from our sins in His own blood, and has made us kings and priests to His God and Father, to Him be glory and dominion forever and ever. Amen.

1 COR 15:57.ROM 8:33-34.LEV 17:11.EX 12:12-13.ROM 8:1.REV 7:13-16.REV 1:5-6

MORNING

God will wipe away every tear . . . there shall be no more death, nor sorrow, . . . for the former things have passed away.

He will swallow up death forever, and the Lord God will wipe away tears from all faces; the rebuke of His people He will take away from all the earth; for the Lord has spoken. ◇ Your sun shall no longer go down, nor shall your moon withdraw itself; for the Lord will be your everlasting light, and the days of your mourning shall be ended. ◇ The inhabitant will not say, "I am sick"; the people who dwell in it will be forgiven their iniquity. ◇ The voice of weeping shall no longer be heard in her, nor the voice of crying. ◇ Sorrow and sighing shall flee away.

I will ransom them from the power of the grave; I will redeem them from death. O Death, I will be your plagues! O Grave, I will be your destruction! ◇ The last enemy that will be destroyed is death. . . . Then shall be brought to pass the saying that is written: "Death is swallowed up in victory."

REV 21:4.IS 25:8.IS 60:20.IS 33:24.IS 65:19.IS 35:10.HOS 13:14.1 COR 15:26,54

EVENING

[God] raised us up together, and made us sit together in the heavenly places in Christ Jesus.

Do not be afraid; . . . I am He who lives, and was dead. ◇ Father, I desire that they also whom You gave Me may be with Me where I am, that they may behold My glory.

For we are members of His body. ◇ He is the head of the body, the church, who is the beginning, the firstborn from the dead. ◇ You are complete in Him, who is the head of all principality and power.

As the children have partaken of flesh and blood, He Himself likewise shared in the same, that through death He might destroy him who had the power of death, that is, the devil, and release those who through fear of death were all their lifetime subject to bondage.

For this corruptible must put on incorruption, and this mortal must put on immortality. Then shall be brought to pass the saying that is written: "Death is swallowed up in victory." . . . Therefore, my beloved brethren, be steadfast, immovable, always abounding in the work of the Lord, knowing that your labor is not in vain in the Lord.

EPH 2:6.REV 1:17-18.JOHN 17:24.EPH 5:30.COL 1:18.COL 2:10.HEB 2:14-15.1 COR 15:53-54,58

MORNING

A servant of Jesus Christ.

You call me Teacher and Lord, and you say well, for so I am. ◊ If anyone serves Me, let him follow Me; and where I am, there My servant will be also. ◊ Take My yoke upon you and learn from Me, for I am gentle and lowly in heart, and you will find rest for your souls. For My yoke is easy and My burden is light.

What things were gain to me, these I have counted loss for Christ. ◊ Having been set free from sin, and having become slaves of God, you have your fruit to holiness, and the end, everlasting life.

No longer do I call you servants, for a servant does not know what his master is doing; but I have called you friends, for all things that I heard from My Father I have made known to you.

Stand fast therefore in the liberty by which Christ has made us free, and do not be entangled again with a yoke of bondage. ◊ For you, brethren, have been called to liberty; only do not use liberty as an opportunity for the flesh.

ROM 1:1.JOHN 13:13.JOHN 12:26.MATT 11:29-30.PHIL 3:7.ROM
6:22.JOHN 15:15.GAL 5:1.GAL 5:13

EVENING

I will bless the Lord who has given me counsel.

His name will be called Wonderful, Counselor. ◊ Counsel is mine, and sound wisdom; I am understanding. ◊ Your word is a lamp to my feet and a light to my path. ◊ Trust in the Lord with all your heart, and lean not on your own understanding; in all your ways acknowledge Him, and He shall direct your paths.

O Lord, I know the way of man is not in himself; it is not in man who walks to direct his own steps. ◊ Your ears shall hear a word behind you, saying, "This is the way, walk in it," whenever you turn to the right hand or whenever you turn to the left. ◊ Commit your works to the Lord, and your thoughts will be established. ◊ A man's steps are of the Lord; how then can a man understand his own way?

You will guide me with Your counsel, and afterward receive me to glory. ◊ Yea, though I walk through the valley of the shadow of death, I will fear no evil; for You are with me; Your rod and Your staff, they comfort me. ◊ For this is God, our God forever and ever; He will be our guide even to death.

PS 16:7.IS 9:6.PROV 8:14.PS 119:105.PROV 3:5-6.JER 10:23.IS
30:21.PROV 16:3.PROV 20:24.PS 73:24.PS 23:4.PS 48:14

MORNING

**I am the Lord your God: Walk in My statutes, keep
My judgments, and do them.**

As He who called you is holy, you also be holy in all your conduct. ◊
He who says he abides in Him ought himself also to walk just as He
walked. ◊ If you know that He is righteous, you know that everyone
who practices righteousness is born of Him. Circumcision is nothing and
uncircumcision is nothing, but keeping the commandments of God is
what matters. ◊ Whoever shall keep the whole law, and yet stumble in
one point, he is guilty of all.

Not that we are sufficient . . . to think of anything as being from
ourselves, but our sufficiency is from God. ◊ Teach me, O Lord, the way
of Your statutes.

Work out your own salvation with fear and trembling; for it is God who
works in you both to will and to do for His good pleasure. ◊ The God of
peace . . . make you complete in every good work to do His will, working
in you what is well pleasing in His sight, through Jesus Christ.

EZEK 20:19.1 PET 1:15.1 JOHN 2:6.1 JOHN 2:29.1 COR 7:19.JAMES
2:10.2 COR 3:5.PS 119:33.PHIL 2:12-13.HEB 13:20-21

EVENING

He gave His only begotten Son.

For indeed He does not give aid to angels, but He does give aid to the
seed of Abraham. Therefore, in all things He had to be made like His
brethren. ◊ Above the firmament over their heads was the likeness of a
throne, in appearance like a sapphire stone; on the likeness of the throne
was a likeness with the appearance of a man high above it. ◊ No one has
ascended to heaven but He who came down from heaven. ◊ Behold My
hands and My feet, that it is I Myself. Handle Me and see, for a spirit does
not have flesh and bones as you see I have.

Christ Jesus, who, being in the form of God, did not consider it robbery
to be equal with God, but made Himself of no reputation, taking the form
of a servant, and coming in the likeness of men. And being found in
appearance as a man, He humbled Himself and became obedient to the
point of death, even the death of the cross. Therefore God also has highly
exalted Him and given Him the name which is above every name, that at
the name of Jesus every knee should bow, of those in heaven, and of
those on earth, and of those under the earth, and that every tongue
should confess that Jesus Christ is Lord, to the glory of God the Father.

JOHN 3:16.HEB 2:16-17.EZEK 1:26.JOHN 3:13.LUKE 24:39.PHIL 2:5-11

MORNING

As the Father has life in Himself, so He has granted the Son to have life in Himself.

Our Savior Jesus Christ . . . has abolished death and brought life and immortality to light through the gospel. ◊ I am the resurrection and the life. ◊ Because I live, you will live also. ◊ We have become partakers of Christ. ◊ Partakers of the Holy Spirit. ◊ Partakers of the divine nature. ◊ The first man Adam became a living being. The last Adam became a life-giving spirit. ◊ Behold, I tell you a mystery: We shall not all sleep, but we shall all be changed—in a moment, in the twinkling of an eye, at the last trumpet. For the trumpet will sound, and the dead will be raised incorruptible, and we shall be changed.

"Holy, holy, holy, Lord God Almighty, who was and is and is to come!" . . . [He] lives forever and ever. ◊ The blessed and only Potentate, the King of kings and Lord of lords, who alone has immortality. ◊ Now to the King eternal . . . be honor and glory forever and ever. Amen.

JOHN 5:26.2 TIM 1:10.JOHN 11:25.JOHN 14:19.HEB 3:14.HEB 6:4.2 PET 1:4.1 COR 15:45.1 COR 15:51-52.REV 4:8-9.1 TIM 6:15-16.1 TIM 1:17

EVENING

Let us not become conceited.

Gideon said . . . "I would like to make a request of you, that each of you would give me the earrings from his plunder." For they had gold earrings, because they were Ishmaelites. So they answered, "We will gladly give them." And they spread out a garment, and each man threw into it the earrings from his plunder. . . . Gideon made it into an ephod and set it up in his city, Ophrah. And all Israel played the harlot with it there. It became a snare to Gideon and to his house.

And do you seek great things for yourself? Do not seek them. ◊ Lest I should be exalted above measure by the abundance of the revelations, a thorn in the flesh was given to me, a messenger of Satan to buffet me, lest I be exalted above measure. . . . Most gladly I will rather boast in my infirmities, that the power of Christ may rest upon me.

Let nothing be done through selfish ambition or conceit, but in lowliness of mind let each esteem others better than himself. ◊ Love suffers long and is kind; love does not envy; love does not parade itself, is not puffed up; does not behave rudely, does not seek its own.

Take My yoke upon you and learn from Me.

GAL 5:26.JUDG 8:24-25,27.JER 45:5.2 COR 12:7,9.PHIL 2:3.1 COR 13:4-5.MATT 11:29

MAY 19

Wash me thoroughly from my iniquity.

I will cleanse them from all their iniquity by which they have sinned against Me, and I will pardon all their iniquities by which they have sinned and by which they have transgressed against Me. ◊ Then I will sprinkle clean water on you, and you shall be clean; I will cleanse you from all your filthiness and from all your idols.

Unless one is born of water and the Spirit, he cannot enter the kingdom of God. ◊ If the blood of bulls and goats and the ashes of a heifer, sprinkling the unclean, sanctifies for the purifying of the flesh, how much more shall the blood of Christ, who through the eternal Spirit offered Himself without spot to God, purge your conscience from dead works to serve the living God?

He saved them for His name's sake, that He might make His mighty power known. ◊ Not unto us, O Lord, not unto us, but to Your name give glory, because of Your mercy, and because of Your truth. . . . We will bless the Lord from this time forth and forevermore. Praise the Lord!

PS 51:2.JER 33:8.EZEK 36:25.JOHN 3:5.HEB 9:13-14.PS 106:8.PS
115:1,18.

EVENING_____

**I thank my God . . . for your fellowship in the gospel
from the first day until now.**

For as the body is one and has many members, but all the members of that one body, being many, are one body, so also is Christ. For by one Spirit we were all baptized into one body—whether Jews or Greeks, whether slaves or free—and have all been made to drink into one Spirit.

God is faithful, by whom you were called into the fellowship of His Son, Jesus Christ our Lord. ◊ That which we have seen and heard we declare to you, that you also may have fellowship with us; and truly our fellowship is with the Father and with His Son Jesus Christ.

If we walk in the light as He is in the light, we have fellowship with one another, and the blood of Jesus Christ His Son cleanses us from all sin. ◊ Jesus . . . lifted up His eyes to heaven, and said: . . . "I do not pray for these alone, but also for those who will believe in Me through their word; that they all may be one, as You, Father, are in Me, and I in You; that they also may be one in Us."

PHIL 1:3,5.1 COR 12:12,13.1 COR 1:9.1 JOHN 1:3.1 JOHN 1:7.JOHN
17:1,20-21

MORNING———————————————————————

Take heed to yourself.

And everyone who competes for the prize is temperate in all things. Now they do it to obtain a perishable crown, but we for an imperishable crown. Therefore I run thus: not with uncertainty. . . . But I discipline my body and bring it into subjection, lest, when I have preached to others, I myself should become disqualified.

Put on the whole armor of God, that you may be able to stand against the wiles of the devil. For we do not wrestle against flesh and blood, but against principalities, against powers, against the rulers of the darkness of this age, against spiritual hosts of wickedness in the heavenly places.

Those who are Christ's have crucified the flesh with its passions and desires. If we live in the Spirit, let us also walk in the Spirit. ◇ For as many as are led by the Spirit of God, these are sons of God. ◇ Meditate on these things; give yourself entirely to them, that your progress may be evident to all.

1 TIM 4:16.1 COR 9:25-27.EPH 6:11-12.GAL 5:24-25.ROM 8:14.1 TIM 4:15

EVENING———————————————————————

**I, the Lord, who call you by your name, am the God
of Israel.**

Jesus said to her, "Mary!" ◇ Fear not, for I have redeemed you; I have called you by your name; you are Mine. ◇ The sheep hear his voice; and he calls his own sheep by name and leads them out. The sheep follow him, for they know his voice.

But Zion said, "The Lord has forsaken me, and my Lord has forgotten me." Can a woman forget her nursing child, and not have compassion on the son of her womb? Surely they may forget, yet I will not forget you. See, I have inscribed you on the palms of My hands.

The Lord knows those who are His. ◇ Seeing then that we have a great High Priest who has passed through the heavens, Jesus the Son of God, let us hold fast our confession. For we do not have a High Priest who cannot sympathize with our weaknesses, but was in all points tempted as we are, yet without sin. Let us therefore come boldly to the throne of grace, that we may obtain mercy and find grace to help in time of need.

He who overcomes shall be clothed in white garments, and I will not blot out his name from the Book of Life.

IS 45:3.JOHN 20:16.IS 43:1.JOHN 10:3-4.IS 49:14-16.2 TIM 2:19.HEB
4:14-16.REV 3:5

MAY 21

MORNING

**My brethren, be strong in the Lord and in the power
of His might.**

"My grace is sufficient for you, for My strength is made perfect in weakness." Therefore most gladly I will rather boast in my infirmities, that the power of Christ may rest upon me. Therefore I take pleasure in infirmities, in reproaches, in needs, in persecutions, in distresses, for Christ's sake. For when I am weak, then I am strong. ◊ I will go in the strength of the Lord God; I will make mention of Your righteousness, of Yours only. ◊ The gospel of Christ, . . . is the power of God to salvation.

I can do all things through Christ who strengthens me. ◊ I also labor, striving according to His working which works in me mightily. ◊ We have this treasure in earthen vessels, that the excellence of the power may be of God and not of us.

The joy of the Lord is your strength. ◊ Strengthened with all might, according to His glorious power, for all patience and longsuffering with joy.

EPH 6:10.2 COR 12:9-10.PS 71:16.ROM 1:16.PHIL 4:13.COL 1:29.2 COR 4:7.NEH 8:10.COL 1:11

EVENING

Christ our Lord.

You shall call His name Jesus, for He will save His people from their sins. ◊ He humbled Himself and became obedient to the point of death, even the death of the cross. Therefore God also has highly exalted Him and given Him the name which is above every name, that at the name of Jesus every knee should bow, of those in heaven, and of those on earth, and of those under the earth.

The Spirit of the Lord God is upon Me, because the Lord has anointed Me to preach good tidings to the poor; He has sent Me to heal the brokenhearted, to proclaim liberty to the captives, and the opening of the prison to those who are bound; to proclaim the acceptable year of the Lord, and the day of vengeance of our God; to comfort all who mourn.

The last Adam became a life-giving spirit. . . . [He] is the Lord from heaven. ◊ My Lord and my God! ◊ You call me Teacher and Lord, and you say well, for so I am. If I then, your Lord and Teacher, have washed your feet, you also ought to wash one another's feet. For I have given you an example, that you should do as I have done to you.

1 COR 1:9.MATT 1:21.PHIL 2:8-10.IS 61:1-2.1 COR 15:45,47.JOHN 20:28.JOHN 13:13-15

MORNING

Peace I leave with you, My peace I give to you; not as the world gives do I give to you.

The world is passing away, and the lust of it. ◇ Surely every man walks about like a shadow; surely they busy themselves in vain; he heaps up riches, and does not know who will gather them. ◇ What fruit did you have then in the things of which you are now ashamed? For the end of those things is death.

Martha, Martha, you are worried and troubled about many things. But one thing is needed, and Mary has chosen that good part, which will not be taken away from her.

These things I have spoken to you, that in Me you may have peace. In the world you will have tribulation; but be of good cheer, I have overcome the world. ◇ The Lord of peace Himself give you peace always in every way. ◇ The Lord bless you and keep you; the Lord make His face shine upon you, and be gracious to you; the Lord lift up His countenance upon you, and give you peace.

JOHN 14:27.1 JOHN 2:17.PS 39:6.ROM 6:21.LUKE 10:41-42.JOHN 16:33.2 THESS 3:16.NUM 6:24-26

EVENING

The Spirit also helps in our weaknesses.

The Helper, the Holy Spirit. ◇ Do you not know that your body is the temple of the Holy Spirit who is in you? ◇ It is God who works in you.

Likewise the Spirit also helps in our weaknesses. For we do not know what we should pray for as we ought, but the Spirit Himself makes intercession for us with groanings which cannot be uttered. Now He who searches the hearts knows what the mind of the Spirit is, because He makes intercession for the saints according to the will of God.

He remembers that we are dust. ◇ A bruised reed He will not break, and smoking flax He will not quench.

The spirit indeed is willing, but the flesh is weak.

The Lord is my shepherd; I shall not want. He makes me to lie down in green pastures; He leads me beside the still waters. He restores my soul; He leads me in the paths of righteousness for His name's sake. Yea, though I walk through the valley of the shadow of death, I will fear no evil.

ROM 8:26.JOHN 14:26.1 COR 6:19.PHIL 2:13.ROM 8:26-27.PS 103:14.IS 42:3.MATT 26:41.PS 23:1-4

MORNING

You shall put the two stones on the shoulders of the ephod as memorial stones for the sons of Israel. So Aaron shall bear their names before the Lord.

He, because He continues forever, has an unchangeable priesthood. Therefore He is also able to save to the uttermost those who come to God through Him, since He ever lives to make intercession for them. ◊ [He] is able to keep you from stumbling, and to present you faultless before the presence of His glory.

Seeing . . . that we have a great High Priest who has passed through the heavens, Jesus the Son of God, let us hold fast our confession. For we do not have a High Priest who cannot sympathize with our weaknesses, but was in all points tempted as we are, yet without sin. Let us therefore come boldly to the throne of grace.

The beloved of the Lord shall dwell in safety by Him, who shelters him all the day long; and he shall dwell between His shoulders.

EX 28:12.HEB 7:24-25.JUDE 1:24.HEB 4:14-16.DEUT 33:12

EVENING

That night the king could not sleep.

You hold my eyelids open. ◊ Who is like the Lord our God, who dwells on high, who humbles Himself to behold the things that are in the heavens and in the earth?

All the inhabitants of the earth are reputed as nothing; He does according to His will in the army of heaven and among the inhabitants of the earth. ◊ Behold, the nations are as a drop in a bucket, and are counted as the small dust on the balance; look, He lifts up the isles as a very little thing. ◊ Your way was in the sea, Your path in the great waters, and Your footsteps were not known. ◊ The wrath of man shall praise You; with the remainder of wrath You shall gird Yourself.

The eyes of the Lord run to and fro throughout the whole earth, to show Himself strong on behalf of those whose heart is loyal to Him. ◊ We know that all things work together for good to those who love God.

Are not two sparrows sold for a copper coin? And not one of them falls to the ground apart from your Father's will. But the very hairs of your head are all numbered.

ESTH 6:1.PS 77:4.PS 113:5-6.DAN 4:35.IS 40:15.PS 77:19.PS 76:10.2 CHR 16:9.ROM 8:28.MATT 10:29-30

MORNING

Do not grieve the Holy Spirit of God, by whom you were sealed for the day of redemption.

The love of the Spirit. ◊ The Helper, the Holy Spirit. ◊ In all their affliction He was afflicted, and the Angel of His Presence saved them; in His love and in His pity He redeemed them; and He bore them and carried them all the days of old. But they rebelled and grieved His Holy Spirit; so He turned Himself against them as an enemy, and He fought against them.

We know that we abide in Him, and He in us, because He has given us of His Spirit. ◊ Having believed, you were sealed with the Holy Spirit of promise, who is the guarantee of our inheritance until the redemption of the purchased possession. ◊ I say then: Walk in the Spirit, and you shall not fulfill the lust of the flesh. For the flesh lusts against the Spirit, and the Spirit against the flesh; and these are contrary to one another, so that you do not do the things that you wish.

The Spirit also helps in our weaknesses.

EPH 4:30.ROM 15:30.JOHN 14:26.IS 63:9-10.1 JOHN 4:13.EPH 1:13-14.GAL 5:16-17.ROM 8:26

EVENING

I will return again to My place till they acknowledge their offense. Then . . . they will diligently seek Me.

Your iniquities have separated you from your God; and your sins have hidden His face from you, so that He will not hear. ◊ I opened for my beloved, but my beloved had turned away and was gone. My heart went out to him when he spoke. I sought him, but I could not find him; I called him, but he gave me no answer. ◊ I was angry and struck him; . . . and he went on backsliding in the way of his heart. I have seen his ways. ◊ Have you not brought this on yourself, in that you have forsaken the Lord your God when He led you in the way?

And he arose and came to his father. But when he was still a great way off, his father saw him and had compassion, and ran and fell on his neck and kissed him. ◊ I will heal their backsliding, I will love them freely, for My anger has turned away from him.

If we confess our sins, He is faithful and just to forgive us our sins and to cleanse us from all unrighteousness.

HOS 5:15.IS 59:2.SONG 5:6.IS 57:17-18.JER 2:17.LUKE 15:20.HOS 14:4.
1 JOHN 1:9

MORNING

How great is Your goodness, which You have laid up for those who fear You.

Since the beginning of the world men have not heard nor perceived by the ear, nor has the eye seen any God besides You, who acts for the one who waits for Him. ◊ Eye has not seen, nor ear heard, nor have entered into the heart of man the things which God has prepared for those who love Him. But God has revealed them to us through His Spirit. ◊ You will show me the path of life; in Your presence is fullness of joy; at Your right hand are pleasures forevermore.

How precious is Your lovingkindness, O God! Therefore the children of men put their trust under the shadow of Your wings. They are abundantly satisfied with the fullness of Your house, and You give them drink from the river of Your pleasures.

Godliness is profitable for all things, having promise of the life that now is and of that which is to come.

PS 31:19.IS 64:4.1 COR 2:9-10.PS 16:11.PS 36:7-8.1 TIM 4:8

EVENING

The Son of God . . . has eyes like a flame of fire.

The heart is deceitful above all things, and desperately wicked; who can know it? I, the Lord, search the heart, I test the mind, even to give every man according to his ways, and according to the fruit of his doings. ◊ You have set our iniquities before You, our secret sins in the light of Your countenance. ◊ The Lord turned and looked at Peter. Then Peter went out and wept bitterly.

Jesus did not commit Himself to them, because He knew all men, and had no need that anyone should testify of man, for He knew what was in man. ◊ He remembers that we are dust. ◊ A bruised reed He will not break, and smoking flax He will not quench.

The Lord knows those who are His. ◊ I am the good shepherd; and I know My sheep, and am known by My own. . . . My sheep hear My voice, and I know them, and they follow Me. And I give them eternal life, and they shall never perish; neither shall anyone snatch them out of My hand. My Father, who has given them to Me, is greater than all; and no one is able to snatch them out of My Father's hand.

REV 2:18.JER 17:9-10.PS 90:8.LUKE 22:61-62.JOHN 2:24-25.PS 103:14.IS 42:3.2 TIM 2:19.JOHN 10:14,27-29

MORNING

Our Lord Jesus . . . that great Shepherd of the sheep.

I am the good shepherd; and I know My sheep, and am known by My own. . . . My sheep hear My voice, and I know them, and they follow Me. And I give them eternal life, and they shall never perish; neither shall anyone snatch them out of My hand.

The Lord is my shepherd; I shall not want. He makes me to lie down in green pastures; He leads me beside the still waters. He restores my soul; He leads me in the paths of righteousness for His name's sake.

All we like sheep have gone astray; we have turned, every one, to his own way; and the Lord has laid on Him the iniquity of us all. ◊ I am the good shepherd. The good shepherd gives His life for the sheep. ◊ I will seek what was lost and bring back what was driven away, bind up the broken and strengthen what was sick. ◊ You were like sheep going astray, but have now returned to the Shepherd and Overseer of your souls.

HEB 13:20.JOHN 10:14,27-28.PS 23:1-3.IS 53:6.JOHN 10:11.EZEK 34:16.1 PET 2:25

EVENING

The city had no need of the sun or of the moon to shine in it, for the glory of God illuminated it, and the Lamb is its light.

I saw a light from heaven, brighter than the sun, shining around me and those who journeyed with me. . . . So I said, "Who are You, Lord?" And He said, "I am Jesus, whom you are persecuting." ◊ Jesus took Peter, James, and John his brother, brought them up on a high mountain by themselves, and was transfigured before them. His face shone like the sun, and His clothes became as white as the light. ◊ The sun shall no longer be your light by day, nor for brightness shall the moon give light to you; but the Lord will be to you an everlasting light, and your God your glory. Your sun shall no longer go down, nor shall your moon withdraw itself; for the Lord will be your everlasting light, and the days of your mourning shall be ended.

But may the God of all grace, who called us to His eternal glory by Christ Jesus, after you have suffered a while, perfect, establish, strengthen, and settle you. ◊ In this you greatly rejoice, though now for a little while, if need be, you have been grieved by various trials.

REV 21:23.ACTS 26:13,15.MATT 17:1-2.IS 60:19-20.1 PET 5:10.1 PET 1:6

MORNING

**The Lord is good, a stronghold in the day of trouble;
and He knows those who trust in Him.**

Praise the Lord of hosts, for the Lord is good, for His mercy endures forever. ◊ God is our refuge and strength, a very present help in trouble. ◊ I will say of the Lord, "He is my refuge and my fortress; my God, in Him I will trust." ◊ Who is like you, a people saved by the Lord, the shield of your help and the sword of your majesty! ◊ As for God, His way is perfect; the word of the Lord is proven; he is a shield to all who trust in Him. For who is God, except the Lord? ◊ And who is a rock, except our God?

If anyone loves God, this one is known by Him. ◊ The solid foundation of God stands, having this seal: "The Lord knows those who are His," and, "Let everyone who names the name of Christ depart from iniquity." ◊ The Lord knows the way of the righteous, but the way of the ungodly shall perish. ◊ You have found grace in My sight, and I know you by name.

NAH 1:7.JER 33:11.PS 46:1.PS 91:2.DEUT 33:29.2 SAM 22:31-32.1 COR
8:3.2 TIM 2:19.PS 1:6.EX 33:17

EVENING

I want you to be without care.

[Cast] all your care upon Him, for He cares for you. ◊ For the eyes of the Lord run to and fro throughout the whole earth, to show Himself strong on behalf of those whose heart is loyal to Him.

Oh, taste and see that the Lord is good; blessed is the man who trusts in Him! ◊ The young lions lack and suffer hunger; but those who seek the Lord shall not lack any good thing. ◊ Therefore I say to you, do not worry about your life, what you will eat or what you will drink; nor about your body, what you will put on. Is not life more than food and the body more than clothing? Look at the birds of the air, for they neither sow nor reap nor gather into barns; yet your heavenly Father feeds them. Are you not of more value than they? ◊ Be anxious for nothing, but in everything by prayer and supplication, with thanksgiving, let your requests be made known to God; and the peace of God, which surpasses all understanding, will guard your hearts and minds through Christ Jesus.

1 COR 7:32.1 PET 5:7.2 CHR 16:9.PS 34:8.PS 34:10.MATT 6:25-26.PHIL
4:6-7

MORNING

We also eagerly wait for the Savior.

The grace of God that brings salvation has appeared to all men, teaching us that, denying ungodliness and worldly lusts, we should live soberly, righteously, and godly in the present age, looking for the blessed hope and glorious appearing of our great God and Savior Jesus Christ, who gave Himself for us, that He might redeem us from every lawless deed and purify for Himself His own special people, zealous for good works. ◊ We, according to His promise, look for new heavens and a new earth in which righteousness dwells. Therefore, beloved, looking forward to these things, be diligent to be found by Him in peace, without spot and blameless.

Christ was offered once to bear the sins of many. To those who eagerly wait for Him He will appear a second time, apart from sin, for salvation. ◊ And it will be said in that day: "Behold, this is our God; we have waited for Him, and He will save us. This is the Lord; we have waited for Him; we will be glad and rejoice in His salvation."

PHIL 3:20.TITUS 2:11-14.2 PET 3:13-14.HEB 9:28.IS 25:9

EVENING

Run in such a way that you may obtain . . . the prize.

Let us lay aside every weight, and the sin which so easily ensnares us, and let us run with endurance the race that is set before us, looking unto Jesus, the author and finisher of our faith.

Having these promises, beloved, let us cleanse ourselves from all filthiness of the flesh and spirit, perfecting holiness in the fear of God.

I press toward the goal. ◊ Therefore I run thus: not with uncertainty. Thus I fight: not as one who beats the air. But I discipline my body and bring it into subjection.

The form of this world is passing away. ◊ We, according to His promise, look for new heavens and a new earth in which righteousness dwells. Therefore, beloved, looking forward to these things, be diligent to be found by Him in peace, without spot and blameless. ◊ Gird up the loins of your mind, be sober, and rest your hope fully upon the grace that is to be brought to you at the revelation of Jesus Christ.

1 COR 9:24.HEB 12:1-2.2 COR 7:1.PHIL 3:14.1 COR 9:26-27.1 COR 7:31.
2 PET 3:13-14.1 PET 1:13

MORNING

**The life of the flesh is in the blood, and I have given
it to you upon the altar to make atonement for your
souls; for it is the blood that makes atonement
for the soul.**

Behold! The Lamb of God who takes away the sin of the world! ◊ The blood of the Lamb. ◊ The precious blood of Christ, as of a lamb without blemish and without spot. ◊ Without shedding of blood there is no remission. ◊ The blood of Jesus Christ His Son cleanses us from all sin.

With His own blood He entered the Most Holy Place once for all, having obtained eternal redemption. ◊ Therefore, brethren, having boldness to enter the Holiest by the blood of Jesus, by a new and living way which He consecrated for us, through the veil, that is, His flesh, . . . let us draw near with a true heart in full assurance of faith.

You were bought at a price; therefore glorify God in your body and in your spirit, which are God's.

LEV 17:11.JOHN 1:29.REV 7:14.1 PET 1:19.HEB 9:22.1 JOHN 1:7.HEB
9:12.HEB 10:19-20,22.1 COR 6:20

EVENING

**Oh, that I had wings like a dove! For then I would fly
away and be at rest.**

When the sun arose, . . . God prepared a vehement east wind; and the sun beat on Jonah's head, so that he grew faint. Then he wished death for himself, and said, "It is better for me to die than to live."

Job opened his mouth and cursed the day of his birth. . . . "Why is light given to him who is in misery, and life to the bitter of soul, who long for death, but it does not come, and search for it more than hidden treasures?" ◊ The Lord is near to those who have a broken heart, and saves such as have a contrite spirit. Many are the afflictions of the righteous, but the Lord delivers him out of them all.

Now My soul is troubled, and what shall I say? "Father, save Me from this hour"? But for this purpose I came to this hour. ◊ Therefore, in all things He had to be made like His brethren, that He might be a merciful and faithful High Priest in things pertaining to God, to make propitiation for the sins of the people. For in that He Himself has suffered, being tempted, He is able to aid those who are tempted.

PS 55:6.JON 4:8.JOB 3:1.JOB 3:20-21.PS 34:18-19.JOHN 12:27.HEB
2:17-18

MORNING

Let us therefore be diligent to enter that rest.

Enter by the narrow gate; for wide is the gate and broad is the way that leads to destruction. . . . Narrow is the gate and difficult is the way which leads to life, and there are few who find it. ◊ The kingdom of heaven suffers violence, and the violent take it by force. ◊ Do not labor for the food which perishes, but for the food which endures to everlasting life, which the Son of Man will give you. ◊ Be even more diligent to make your calling and election sure, . . . for so an entrance will be supplied to you abundantly into the everlasting kingdom of our Lord and Savior Jesus Christ.

Run in such a way that you may obtain it. And everyone who competes for the prize is temperate in all things. Now they do it to obtain a perishable crown, but we for an imperishable crown.

For he who has entered His rest has himself also ceased from his works as God did from His. ◊ The Lord will be to you an everlasting light, and your God your glory.

HEB 4:11.MATT 7:13-14.MATT 11:12.JOHN 6:27.2 PET 1:10-11.1 COR
9:24-25.HEB 4:10.IS 60:19

EVENING

You always hear Me.

Jesus lifted up His eyes and said, "Father, I thank You that You have heard Me." ◊ "Father, glorify Your name." Then a voice came from heaven, saying, "I have both glorified it and will glorify it again." ◊ I have come . . . to do Your will. ◊ Not My will, but Yours, be done.

Love has been perfected among us in this: that we may have boldness in the day of judgment; because as He is, so are we in this world. ◊ Now this is the confidence that we have in Him, that if we ask anything according to His will, He hears us.

Whatever we ask we receive from Him, because we keep His commandments and do those things that are pleasing in His sight.

But without faith it is impossible to please Him, for he who comes to God must believe that He is, and that He is a rewarder of those who diligently seek Him.

He is also able to save to the uttermost those who come to God through Him, since He ever lives to make intercession for them. ◊ If anyone sins, we have an Advocate with the Father, Jesus Christ the righteous.

JOHN 11:42.JOHN 11:41.JOHN 12:28.HEB 10:7.LUKE 22:42.1 JOHN
4:17.1 JOHN 5:14.1 JOHN 3:22.HEB 11:6.HEB 7:25.1 JOHN 2:1

MAY 31

MORNING_____

**Your name shall . . . be called . . . Israel; for you
have struggled with God and with men,
and have prevailed.**

In his strength he struggled with God. Yes he struggled with the Angel
and prevailed; he wept, and sought favor from Him. ◊ [Abraham] did
not waver at the promise of God through unbelief, but was strengthened
in faith, giving glory to God.

Have faith in God. For assuredly, I say to you, whoever says to this
mountain, "Be removed and be cast into the sea," and does not doubt in
his heart, but believes that those things he says will come to pass, he will
have whatever he says. Therefore I say to you, whatever things you ask
when you pray, believe that you receive them, and you will have them.
◊ If you can believe, all things are possible to him who believes. ◊
Blessed is she who believed, for there will be a fulfillment of those things
which were told her from the Lord.

Lord, increase our faith.

GEN 32:28.HOS 12:3-4.ROM 4:20.MARK 11:22-24.MARK 9:23.LUKE
1:45.LUKE 17:5

EVENING_____

Little children, abide in Him.

Let him ask in faith, with no doubting, for he who doubts is like a wave
of the sea driven and tossed by the wind. Let not that man suppose that
he will receive anything from the Lord.

I marvel that you are turning away so soon from Him who called you in
the grace of Christ, to a different gospel. ◊ You have become estranged
from Christ, you who attempt to be justified by law; you have fallen from
grace. You ran well. Who hindered you from obeying the truth?

Abide in Me, and I in you. As the branch cannot bear fruit of itself,
unless it abides in the vine, neither can you, unless you abide in Me. . . . If
you abide in Me, and My words abide in you, you will ask what you
desire, and it shall be done for you. ◊ For all the promises of God in Him
are Yes, and in Him Amen, to the glory of God through us.

1 JOHN 2:28.JAMES 1:6-7.GAL 1:6.GAL 5:4.GAL 5:7.JOHN 15:4,7.
2 COR 1:20

MORNING

**The fruit of the Spirit is love, joy, peace,
longsuffering, kindness, goodness, faithfulness.**

The Lord, the Lord God, merciful and gracious, longsuffering, and abounding in goodness and truth.

Walk worthy of the calling with which you were called, with all lowliness and gentleness, with longsuffering, bearing with one another in love. ◇ Be kind to one another, tenderhearted, forgiving one another, just as God in Christ also forgave you. ◇ The wisdom that is from above is first pure, then peaceable, gentle, willing to yield, full of mercy and good fruits. ◇ Love suffers long and is kind.

In due season we shall reap if we do not lose heart. ◇ Therefore be patient, brethren, until the coming of the Lord. See how the farmer waits for the precious fruit of the earth, waiting patiently for it until it receives the early and latter rain. You also be patient. Establish your hearts, for the coming of the Lord is at hand.

GAL 5:22.EX 34:6.EPH 4:1-2.EPH 4:32.JAMES 3:17.1 COR 13:4.GAL
6:9.JAMES 5:7-8

EVENING

Immanuel, . . . "God with us."

Will God indeed dwell with men on the earth? Behold, heaven and the heaven of heavens cannot contain You. ◇ The Word became flesh and dwelt among us, and we beheld His glory, the glory as of the only begotten of the Father, full of grace and truth. ◇ God was manifested in the flesh.

God has in these last days spoken to us by His Son, whom He has appointed heir of all things, through whom also He made the worlds.

At evening, . . . when the doors were shut where the disciples were assembled, . . . Jesus came and stood in the midst. . . . He showed them His hands and His side. Then the disciples were glad when they saw the Lord. . . . After eight days His disciples were again inside, and Thomas with them. Jesus came, the doors being shut, and stood in the midst, and said, "Peace to you!" Then He said to Thomas, "Reach your finger here, and look at My hands; and reach your hand here, and put it into My side. Do not be unbelieving, but believing." And Thomas answered and said to Him, "My Lord and my God!" ◇ Unto us a Son is given; . . . the . . . Mighty God.

MATT 1:23.2 CHR 6:18.JOHN 1:14.1 TIM 3:16.HEB 1:2.JOHN 20:19,20,
26-28.IS 9:6

JUNE 2

MORNING————————————————————

**Thus you shall eat it: with a belt on your waist. . . .
So you shall eat it in haste. It is the Lord's Passover.**

Arise and depart, for this is not your rest. ◊ Here we have no continuing city, but we seek the one to come. ◊ There remains therefore a rest for the people of God.

Let your waist be girded and your lamps burning; and you yourselves be like men who wait for their master, when he will return from the wedding, that when he comes and knocks they may open to him immediately. Blessed are those servants whom the master, when he comes, will find watching. ◊ Gird up the loins of your mind, be sober, and rest your hope fully upon the grace that is to be brought to you at the revelation of Jesus Christ. ◊ One thing I do, forgetting those things which are behind . . . I press toward the goal for the prize of the upward call of God in Christ Jesus. Therefore let us, as many as are mature, have this mind.

EX 12:11.MIC 2:10.HEB 13:14.HEB 4:9.LUKE 12:35-37.1 PET 1:13.PHIL
3:13-15

EVENING————————————————————

**You, O Lord, are the portion of my inheritance and
my cup.**

If children, then heirs. ◊ All things are yours. ◊ My beloved is mine. ◊ The Son of God. . . . loved me and gave Himself for me.

You shall have no inheritance in their land, nor shall you have any portion among them; I am your portion and your inheritance.

Whom have I in heaven but You? And there is none upon earth that I desire besides You. My flesh and my heart fail; but God is the strength of my heart and my portion forever.

Yea, though I walk through the valley of the shadow of death, I will fear no evil; for You are with me. ◊ I know whom I have believed and am persuaded that He is able to keep what I have committed to Him until that Day.

O God, You are my God; early will I seek You; my soul thirsts for You; my flesh longs for You in a dry and thirsty land where there is no water. ◊ Pray to Me, and I will listen to you. And you will seek Me and find Me, when you search for Me with all your heart. I will be found by you, says the Lord.

PS 16:5.ROM 8:17.1 COR 3:21.SONG 2:16.GAL 2:20.NUM 18:20.PS
73:25-26.PS 23:4.2 TIM 1:12.PS 63:1.JER 29:12-14

MORNING

Watch therefore, for you know neither the day nor the hour in which the Son of Man is coming.

Take heed to yourselves, lest your hearts be weighed down with carousing, drunkenness, and cares of this life, and that Day come on you unexpectedly. For it will come as a snare on all those who dwell on the face of the whole earth. Watch therefore, and pray always that you may be counted worthy to escape all these things that will come to pass, and to stand before the Son of Man.

The day of the Lord so comes as a thief in the night. For when they say, "Peace and safety!" then sudden destruction comes upon them, as labor pains upon a pregnant woman. And they shall not escape. But you, brethren, are not in darkness, so that this Day should overtake you as a thief. You are all sons of light and sons of the day. We are not of the night nor of darkness. Therefore let us not sleep, as others do, but let us watch and be sober.

MATT 25:13.LUKE 21:34-36.1 THESS 5:2-6

EVENING

I am Almighty God; walk before Me and be blameless.

Not that I . . . am already perfected; but I press on, that I may lay hold of that for which Christ Jesus has also laid hold of me. Brethren, I do not count myself to have apprehended; but one thing I do, forgetting those things which are behind and reaching forward to those things which are ahead, I press toward the goal for the prize of the upward call of God in Christ Jesus.

Grow in the grace and knowledge of our Lord and Savior Jesus Christ. ◊ We all, with unveiled face, beholding as in a mirror the glory of the Lord, are being transformed into the same image from glory to glory, just as by the Spirit of the Lord.

The path of the just is like the shining sun, that shines ever brighter unto the perfect day. ◊ Jesus . . . lifted up His eyes to heaven, and said: . . . "I do not pray that You should take them out of the world, but that You should keep them from the evil one. . . . I in them, and You in Me; that they may be made perfect in one."

GEN 17:1.PHIL 3:12-14.2 PET 3:18.2 COR 3:18.PROV 4:18.JOHN
17:1,15,23

JUNE 4

**The glory of this latter temple shall be greater than
the former, . . .and in this place I will give peace.**

The house that is to be built for the Lord must be exceedingly
magnificent, famous and glorious throughout all countries. ◇ The glory
of the Lord . . . filled the Lord's house.

"Destroy this temple, and in three days I will raise it up." . . . He was
speaking of the temple of His body. ◇ What was made glorious had no
glory in this respect, because of the glory that excels. ◇ The Word
became flesh and dwelt among us, and we beheld His glory, the glory as
of the only begotten of the Father, full of grace and truth. ◇ God . . . has
in these last days spoken to us by His Son, whom He has appointed heir
of all things, through whom also He made the worlds.

Glory to God in the highest, and on earth peace, good will toward men!
◇ Prince of Peace. ◇ He Himself is our peace. ◇ The peace of God,
which surpasses all understanding, will guard your hearts and minds
through Christ Jesus.

HAG 2:9.1 CHR 22:5.2 CHR 7:2.JOHN 2:19,21.2 COR 3:10.JOHN
1:14.HEB 1:1-2.LUKE 2:14.IS 9:6.EPH 2:14.PHIL 4:7

Put on the armor of light.

Put on the Lord Jesus Christ. ◇ Indeed I also count all things loss for
the excellence of the knowledge of Christ Jesus my Lord, for whom I have
suffered the loss of all things, and count them as rubbish, that I may gain
Christ and be found in Him, not having my own righteousness, which is
from the law, but that which is through faith in Christ, the righteousness
which is from God by faith. ◇ The righteousness of God . . . is through
faith in Jesus Christ to all and on all who believe.

He has clothed me with the garments of salvation, He has covered me
with the robe of righteousness. ◇ I will go in the strength of the Lord
God; I will make mention of Your righteousness, of Yours only.

For you were once darkness, but now you are light in the Lord. Walk as
children of light. . . . Have no fellowship with the unfruitful works of
darkness, but rather expose them. . . . All things that are exposed are
made manifest by the light. . . . Therefore He says: "Awake, you who
sleep, arise from the dead, and Christ will give you light." See then that
you walk circumspectly, not as fools but as wise.

ROM 13:12.ROM 13:14.PHIL 3:8-9.ROM 3:22.IS 61:10.PS 71:16.EPH
5:8.EPH 5:11,13-15

MORNING

**When you have done all those things which you are
commanded, say, "We are unprofitable servants."**

Where is boasting then? It is excluded. By what law? Of works? No, but
by the law of faith. ◊ What do you have that you did not receive? Now if
you did indeed receive it, why do you glory as if you had not received it?
◊ For by grace you have been saved through faith, and that not of
yourselves; it is the gift of God, not of works, lest anyone should boast.
For we are His workmanship, created in Christ Jesus for good works,
which God prepared beforehand that we should walk in them.

By the grace of God I am what I am, and His grace toward me was not
in vain; but I labored more abundantly than they all, yet not I, but the
grace of God which was with me. ◊ For of Him and through Him and to
Him are all things. ◊ Of Your own we have given You.

Do not enter into judgment with Your servant, for in Your sight no one
living is righteous.

LUKE 17:10.ROM 3:27.1 COR 4:7.EPH 2:8-10.1 COR 15:10.ROM 11:36.
1 CHR 29:14.PS 143:2

EVENING

He remembers that we are dust.

The Lord God formed man of the dust of the ground, and breathed into
his nostrils the breath of life; and man became a living being.

I will praise You, for I am fearfully and wonderfully made; marvelous
are Your works, and that my soul knows very well. My frame was not
hidden from You, when I was made in secret. . . . Your eyes saw my
substance, being yet unformed. And in Your book they all were written,
the days fashioned for me, when as yet there were none of them.

Have we not all one Father? Has not one God created us? ◊ For in Him
we live and move and have our being. ◊ As a father pities his children,
so the Lord pities those who fear Him. . . . He remembers that we are
dust. As for man, his days are like grass; as a flower of the field, so he
flourishes. For the wind passes over it, and it is gone, and its place
remembers it no more.

He, being full of compassion, forgave their iniquity, and did not
destroy them. Yes, many a time He turned His anger away, . . . for He
remembered that they were but flesh, a breath that passes away and does
not come again.

PS 103:14.GEN 2:7.PS 139:14-16.PS 139:13.MAL 2:10.ACTS 17:28.PS
103:13-16.PS 78:38-39

JUNE 6

MORNING

He will quiet you in His love.

The Lord did not set His love on you nor choose you because you were more in number than any other people, for you were the least of all peoples; but because the Lord loves you. ◊ We love Him because He first loved us. ◊ You . . . He has reconciled in the body of His flesh through death, to present you holy, and blameless, and irreproachable in His sight.

In this is love, not that we loved God, but that He loved us and sent His Son to be the propitiation for our sins. ◊ God demonstrates His own love toward us, in that while we were still sinners, Christ died for us.

Suddenly a voice came from heaven, saying, "This is My beloved Son, in whom I am well pleased." ◊ Therefore My Father loves Me, because I lay down My life that I may take it again. ◊ His Son . . . who being the brightness of His glory and the express image of His person, and upholding all things by the word of His power, when He had by Himself purged our sins, sat down at the right hand of the Majesty on high.

ZEPH 3:17.DEUT 7:7-8.1 JOHN 4:19.COL 1:21-22.1 JOHN 4:10.ROM
5:8.MATT 3:17.JOHN 10:17.HEB 1:2-3

EVENING

Enter the Holiest by a new and living way.

Cain went out from the presence of the Lord. ◊ Your iniquities have separated you from your God; and your sins have hidden His face from you. ◊ Pursue . . . holiness, without which no one will see the Lord.

I am the way, the truth, and the life. No one comes to the Father except through Me. ◊ Our Savior Jesus Christ . . . has abolished death and brought life and immortality to light through the gospel.

The way into the Holiest of All was not yet made manifest while the first tabernacle was still standing. ◊ He Himself is our peace, who has made both one, and has broken down the middle wall of division between us. ◊ The veil of the temple was torn in two from top to bottom.

Narrow is the gate and difficult is the way which leads to life, and there are few who find it. ◊ You will show me the path of life; in Your presence is fullness of joy; at Your right hand are pleasures forevermore.

HEB 10:19-20.GEN 4:16.IS 59:2.HEB 12:14.JOHN 14:6.2 TIM 1:10.HEB
9:8.EPH 2:14.MATT 27:51.MATT 7:14.PS 16:11

MORNING

Men always ought to pray and not lose heart.

Which of you shall have a friend, and go to him at midnight and say to him, "Friend, lend me three loaves; for a friend of mine has come to me on his journey, and I have nothing to set before him"; and he will answer from within and say, "Do not trouble me; the door is now shut, and my children are with me in bed; I cannot rise and give to you"? I say to you, though he will not rise and give to him because he is his friend, yet because of his persistence he will rise and give him as many as he needs. ◊ [Pray] always with all prayer and supplication in the Spirit, being watchful to this end with all perseverance and supplication for all the saints.

"I will not let You go unless You bless me!" . . . "You have struggled with God and with men, and have prevailed." ◊ Continue earnestly in prayer, being vigilant in it with thanksgiving.

[Jesus] went out to the mountain to pray, and continued all night in prayer to God.

LUKE 18:1.LUKE 11:5-8.EPH 6:18.GEN 32:26,28.COL 4:2.LUKE 6:12

EVENING

Forgive all my sins.

"Come now, and let us reason together," says the Lord, "though your sins are like scarlet, they shall be as white as snow; though they are red like crimson, they shall be as wool."

Be of good cheer; your sins are forgiven you. ◊ I, even I, am He who blots out your transgressions for My own sake; and I will not remember your sins.

The Son of Man has power on earth to forgive sins. ◊ In Him we have redemption through His blood, the forgiveness of sins, according to the riches of His grace. ◊ Not by works of righteousness which we have done, but according to His mercy He saved us, through the washing of regeneration and renewing of the Holy Spirit, whom He poured out on us abundantly through Jesus Christ our Savior. ◊ [He has] forgiven you all trespasses, having wiped out the handwriting of requirements that was against us, which was contrary to us. He has taken it out of the way, having nailed it to the cross.

Bless the Lord, O my soul, . . . who forgives all your iniquities.

PS 25:18.IS 1:18.MATT 9:2.IS 43:25.MATT 9:6.EPH 1:7.TITUS 3:5-6.COL
2:13-14.PS 103:2-3

JUNE 8

The Lord made all he did to prosper in his hand.

Blessed is every one who fears the Lord, who walks in His ways. When you eat the labor of your hands, you shall be happy, and it shall be well with you. ◊ Trust in the Lord, and do good; dwell in the land, and feed on His faithfulness. Delight yourself also in the Lord, and He shall give you the desires of your heart. ◊ Do not be afraid, nor be dismayed, for the Lord your God is with you wherever you go.

Seek first the kingdom of God and His righteousness, and all these things shall be added to you.

As long as he sought the Lord, God made him prosper. ◊ Beware that you do not forget the Lord your God by not keeping His commandments, His judgments, and His statutes which I command you today, . . . then you say in your heart, "My power and the might of my hand have gained me this wealth." ◊ Is not the Lord your God with you? And has He not given you rest on every side?

GEN 39:3.PS 128:1-2.PS 37:3-4.JOSH 1:9.MATT 6:33.2 CHR 26:5.DEUT 8:11,17.1 CHR 22:18

Why do you reason about these things in your hearts?

Not being weak in faith, [Abraham] did not consider his own body, already dead (since he was about a hundred years old), and the deadness of Sarah's womb. He did not waver at the promise of God through unbelief, but was strengthened in faith, giving glory to God.

Which is easier, to say to the paralytic, "Your sins are forgiven you," or to say, "Arise, take up your bed and walk"? ◊ If you can believe, all things are possible to him who believes.

All authority has been given to Me in heaven and on earth. ◊ Why are you so fearful? How is it that you have no faith? ◊ Look at the birds of the air, . . . your heavenly Father feeds them. Are you not of more value than they? ◊ Why do you reason among yourselves because you have brought no bread? Do you not . . . remember the five loaves of the five thousand?

My God shall supply all your need according to His riches in glory by Christ Jesus.

MARK 2:8.ROM 4:19-20.MARK 2:9.MARK 9:23.MATT 28:18.MARK 4:40.MATT 6:26.MATT 16:8-9.PHIL 4:19

MORNING

No man ever spoke like this Man!

You are fairer than the sons of men; grace is poured upon Your lips; therefore God has blessed You forever. ◊ The Lord God has given Me the tongue of the learned, that I should know how to speak a word in season to him who is weary. ◊ His mouth is most sweet, yes, he is altogether lovely. This is my beloved, and this is my friend.

All bore witness to Him, and marveled at the gracious words which proceeded out of His mouth. ◊ He taught them as one having authority, and not as the scribes.

Let the word of Christ dwell in you richly in all wisdom. ◊ The sword of the Spirit . . . is the word of God. ◊ The word of God is living and powerful, and sharper than any two-edged sword. ◊ The weapons of our warfare are not carnal but mighty in God for pulling down strongholds, casting down arguments and every high thing that exalts itself against the knowledge of God, bringing every thought into captivity to the obedience of Christ.

JOHN 7:46.PS 45:2.IS 50:4.SONG 5:16.LUKE 4:22.MATT 7:29.COL 3:16.EPH 6:17.HEB 4:12.2 COR 10:4-5

EVENING

The triumphing of the wicked is short.

You shall bruise His heel. ◊ This is your hour, and the power of darkness. ◊ As the children have partaken of flesh and blood, He Himself likewise shared in the same, that through death He might destroy him who had the power of death, that is, the devil. ◊ Having disarmed principalities and powers, He made a public spectacle of them, triumphing over them in it.

Be sober, be vigilant; because your adversary the devil walks about like a roaring lion, seeking whom he may devour. Resist him, steadfast in the faith. ◊ Resist the devil and he will flee from you.

The wicked plots against the just, and gnashes at him with his teeth. The Lord laughs at him, for He sees that his day is coming. ◊ The God of peace will crush Satan under your feet shortly. ◊ The devil . . . was cast into the lake of fire and brimstone. . . . [He] will be tormented day and night forever and ever.

JOB 20:5.GEN 3:15.LUKE 22:53.HEB 2:14.COL 2:15.1 PET 5:8-9.JAMES 4:7.PS 37:12-13.ROM 16:20.REV 20:10

JUNE 10

The younger son . . . journeyed to a far country, and there wasted his possessions with prodigal living.

Such were some of you. But you were washed, but you were sanctified, but you were justified in the name of the Lord Jesus and by the Spirit of our God. ◊ We . . . were by nature children of wrath, just as the others. But God, who is rich in mercy, because of His great love with which He loved us, even when we were dead in trespasses, made us alive together with Christ (by grace you have been saved), and raised us up together, and made us sit together in the heavenly places in Christ Jesus.

In this is love, not that we loved God, but that He loved us and sent His Son to be the propitiation for our sins.

God demonstrates His own love toward us, in that while we were still sinners, Christ died for us. . . . If when we were enemies we were reconciled to God through the death of His Son, much more, having been reconciled, we shall be saved by His life.

LUKE 15:13.1 COR 6:11.EPH 2:3-6.1 JOHN 4:10.ROM 5:8,10

EVENING

As Christ forgave you, so you also must do.

There was a certain creditor who had two debtors. One owed five hundred denarii, and the other fifty. And when they had nothing with which to repay, he freely forgave them both. ◊ "I forgave you all that debt. . . . Should you not also have had compassion on your fellow servant, just as I had pity on you?"

And whenever you stand praying, if you have anything against anyone, forgive him, that your Father in heaven may also forgive you your trespasses. But if you do not forgive, neither will your Father in heaven forgive your trespasses. ◊ As the elect of God, holy and beloved, put on tender mercies, kindness, humbleness of mind, meekness, longsuffering; bearing with one another, and forgiving one another, if anyone has a complaint against another.

"Lord, how often shall my brother sin against me, and I forgive him? Up to seven times?" Jesus said to him, "I do not say to you, up to seven times, but up to seventy times seven."

Love . . . is the bond of perfection.

COL 3:13.LUKE 7:41-42.MATT 18:32-33.MARK 11:25-26.COL.3:12-13.MATT 18:21-22.COL 3:14

MORNING

**He arose and came to his father. But when he was
still a great way off, his father saw him and had
compassion, and ran and fell on his neck
and kissed him.**

The Lord is merciful and gracious, slow to anger, and abounding in mercy. He will not always strive with us, nor will He keep His anger forever. He has not dealt with us according to our sins, nor punished us according to our iniquities. For as the heavens are high above the earth, so great is His mercy toward those who fear Him; as far as the east is from the west, so far has He removed our transgressions from us. As a father pities his children, so the Lord pities those who fear Him.

You received the Spirit of adoption by whom we cry out, "Abba, Father." The Spirit Himself bears witness with our spirit that we are children of God. ◊ You who once were far off have been made near by the blood of Christ. . . . Now, therefore, you are no longer strangers and foreigners, but fellow citizens with the saints and members of the household of God.

LUKE 15:20.PS 103:8-13.ROM 8:15-16.EPH 2:13,19

EVENING

Behold, I make all things new.

Unless one is born again, he cannot see the kingdom of God. ◊ If anyone is in Christ, he is a new creation; old things have passed away; behold, all things have become new.

I will give you a new heart and put a new spirit within you; I will take the heart of stone out of your flesh and give you a heart of flesh. ◊ Purge out the old leaven, that you may be a new lump. ◊ The new man . . . was created according to God, in righteousness and true holiness.

You shall be called by a new name, which the mouth of the Lord will name.

Behold, I create new heavens and a new earth; and the former shall not be remembered or come to mind. ◊ Since all these things will be dissolved, what manner of persons ought you to be in holy conduct and godliness?

REV 21:5.JOHN 3:3.2 COR 5:17.EZEK 36:26.1 COR 5:7.EPH 4:24.IS
62:2.IS 65:17.2 PET 3:11

JUNE 12

Everything that can endure fire, you shall put through the fire, and it shall be clean.

The Lord your God is testing you to know whether you love the Lord your God with all your heart and with all your soul. ◊ He will sit as a refiner and a purifier of silver; He will purify the sons of Levi, and purge them as gold and silver, that they may offer to the Lord an offering in righteousness. ◊ Each one's work will become manifest; for the Day will declare it, because it will be revealed by fire; and the fire will test each one's work, of what sort it is.

I will turn My hand against you, and thoroughly purge away your dross, and take away all your alloy. ◊ I will refine them and try them.

You, O God, have proved us; You have refined us as silver is refined. . . . We went through fire and through water; but You brought us out to rich fulfillment.

When you walk through the fire, you shall not be burned, nor shall the flame scorch you.

NUM 31:23.DEUT 13:3.MAL 3:3.1 COR 3:13.IS 1:25.JER 9:7.PS 66:10,12.IS 43:2

EVENING

We, having died to sins, might live for righteousness.

Put off, concerning your former conduct, the old man which grows corrupt according to the deceitful lusts, and be renewed in the spirit of your mind, and . . . put on the new man which was created according to God, in righteousness and true holiness.

You died, and your life is hidden with Christ in God. ◊ As Christ was raised from the dead by the glory of the Father, even so we also should walk in newness of life. . . . Knowing this, that our old man was crucified with Him, that the body of sin might be done away with, that we should no longer be slaves of sin. For he who has died has been freed from sin. Likewise you also, reckon yourselves to be dead indeed to sin, but alive to God in Christ Jesus our Lord. . . . Therefore do not let sin reign in your mortal body, that you should obey it in its lusts. But present yourselves to God as being alive from the dead, and your members as instruments of righteousness to God.

1 PET 2:24.EPH 4:22-24.COL 3:3.ROM 6:4,6-7,11-13

MORNING

Abide in Me, and I in you.

I have been crucified with Christ; it is no longer I who live, but Christ lives in me; and the life which I now live in the flesh I live by faith in the Son of God, who loved me and gave Himself for me.

For I know that in me (that is, in my flesh) nothing good dwells; for to will is present with me, but how to perform what is good I do not find. . . . O wretched man that I am! Who will deliver me from this body of death? I thank God—through Jesus Christ our Lord! ◊ If Christ is in you, the body is dead because of sin, but the Spirit is life because of righteousness. ◊ Indeed you continue in the faith, grounded and steadfast, and are not moved away from the hope of the gospel which you heard.

Little children, abide in Him, that when He appears, we may have confidence and not be ashamed before Him at His coming. ◊ He who says he abides in Him ought himself also to walk just as He walked.

JOHN 15:4.GAL 2:20.ROM 7:18,24-25.ROM 8:10.COL 1:23.1 JOHN
2:28.1 JOHN 2:6

EVENING

Do you believe in the Son of God?

Who is He, Lord, that I may believe in Him?

[He is] the brightness of [God's] glory and the express image of His person. ◊ He . . . is the blessed and only Potentate, the King of kings and Lord of lords, who alone has immortality, dwelling in unapproachable light, whom no man has seen or can see, to whom be honor and everlasting power. Amen. ◊ "I am the Alpha and the Omega, the Beginning and the End," says the Lord , "who is and who was and who is to come, the Almighty."

Lord, I believe! ◊ I know whom I have believed and am persuaded that He is able to keep what I have committed to Him until that Day.

Behold, I lay in Zion a chief cornerstone, elect, precious, and he who believes on Him will by no means be put to shame. Therefore, to you who believe, He is precious.

JOHN 9:35.JOHN 9:36.HEB 1:3.1 TIM 6:15-16.REV 1:8.JOHN 9:38.2 TIM
1:12.1 PET 2:6-7

JUNE 14

_____

As the sufferings of Christ abound in us, so our consolation also abounds through Christ.

I have suffered the loss of all things . . . that I may know . . . the fellowship of His sufferings. ◊ Rejoice to the extent that you partake of Christ's sufferings, that when His glory is revealed, you may also be glad with exceeding joy. ◊ For if we died with Him, we shall also live with Him. ◊ If children, then heirs—heirs of God and joint heirs with Christ, if indeed we suffer with Him, that we may also be glorified together.

God, determining to show more abundantly to the heirs of promise the immutability of His counsel, confirmed it by an oath, that by two immutable things, in which it is impossible for God to lie, we might have strong consolation, who have fled for refuge to lay hold of the hope set before us. ◊ Our Lord Jesus Christ Himself, and our God and Father, who has loved us and given us everlasting consolation and good hope by grace, comfort your hearts and establish you in every good word and work.

2 COR 1:5.PHIL 3:8,10.1 PET 4:13.2 TIM 2:11.ROM 8:17.HEB 6:17-18.
2 THESS 2:16-17

EVENING_____

Martha, Martha, you are worried and troubled about many things.

Consider the ravens, for they neither sow nor reap. . . . Consider the lilies, how they grow: they neither toil nor spin. . . . Do not seek what you should eat or what you should drink, nor have an anxious mind. . . . Your Father knows that you need these things.

Having food and clothing, with these we shall be content. But those who desire to be rich fall into temptation and a snare, and into many foolish and harmful lusts which drown men in destruction and perdition. For the love of money is a root of all kinds of evil, for which some have strayed from the faith in their greediness, and pierced themselves through with many sorrows.

The cares of this world, the deceitfulness of riches, and the desires for other things entering in choke the word, and it becomes unfruitful.

Let us lay aside every weight, and the sin which so easily ensnares us, and let us run with endurance the race that is set before us.

LUKE 10:41.LUKE 12:24,27,29-30.1 TIM 6:8-10.MARK 4:19.HEB 12:1

MORNING

**The secret things belong to the Lord our God, but
those things which are revealed belong to us.**

Lord, my heart is not haughty, nor my eyes lofty. Neither do I concern myself with great matters, nor with things too profound for me. Surely I have calmed and quieted my soul, like a weaned child with his mother; like a weaned child is my soul within me.

The secret of the Lord is with those who fear Him, and He will show them His covenant. ◇ There is a God in heaven who reveals secrets. ◇ Indeed these are the mere edges of His ways, and how small a whisper we hear of Him!

No longer do I call you servants, for a servant does not know what his master is doing; but I have called you friends, for all things that I heard from My Father I have made known to you. ◇ If you love Me, keep My commandments. And I will pray the Father, and He will give you another Helper, that He may abide with you forever, even the Spirit of truth.

DEUT 29:29. PS 131:1-2. PS 25:14. DAN 2:28. JOB 26:14. JOHN 15:15. JOHN 14:15-17

EVENING

**The Spirit . . . makes intercession for the saints
according to the will of God.**

Most assuredly, I say to you, whatever you ask the Father in My name He will give you. Until now you have asked nothing in My name. Ask, and you will receive, that your joy may be full. ◇ [Pray] always with all prayer and supplication in the Spirit.

This is the confidence that we have in Him, that if we ask anything according to His will, He hears us. And if we know that He hears us, whatever we ask, we know that we have the petitions that we have asked of Him. ◇ This is the will of God, your sanctification. . . . God did not call us to uncleanness, but in holiness . . . who has also given us His Holy Spirit.

Rejoice always, pray without ceasing, in everything give thanks; for this is the will of God in Christ Jesus for you. Do not quench the Spirit.

ROM 8:27. JOHN 16:23-24. EPH 6:18.1 JOHN 5:14-15.1 THESS 4:3,7-8.1. THESS 5:16-19

JUNE 16

MORNING

See then that you walk circumspectly, not as fools but as wise, redeeming the time, because the days are evil.

Take diligent heed to do the commandment and the law, . . . to love the Lord your God, to walk in all His ways, to keep His commandments, to hold fast to Him, and to serve Him with all your heart and with all your soul. ◊ Walk in wisdom toward those who are outside, redeeming the time. Let your speech always be with grace, seasoned with salt, that you may know how you ought to answer each one. ◊ Abstain from every form of evil.

While the bridegroom was delayed, they all slumbered and slept. And at midnight a cry was heard: "Behold, the bridegroom is coming; go out to meet him!" ◊ Watch therefore, for you know neither the day nor the hour in which the Son of Man is coming.

Brethren, be even more diligent to make your calling and election sure, for if you do these things you will never stumble. ◊ Blessed are those servants whom the master, when he comes, will find watching.

EPH 5:15-16.JOSH 22:5.COL 4:5-6.1 THESS 5:22.MATT 25:5-6.MATT 25:13.2 PET 1:10.LUKE 12:37

EVENING

Hold fast what you have, that no one may take your crown.

"If only I may touch His garment, I shall be made well." ◊ "Lord, if You are willing, You can make me clean." . . . "I am willing; be cleansed." ◊ If you have . . . faith as a mustard seed . . . nothing will be impossible for you.

Do not cast away your confidence, which has great reward. ◊ Work out your own salvation with fear and trembling; for it is God who works in you both to will and to do for His good pleasure.

First the blade, then the head, after that the full grain in the head. ◊ Let us know, let us pursue the knowledge of the Lord. ◊ The kingdom of heaven suffers violence, and the violent take it by force. ◊ Run in such a way that you may obtain it.

I have fought the good fight, I have finished the race, I have kept the faith. Finally, there is laid up for me the crown of righteousness, which the Lord, the righteous Judge, will give to me on that Day.

REV 3:11.MATT 9:21.MATT 8:2-3.MATT 17:20.HEB 10:35.PHIL 2:12-13.MARK 4:28.HOS 6:3.MATT 11:12.1 COR 9:24.2 TIM 4:7-8

MORNING

In everything by prayer and supplication, with thanksgiving, let your requests be made known to God.

I love the Lord, because He has heard My voice and my supplications. Because He has inclined His ear to me, therefore I will call upon Him as long as I live.

When you pray, do not use vain repetitions as the heathen do. For they think that they will be heard for their many words. ◊ The Spirit . . . helps in our weaknesses. For we do not know what we should pray for as we ought, but the Spirit Himself makes intercession for us with groanings which cannot be uttered.

Therefore I desire that the men pray everywhere, lifting up holy hands, without wrath and doubting. ◊ Praying always with all prayer and supplication in the Spirit, being watchful to this end with all perseverance and supplication for all the saints.

If two of you agree on earth concerning anything that they ask, it will be done for them by My Father in heaven.

PHIL 4:6.PS 116:1-2.MATT 6:7.ROM 8:26.1 TIM 2:8.EPH 6:18.MATT 18:19

EVENING

All Your works shall praise You, O Lord, and Your saints shall bless You.

Bless the Lord, O my soul; and all that is within me, bless His holy name! Bless the Lord, O my soul, and forget not all His benefits. ◊ I will bless the Lord at all times; His praise shall continually be in my mouth. ◊ Every day I will bless You, and I will praise Your name forever and ever.

Because Your lovingkindness is better than life, my lips shall praise You. Thus I will bless You while I live; I will lift up my hands in Your name. My soul shall be satisfied as with marrow and fatness, and my mouth shall praise You with joyful lips.

My soul magnifies the Lord, and my spirit has rejoiced in God my Savior.

You are worthy, O Lord, to receive glory and honor and power; for You created all things, and by Your will they exist and were created.

PS 145:10.PS 103:1-2.PS 34:1.PS 145:2.PS 63:3-5.LUKE 1:46-47.REV 4:11

JUNE 18

**You shall put the mercy seat on top of the ark, . . .
and there I will meet with you.**

The way into the Holiest of All was not yet made manifest. ◊ Jesus, when He had cried out again with a loud voice, yielded up His spirit. And behold, the veil of the temple was torn in two from top to bottom.

Brethren, having boldness to enter the Holiest by the blood of Jesus, by a new and living way which He consecrated for us, through the veil, that is, His flesh, . . . let us draw near with a true heart in full assurance of faith, having our hearts sprinkled from an evil conscience and our bodies washed with pure water. ◊ Let us therefore come boldly to the throne of grace, that we may obtain mercy and find grace to help in time of need.

Christ Jesus, . . . whom God set forth to be a propitiation by His blood, through faith, to demonstrate His righteousness, because in His forbearance God had passed over the sins that were previously committed. ◊ Through Him we . . . have access by one Spirit to the Father.

EX 25:21-22.HEB 9:8.MATT 27:50-51.HEB 10:19-20,22.HEB 4:16.ROM
3:24-25.EPH 2:18

Faith as a mustard seed.

Barak said to [Deborah], "If you will go with me, then I will go; but if you will not go with me, I will not go." . . . On that day God subdued Jabin king of Canaan. ◊ Gideon . . . feared his father's household and the men of the city too much to do it by day. . . . He did it by night. . . . Then Gideon said to God, "If You will save Israel by my hand as You have said . . . let me test, I pray." . . . And God did so.

You have a little strength, have kept My word, and have not denied My name. ◊ Who has despised the day of small things?

We are bound to thank God always for you, brethren, as it is fitting, because your faith grows exceedingly. ◊ Lord, increase our faith. ◊ I will be like the dew to Israel; he shall grow like the lily, and lengthen his roots like Lebanon. His branches shall spread; his beauty shall be like an olive tree, and his fragrance like Lebanon.

MATT 17:20.JUDG 4:8,23.JUDG 6:27,36,39-40.REV 3:8.ZECH 4:10.
2 THESS 1:3.LUKE 17:5.HOS 14:5-6

MORNING

Pursue . . . holiness, without which no one will see the Lord.

Unless one is born again, he cannot see the kingdom of God. ◊ There shall by no means enter it anything that defiles. ◊ There is no spot in you.

You shall be holy, for I the Lord your God am holy. ◊ As obedient children, not conforming yourselves to the former lusts, as in your ignorance; but as He who called you is holy, you also be holy in all your conduct, because it is written, "Be holy, for I am holy." And if you call on the Father, who without partiality judges according to each one's work, conduct yourselves throughout the time of your sojourning here in fear. ◊ Put off, concerning your former conduct, the old man which grows corrupt according to the deceitful lusts, and be renewed in the spirit of your mind, and . . . put on the new man which was created according to God, in righteousness and true holiness. ◊ He chose us in Him before the foundation of the world, that we should be holy and without blame before Him in love.

HEB 12:14.JOHN 3:3.REV 21:27.SONG 4:7.LEV 19:2.1 PET 1:14-17.EPH 4:22-24.EPH 1:4

EVENING

Buy from Me gold refined in the fire.

There is no one who has left house or brothers or sisters or father or mother or wife or children or lands, for My sake and the gospel's, who shall not receive a hundredfold now in this time—houses and brothers and sisters and mothers and children and lands, with persecutions and in the age to come, eternal life.

Beloved, do not think it strange concerning the fiery trial which is to try you, as though some strange thing happened to you. ◊ Now for a little while, if need be, you have been grieved by various trials, that the genuineness of your faith, being much more precious than gold that perishes, though it is tested by fire, may be found to praise, honor, and glory at the revelation of Jesus Christ.

The God of all grace, who called us to His eternal glory by Christ Jesus, after you have suffered a while, perfect, establish, strengthen, and settle you. ◊ In the world you will have tribulation; but be of good cheer, I have overcome the world.

REV 3:18.MARK 10:29-30.1 PET 4:12.1 PET 1:6-7.1 PET 5:10.JOHN 16:33

JUNE 20

Take this child away and nurse him for me, and I will give you your wages.

Go into the vineyard, and whatever is right I will give you. ◊ Whoever gives you a cup of water to drink in My name, because you belong to Christ, assuredly, I say to you, he will by no means lose his reward. ◊ The generous soul will be made rich, and he who waters will also be watered himself. ◊ God is not unjust to forget your work and labor of love . . . in that you have ministered to the saints, and do minister.

Each one will receive his own reward according to his own labor.

"Lord, when did we see You hungry and feed You, or thirsty and give You drink? When did we see You a stranger and take You in, or naked and clothe You?" And the King will answer and say to them, ". . . inasmuch as you did it to one of the least of these My brethren, you did it to Me." ◊ Come, you blessed of My Father, inherit the kingdom prepared for you from the foundation of the world.

EX 2:9.MATT 20:4.MARK 9:41.PROV 11:25.HEB 6:10.1 COR 3:8.MATT 25:37-38,40.MATT 25:34

You comprehend my path and my lying down.

Jacob awoke from his sleep and said, "Surely the Lord is in this place, and I did not know it." And he was afraid and said, "How awesome is this place! This is none other than the house of God, and this is the gate of heaven!"

For the eyes of the Lord run to and fro throughout the whole earth, to show Himself strong on behalf of those whose heart is loyal to Him.

I will both lie down in peace, and sleep; for You alone, O Lord, make me dwell in safety.

Because you have made the Lord, who is my refuge, even the Most High, your habitation, no evil shall befall you, nor shall any plague come near your dwelling; for He shall give His angels charge over you, to keep you in all your ways. ◊ When you lie down, you will not be afraid; yes, you will lie down and your sleep will be sweet. ◊ So He gives His beloved sleep.

PS 139:3.GEN 28:16-17.2 CHR 16:9.PS 4:8.PS 91:9-11.PROV 3:24.PS 127:2

MORNING

**Christ also suffered for us, leaving us an example,
that you should follow His steps.**

Even the Son of Man did not come to be served, but to serve. ◊ Whoever of you desires to be first shall be slave of all.

Jesus of Nazareth . . . went about doing good. ◊ Bear one another's burdens, and so fulfill the law of Christ.

The meekness and gentleness of Christ. ◊ In lowliness of mind let each esteem others better than himself.

Father, forgive them, for they do not know what they do. ◊ Be kind to one another, tenderhearted, forgiving one another, just as God in Christ also forgave you.

He who says he abides in Him ought himself also to walk just as He walked. ◊ [Look] unto Jesus, the author and finisher of our faith, who for the joy that was set before Him endured the cross, despising the shame, and has sat down at the right hand of the throne of God.

1 PET 2:21.MARK 10:45.MARK 10:44.ACTS 10:38.GAL 6:2.2 COR 10:1.PHIL 2:3.LUKE 23:34.EPH 4:32.1 JOHN 2:6.HEB 12:2

EVENING

**I sought him, but I could not find him; I called him,
but he gave me no answer.**

"O Lord, what shall I say when Israel turns its back before its enemies?" . . . So the Lord said to Joshua: "Get up! Why do you lie thus on your face? Israel has sinned. . . . For they have even taken some of the accursed things, . . . and they have also put it among their own stuff."

Behold, the Lord's hand is not shortened, that it cannot save; nor His ear heavy, that it cannot hear. But your iniquities have separated you from your God; and your sins have hidden His face from you, so that He will not hear.

If I regard iniquity in my heart, the Lord will not hear.

Beloved, if our heart does not condemn us, we have confidence toward God. And whatever we ask we receive from Him, because we keep His commandments and do those things that are pleasing in His sight.

SONG 5:6.JOSH 7:8,10-11.IS 59:1-2.PS 66:18.1 JOHN 3:21-22

JUNE 22

——————————————————————

You died, and your life is hidden with Christ in God.

How shall we who died to sin live any longer in it? ◊ I have been crucified with Christ; it is no longer I who live, but Christ lives in me; and the life which I now live in the flesh I live by faith in the Son of God, who loved me and gave Himself for me. ◊ He died for all, that those who live should live no longer for themselves, but for Him who died for them and rose again. ◊ If anyone is in Christ, he is a new creation; old things have passed away; behold, all things have become new.

We are in Him who is true, in His Son Jesus Christ. ◊ They all may be one as You, Father, are in Me, and I in You; that they also may be one in Us. ◊ You are the body of Christ, and members individually. ◊ Because I live, you will live also.

To him who overcomes I will give some of the hidden manna to eat. And I will give him a white stone, and on the stone a new name written which no one knows except him who receives it.

COL 3:3.ROM 6:2.GAL 2:20.2 COR 5:15.2 COR 5:17.1 JOHN 5:20.JOHN 17:21.1 COR 12:27.JOHN 14:19.REV 2:17

——————————————————————

See how He loved.

He died for all. ◊ Greater love has no one than this, than to lay down one's life for his friends.

He . . . lives to make intercession for them. ◊ I go to prepare a place for you.

I will come again and receive you to Myself; that where I am, there you may be also. ◊ Father, I desire that they also whom You gave Me may be with Me where I am. ◊ Having loved His own who were in the world, He loved them to the end.

We love Him because He first loved us. ◊ The love of Christ constrains us, because we judge thus: that if One died for all, then all died; and He died for all, that those who live should live no longer for themselves, but for Him who died for them and rose again.

If you keep My commandments, you will abide in My love, just as I have kept My Father's commandments and abide in His love.

JOHN 11:36.2 COR 5:15.JOHN 15:13.HEB 7:25.JOHN 14:2.JOHN 14:3.JOHN 17:24.JOHN 13:1.1 JOHN 4:19.2 COR 5:14-15.JOHN 15:10

MORNING

I will pray the Father, and He will give you another Helper, . . . even the Spirit of truth.

It is to your advantage that I go away; for if I do not go away, the Helper will not come to you; but if I depart, I will send Him to you.

The Spirit Himself bears witness with our spirit that we are children of God. ◊ You did not receive the spirit of bondage again to fear, but you received the Spirit of adoption by whom we cry out, "Abba, Father." ◊ The Spirit . . . helps in our weaknesses. For we do not know what we should pray for as we ought, but the Spirit Himself makes intercession for us with groanings which cannot be uttered.

The God of hope fill you with all joy and peace in believing, that you may abound in hope by the power of the Holy Spirit. ◊ Hope does not disappoint, because the love of God has been poured out in our hearts by the Holy Spirit who was given to us.

By this we know that we abide in Him, and He in us, because He has given us of His Spirit.

JOHN 14:16-17.JOHN 16:7.ROM 8:16.ROM 8:15.ROM 8:26.ROM
15:13.ROM 5:5.1 JOHN 4:13

EVENING

Shall I not seek security for you, that it may be well with you?

There remains . . . a rest for the people of God. ◊ My people will dwell in a peaceful habitation, in secure dwellings, and in quiet resting places. ◊ There the wicked cease from troubling, and there the weary are at rest. ◊ They . . . rest from their labors.

The forerunner has entered for us, even Jesus, having become High Priest forever according to the order of Melchizedek.

Come to Me, all you who labor and are heavy laden, and I will give you rest. Take My yoke upon you and learn from Me, for I am gentle and lowly in heart, and you will find rest for your souls. For My yoke is easy and My burden is light. ◊ In returning and rest you shall be saved; in quietness and confidence shall be your strength.

The Lord is my shepherd; I shall not want. He makes me to lie down in green pastures; He leads me beside the still waters.

RUTH 3:1.HEB 4:9.IS 32:18.JOB 3:17.REV 14:13.HEB 6:20.MATT
11:28-30.IS 30:15.PS 23:1-2

JUNE 24

MORNING_____

> **The ark of the covenant of the Lord went before them
> . . . to search out a resting place for them.**

My times are in Your hand. ◇ He will choose our inheritance for us. ◇ Lead me, O Lord, in Your righteousness, . . . make Your way straight before my face.

Commit your way to the Lord, trust also in Him, and He shall bring it to pass. ◇ In all your ways acknowledge Him, and He shall direct your paths. ◇ Your ears shall hear a word behind you, saying, "This is the way, walk in it," whenever you turn to the right hand or whenever you turn to the left.

The Lord is my shepherd; I shall not want. He makes me to lie down in green pastures; He leads me beside the still waters. ◇ As a father pities his children, so the Lord pities those who fear Him. For He knows our frame; He remembers that we are dust. ◇ Your heavenly Father knows that you need all these things. ◇ [Cast] all your care upon Him, for He cares for you.

NUM 10:33.PS 31:15.PS 47:4.PS 5:8.PS 37:5.PROV 3:6.IS 30:21.PS
23:1-2.PS 103:13-14.MATT 6:32.1 PET 5:7

EVENING_____

> **"Rabbi . . . , where are You staying?" He said to
> them, "Come and see."**

In My Father's house are many mansions; if it were not so, I would have told you. I go to prepare a place for you. And if I go and prepare a place for you, I will come again and receive you to Myself; that where I am, there you may be also. ◇ To him who overcomes I will grant to sit with Me on My throne.

Thus says the High and Lofty One who inhabits eternity, whose name is Holy: "I dwell in the high and holy place, with him who has a contrite and humble spirit, to revive the spirit of the humble, and to revive the heart of the contrite ones."

Behold, I stand at the door and knock. If anyone hears My voice and opens the door, I will come in to him and dine with him, and he with Me.

Lo, I am with you always, even to the end of the age. ◇ How precious is Your lovingkindness, O God! Therefore the children of men put their trust under the shadow of Your wings.

JOHN 1:38-39.JOHN 14:2-3.REV 3:21.IS 57:15.REV 3:20.MATT 28:20.PS
36:7

MORNING

When He is revealed, we shall be like Him, for we shall see Him as He is.

As many as received Him, to them He gave the right to become children of God, even to those who believe in His name. ◊ By which have been given to us exceedingly great and precious promises, that through these you may be partakers of the divine nature, having escaped the corruption that is in the world through lust.

Since the beginning of the world men have not heard nor perceived by the ear, nor has the eye seen any God besides You, who acts for the one who waits for Him.

Now we see in a mirror, dimly, but then face to face. Now I know in part, but then I shall know just as I also am known. ◊ Christ . . . will transform our lowly body that it may be conformed to His glorious body, according to the working by which He is able even to subdue all things to Himself. ◊ As for me, I will see Your face in righteousness; I shall be satisfied when I awake in Your likeness.

1 JOHN 3:2.JOHN 1:12.2 PET 1:4.IS 64:4.1 COR 13:12.PHIL 3:20-21.PS
17:15

EVENING

**"The Man . . . is My Companion,"
says the Lord of hosts.**

In Him dwells all the fullness of the Godhead bodily. ◊ I have given help to one who is mighty; I have exalted one chosen from the people. ◊ I have trodden the winepress alone, and from the peoples no one was with Me.

Great is the mystery of godliness: God was manifested in the flesh. ◊ Unto us a Child is born, unto us a Son is given; and the government will be upon His shoulder. And His name will be called Wonderful, Counselor, Mighty God, Everlasting Father, Prince of Peace.

The brightness of His glory and the express image of His person, and upholding all things by the word of His power, when He had by Himself purged our sins, sat down at the right hand of the Majesty on high. ◊ To the Son He says: "Your throne, O God, is forever and ever."

Let all the angels of God worship Him.

King of kings and Lord of lords.

ZECH 13:7.COL 2:9.PS 89:19.IS 63:3.1 TIM 3:16.IS 9:6.HEB 1:3.HEB
1:8.HEB 1:6.REV 19:16

JUNE 26

**"Oh, that You would bless me indeed, . . . and that
You would keep me from evil." . . . So God granted
him what he requested.**

The blessing of the Lord makes one rich, and He adds no sorrow with it. ◊ When He gives quietness, who then can make trouble? And when He hides His face, who then can see Him?

Salvation belongs to the Lord. Your blessing is upon Your people. ◊ How great is Your goodness, which You have laid up for those who fear You, which You have prepared for those who trust in You in the presence of the sons of men! ◊ I do not pray that You should take them out of the world, but that You should keep them from the evil one.

Ask, and it will be given to you; seek, and you will find; knock, and it will be opened to you. For everyone who asks receives, and he who seeks finds, and to him who knocks it will be opened. ◊ The Lord redeems the soul of His servants, and none of those who trust in Him shall be condemned.

1 CHR 4:10.PROV 10:22.JOB 34:29.PS 3:8.PS 31:19.JOHN 17:15.MATT
7:7-8.PS 34:22

EVENING

**It is a night of solemn observance to the Lord for
bringing them out of the land of Egypt.**

The Lord Jesus on the same night in which He was betrayed took bread; and when He had given thanks, He broke it and said, "Take, eat; this is My body which is broken for you; do this in remembrance of Me." In the same manner He also took the cup after supper, saying, "This cup is the new covenant in My blood. This do, as often as you drink it, in remembrance of Me."

He knelt down and prayed. . . . And being in agony, He prayed more earnestly. And His sweat became like great drops of blood falling down to the ground.

It was the Preparation Day of the Passover, and about the sixth hour . . . they took Jesus and led Him away . . . to a place called . . . Golgotha, where they crucified Him.

Christ, our Passover, was sacrificed for us. Therefore let us keep the feast.

EX 12:42.1 COR 11:23-25.LUKE 22:41,44.JOHN 19:14,16-18.1 COR 5:7-8

MORNING

Who is able to stand?

But who can endure the day of His coming? And who can stand when He appears? For He is like a refiner's fire and like fuller's soap.

I looked, and behold, a great multitude which no one could number, of all nations, tribes, peoples, and tongues, standing before the throne and before the Lamb, clothed with white robes, with palm branches in their hands. . . . These are the ones who come out of the great tribulation, and washed their robes and made them white in the blood of the Lamb. . . . They shall neither hunger anymore nor thirst anymore; the sun shall not strike them, nor any heat; for the Lamb who is in the midst of the throne will shepherd them and lead them to living fountains of waters. And God will wipe away every tear from their eyes.

There is . . . no condemnation to those who are in Christ Jesus, who do not walk according to the flesh, but according to the Spirit. ◊ Stand fast therefore in the liberty by which Christ has made us free.

REV 6:17.MAL 3:2.REV 7:9,14,16-17.ROM 8:1.GAL 5:1

EVENING

Do not enter into judgment with Your servant, for in Your sight no one living is righteous.

"Come now, and let us reason together," says the Lord, "though your sins are like scarlet, they shall be as white as snow; though they are red like crimson, they shall be as wool."

Let him take hold of My strength, that he may make peace with Me; and he shall make peace with Me. ◊ Now acquaint yourself with Him, and be at peace.

Having been justified by faith, we have peace with God through our Lord Jesus Christ. ◊ A man is not justified by the works of the law but by faith in Jesus Christ. ◊ By the deeds of the law no flesh will be justified in His sight.

By Him everyone who believes is justified from all things from which you could not be justified by the law of Moses. Thanks be to God, who gives us the victory through our Lord Jesus Christ.

PS 143:2.IS 1:18.IS 27:5.JOB 22:21.ROM 5:1.GAL 2:16.ROM 3:20.ACTS 13:39.1 COR 15:57

JUNE 28

I know that my Redeemer lives.

If when we were enemies we were reconciled to God through the death of His Son, much more, having been reconciled, we shall be saved by His life. ◊ But He, because He continues forever, has an unchangeable priesthood. Therefore He is also able to save to the uttermost those who come to God through Him, since He ever lives to make intercession for them.

Because I live, you will live also. ◊ If in this life only we have hope in Christ, we are of all men the most pitiable. But now Christ is risen from the dead, and has become the firstfruits of those who have fallen asleep.

"The Redeemer will come to Zion, and to those who turn from transgression in Jacob," says the Lord. ◊ We have redemption through His blood, the forgiveness of sins, according to the riches of His grace. ◊ You were not redeemed with corruptible things, like silver or gold, from your aimless conduct received by tradition from your fathers, but with the precious blood of Christ, as of a lamb without blemish and without spot.

JOB 19:25.ROM 5:10.HEB 7:24-25.JOHN 14:19.1 COR 15:19-20.IS 59:20.EPH 1:7.1 PET 1:18-19

EVENING

The Spirit expressly says that in latter times some will depart from the faith, giving heed to deceiving spirits.

Therefore take heed how you hear. ◊ Let the word of Christ dwell in you richly in all wisdom. ◊ Above all, [take] the shield of faith with which you will be able to quench all the fiery darts of the wicked one.

Great peace have those who love Your law, and nothing causes them to stumble.

How sweet are Your words to my taste, sweeter than honey to my mouth! Through Your precepts I get understanding; therefore I hate every false way.

Your word is a lamp to my feet and a light to my path. ◊ I have more understanding than all my teachers, for Your testimonies are my meditation.

Satan himself transforms himself into an angel of light. ◊ But even if we, or an angel from heaven, preach any other gospel to you than what we have preached to you, let him be accursed.

1 TIM 4:1.LUKE 8:18.COL 3:16.EPH 6:16.PS 119:165.PS 119:103-104.PS 119:105.PS 119:99.2 COR 11:14.GAL 1:8

MORNING

His commandments are not burdensome.

This is the will of Him who sent Me, that everyone who sees the Son and believes in Him may have everlasting life. ◊ Whatever we ask we receive from Him, because we keep His commandments and do those things that are pleasing in His sight.

My yoke is easy and My burden is light. ◊ If you love Me, keep My commandments. ◊ He who has My commandments and keeps them, it is he who loves Me. And he who loves Me will be loved by My Father, and I will love him and manifest Myself to him.

Happy is the man who finds wisdom, and the man who gains understanding. . . . Her ways are ways of pleasantness, and all her paths are peace. ◊ Great peace have those who love Your law, and nothing causes them to stumble. ◊ I delight in the law of God according to the inward man.

This is His commandment: that we should believe on the name of His Son Jesus Christ and love one another. ◊ Love does no harm to a neighbor; therefore love is the fulfillment of the law.

1 JOHN 5:3.JOHN 6:40.1 JOHN 3:22.MATT 11:30.JOHN 14:15.JOHN
14:21.PROV 3:13,17.PS 119:165.ROM 7:22.1 JOHN 3:23.ROM 13:10

EVENING

Do not remember the sins of my youth,
nor my transgressions.

I have blotted out, like a thick cloud, your transgressions, and like a cloud, your sins. ◊ I, even I, am He who blots out your transgressions for My own sake; and I will not remember your sins. ◊ "Come now, and let us reason together," says the Lord, "though your sins are like scarlet, they shall be as white as snow; though they are red like crimson, they shall be as wool." ◊ I will forgive their iniquity, and their sin I will remember no more. ◊ You will cast all our sins into the depths of the sea.

You have lovingly delivered my soul from the pit of corruption, for You have cast all my sins behind Your back. ◊ Who is a God like You, pardoning iniquity . . . ? He does not retain His anger forever, because He delights in mercy. ◊ To Him who loved us and washed us from our sins in His own blood, . . . to Him be glory and dominion forever and ever. Amen.

PS 25:7.IS 44:22.IS 43:25.IS 1:18.JER 31:34.MIC 7:19.IS 38:17.MIC
7:18.REV 1:5-6

MORNING

As many as I love, I rebuke and chasten.

My son, do not despise the chastening of the Lord, nor be discouraged when you are rebuked by Him; for whom the Lord loves He chastens, and scourges every son whom He receives. ◊ Just as a father the son in whom he delights. ◊ He bruises, but He binds up; He wounds, but His hands make whole. ◊ Humble yourselves under the mighty hand of God, that He may exalt you in due time. ◊ I have tested you in the furnace of affliction.

He does not afflict willingly, nor grieve the children of men. ◊ He has not dealt with us according to our sins, nor punished us according to our iniquities. For as the heavens are high above the earth, so great is His mercy toward those who fear Him; as far as the east is from the west, so far has He removed our transgressions from us. As a father pities his children, so the Lord pities those who fear Him. For He knows our frame; He remembers that we are dust.

REV 3:19.HEB 12:5-6.PROV 3:12.JOB 5:18.1 PET 5:6.IS 48:10.LAM 3:33.PS 103:10-14

EVENING

God is in heaven, and you on earth; therefore let your words be few.

But when you pray, do not use vain repetitions as the heathen do. For they think that they will be heard for their many words. Therefore do not be like them. For your Father knows the things you have need of before you ask Him.

They . . . called on the name of Baal from morning even till noon, saying, "O Baal, hear us!"

Two men went up to the temple to pray, one a Pharisee and the other a tax collector. The Pharisee stood and prayed thus with himself, "God, I thank You that I am not like other men—extortioners, unjust, adulterers, or even as this tax collector. . . ." And the tax collector, standing afar off, would not so much as raise his eyes to heaven, but beat his breast, saying, "God be merciful to me a sinner!" I tell you, this man went down to his house justified rather than the other.

Lord, teach us to pray.

ECCL 5:2.MATT 6:7-8.1 KIN 18:26.LUKE 18:10-14.LUKE 11:1

MORNING

The fruit of the Spirit is . . . goodness.

Be followers of God as dear children. ◊ Love your enemies, bless those who curse you, do good to those who hate you, and pray for those who spitefully use you and persecute you, that you may be sons of your Father in heaven; for He makes His sun rise on the evil and on the good, and sends rain on the just and on the unjust. ◊ Be merciful, just as your Father also is merciful.

The fruit of the Spirit is in all goodness, righteousness, and truth.

When the kindness and the love of God our Savior toward man appeared, not by works of righteousness which we have done, but according to His mercy He saved us, through the washing of regeneration and renewing of the Holy Spirit, whom He poured out on us abundantly through Jesus Christ our Savior. ◊ The Lord is good to all, and His tender mercies are over all His works. ◊ He who did not spare His own Son, but delivered Him up for us all, how shall He not with Him also freely give us all things?

GAL 5:22.EPH 5:1.MATT 5:44-45.LUKE 6:36.EPH 5:9.TITUS 3:4-6.PS 145:9.ROM 8:32

EVENING

Then Samuel took a stone . . . and called its name Ebenezer, saying, "Thus far the Lord has helped us."

I was brought low, and He saved me. ◊ Blessed be the Lord, because He has heard the voice of my supplications! The Lord is my strength and my shield; my heart trusted in Him, and I am helped; therefore my heart greatly rejoices, and with my song I will praise Him.

It is better to trust in the Lord than to put confidence in man. It is better to trust in the Lord than to put confidence in princes. ◊ Happy is he who has the God of Jacob for his help, whose hope is in the Lord his God. ◊ He led them forth by the right way, that they might go to a city for habitation. ◊ Not a word failed of any good thing which the Lord had spoken to the house of Israel. All came to pass.

"When I sent you without money bag, sack, and sandals, did you lack anything?" So they said, "Nothing." ◊ Because You have been my help, therefore in the shadow of Your wings I will rejoice.

1 SAM 7:12.PS 116:6.PS 28:6-7.PS 118:8-9.PS 146:5.PS 107:7.JOSH 21:45.LUKE 22:35.PS 63:7

JULY 2

_____

This is the ordinance of the Passover: No outsider shall eat it.

We have an altar from which those who serve the tabernacle have no right to eat. ◊ Unless one is born again, he cannot see the kingdom of God. ◊ At that time you were without Christ, being aliens from the commonwealth of Israel and strangers from the covenants of promise, . . . but now in Christ Jesus you who once were far off have been made near by the blood of Christ.

For He Himself is our peace, who has made both one, . . . having abolished in His flesh the enmity, that is, the law of commandments contained in ordinances, so as to create in Himself one new man from the two, thus making peace.

Now, therefore, you are no longer strangers and foreigners, but fellow citizens with the saints and members of the household of God.

If anyone hears My voice and opens the door, I will come in to him and dine with him, and he with Me.

EX 12:43.HEB 13:10.JOHN 3:3.EPH 2:12-13.EPH 2:14-15.EPH 2:19.REV 3:20

EVENING_____

[Jesus] prayed the third time, saying the same words.

[Christ], in the days of His flesh, . . . offered up prayers and supplications, with vehement cries and tears to Him who was able to save Him from death.

Let us know, let us pursue the knowledge of the Lord. ◊ [Continue] steadfastly in prayer. ◊ Praying always with all prayer and supplication in the Spirit, being watchful to this end with all perseverance and supplication. ◊ By prayer and supplication, with thanksgiving, let your requests be made known to God; and the peace of God, which surpasses all understanding, will guard your hearts and minds through Christ Jesus.

Nevertheless, not as I will, but as You will. ◊ This is the confidence that we have in Him, that if we ask anything according to His will, He hears us.

Delight yourself . . . in the Lord, and He shall give you the desires of your heart. Commit your way to the Lord, trust also in Him, and He shall bring it to pass.

MATT 26:44.HEB 5:7.HOS 6:3.ROM 12:12.EPH 6:18.PHIL 4:6-7.MATT 26:39.1 JOHN 5:14.PS 37:4-5

MORNING

If children, then heirs—heirs of God and joint heirs with Christ.

If you are Christ's, then you are Abraham's seed, and heirs according to the promise.

Behold what manner of love the Father has bestowed on us, that we should be called children of God! ◊ Therefore you are no longer a slave but a son, and if a son, then an heir of God through Christ. ◊ [God] predestined us to adoption as sons by Jesus Christ to Himself, according to the good pleasure of His will.

Father, I desire that they also whom You gave Me may be with Me where I am, that they may behold My glory which You have given Me.

And he who overcomes, and keeps My works until the end, to him I will give power over the nations. ◊ To him who overcomes I will grant to sit with Me on My throne, as I also overcame and sat down with My Father on His throne.

ROM 8:17.GAL 3:29.1 JOHN 3:1.GAL 4:7.EPH 1:5.JOHN 17:24.REV 2:26.REV 3:21

EVENING

Things which are despised God has chosen.

Look, are not all these who speak Galileans?

Jesus . . . saw two brothers . . . casting a net into the sea; for they were fishermen. And He said to them, "Follow Me." ◊ Now when they saw the boldness of Peter and John, and perceived that they were uneducated and untrained men, they marveled. And they realized that they had been with Jesus.

My speech and my preaching were not with persuasive words of human wisdom, but in demonstration of the Spirit and of power, that your faith should not be in the wisdom of men but in the power of God.

You did not choose Me, but I chose you and appointed you that you should go and bear fruit. ◊ He who abides in Me, and I in him, bears much fruit; for without Me you can do nothing. ◊ We have this treasure in earthen vessels, that the excellence of the power may be of God.

1 COR 1:28.ACTS 2:7.MATT 4:18-19.ACTS 4:13.1 COR 2:4-5.JOHN 15:16.JOHN 15:5.2 COR 4:7

JULY 4

Leaning on Jesus' bosom.

As one whom his mother comforts, so I will comfort you. ◊ Then they brought young children to Him, that He might touch them. . . . And He took them up in His arms, put His hands on them, and blessed them. ◊ Jesus called His disciples to Him and said, "I have compassion on the multitude, because they have now continued with Me three days and have nothing to eat. And I do not want to send them away hungry, lest they faint on the way." ◊ We . . . have a High Priest . . . tempted as we are. ◊ In His love and in His pity He redeemed them.

I will not leave you orphans; I will come to you. ◊ Can a woman forget her nursing child, and not have compassion on the son of her womb? Surely they may forget, yet I will not forget you.

The Lamb who is in the midst of the throne will shepherd them and lead them to living fountains of waters. And God will wipe away every tear from their eyes.

JOHN 13:23.IS 66:13.MARK 10:13,16.MATT 15:32.HEB 4:15.IS
63:9.JOHN 14:18.IS 49:15.REV 7:17

Jesus Christ the righteous. The propitiation
for our sins.

The faces of the cherubim shall be toward the mercy seat. You shall put the mercy seat on top of the ark, and in the ark you shall put the Testimony that I will give you. I will meet with you, and I will speak with you from above the mercy seat.

Surely His salvation is near to those who fear Him. . . . Mercy and truth have met together; righteousness and peace have kissed each other.

If You, Lord, should mark iniquities, O Lord, who could stand? But there is forgiveness with You, that You may be feared. . . . O Israel, hope in the Lord; for with the Lord there is mercy, and with Him is abundant redemption. And He shall redeem Israel from all his iniquities. ◊ All have sinned and fall short of the glory of God, being justified freely by His grace through the redemption that is in Christ Jesus, whom God set forth to be a propitiation by His blood, through faith, to demonstrate His righteousness.

1 JOHN 2:1-2.EX 25:20-22.PS 85:9-10.PS 130:3-4,7-8.ROM 3:23-25

MORNING

We have known and believed the love that God has for us.

God, who is rich in mercy, because of His great love with which He loved us, even when we were dead in trespasses, made us alive together with Christ (by grace you have been saved), and raised us up together, and made us sit together in the heavenly places in Christ Jesus, that in the ages to come He might show the exceeding riches of His grace in His kindness toward us in Christ Jesus.

God so loved the world that He gave His only begotten Son, that whoever believes in Him should not perish but have everlasting life. ◊ He who did not spare His own Son, but delivered Him up for us all, how shall He not with Him also freely give us all things? ◊ The Lord is good to all, and His tender mercies are over all His works.

We love Him because He first loved us.

Blessed is she who believed, for there will be a fulfillment of those things which were told her from the Lord.

1 JOHN 4:16.EPH 2:4-7.JOHN 3:16.ROM 8:32.PS 145:9.1 JOHN 4:19.LUKE 1:45

EVENING

Do not set your mind on high things, but associate with the humble.

My brethren, do not hold the faith of our Lord Jesus Christ, the Lord of glory, with partiality. . . . Has God not chosen the poor of this world to be rich in faith and heirs of the kingdom which He promised to those who love Him?

Let no one seek his own, but each one the other's well-being. ◊ Having food and clothing, with these we shall be content. But those who desire to be rich fall into temptation and a snare, and into many foolish and harmful lusts which drown men in destruction and perdition.

God has chosen the foolish things of the world to put to shame the wise, and God has chosen the weak things of the world to put to shame the things which are mighty; and the base things of the world and the things which are despised God has chosen and the things which are not, to bring to nothing the things that are, that no flesh should glory in His presence.

Lord, my heart is not haughty, nor my eyes lofty.

ROM 12:16.JAMES 2:1,5.1 COR 10:24.1 TIM 6:8-9.1 COR 1:27-29.PS 131:1

JULY 6

MORNING

Let your speech always be with grace.

A word fitly spoken is like apples of gold in settings of silver. Like an earring of gold and an ornament of fine gold is a wise reprover to an obedient ear. ◊ Let no corrupt communication proceed out of your mouth, but what is good for necessary edification, that it may impart grace to the hearers. ◊ A good man out of the good treasure of his heart brings forth good things, and an evil man out of the evil treasure brings forth evil things. . . . By your words you will be justified. ◊ The tongue of the wise promotes health.

Those who feared the Lord spoke to one another, and the Lord listened and heard them; so a book of remembrance was written before Him for those who fear the Lord and who meditate on His name.

If you take out the precious from the vile, you shall be as My mouth. ◊ But as you abound in everything in faith, in speech, in knowledge, in all diligence, . . . see that you abound in this grace also.

COL 4:6.PROV 25:11-12.EPH 4:29.MATT 12:35,37.PROV 12:18.MAL 3:16.JER 15:19.2 COR 8:7

EVENING

Your lovingkindness is before my eyes.

The Lord is gracious and full of compassion, slow to anger and great in mercy. ◊ Your Father in heaven . . . makes His sun rise on the evil and on the good, and sends rain on the just and on the unjust.

Be followers of God as dear children. And walk in love, as Christ also has loved us and given Himself for us, an offering and a sacrifice to God for a sweet-smelling aroma. ◊ Be kind to one another, tenderhearted, forgiving one another, just as God in Christ also forgave you. ◊ Since you have purified your souls in obeying the truth through the Spirit in sincere love of the brethren, love one another fervently with a pure heart. ◊ The love of Christ constrains us.

Love your enemies, do good, and lend, hoping for nothing in return; and your reward will be great, and you will be sons of the Highest. For He is kind to the unthankful and evil. Therefore be merciful, just as your Father also is merciful.

PS 26:3.PS 145:8.MATT 5:45.EPH 5:1-2.EPH 4:32.1 PET 1:22.2 COR 5:14.LUKE 6:35-36

MORNING

**Then Jesus was led up by the Spirit into the
wilderness to be tempted by the devil.**

In the days of His flesh, when He had offered up prayers and
supplications, with vehement cries and tears to Him who was able to
save Him from death, and was heard because of His godly fear, though
He was a Son, yet He learned obedience by the things which He suffered.
And having been perfected, He became the author of eternal salvation to
all who obey Him. ◊ We do not have a High Priest who cannot
sympathize with our weaknesses, but was in all points tempted as we
are, yet without sin.

No temptation has overtaken you except such as is common to man;
but God is faithful, who will not allow you to be tempted beyond what
you are able, but with the temptation will also make the way of escape,
that you may be able to bear it. ◊ My grace is sufficient for you, for My
strength is made perfect in weakness.

MATT 4:1.HEB 5:7-9.HEB 4:15.1 COR 10:13.2 COR 12:9

EVENING

**The Son of Man did not come to be served, but to
serve, and to give His life a ransom for many.**

If the blood of bulls and goats and the ashes of a heifer, sprinkling the
unclean, sanctifies for the purifying of the flesh, how much more shall
the blood of Christ, who through the eternal Spirit offered Himself
without spot to God, purge your conscience from dead works to serve the
living God?

He was led as a lamb to the slaughter. ◊ I lay down My life for the
sheep. . . . No one takes it from Me, but I lay it down of Myself. I have
power to lay it down, and I have power to take it again.

The life of the flesh is in the blood, and I have given it to you upon the
altar to make atonement for your souls; for it is the blood that makes
atonement for the soul. ◊ Without shedding of blood there is no
remission.

While we were still sinners, Christ died for us. Much more then,
having now been justified by His blood, we shall be saved from wrath
through Him.

MATT 20:28.HEB 9:13-14.IS 53:7.JOHN 10:15,18.LEV 17:11.HEB
9:22.ROM 5:8-9

JULY 8

MORNING

**If we confess our sins, He is faithful and just
to forgive us our sins and to cleanse us from
all unrighteousness.**

I acknowledge my transgressions, and my sin is ever before me. Against You, You only, have I sinned, and done this evil in Your sight.

And he arose and came to his father. But when he was still a great way off, his father saw him and had compassion, and ran and fell on his neck and kissed him. ◊ I have blotted out, like a thick cloud, your transgressions, and like a cloud, your sins. Return to Me, for I have redeemed you. ◊ Your sins are forgiven you for His name's sake. ◊ God in Christ also forgave you. ◊ That He might be just and the justifier of the one who has faith in Jesus.

Then I will sprinkle clean water on you, and you shall be clean. ◊ They shall walk with Me in white, for they are worthy.

This is He who came by water and blood—Jesus Christ; not only by water, but by water and blood.

1 JOHN 1:9.PS 51:3-4.LUKE 15:20.IS 44:22.1 JOHN 2:12.EPH 4:32.ROM
3:26.EZEK 36:25.REV 3:4.1 JOHN 5:6

EVENING

**Shall the throne of iniquity . . . have fellowship
with You?**

Truly our fellowship is with the Father and with His Son Jesus Christ. ◊ Beloved, now we are children of God; and it has not yet been revealed what we shall be, but we know that when He is revealed, we shall be like Him, for we shall see Him as He is. And everyone who has this hope in Him purifies himself, just as He is pure.

The ruler of this world is coming, and he has nothing in Me. ◊ A High Priest . . . holy, harmless, undefiled.

We do not wrestle against flesh and blood, but against principalities, against powers, against the rulers of the darkness of this age, against spiritual hosts of wickedness in the heavenly places. ◊ The prince of the power of the air, the spirit who now works in the sons of disobedience.

Whoever is born of God does not sin; but he who has been born of God keeps himself, and the wicked one does not touch him. We know that we are of God, and the whole world lies under the sway of the wicked one.

PS 94:20.1 JOHN 1:3.1 JOHN 3:2-3.JOHN 14:30.HEB 7:26.EPH 6:12.EPH
2:2.1 JOHN 5:18-19

MORNING

I have removed your iniquity from you, and I will clothe you with rich robes.

Blessed is he whose transgression is forgiven, whose sin is covered. ◊ We are all like an unclean thing. ◊ I know that in me (that is, in my flesh) nothing good dwells; for to will is present with me, but how to perform what is good I do not find.

As many of you as were baptized into Christ have put on Christ. ◊ You have put off the old man with his deeds, and have put on the new man who is renewed in knowledge according to the image of Him who created him. ◊ Not having my own righteousness, which is from the law, but . . . the righteousness which is from God by faith.

Bring out the best robe and put it on him. ◊ The fine linen is the righteous acts of the saints. ◊ I will greatly rejoice in the Lord, my soul shall be joyful in my God; for He has clothed me with the garments of salvation, He has covered me with the robe of righteousness.

ZECH 3:4.PS 32:1.IS 64:6.ROM 7:18.GAL 3:27.COL 3:9-10.PHIL 3:9.LUKE 15:22.REV 19:8.IS 61:10

EVENING

The Day will declare it.

Judge nothing before the time, until the Lord comes, who will both bring to light the hidden things of darkness and reveal the counsels of the hearts; and then each one's praise will come from God.

Why do you judge your brother? Or why do you show contempt for your brother? For we shall all stand before the judgment seat of Christ. . . . So then each of us shall give account of himself to God. Therefore let us not judge one another anymore.

God will judge the secrets of men by Jesus Christ. ◊ The Father judges no one, but has committed all judgment to the Son. . . . [He] has given Him authority to execute judgment also, because He is the Son of Man.

The Great, the Mighty God, whose name is the Lord of hosts. You are great in counsel and mighty in work, for your eyes are open to all the ways of the sons of men, to give everyone according to his ways and according to the fruit of his doings.

1 COR 3:13.1 COR 4:5.ROM 14:10,12-13.ROM 2:16.JOHN 5:22,27.JER 32:18-19

JULY 10

_____

A disciple is not above his teacher.

You call me Teacher and Lord, and you say well, for so I am.

It is enough for a disciple that he be like his teacher, and a servant like his master. ◊ If they persecuted Me, they will also persecute you. If they kept My word, they will keep yours also. ◊ I have given them Your word; and the world has hated them because they are not of the world, just as I am not of the world.

Consider Him who endured such hostility from sinners against Himself, lest you become weary and discouraged in your souls. You have not yet resisted to bloodshed, striving against sin.

Let us run with endurance the race that is set before us, looking unto Jesus, the author and finisher of our faith, who for the joy that was set before Him endured the cross, despising the shame, and has sat down at the right hand of the throne of God. ◊ Therefore, since Christ suffered for us in the flesh, arm yourselves also with the same mind.

MATT 10:24.JOHN 13:13.MATT 10:25.JOHN 15:20.JOHN 17:14.HEB
12:3-4.HEB 12:1-2.1 PET 4:1

EVENING_____

My son, give me your heart.

Oh, that they had such a heart in them that they would fear Me and always keep all My commandments, that it might be well with them and with their children forever!

Your heart is not right in the sight of God. ◊ Because the carnal mind is enmity against God; for it is not subject to the law of God, nor indeed can be. So then, those who are in the flesh cannot please God.

They . . . first gave themselves to the Lord. ◊ In every work that [Hezekiah] began . . . to seek his God, he did it with all his heart. So he prospered.

Keep your heart with all diligence, for out of it spring the issues of life.

Whatever you do, do it heartily, as to the Lord. ◊ As servants of Christ, doing the will of God from the heart, with good will doing service, as to the Lord, and not to men.

I will run in the way of Your commandments, for You shall enlarge my heart.

PROV 23:26.DEUT 5:29.ACTS 8:21.ROM 8:7-8.2 COR 8:5.2 CHR
31:21.PROV 4:23.COL 3:23.EPH 6:6-7.PS 119:32

MORNING

I am with you to save you.

Shall the prey be taken from the mighty, or the captives of the righteous be delivered? But thus says the Lord: "Even the captives of the mighty shall be taken away, and the prey of the terrible be delivered; for I will contend with him who contends with you. . . . All flesh shall know that I, the Lord, am your Savior, and your Redeemer, the Mighty One of Jacob." ◊ Fear not, for I am with you; be not dismayed, for I am your God. I will strengthen you, yes, I will help you, I will uphold you with My righteous right hand.

We do not have a High Priest who cannot sympathize with our weaknesses, but was in all points tempted as we are, yet without sin. ◊ In that He Himself has suffered, being tempted, He is able to aid those who are tempted. ◊ The steps of a good man are ordered by the Lord, and He delights in his way. Though he fall, he shall not be utterly cast down; for the Lord upholds him with His hand.

JER 15:20.IS 49:24-26.IS 41:10.HEB 4:15.HEB 2:18.PS 37:23-24

EVENING

He satisfies the longing soul, and fills the hungry soul with goodness.

You have tasted that the Lord is gracious.

O God, You are my God; early will I seek You; my soul thirsts for You; my flesh longs for You in a dry and thirsty land where there is no water. So I have looked for You in the sanctuary, to see Your power and Your glory. ◊ My soul longs, yes, even faints for the courts of the Lord; my heart and my flesh cry out for the living God. ◊ Having a desire to depart and be with Christ, which is far better.

I shall be satisfied when I awake in Your likeness. ◊ They shall neither hunger anymore nor thirst anymore; the sun shall not strike them, nor any heat; for the Lamb who is in the midst of the throne will shepherd them and lead them to living fountains of waters. And God will wipe away every tear from their eyes. ◊ They are abundantly satisfied with the fullness of Your house, and You give them drink from the river of Your pleasures. ◊ "My people shall be satisfied with My goodness," says the Lord.

PS 107:9.1 PET 2:3.PS 63:1-2.PS 84:2.PHIL 1:23.PS 17:15.REV 7:16-17.PS 36:8.JER 31:14

JULY 12

MORNING_____

My Presence will go with you, and I will
give you rest.

Be strong and of good courage, do not fear nor be afraid of them; for the Lord your God, He is the One who goes with you. He will not leave you nor forsake you. . . . The Lord, He is the one who goes before you. He will be with you, He will not leave you nor forsake you; do not fear nor be dismayed. ◊ Have I not commanded you? Be strong and of good courage; do not be afraid, nor be dismayed, for the Lord your God is with you wherever you go. ◊ In all your ways acknowledge Him, and He shall direct your paths.

He Himself has said, "I will never leave you nor forsake you." . . . So we may boldly say: "The Lord is my helper; I will not fear. What can man do to me?" ◊ Our sufficiency is from God.

Do not lead us into temptation. ◊ O Lord, I know the way of man is not in himself; it is not in man who walks to direct his own steps. ◊ My times are in Your hand.

EX 33:14.DEUT 31:6,8.JOSH 1:9.PROV 3:6.HEB 13:5-6.2 COR 3:5.MATT
6:13.JER 10:23.PS 31:15

EVENING_____

Let us consider one another in order to stir up love
and good works.

How forceful are right words! ◊ I stir up your pure minds by way of reminder.

Those who feared the Lord spoke to one another, and the Lord listened and heard them; so a book of remembrance was written before Him for those who fear the Lord and who meditate on His name. ◊ If two of you agree on earth concerning anything that they ask, it will be done for them by My Father in heaven.

The Lord God said, "It is not good that man should be alone." ◊ Two are better than one, because they have a good reward for their labor. For if they fall, one will lift up his companion. But woe to him who is alone when he falls, for he has no one to help him up.

Let us not . . . put a stumbling block or a cause to fall in our brother's way. ◊ Bear one another's burdens, and so fulfill the law of Christ. ◊ [Consider] yourself lest you also be tempted.

HEB 10:24.JOB 6:25.2 PET 3:1.MAL 3:16.MATT 18:19.GEN 2:18.ECCL
4:9-10.ROM 14:13.GAL 6:2.GAL 6:1

MORNING

I am my beloved's, and his desire is toward me.

I know whom I have believed and am persuaded that He is able to keep what I have committed to Him until that Day. ◊ I am persuaded that neither death nor life, nor angels nor principalities nor powers, nor things present nor things to come, nor height nor depth, nor any other created thing, shall be able to separate us from the love of God which is in Christ Jesus our Lord. ◊ Those whom You gave Me I have kept; and none of them is lost.

The Lord takes pleasure in His people. ◊ My delight was with the sons of men. ◊ His great love with which He loved us. ◊ Greater love has no one than this, than to lay down one's life for his friends.

You were bought at a price; therefore glorify God in your body and in your spirit, which are God's. ◊ If we live, we live to the Lord; and if we die, we die to the Lord. Therefore, whether we live or die, we are the Lord's.

SONG 7:10.2 TIM 1:12.ROM 8:38-39.JOHN 17:12.PS 149:4.PROV 8:31.EPH 2:4.JOHN 15:13.1 COR 6:20.ROM 14:8

EVENING

Search from the book of the Lord.

Lay up these words of mine in your heart and in your soul, and bind them as a sign on your hand, and they shall be as frontlets between your eyes. ◊ This Book of the Law shall not depart from your mouth, but you shall meditate in it day and night, that you may observe to do according to all that is written in it. For then you will make your way prosperous, and then you will have good success.

The law of his God is in his heart; none of his steps shall slide. ◊ By the word of Your lips, I have kept myself from the paths of the destroyer. ◊ Your word I have hidden in my heart, that I might not sin against You.

We also have the prophetic word made more sure, which you do well to heed as a light that shines in a dark place, until the day dawns and the morning star rises in your hearts. ◊ That we through the patience and comfort of the Scriptures might have hope.

IS 34:16.DEUT 11:18.JOSH 1:8.PS 37:31.PS 17:4.PS 119:11.2 PET 1:19.ROM 15:4

JULY 14

MORNING

Out of the abundance of the heart the mouth speaks.

Let the word of Christ dwell in you richly in all wisdom.

Keep your heart with all diligence, for out of it spring the issues of life. ◊ Death and life are in the power of the tongue. ◊ The mouth of the righteous speaks wisdom, and his tongue talks of justice. The law of his God is in his heart; none of his steps shall slide. Let no corrupt communication proceed out of your mouth, but what is good for necessary edification, that it may impart grace to the hearers.

For we cannot but speak the things which we have seen and heard. ◊ I believed, therefore I spoke.

Whoever confesses Me before men, him I will also confess before My Father who is in heaven. ◊ With the heart one believes to righteousness, and with the mouth confession is made to salvation.

MATT 12:34.COL 3:16.PROV 4:23.PROV 18:21.PS 37:30-31.EPH
4:29.ACTS 4:20.PS 116:10.MATT 10:32.ROM 10:10

EVENING

I hope to see you shortly, and we shall speak face to face.

Oh, that You would rend the heavens! That You would come down! ◊ As the deer pants for the water brooks, so pants my soul for You, O God. My soul thirsts for God, for the living God. When shall I come and appear before God? ◊ Make haste, my beloved, and be like a gazelle or a young stag on the mountains of spices.

Our citizenship is in heaven, from which we also eagerly wait for the Savior, the Lord Jesus Christ. ◊ Looking for the blessed hope and glorious appearing of our great God and Savior Jesus Christ. ◊ God our Savior and the Lord Jesus Christ, our hope. ◊ Whom having not seen you love.

He who testifies to these things says, "Surely I am coming quickly." Amen. Even so, come, Lord Jesus! ◊ It will be said in that day: "Behold, this is our God; we have waited for Him, and He will save us. This is the Lord; we have waited for Him; we will be glad and rejoice in His salvation."

3 JOHN 1:14.IS 64:1.PS 42:1-2.SONG 8:14.PHIL 3:20.TITUS 2:13.1 TIM
1:1.1 PET 1:8.REV 22:20.IS 25:9

MORNING

Your will be done on earth as it is in heaven.

Bless the Lord, you His angels, who excel in strength, who do His word, heeding the voice of His word. Bless the Lord, all you His hosts, you ministers of His, who do His pleasure.

I have come down from heaven, not to do My own will, but the will of Him who sent Me. ◊ I delight to do Your will, O my God, and Your law is within my heart. ◊ O My Father, if this cup cannot pass away from Me unless I drink it, Your will be done.

Not everyone who says to Me, "Lord, Lord," shall enter the kingdom of heaven, but he who does the will of My Father in heaven. ◊ Not the hearers of the law are just in the sight of God, but the doers of the law will be justified. ◊ If you know these things, happy are you if you do them. ◊ To him who knows to do good and does not do it, to him it is sin.

Do not be conformed to this world, but be transformed by the renewing of your mind.

MATT 6:10.PS 103:20-21.JOHN 6:38.PS 40:8.MATT 26:42.MATT 7:21.ROM 2:13.JOHN 13:17.JAMES 4:17.ROM 12:2

EVENING

The ear tests words as the palate tastes food.

Beloved, do not believe every spirit, but test the spirits, whether they are of God; because many false prophets have gone out into the world. ◊ Do not judge according to appearance, but judge with righteous judgment. ◊ I speak as to wise men; judge for yourselves what I say. ◊ Let the word of Christ dwell in you richly in all wisdom.

He who has an ear, let him hear what the Spirit says. ◊ He who is spiritual judges all things.

Take heed what you hear. ◊ I know your works, . . . you have tested those who say they are apostles and are not, and have found them liars. ◊ Test all things; hold fast what is good.

He calls his own sheep by name and leads them out. And when he brings out his own sheep, he goes before them; and the sheep follow him, for they know his voice. Yet they will by no means follow a stranger, but will flee from him, for they do not know the voice of strangers.

JOB 34:3.1 JOHN 4:1.JOHN 7:24.1 COR 10:15.COL 3:16.REV 2:29.1 COR 2:15.MARK 4:24.REV 2:2.1 THESS 5:21.JOHN 10:3-5

JULY 16

MORNING

You shall be to Me a kingdom of priests and a holy nation.

You were slain, and have redeemed us to God by Your blood out of every tribe and tongue and people and nation, and have made us kings and priests to our God. ◊ You are a chosen generation, a royal priesthood, a holy nation, His own special people, that you may proclaim the praises of Him who called you out of darkness into His marvelous light.

You shall be named the Priests of the Lord, men shall call you the Servants of our God. ◊ Priests of God and of Christ.

Therefore, holy brethren, partakers of the heavenly calling, consider the Apostle and High Priest of our confession, Christ Jesus. ◊ Therefore by Him let us continually offer the sacrifice of praise to God, that is, the fruit of our lips, giving thanks to His name.

For we are His workmanship, created in Christ Jesus for good works, which God prepared beforehand that we should walk in them. ◊ The temple of God is holy, which temple you are.

EX 19:6.REV 5:9-10.1 PET 2:9.IS 61:6.REV 20:6.HEB 3:1.HEB 13:15.EPH 2:10.1 COR 3:17

EVENING

We made our prayer to our God, and . . . set a watch against them.

Watch and pray, lest you enter into temptation. ◊ Continue earnestly in prayer, being vigilant in it with thanksgiving. ◊ [Cast] all your care upon Him, for He cares for you. Be sober, be vigilant; because your adversary the devil walks about like a roaring lion, seeking whom he may devour. Resist him, steadfast in the faith.

Why do you call Me "Lord, Lord," and do not do the things which I say? ◊ But be doers of the word, and not hearers only, deceiving yourselves.

Why do you cry to Me? Tell the children of Israel to go forward.

Be anxious for nothing, but in everything by prayer and supplication, with thanksgiving, let your requests be made known to God; and the peace of God, which surpasses all understanding, will guard your hearts and minds through Christ Jesus.

NEH 4:9.MATT 26:41.COL 4:2.1 PET 5:7-9.LUKE 6:46.JAMES 1:22.EX 14:15.PHIL 4:6-7

MORNING

**You are a gracious and merciful God, slow to anger
and abundant in lovingkindness, One who relents
from doing harm.**

I pray, let the power of my Lord be great, just as You have spoken, saying, "The Lord is longsuffering and abundant in mercy, forgiving iniquity and transgression; but He by no means clears the guilty, visiting the iniquity of the fathers on the children to the third and fourth generation."

Oh, do not remember former iniquities against us! Let Your tender mercies come speedily to meet us. . . . Help us, O God of our salvation, for the glory of Your name; and deliver us, and provide atonement for our sins, for Your name's sake! ◊ O Lord, though our iniquities testify against us, do it for Your name's sake; for our backslidings are many, we have sinned against You. ◊ We acknowledge, O Lord, our wickedness and the iniquity of our fathers, for we have sinned against You.

If You, Lord, should mark iniquities, O Lord, who could stand? But there is forgiveness with You, that You may be feared.

JON 4:2.NUM 14:17-18.PS 79:8-9.JER 14:7.JER 14:20.PS 130:3-4

EVENING

**God . . . chose you for salvation through sanctification
by the Spirit.**

Awake, O north wind, and come, O south! Blow upon my garden, that its spices may flow out.

Observe this very thing, that you sorrowed in a godly manner: What diligence it produced in you, what clearing of yourselves, what indignation, what fear, what vehement desire, what zeal, what vindication! ◊ The fruit of the Spirit is in all goodness, righteousness, and truth, proving what is acceptable to the Lord.

The Helper, the Holy Spirit . . . will teach you. ◊ The love of God has been poured out in our hearts by the Holy Spirit who was given to us.

The fruit of the Spirit is love, joy, peace.

In a great trial of affliction the abundance of their joy and their deep poverty abounded in the riches of their liberality.

One and the same Spirit works all these things, distributing to each one individually as He wills.

2 THESS 2:13.SONG 4:16.2 COR 7:11.EPH 5:9-10.JOHN 14:26.ROM
5:5.GAL 5:22.2 COR 8:2.1 COR 12:11

JULY 18

MORNING

He calls his own sheep by name and leads them out.

The solid foundation of God stands, having this seal: "The Lord knows those who are His," and, "Let everyone who names the name of Christ depart from iniquity." ◊ Many will say to Me in that day, "Lord, Lord, have we not prophesied in Your name, cast out demons in Your name, and done many wonders in Your name?" And then I will declare to them, "I never knew you; depart from Me, you who practice lawlessness!" ◊ The Lord knows the way of the righteous, but the way of the ungodly shall perish.

See, I have inscribed you on the palms of My hands; your walls are continually before Me. ◊ Set me as a seal upon your heart, as a seal upon your arm. ◊ The Lord is good, a stronghold in the day of trouble; and He knows those who trust in Him.

I go to prepare a place for you. And if I go and prepare a place for you, I will come again and receive you to Myself; that where I am, there you may be also.

JOHN 10:3.2 TIM 2:19.MATT 7:22-23.PS 1:6.IS 49:16.SONG 8:6.NAH 1:7.JOHN 14:2-3

EVENING

She has done what she could.

This poor widow has put in more than all. ◊ Whoever gives you a cup of water to drink in My name, because you belong to Christ, assuredly, I say to you, he will by no means lose his reward. ◊ If there is first a willing mind, it is accepted according to what one has, and not according to what he does not have.

Let us not love in word or in tongue, but in deed and in truth. ◊ If a brother or sister is naked and destitute of daily food, . . . and one of you says to them, "Depart in peace, be warmed and filled," but you do not give them the things which are needed for the body, what does it profit? ◊ He who sows bountifully will also reap bountifully. So let each one give as he purposes in his heart, not grudgingly or of necessity; for God loves a cheerful giver.

When you have done all those things which you are commanded, say, "We are unprofitable servants. We have done what was our duty to do."

MARK 14:8.LUKE 21:3.MARK 9:41.2 COR 8:12.1 JOHN 3:18.JAMES 2:15-16.2 COR 9:6-7.LUKE 17:10

MORNING

**He who is mighty has done great things for me, and
holy is His name.**

Who is like You, O Lord, among the gods? Who is like You, glorious in holiness, fearful in praises, doing wonders? ◊ Among the gods there is none like You, O Lord; nor are there any works like Your works. ◊ Who shall not fear You, O Lord, and glorify Your name? For You alone are holy. ◊ Hallowed be Your name.

Blessed is the Lord God of Israel, for He has visited and redeemed His people.

Who is this who comes from Edom, with dyed garments from Bozrah, this One who is glorious in His apparel, traveling in the greatness of His strength? I who speak in righteousness, mighty to save. ◊ I have given help to one who is mighty; I have exalted one chosen from the people.

Now to Him who is able to do exceedingly abundantly above all that we ask or think, according to the power that works in us, . . . be glory.

LUKE 1:49.EX 15:11.PS 86:8.REV 15:4.MATT 6:9.LUKE 1:68.IS 63:1.PS
89:19.EPH 3:20-21

EVENING

**To dwell together in unity . . . is like the dew
of Hermon.**

Mount Sion (that is, Hermon). ◊ There the Lord commanded the blessing—life forevermore. ◊ I will be like the dew to Israel; He shall grow like the lily, and lengthen his roots like Lebanon.

Let my teaching drop as the rain, my speech distill as the dew, as raindrops on the tender herb, and as showers on the grass. ◊ As the rain comes down, and the snow from heaven, and do not return there, but water the earth, and make it bring forth and bud, that it may give seed to the sower and bread to the eater, . . . so shall My word be that goes forth from My mouth; it shall not return to Me void, but it shall accomplish what I please, and it shall prosper in the thing for which I sent it.

God does not give the Spirit by measure. ◊ And of His fullness we have all received, and grace for grace. ◊ It is like the precious oil upon the head, running down on the beard . . . of Aaron, running down on the edge of his garments.

PS 133:1,3.DEUT 4:48.PS 133:3.HOS 14:5.DEUT 32:2.IS 55:10-11.JOHN
3:34.JOHN 1:16.PS 133:2

JULY 20

MORNING

They are not of the world, just as I am not of the world.

He is despised and rejected by men, a man of sorrows and acquainted with grief. ◊ In the world you will have tribulation; but be of good cheer, I have overcome the world.

Such a High Priest was fitting for us, who is holy, harmless, undefiled, separate from sinners. ◊ That you may become blameless and harmless, children of God without fault in the midst of a crooked and perverse generation.

Jesus of Nazareth . . . went about doing good and healing all who were oppressed by the devil, for God was with Him. ◊ Therefore, as we have opportunity, let us do good to all, especially to those who are of the household of faith.

That was the true Light which gives light to every man who comes into the world. ◊ You are the light of the world. A city that is set on a hill cannot be hidden. . . . Let your light so shine before men, that they may see your good works and glorify your Father in heaven.

JOHN 17:16.IS 53:3.JOHN 16:33.HEB 7:26.PHIL 2:15.ACTS 10:38.GAL
6:10.JOHN 1:9.MATT 5:14,16

EVENING

He who is of a merry heart has a continual feast.

The joy of the Lord is your strength. ◊ The kingdom of God is not food and drink, but righteousness and peace and joy in the Holy Spirit. ◊ Be filled with the Spirit, speaking to one another in psalms and hymns and spiritual songs, singing and making melody in your heart to the Lord, giving thanks always for all things to God the Father in the name of our Lord Jesus Christ.

By Him let us continually offer the sacrifice of praise to God, that is, the fruit of our lips, giving thanks to His name.

Though the fig tree may not blossom, nor fruit be on the vines; though the labor of the olive may fail, and the fields yield no food; though the flock be cut off from the fold, and there be no herd in the stalls—yet I will rejoice in the Lord, I will joy in the God of my salvation. ◊ Sorrowful, yet always rejoicing. ◊ We also glory in tribulations.

PROV 15:15.NEH 8:10.ROM 14:17.EPH 5:18-20.HEB 13:15.HAB 3:17-
18.2 COR 6:10.ROM 5:3

MORNING

What is the profit of circumcision?

Much in every way! ◊ Circumcise yourselves to the Lord, and take away the foreskins of your hearts. ◊ If their uncircumcised hearts are humbled, and they accept their guilt—then I will remember My covenant with Jacob, and My covenant with Isaac and My covenant with Abraham I will remember.

Jesus Christ has become a servant to the circumcision for the truth of God, to confirm the promises made to the fathers. ◊ In Him you were also circumcised with the circumcision made without hands, by putting off the body of the sins of the flesh, by the circumcision of Christ. ◊ You, being dead in your trespasses and the uncircumcision of your flesh, He has made alive together with Him, having forgiven you all trespasses.

Put off, concerning your former conduct, the old man which grows corrupt according to the deceitful lusts, and be renewed in the spirit of your mind, and . . . put on the new man which was created according to God, in righteousness and true holiness.

ROM 3:1.ROM 3:2.JER 4:4.LEV 26:41-42.ROM 15:8.COL 2:11.COL 2:13.EPH 4:22-24

EVENING

The veil of the temple was torn in two from top to bottom.

The Lord Jesus on the same night in which He was betrayed took bread; and when He had given thanks, He broke it and said, "Take, eat; this is My body which is broken for you; do this in remembrance of Me." ◊ The bread that I shall give is My flesh, which I shall give for the life of the world.

Unless you eat the flesh of the Son of Man and drink His blood, you have no life in you. Whoever eats My flesh and drinks My blood has eternal life. . . . He who eats My flesh and drinks My blood abides in Me, and I in him. As the living Father sent Me, and I live because of the Father, so he who feeds on Me will live because of Me. ◊ Does this offend you? What then if you should see the Son of Man ascend where He was before? It is the Spirit who gives life; the flesh profits nothing.

Enter the Holiest . . . by a new and living way which He consecrated for us, through the veil, that is, His flesh. . . . Let us draw near.

MATT 27:51.1 COR 11:23-24.JOHN 6:51.JOHN 6:53-54,56-57.JOHN 6:61-63.HEB 10:20,22

JULY 22

For the death that He died, He died to sin once for all; but the life that He lives, He lives to God.

He was numbered with the transgressors. ◊ Christ was offered once to bear the sins of many. ◊ [He] Himself bore our sins in His own body on the tree, that we, having died to sins, might live for righteousness—by whose stripes you were healed. ◊ By one offering He has perfected forever those who are being sanctified.

But He, because He continues forever, has an unchangeable priesthood. Therefore He is also able to save to the uttermost those who come to God through Him, since He ever lives to make intercession for them. ◊ While we were still sinners, Christ died for us. Much more then, having now been justified by His blood, we shall be saved from wrath through Him.

Therefore, since Christ suffered for us in the flesh, arm yourselves also with the same mind, for he who has suffered in the flesh has ceased from sin, that he no longer should live the rest of his time in the flesh for the lusts of men, but for the will of God.

ROM 6:10.IS 53:12.HEB 9:28.1 PET 2:24.HEB 10:14.HEB 7:24-25.ROM 5:8-9.1 PET 4:1-2

Keep yourselves in the love of God.

Abide in Me, and I in you. As the branch cannot bear fruit of itself, unless it abides in the vine, neither can you, unless you abide in Me. I am the vine, you are the branches. He who abides in Me, and I in him, bears much fruit; for without Me you can do nothing.

The fruit of the Spirit is love.

By this My Father is glorified, that you bear much fruit; so you will be My disciples. As the Father loved Me, I also have loved you; abide in My love. If you keep My commandments, you will abide in My love, just as I have kept My Father's commandments and abide in His love. ◊ Whoever keeps His word, truly the love of God is perfected in him.

This is My commandment, that you love one another as I have loved you. ◊ God demonstrates His own love toward us, in that while we were still sinners, Christ died for us. ◊ God is love, and he who abides in love abides in God, and God in him.

JUDE 1:21.JOHN 15:4-5.GAL 5:22.JOHN 15:8-10.1 JOHN 2:5.JOHN 15:12.ROM 5:8.1 JOHN 4:16

MORNING

Then comes the end.

Of that day and hour no one knows, neither the angels in heaven, nor the Son, but only the Father. Take heed, watch and pray; for you do not know when the time is. And what I say to you, I say to all: Watch! ◊ The Lord is not slack concerning His promise, as some count slackness, but is longsuffering toward us, not willing that any should perish but that all should come to repentance. ◊ The coming of the Lord is at hand. . . . The Judge is standing at the door! ◊ Surely I am coming quickly.

Therefore, since all these things will be dissolved, what manner of persons ought you to be in holy conduct and godliness?

The end of all things is at hand; therefore be serious and watchful in your prayers. ◊ Let your waist be girded and your lamps burning; and you yourselves be like men who wait for their master, when he will return from the wedding, that when he comes and knocks they may open to him immediately.

1 COR 15:24.MARK 13:32-33.MARK 13:37.2 PET 3:9.JAMES 5:8-9.REV 22:20.PET 3:11.1 PET 4:7.LUKE 12:35-36

EVENING

Brethren, pray for us.

Is anyone among you sick? Let him call for the elders of the church, and let them pray over him. . . . And the prayer of faith will save the sick, and the Lord will raise him up. . . . Pray for one another, that you may be healed. The effective, fervent prayer of a righteous man avails much. Elijah was a man with a nature like ours, and he prayed earnestly that it would not rain; and it did not rain on the land for three years and six months. And he prayed again, and the heaven gave rain, and the earth produced its fruit.

[Pray] always with all prayer and supplication in the Spirit, being watchful to this end with all perseverance and supplication for all the saints.

Without ceasing I make mention of you always in my prayers. ◊ Always laboring fervently for you in prayers, that you may stand perfect and complete in all the will of God.

1 THESS 5:25.JAMES 5:14-18.EPH 6:18.ROM 1:9.COL 4:12

JULY 24

[Be] patient in tribulation.

It is the Lord. Let Him do what seems good to Him. ◊ For though I were righteous, I could not answer Him; I would beg mercy of my Judge. ◊ The Lord gave, and the Lord has taken away; blessed be the name of the Lord. ◊ Shall we indeed accept good from God, and shall we not accept adversity?

Jesus wept. ◊ A man of sorrows and acquainted with grief. . . . Surely He has borne our griefs and carried our sorrows.

Whom the Lord loves He chastens, and scourges every son whom He receives. . . . Now no chastening seems to be joyful for the present, but grievous; nevertheless, afterward it yields the peaceable fruit of righteousness to those who have been trained by it. ◊ [Be] strengthened with all might, according to His glorious power, for all patience and longsuffering with joy. ◊ In the world you will have tribulation; but be of good cheer, I have overcome the world.

ROM 12:12.1 SAM 3:18.JOB 9:15.JOB 1:21.JOB 2:10.JOHN 11:35.IS 53:3-4.HEB 12:6,11.COL 1:11.JOHN 16:33

EVENING

He did not waver at the promise of God through unbelief.

Have faith in God. . . . Whoever says to this mountain, "Be removed and be cast into the sea," and does not doubt in his heart, but believes that those things he says will come to pass, he will have whatever he says. Therefore I say to you, whatever things you ask when you pray, believe that you receive them, and you will have them. ◊ Without faith it is impossible to please Him, for he who comes to God must believe that He is, and that He is a rewarder of those who diligently seek Him.

He who had received the promises offered up his only begotten son, of whom it was said, "In Isaac your seed shall be called," accounting that God was able to raise him up, even from the dead. ◊ [Abraham was] fully convinced that what He had promised He was also able to perform.

Is anything too hard for the Lord? ◊ With God all things are possible. ◊ Lord, increase our faith.

ROM 4:20.MARK 11:22-24.HEB 11:6.HEB 11:17-19.ROM 4:21.GEN 18:14.MATT 19:26.LUKE 17:5

MORNING

We know that we have passed from death to life.

He who hears My word and believes in Him who sent Me has everlasting life, and shall not come into judgment, but has passed from death into life. ◊ He who has the Son has life; he who does not have the Son of God does not have life.

He who establishes us with you in Christ and has anointed us is God, who also has sealed us and given us the Spirit in our hearts as a deposit. ◊ By this we know that we are of the truth, and shall assure our hearts before Him. . . . Beloved, if our heart does not condemn us, we have confidence toward God. ◊ We know that we are of God, and the whole world lies under the sway of the wicked one.

You He made alive, who were dead in trespasses and sins. ◊ [He] made us alive together with Christ. ◊ He has delivered us from the power of darkness and translated us into the kingdom of the Son of His love.

1 JOHN 3:14.JOHN 5:24.1 JOHN 5:12.2 COR 1:21-22.1 JOHN 3:19,
21.JOHN 5:19.EPH 2:1.EPH 2:5.COL 1:13

EVENING

You will show me the path of life.

Thus says the Lord: "Behold, I set before you the way of life and the way of death." ◊ I will teach you the good and the right way. ◊ I am the way, the truth, and the life. No one comes to the Father except through Me. ◊ Follow Me.

There is a way which seems right to a man, but its end is the way of death. ◊ Enter by the narrow gate; for wide is the gate and broad is the way that leads to destruction, and there are many who go in by it. Because narrow is the gate and difficult is the way which leads to life, and there are few who find it.

A highway shall be there, and a road, and it shall be called the Highway of Holiness. The unclean shall not pass over it, but it shall be for others. Whoever walks the road, although a fool, shall not go astray. ◊ Let us know, let us pursue the knowledge of the Lord.

In My Father's house are many mansions; if it were not so, I would have told you. I go to prepare a place for you.

PS 16:11.JER 21:8.1 SAM 12:23.JOHN 14:6.MATT 4:19.PROV
14:12.MATT 7:13-14.IS 35:8.HOS 6:3.JOHN 14:2

MORNING

**By faith Abraham obeyed when he was called to go
out to the place which he would afterward receive as
an inheritance.**

He will choose our inheritance for us. ◊ He encircled him, He instructed him, He kept him as the apple of His eye. As an eagle stirs up its nest, hovers over its young, spreading out its wings, taking them up, carrying them on its wings, so the Lord alone led him, and there was no foreign god with him.

I am the Lord your God, who teaches you to profit, who leads you by the way you should go. ◊ Who teaches like Him?

We walk by faith, not by sight. ◊ Here we have no continuing city, but we seek the one to come. ◊ Beloved, I beg you as sojourners and pilgrims, abstain from fleshly lusts which war against the soul. ◊ Arise and depart, for this is not your rest; because it is defiled, it shall destroy you, even with utter destruction.

HEB 11:8.PS 47:4.DEUT 32:10-12.IS 48:17.JOB 36:22.2 COR 5:7.HEB
13:14.1 PET 2:11.MIC 2:10

EVENING

Give thanks at the remembrance of His holy name.

The heavens are not pure in His sight, . . . how much less man, who is abominable and filthy, who drinks iniquity like water! ◊ The stars are not pure in His sight, . . . how much less man, who is a maggot?

Who is like You, O Lord, among the gods? Who is like You, glorious in holiness? ◊ Holy, holy, holy is the Lord of hosts.

As He who called you is holy, you also be holy in all your conduct, . . . because it is written, "Be holy, for I am holy." ◊ Be partakers of His holiness.

The temple of God is holy, which temple you are. ◊ What manner of persons ought you to be in holy conduct and godliness? . . . Be found by Him in peace, without spot and blameless.

Let no corrupt communication proceed out of your mouth, but what is good for necessary edification. . . . And do not grieve the Holy Spirit of God, by whom you were sealed for the day of redemption.

PS 97:12.JOB 15:15-16.JOB 25:5-6.EX 15:11.IS 6:3.1 PET 1:15-16.HEB
12:10.1 COR 3:17.2 PET 3:11,14.EPH 4:29-30

MORNING

Christ, who is the image of God.

The glory of the Lord shall be revealed, and all flesh shall see it together. ◇ No one has seen God at any time. The only begotten Son, who is in the bosom of the Father, He has declared Him. ◇ And the Word became flesh and dwelt among us, and we beheld His glory, the glory as of the only begotten of the Father, full of grace and truth. ◇ He who has seen Me has seen the Father. ◇ The brightness of His glory and the express image of His person. ◇ God was manifested in the flesh.

In whom we have redemption through His blood, the forgiveness of sins. He is the image of the invisible God, the firstborn over all creation. ◇ Whom He foreknew, He also predestined to be conformed to the image of His Son, that He might be the firstborn among many brethren.

As we have borne the image of the man of dust, we shall also bear the image of the heavenly Man.

2 COR 4:4.IS 40:5.JOHN 1:18.JOHN 1:14.JOHN 14:9.HEB 1:3.1 TIM
3:16.COL 1:14-15.ROM 8:29.1 COR 15:49

EVENING

You have armed me with strength for the battle.

When I am weak, then I am strong.

Asa cried out to the Lord his God, and said, "Lord, it is nothing for You to help, whether with many or with those who have no power; help us, O Lord our God, for we rest on You, and in Your name we go against this multitude. O Lord, You are our God; do not let man prevail against You!" ◇ Jehoshaphat cried out, and the Lord helped him.

It is better to trust in the Lord than to put confidence in man. It is better to trust in the Lord than to put confidence in princes. ◇ No king is saved by the multitude of an army; a mighty man is not delivered by great strength. A horse is a vain hope for safety; neither shall it deliver any by its great strength.

We do not wrestle against flesh and blood, but against principalities, against powers, against the rulers of the darkness of this age, against spiritual hosts of wickedness in the heavenly places. Therefore take up the whole armor of God.

PS 18:39.2 COR 12:10.2 CHR 14:11.2 CHR 18:31.PS 118:8-9.PS
33:16-17.EPH 6:12-13

MORNING

Walk in love.

A new commandment I give to you, that you love one another; as I have loved you, that you also love one another. ◊ Above all things have fervent love for one another, for love will cover a multitude of sins. ◊ Love covers all sins.

Whenever you stand praying, if you have anything against anyone, forgive him, that your Father in heaven may also forgive you your trespasses. ◊ Love your enemies, do good, and lend, hoping for nothing in return. ◊ Do not rejoice when your enemy falls, and do not let your heart be glad when he stumbles. ◊ Not returning evil for evil or reviling for reviling, but on the contrary blessing, knowing that you were called to this, that you may inherit a blessing. ◊ If it is possible, as much as depends on you, live peaceably with all men. ◊ Be kind to one another, tenderhearted, forgiving one another, just as God in Christ also forgave you.

My little children, let us not love in word or in tongue, but in deed and in truth.

EPH 5:2.JOHN 13:34.1 PET 4:8.PROV 10:12.MARK 11:25.LUKE 6:35.PROV 24:17.PET 3:9.ROM 12:18.EPH 4:32.1 JOHN 3:18

EVENING

Let your requests be made known to God.

Abba, Father, all things are possible for You. Take this cup away from Me; nevertheless, not what I will, but what You will. ◊ A thorn in the flesh was given to me. . . . Concerning this thing I pleaded with the Lord three times that it might depart from me. And He said to me, "My grace is sufficient for you, for My strength is made perfect in weakness." Therefore most gladly I will rather boast in my infirmities.

I pour out my complaint before Him; I declare before Him my trouble. ◊ Hannah . . . was in bitterness of soul, and prayed to the Lord and wept in anguish. She made a vow and said, "O Lord of hosts, if You will indeed look on the affliction of your maidservant and . . . will give your maidservant a male child, then I will give him to the Lord all the days of his life." . . . So it came to pass.

We do not know what we should pray for as we ought. ◊ He will choose our inheritance for us.

PHIL 4:6.MARK 14:36.2 COR 12:7-9.PS 142:2.1 SAM 1:9-11,20.ROM 8:26.PS 47:4

MORNING———————————————————————————

**Oh, that You would rend the heavens! That You
would come down!**

Make haste, my beloved, and be like a gazelle or a young stag on the
mountains of spices. ◊ We ourselves groan within ourselves, eagerly
waiting for the adoption, the redemption of our body. ◊ Bow down Your
heavens, O Lord, and come down; touch the mountains, and they shall
smoke.

This same Jesus, who was taken up from you into heaven, will so come
in like manner as you saw Him go into heaven. ◊ To those who eagerly
wait for Him He will appear a second time, apart from sin, for salvation.
◊ It will be said in that day: "Behold, this is our God; we have waited for
Him, and He will save us. This is the Lord; we have waited for Him; we
will be glad and rejoice in His salvation."

He who testifies to these things says, "Surely I am coming quickly."
Amen. Even so, come, Lord Jesus! ◊ The blessed hope and glorious
appearing of our great God and Savior Jesus Christ. ◊ Our citizenship is
in heaven.

IS 64:1. SONG 8:14. ROM 8:23. PS 144:5. ACTS 1:11. HEB 9:28. IS 25:9. REV
22:20. TITUS 2:13. PHIL 3:20

EVENING———————————————————————————

**You have given me the heritage of those who fear
Your name.**

"No weapon formed against you shall prosper, and every tongue
which rises against you in judgment you shall condemn. This is the
heritage of the servants of the Lord, and their righteousness is from Me,"
says the Lord. ◊ The angel of the Lord encamps all around those who
fear Him, and delivers them. Oh, taste and see that the Lord is good;
blessed is the man who trusts in Him! . . . Oh, fear the Lord, you His
saints! There is no want to those who fear Him. The young lions lack and
suffer hunger; but those who seek the Lord shall not lack any good thing.
◊ The lines have fallen to me in pleasant places; yes, I have a good
inheritance.

To you who fear My name the Sun of Righteousness shall arise with
healing in His wings; and you shall go out and grow fat like stall-fed
calves. ◊ He who did not spare His own Son, but delivered Him up for
us all, how shall He not with Him also freely give us all things?

PS 61:5. IS 54:17. PS 34:7-10. PS 16:6. MAL 4:2. ROM 8:32

MORNING

Seek those things which are above, where Christ is, sitting at the right hand of God.

Get wisdom! Get understanding! ◇ The wisdom that is from above. ◇ The deep says, "It is not in me"; and the sea says, "It is not with me." ◇ We were buried with Him through baptism into death, that just as Christ was raised from the dead by the glory of the Father, even so we also should walk in newness of life. For if we have been united together in the likeness of His death, certainly we also shall be in the likeness of His resurrection.

Let us lay aside every weight, and the sin which so easily ensnares us, and let us run with endurance the race that is set before us. ◇ God . . . made us alive together with Christ . . . and raised us up together, and made us sit together in the heavenly places in Christ Jesus.

Those who say such things declare plainly that they seek a homeland. ◇ Seek the Lord, all you meek of the earth, who have upheld His justice. Seek righteousness, seek humility.

COL 3:1.PROV 4:5.JAMES 3:17.JOB 28:14.ROM 6:4-5.HEB 12:1.EPH 2:4-6.HEB 11:14.ZEPH 2:3

EVENING

Nicodemus . . . came to Jesus by night.

Peter followed Him at a distance. ◇ Among the rulers many believed in Him, but because of the Pharisees they did not confess Him, lest they should be put out of the synagogue; for they loved the praise of men more than the praise of God. ◇ The fear of man brings a snare, but whoever trusts in the Lord shall be safe.

The one who comes to Me I will by no means cast out. ◇ A bruised reed He will not break, and smoking flax He will not quench. ◇ If you have faith as a mustard seed . . . nothing will be impossible for you.

God has not given us a spirit of fear, but of power and of love and of a sound mind. Therefore do not be ashamed of the testimony of our Lord. ◇ Little children, abide in Him, that when He appears, we may have confidence and not be ashamed before Him at His coming. ◇ Whoever confesses Me before men, him I will also confess before My Father who is in heaven.

JOHN 7:50.MATT 26:58.JOHN 12:42-43.PROV 29:25.JOHN 6:37.IS 42:3.MATT 17:20.2 TIM 1:7-8.1 JOHN 2:28.MATT 10:32

MORNING

Endure hardship as a good soldier of Jesus Christ.

I have given him as a witness to the people, a leader and commander for the people. ◊ It was fitting for Him, for whom are all things and by whom are all things, in bringing many sons to glory, to make the author of their salvation perfect through sufferings. ◊ We must through many tribulations enter the kingdom of God.

We do not wrestle against flesh and blood, but against principalities, against powers, against the rulers of the darkness of this age, against spiritual hosts of wickedness in the heavenly places. Therefore take up the whole armor of God. ◊ We do not war according to the flesh. For the weapons of our warfare are not carnal but mighty in God for pulling down strongholds.

May the God of all grace, who called us to His eternal glory by Christ Jesus, after you have suffered a while, perfect, establish, strengthen, and settle you.

2 TIM 2:3. IS 55:4. HEB 2:10. ACTS 14:22. EPH 6:12-13. 2 COR 10:3-4. 1 PET 5:10

EVENING

Keep the the unity of the Spirit.

There is one body and one Spirit. ◊ Through Him we both have access by one Spirit to the Father. Now, therefore, you are no longer strangers and foreigners, but fellow citizens with the saints and members of the household of God, having been built on the foundation of the apostles and prophets, Jesus Christ Himself being the chief cornerstone, in whom the whole building, being joined together, grows into a holy temple in the Lord, in whom you also are being built together for a habitation of God in the Spirit.

Behold, how good and how pleasant it is for brethren to dwell together in unity! It is like the precious oil upon the head, running down on the beard, the beard of Aaron, running down on the edge of his garments.

Since you have purified your souls in obeying the truth through the Spirit in sincere love of the brethren, love one another fervently with a pure heart.

EPH 4:3. EPH 4:4. EPH 2:18-22. PS 133:1-2. 1 PET 1:22

MORNING

The fruit of the Spirit is . . . faithfulness.

By grace you have been saved through faith, and that not of yourselves; it is the gift of God. ◊ Without faith it is impossible to please Him. ◊ He who believes in Him is not condemned; but he who does not believe is already, because he has not believed in the name of the only begotten Son of God. ◊ Lord, I believe; help my unbelief!

Whoever keeps His word, truly the love of God is perfected in him. By this we know that we are in Him. ◊ Faith working through love. ◊ Faith without works is dead.

We walk by faith, not by sight. ◊ I have been crucified with Christ; it is no longer I who live, but Christ lives in me; and the life which I now live in the flesh I live by faith in the Son of God, who loved me and gave Himself for me. ◊ Jesus Christ whom having not seen you love. Though now you do not see Him, yet believing, you rejoice with joy inexpressible and full of glory, receiving the end of your faith—the salvation of your souls.

GAL 5:22.EPH 2:8.HEB 11:6.JOHN 3:18.MARK 9:24.1 JOHN 2:5.GAL 5:6.JAMES 2:20.2 COR 5:7.GAL 2:20.1 PET 1:7-9

EVENING

The Lord is very compassionate and merciful.

As a father pities his children, so the Lord pities those who fear Him. ◊ The Lord is gracious and full of compassion. He will ever be mindful of His covenant.

He who keeps you will not slumber. Behold, He who keeps Israel shall neither slumber nor sleep. ◊ As an eagle stirs up its nest, hovers over its young, spreading out its wings, taking them up, carrying them on its wings, . . . so the Lord alone led him, and there was no foreign god with him.

His compassions fail not. They are new every morning; great is Your faithfulness.

When Jesus went out He saw a great multitude; and He was moved with compassion for them, and healed their sick. ◊ The same yesterday, today, and forever.

The very hairs of your head are all numbered. ◊ Are not two sparrows sold for a copper coin? And not one of them falls to the ground apart from your Father's will. ◊ Do not fear therefore.

JAMES 5:11.PS 103:13.PS 111:4-5.PS 121:3-4.DEUT 32:11-12.LAM 3:22-23.MATT 14:14.HEB 13:8.MATT 10:30.MATT 10:29.MATT 10:31

MORNING

The Lamb slain from the foundation of the world.

Your lamb shall be without blemish. . . . Then the whole assembly of the congregation of Israel shall kill it at twilight. And they shall take some of the blood and put it on the two doorposts and on the lintel of the houses where they eat it. . . . And when I see the blood, I will pass over you. ◊ The blood of sprinkling. ◊ Christ, our Passover, was sacrificed for us. ◊ Being delivered by the determined counsel and foreknowledge of God. ◊ God . . . saved us . . . according to His own purpose and grace which was given to us in Christ Jesus before time began.

We have redemption through His blood, the forgiveness of sins.

Therefore, since Christ suffered for us in the flesh, arm yourselves also with the same mind, for he who has suffered in the flesh has ceased from sin, that he no longer should live the rest of his time in the flesh for the lusts of men, but for the will of God.

REV 13:8.EX 12:5-7,13.HEB 12:24.1 COR 5:7.ACTS 2:23.2 TIM 1:9.EPH 1:7.1 PET 4:1-2

EVENING

I have trodden the winepress alone.

Who is like You, O Lord, among the gods? Who is like You, glorious in holiness, fearful in praises, doing wonders? ◊ He saw that there was no man, and wondered that there was no intercessor; therefore His own arm brought salvation for Him; and His own righteousness, it sustained Him. ◊ [He] Himself bore our sins in His own body on the tree. ◊ Having become a curse for us.

Oh, sing to the Lord a new song! For He has done marvelous things; His right hand and His holy arm have gained Him the victory. ◊ Having disarmed principalities and powers, He made a public spectacle of them, triumphing over them in it. ◊ He shall see the travail of His soul, and be satisfied. By His knowledge My righteous Servant shall justify many, for He shall bear their iniquities.

O my soul, march on in strength! ◊ We are more than conquerors through Him who loved us. ◊ They overcame . . . by the blood of the Lamb and by the word of their testimony.

IS 63:3.EX 15:11.IS 59:16.1 PET 2:24.GAL 3:13.PS 98:1.COL 2:15.IS 53:11.JUDG 5:21.ROM 8:37.REV 12:11

AUGUST 3

_____

His mercy is on those who fear Him.

Oh, how great is Your goodness, which You have laid up for those who fear You, which You have prepared for those who trust in You in the presence of the sons of men! You shall hide them in the secret place of Your presence from the plots of man; You shall keep them secretly in a pavilion from the strife of tongues.

If you call on the Father, who without partiality judges according to each one's work, conduct yourselves throughout the time of your sojourning here in fear. ◊ The Lord is near to all who call upon Him . . . in truth. He will fulfill the desire of those who fear Him; He also will hear their cry and save them.

"Because your heart was tender, and you humbled yourself before the Lord . . . and you tore your clothes and wept before Me, I also have heard you," says the Lord. ◊ On this one will I look: on him who is poor and of a contrite spirit, and who trembles at My word. ◊ The Lord is near to those who have a broken heart, and saves such as have a contrite spirit.

LUKE 1:50.PS 31:19-20.1 PET 1:17.PS 145:18-19.2 KIN 22:19.IS 66:2.PS
34:18

EVENING_____

Those who honor Me I will honor.

Whoever confesses Me before men, him I will also confess before My Father who is in heaven. ◊ He who loves father or mother more than Me is not worthy of Me. And he who loves son or daughter more than Me is not worthy of Me. And he who does not take his cross and follow after Me is not worthy of Me. He who finds his life will lose it, and he who loses his life for My sake will find it.

Blessed is the man who endures temptation; for when he has been proved, he will receive the crown of life which the Lord has promised to those who love Him.

Do not fear any of those things which you are about to suffer. Be faithful until death, and I will give you the crown of life.

Our light affliction, which is but for a moment, is working for us a far more exceeding and eternal weight of glory. ◊ Praise, honor, and glory at the revelation of Jesus Christ.

1 SAM 2:30.MATT 10:32.MATT 10:37-39.JAMES 1:12.REV 2:10.2 COR
4:17.1 PET 1:7

MORNING

"It is finished!" And bowing His head, He gave up His spirit.

Jesus, the author and finisher of our faith. ◊ I have glorified You on the earth. I have finished the work which You have given Me to do. ◊ We have been sanctified through the offering of the body of Jesus Christ once for all. And every priest stands ministering daily and offering repeatedly the same sacrifices, which can never take away sins. But this Man, after He had offered one sacrifice for sins forever, sat down at the right hand of God, from that time waiting till His enemies are made His footstool. For by one offering He has perfected forever those who are being sanctified. ◊ Having wiped out the handwriting of requirements that was against us, which was contrary to us. And He has taken it out of the way, having nailed it to the cross.

I lay down My life that I may take it again. No one takes it from Me, but I lay it down of Myself. I have power to lay it down, and I have power to take it again. ◊ Greater love has no one than this, than to lay down one's life for his friends.

JOHN 19:30.HEB 12:2.JOHN 17:4.HEB 10:10-14.COL 2:14.JOHN 10:17-18.JOHN 15:13

EVENING

He sent from above, He took me; He drew me out of many waters.

He also brought me up out of a horrible pit, out of the miry clay, and set my feet upon a rock, and established my steps. ◊ You He made alive, who were dead in trespasses and sins, in which you once walked according to the course of this world. . . . We all once conducted ourselves in the lusts of our flesh.

Hear my cry, O God; attend to my prayer. From the end of the earth I will cry to You, when my heart is overwhelmed. ◊ Out of the belly of Sheol I cried, and You heard my voice. For You cast me into the deep, into the heart of the seas, and the floods surrounded me; all Your billows and Your waves passed over me. ◊ We went through fire and through water; but You brought us out to rich fulfillment.

When you pass through the waters, I will be with you; and through the rivers, they shall not overflow you.

PS 18:16.PS 40:2.EPH 2:1-3.PS 61:1-2.JON 2:2-3.PS 66:12.IS 43:2

AUGUST 5

MORNING

Walk in newness of life.

As you presented your members as slaves of uncleanness, and of lawlessness leading to more lawlessness, so now present your members as slaves of righteousness for holiness. ◊ I beseech you . . . brethren, by the mercies of God, that you present your bodies a living sacrifice, holy, acceptable to God, which is your reasonable service. And do not be conformed to this world, but be transformed by the renewing of your mind.

If anyone is in Christ, he is a new creation; old things have passed away; behold, all things have become new. ◊ In Christ Jesus neither circumcision nor uncircumcision avails anything, but a new creation. And as many as walk according to this rule, peace and mercy be upon them. ◊ This I say, therefore, and testify in the Lord, that you should no longer walk as the rest of the Gentiles walk, in the futility of their mind. ◊ You have not so learned Christ, if indeed you have heard Him and have been taught by Him, as the truth is in Jesus. . . . Put on the new man which was created according to God, in righteousness and true holiness.

ROM 6:4.ROM 6:19.ROM 12:1-2.2 COR 5:17.GAL 6:15-16.EPH 4:17.EPH 4:20-21,24

EVENING

Your will be done.

O Lord, I know the way of man is not in himself; it is not in man who walks to direct his own steps. ◊ Not as I will, but as You will. ◊ Surely I have calmed and quieted my soul, like a weaned child with his mother; like a weaned child is my soul within me.

We do not know what we should pray for as we ought, but the Spirit Himself makes intercession for us with groanings which cannot be uttered. Now He who searches the hearts knows what the mind of the Spirit is, because He makes intercession for the saints according to the will of God.

You do not know what you ask. ◊ He gave them their request, but sent leanness into their soul. ◊ These things became our examples, to the intent that we should not lust after evil things as they also lusted.

I want you to be without care. ◊ You will keep him in perfect peace, whose mind is stayed on You, because he trusts in You.

MATT 26:42.JER 10:23.MATT 26:39.PS 131:2.ROM 8:26-27.MATT 20:22.PS 106:15.1 COR 10:6.1 COR 7:32.IS 26:3

MORNING

For whom the Lord loves He corrects.

Now see that I, even I, am He, and there is no God besides Me; I kill and I make alive; I wound and I heal; nor is there any who can deliver from My hand. ◊ I know the thoughts that I think toward you, says the Lord, thoughts of peace and not of evil, to give you a future and a hope. ◊ "My thoughts are not your thoughts, nor are your ways My ways," says the Lord.

I will allure her, will bring her into the wilderness, and speak comfort to her. ◊ As a man chastens his son, so the Lord your God chastens you. ◊ Now no chastening seems to be joyful for the present, but grievous; nevertheless, afterward it yields the peaceable fruit of righteousness to those who have been trained by it. ◊ Humble yourselves under the mighty hand of God, that He may exalt you in due time.

I know, O Lord, that Your judgments are right, and that in faithfulness You have afflicted me.

PROV 3:12.DEUT 32:39.JER 29:11.IS 55:8.HOS 2:14.DEUT 8:5.HEB 12:11.1 PET 5:6.PS 119:75

EVENING

The earth is the Lord's, and all its fullness.

She did not know that I gave her grain, new wine, and oil, and multiplied her silver and gold. . . . Therefore I will return and take away my grain in its time and My new wine in its season, and will take back My wool and My linen.

All things come from You, and of Your own we have given You. For we are aliens and pilgrims before You, as were all our fathers; our days on earth are as a shadow, and without hope. O Lord our God, all this abundance . . . is from Your hand, and is all Your own. ◊ Of Him and through Him and to Him are all things, to whom be glory forever. Amen.

The living God . . . gives us richly all things to enjoy. ◊ Every creature of God is good, and nothing is to be refused if it is received with thanksgiving; for it is sanctified by the word of God and prayer.

My God shall supply all your need according to His riches in glory by Christ Jesus.

PS 24:1.HOS 2:8-9.1 CHR 29:14-16.ROM 11:36.1 TIM 6:17.1 TIM 4:4-5.PHIL 4:19

AUGUST 7

The Helper, the Holy Spirit, . . . whom the Father will send in My name.

If you knew the gift of God, and who it is who says to you, "Give Me a drink," you would have asked Him, and He would have given you living water. ◊ If you . . . being evil, know how to give good gifts to your children, how much more will your heavenly Father give the Holy Spirit to those who ask Him! ◊ Most assuredly, I say to you, whatever you ask the Father in My name He will give you. Until now you have asked nothing in My name. Ask, and you will receive, that your joy may be full. ◊ You do not have because you do not ask.

When . . . the Spirit of truth, has come, He will guide you into all truth; for He will not speak on His own authority, but whatever He hears He will speak; and He will tell you things to come. He will glorify Me, for He will take of what is Mine and declare it to you.

They rebelled and grieved His Holy Spirit; so He turned Himself against them as an enemy, and He fought against them.

JOHN 14:26.JOHN 4:10.LUKE 11:13.JOHN 16:23-24.JAMES 4:2.JOHN 16:13-14.IS 63:10

EVENING

What do you think about the Christ?

Lift up your heads, O you gates! And lift them up, you everlasting doors! And the King of glory shall come in. Who is this King of glory? The Lord of hosts, He is the King of glory. ◊ He has on His robe and on His thigh a name written: KING OF KINGS AND LORD OF LORDS.

To you who believe, He is precious; but to those who are disobedient, the stone which the builders rejected has become the chief cornerstone. ◊ We preach Christ crucified, to the Jews a stumbling block and to the Greeks foolishness, but to those who are called, both Jews and Greeks, Christ the power of God and the wisdom of God.

I also count all things loss for the excellence of the knowledge of Christ Jesus my Lord, for whom I have suffered the loss of all things, and count them as rubbish, that I may gain Christ. ◊ Lord, You know all things; You know that I love You.

MATT 22:42.PS 24:9-10.REV 19:16.1 PET 2:7.1 COR 1:23-24.PHIL 3:8.JOHN 21:17

MORNING

**The path of the just is like the shining sun, that
shines ever brighter unto the perfect day.**

Not that I have already attained, or am already perfected; but I press on, that I may lay hold of that for which Christ Jesus has also laid hold of me. ◊ Let us know, let us pursue the knowledge of the Lord.

Then the righteous will shine forth as the sun in the kingdom of their Father. ◊ We all, with unveiled face, beholding as in a mirror the glory of the Lord, are being transformed into the same image from glory to glory, just as by the Spirit of the Lord. ◊ When that which is perfect has come, then that which is in part will be done away. . . . For now we see in a mirror, dimly, but then face to face. Now I know in part, but then I shall know just as I also am known. ◊ Beloved, now we are children of God; and it has not yet been revealed what we shall be, but we know that when He is revealed, we shall be like Him, for we shall see Him as He is. And everyone who has this hope in Him purifies himself, just as He is pure.

PROV 4:18.PHIL 3:12.HOS 6:3.MATT 13:43.2 COR 3:18.1 COR 13:10,12.1 JOHN 3:2-3

EVENING

**Whoever calls upon the name of the Lord
shall be saved.**

The one who comes to Me I will by no means cast out. ◊ "Lord, remember me when You come into Your kingdom." And Jesus said to him, "Assuredly, I say to you, today you will be with Me in Paradise." ◊ "What do you want Me to do for you?" They said to Him, "Lord, that our eyes may be opened." So Jesus had compassion and touched their eyes. And immediately their eyes received sight, and they followed Him.

If you then, being evil, know how to give good gifts to your children, how much more will your heavenly Father give the Holy Spirit to those who ask Him! ◊ I will put My Spirit within you. ◊ Thus says the Lord God: "I will also let the house of Israel inquire of Me to do this."

This is the confidence that we have in Him, that if we ask anything according to His will, He hears us. And if we know that He hears us, whatever we ask, we know that we have the petitions that we have asked of Him.

ROM 10:13.JOHN 6:37.LUKE 23:42-43.MATT 20:32-34.LUKE 11:13.EZEK 36:27.EZEK 36:37.1 JOHN 5:14-15

AUGUST 9

You are all fair, my love, and there is no spot in you.

The whole head is sick, and the whole heart faints. From the sole of the foot even to the head, there is no soundness in it, but wounds and bruises and putrefying sores; they have not been closed or bound up, or soothed with ointment. ◊ We are all like an unclean thing, and all our righteousnesses are like filthy rags. ◊ I know that in me (that is, in my flesh) nothing good dwells.

You were washed, . . . you were sanctified, . . . you were justified in the name of the Lord Jesus and by the Spirit of our God. ◊ The royal daughter is all glorious within. ◊ "Your beauty . . . was perfect through My splendor which I had bestowed on you," says the Lord God.

Let the beauty of the Lord our God be upon us.

These are the ones who . . . washed their robes and made them white in the blood of the Lamb. ◊ A glorious church, not having spot or wrinkle or any such thing, but . . . holy and without blemish. ◊ You are complete in Him.

SONG 4:7.IS 1:5-6.IS 64:6.ROM 7:18.1 COR 6:11.PS 45:13.EZEK 16:14.PS 90:17.REV 7:14.EPH 5:27.COL 2:10

Broken cisterns that can hold no water.

Eve . . . bore Cain, and said, "I have gotten a man from the Lord."

"Come, let us build ourselves a city, and a tower whose top is in the heavens." . . . The Lord scattered them. ◊ Lot chose for himself all the plain of Jordan. . . . It was well watered everywhere . . . like the garden of the Lord. . . . But the men of Sodom were exceedingly wicked and sinful against the Lord.

I set my heart to know wisdom and to know madness and folly. I perceived that this also is grasping for the wind. For in much wisdom is much grief, and he who increases knowledge increases sorrow. . . . I made my works great, I built myself houses, and planted myself vineyards. . . . I also gathered for myself silver and gold. . . . Then I looked on all . . . and indeed all was vanity and grasping for the wind.

If anyone thirsts, let him come to Me and drink. ◊ He satisfies the longing soul, and fills the hungry soul with goodness.

Set your mind on things above, not on things on the earth.

JER 2:13.GEN 4:1.GEN 11:4,8.GEN 13:11,10,13.ECCL 1:17-18;2:4,8, 11.JOHN 7:37.PS 107:9.COL 3:2

MORNING

**I do not pray that You should take them out of the
world, but that You should keep them from
the evil one.**

Blameless and harmless, children of God without fault in the midst of a crooked and perverse generation, among whom you shine as lights in the world. ◊ You are the salt of the earth; . . . the light of the world. ◊ Let your light so shine before men, that they may see your good works and glorify your Father in heaven.

I also withheld you from sinning against Me.

The Lord is faithful, who will establish you and guard you from the evil one. ◊ I did not do so, because of the fear of God. ◊ [He] gave Himself for our sins, that He might deliver us from this present evil age, according to the will of our God and Father. ◊ Now to Him who is able to keep you from stumbling, and to present you faultless before the presence of His glory with exceeding joy, to God our Savior, who alone is wise, be glory and majesty, dominion and power, both now and forever. Amen.

JOHN 17:15.PHIL 2:15.MATT 5:13-14.MATT 5:16.GEN 20:6.2 THESS 3:3.NEH 5:15.GAL 1:4.JUDE 1:24-25

EVENING

Whoever trusts in the Lord shall be safe.

The Lord is exalted, for He dwells on high. ◊ The Lord is high above all nations, and His glory above the heavens. . . . He raises the poor out of the dust, and lifts the needy out of the ash heap, that He may seat him with princes.

God, who is rich in mercy, because of His great love with which He loved us, even when we were dead in trespasses, made us alive together with Christ (by grace you have been saved), and raised us up together, and made us sit together in the heavenly places in Christ Jesus.

He who did not spare His own Son, but delivered Him up for us all, how shall He not with Him also freely give us all things? . . . For I am persuaded that neither death nor life, nor angels nor principalities nor powers, nor things present nor things to come, nor height nor depth, nor any other created thing, shall be able to separate us from the love of God which is in Christ Jesus our Lord.

PROV 29:25.IS 33:5.PS 113:4,7-8.EPH 2:4-6.ROM 8:32,38-39

MORNING_____

That through death He might destroy him who had the power of death.

Our Savior Jesus Christ . . . has abolished death and brought life and immortality to light through the gospel. ◊ He will swallow up death forever, and the Lord God will wipe away tears from all faces; the rebuke of His people He will take away from all the earth; for the Lord has spoken. ◊ When this corruptible has put on incorruption, and this mortal has put on immortality, then shall be brought to pass the saying that is written: "Death is swallowed up in victory." "O Death, where is your sting? O Hades, where is your victory?" The sting of death is sin, and the strength of sin is the law. But thanks be to God, who gives us the victory through our Lord Jesus Christ.

God has not given us a spirit of fear, but of power and of love and of a sound mind. ◊ Yea, though I walk through the valley of the shadow of death, I will fear no evil; for You are with me; Your rod and Your staff, they comfort me.

HEB 2:14.2 TIM 1:10.IS 25:8.1 COR 15:54-57.2 TIM 1:7.PS 23:4

EVENING_____

Where is the way to the dwelling of light?

God is light and in Him is no darkness at all. ◊ As long as I am in the world, I am the light of the world.

If we say that we have fellowship with Him, and walk in darkness, we lie and do not practice the truth. But if we walk in the light as He is in the light, we have fellowship with one another, and the blood of Jesus Christ His Son cleanses us from all sin. ◊ The Father . . . has qualified us to be partakers of the inheritance of the saints in the light. He has delivered us from the power of darkness and translated us into the kingdom of the Son of His love, in whom we have redemption through His blood, the forgiveness of sins.

You are all sons of light and sons of the day. We are not of the night nor of darkness. ◊ You are the light of the world. A city that is set on a hill cannot be hidden. . . . Let your light so shine before men, that they may see your good works and glorify your Father in heaven.

JOB 38:19.1 JOHN 1:5.JOHN 9:5.1 JOHN 1:6-7.COL 1:12-14.1 THESS
5:5.MATT 5:14,16

MORNING

The Lord will not cast off forever. Though He causes grief, yet He will show compassion.

"Do not fear, O Jacob My servant," . . . says the Lord, "for I am with you; . . . I will not make a complete end of you. I will rightly correct you." ◇ "For a mere moment I have forsaken you, but with great mercies I will gather you. With a little wrath I hid My face from you for a moment; but with everlasting kindness I will have mercy on you," says the Lord, your Redeemer. . . . "For the mountains shall depart and the hills be removed, but My kindness shall not depart from you, nor shall My covenant of peace be removed," says the Lord, who has mercy on you. "O you afflicted one, tossed with tempest, and not comforted, behold, I will lay your stones with colorful gems, and lay your foundations with sapphires."

I will bear the indignation of the Lord, because I have sinned against Him, until He pleads my case and executes justice for me; He will bring me forth to the light, and I will see His righteousness.

LAM 3:31-32.JER 46:28.IS 54:7-8,10-11.MIC 7:9

EVENING

God has chosen the weak things of the world to put to shame the things which are mighty.

When the children of Israel cried out to the Lord, the Lord raised up a deliverer for them: Ehud . . . a left-handed man. . . . After him was Shamgar . . . who killed six hundred men of the Philistines with an ox goad; and he also delivered Israel.

The Lord turned to [Gideon] and said, "Go in this might of yours. . . . Have I not sent you?" So he said to Him, "O my Lord, how can I save Israel? Indeed my clan is the weakest in Manasseh, and I am the least in my father's house."

The Lord said to Gideon, "The people who are with you are too many for Me . . . lest Israel claim glory for itself against Me, saying, 'My own hand has saved me.' "

"Not by might nor by power, but by My Spirit," says the Lord of hosts. ◇ My brethren, be strong in the Lord and in the power of His might.

1 COR 1:27.JUDG 3:15,31.JUDG 6:14-15.JUDG 7:2.ZECH 4:6.EPH 6:10

AUGUST 13

He has prepared a city for them.

If I go and prepare a place for you, I will come again and receive you to Myself; that where I am, there you may be also. ◊ An inheritance incorruptible and undefiled and that does not fade away, reserved in heaven for you. ◊ Here we have no continuing city, but we seek the one to come.

This same Jesus, who was taken up from you into heaven, will so come in like manner as you saw Him go into heaven. ◊ See how the farmer waits for the precious fruit of the earth, waiting patiently for it until it receives the early and latter rain. You also be patient. Establish your hearts, for the coming of the Lord is at hand. ◊ Yet a little while, and He who is coming will come and will not tarry.

We who are alive and remain shall be caught up together with them in the clouds to meet the Lord in the air. And thus we shall always be with the Lord. Therefore comfort one another with these words.

HEB 11:16. JOHN 14:3. 1 PET 1:4. HEB 13:14. ACTS 1:11. JAMES 5:7-8. HEB 10:37. 1 THESS 4:17-18

Base things of the world . . . God has chosen.

Do not be deceived. Neither fornicators, nor idolaters, nor adulterers, nor homosexuals, nor sodomites, nor thieves, nor covetous, nor drunkards, nor revilers, nor extortioners will inherit the kingdom of God. And such were some of you. But you were washed, but you were sanctified, but you were justified in the name of the Lord Jesus and by the Spirit of our God.

You He made alive, who were dead in trespasses and sins, in which you once walked according to the course of this world, . . . among whom also we all once conducted ourselves in the lusts of our flesh, fulfilling the desires of the flesh and of the mind.

According to His mercy He saved us, through the washing of regeneration and renewing of the Holy Spirit, whom He poured out on us abundantly through Jesus Christ our Savior.

"For My thoughts are not your thoughts, nor are your ways My ways," says the Lord.

1 COR 1:28. 1 COR 6:9-11. EPH 2:1-3. TITUS 3:5-6. IS 55:8

MORNING

The joy of the Lord is your strength.

Sing, O heavens! Be joyful, O earth! And break out in singing, O mountains! For the Lord has comforted His people, and will have mercy on His afflicted. ◊ Behold, God is my salvation, I will trust and not be afraid; for YAH, the Lord, is my strength and my song; He also has become my salvation. ◊ The Lord is my strength and my shield; my heart trusted in Him, and I am helped; therefore my heart greatly rejoices, and with my song I will praise Him. ◊ My soul shall be joyful in my God; for He has clothed me with the garments of salvation, He has covered me with the robe of righteousness, as a bridegroom decks himself with ornaments, and as a bride adorns herself with her jewels.

Therefore I have reason to glory in Christ Jesus in the things which pertain to God. ◊ We . . . rejoice in God through our Lord Jesus Christ, through whom we have now received the reconciliation. ◊ I will joy in the God of my salvation.

NEH 8:10.IS 49:13.IS 12:2.PS 28:7.IS 61:10.ROM 15:17.ROM 5:11.HAB 3:18

EVENING

He has made with me an everlasting covenant, ordered in all things and secure.

I know whom I have believed and am persuaded that He is able to keep what I have committed to Him until that Day.

Blessed be the God and Father of our Lord Jesus Christ, who has blessed us with every spiritual blessing in the heavenly places in Christ, just as He chose us in Him before the foundation of the world, that we should be holy and without blame before Him in love, having predestined us to adoption as sons by Jesus Christ to Himself, according to the good pleasure of His will.

We know that all things work together for good to those who love God, to those who are the called according to His purpose. For whom He foreknew, He also predestined to be conformed to the image of His Son. . . . Moreover whom He predestined, these He also called; whom He called, these He also justified; and whom He justified, these He also glorified.

2 SAM 23:5.2 TIM 1:12.EPH 1:3-5.ROM 8:28-30

AUGUST 15

**The God of peace . . . make you complete in every
good work to do His will.**

Become complete. Be of good comfort, be of one mind, live in peace; and the God of love and peace will be with you.

By grace you have been saved through faith, and that not of yourselves; it is the gift of God, not of works, lest anyone should boast. ◊ Every good gift and every perfect gift is from above, and comes down from the Father of lights, with whom there is no variation or shadow of turning.

Work out your own salvation with fear and trembling; for it is God who works in you both to will and to do for His good pleasure. ◊ Be transformed by the renewing of your mind, that you may prove what is that good and acceptable and perfect will of God. ◊ [Be] filled with the fruits of righteousness which are by Jesus Christ, to the glory and praise of God.

Not that we are sufficient of ourselves to think of anything as being from ourselves, but our sufficiency is from God.

HEB 13:20-21.2 COR 13:11.EPH 2:8-9.JAMES 1:17.PHIL 2:12-13.ROM
12:2.PHIL 1:11.2 COR 3:5

EVENING

**I will allure her, will bring her into the wilderness,
and speak comfort to her.**

Come out from among them and be separate, says the Lord. Do not touch what is unclean, and I will receive you. . . . I will be a Father to you, and you shall be My sons and daughters, says the Lord Almighty. ◊ Therefore, having these promises, beloved, let us cleanse ourselves from all filthiness of the flesh and spirit, perfecting holiness in the fear of God.

Jesus . . . that He might sanctify the people with His own blood, suffered outside the gate. Therefore let us go forth to Him, outside the camp, bearing His reproach.

[Jesus] said, . . . "Come aside by yourselves to a deserted place and rest a while." ◊ The Lord is my shepherd; I shall not want. He makes me to lie down in green pastures; He leads me beside the still waters. He restores my soul; He leads me in the paths of righteousness for His name's sake.

HOS 2:14.2 COR 6:17-18.2 COR 7:1.HEB 13:12-13.MARK 6:31.PS 23:1-3

MORNING

**The house that is to be built for the Lord must be
exceedingly magnificent.**

You . . . as living stones, are being built up a spiritual house. ◊ Do you not know that you are the temple of God and that the Spirit of God dwells in you? If anyone defiles the temple of God, God will destroy him. For the temple of God is holy, which temple you are. ◊ Your body is the temple of the Holy Spirit who is in you, whom you have from God, and you are not your own. For you were bought at a price; therefore glorify God in your body and in your spirit, which are God's. ◊ What agreement has the temple of God with idols? For you are the temple of the living God. As God has said: "I will dwell in them and walk among them. I will be their God, and they shall be My people." ◊ You . . . having been built on the foundation of the apostles and prophets, Jesus Christ Himself being the chief cornerstone, in whom the whole building, being joined together, grows into a holy temple in the Lord, in whom you also are being built together for a habitation of God in the Spirit.

1 CHR 22:5.1 PET 2:5.1 COR 3:16-17.1 COR 6:19-20.2 COR 6:16.EPH
2:19-22

EVENING

He is before all things.

The Amen, . . . the Beginning of the creation of God. ◊ The beginning, the firstborn from the dead, that in all things He may have the preeminence.

The Lord possessed me [wisdom] at the beginning of His way, before His works of old. I have been established from everlasting, from the beginning, before there was ever an earth. . . . When He prepared the heavens, I was there, when He drew a circle on the face of the deep, . . . when He assigned to the sea its limit, so that the waters would not transgress His command, . . . I was daily His delight, rejoicing always before Him. ◊ Indeed before the day was, I am He.

The Lamb slain from the foundation of the world. ◊ The author and finisher of our faith, who for the joy that was set before Him endured the cross, despising the shame, and has sat down at the right hand of the throne of God.

COL 1:17.REV 3:14.COL 1:18.PROV 8:22-23,27-30.IS 43:13.REV
13:8.HEB 12:2

AUGUST 17

MORNING_____

Pray for one another, that you may be healed.

Abraham answered and said, "Indeed now, I who am but dust and ashes have taken it upon myself to speak to the Lord: Suppose there were five less than the fifty righteous; would You destroy all of the city for lack of five?" And He said, "If I find there forty-five, I will not destroy it."

Father, forgive them, for they do not know what they do. ◊ Pray for those who spitefully use you and persecute you.

I pray for them. I do not pray for the world but for those whom You have given Me, for they are Yours. . . . I do not pray for these alone, but also for those who will believe in Me through their word. ◊ Bear one another's burdens, and so fulfill the law of Christ.

The effective, fervent prayer of a righteous man avails much. Elijah was a man with a nature like ours, and he prayed earnestly that it would not rain; and it did not rain on the land for three years and six months.

JAMES 5:16.GEN 18:27-28.LUKE 23:34.MATT 5:44.JOHN 17:9,20.GAL
6:2.JAMES 5:16-17

EVENING_____

**As for man, his days are like grass; as a flower of the
field, so he flourishes. For the wind passes over it,
and it is gone, and its place remembers it no more.**

So teach us to number our days, that we may gain a heart of wisdom. ◊ What will it profit a man if he gains the whole world, and loses his own soul?

Surely the people are grass. The grass withers, the flower fades, but the word of our God stands forever. ◊ The world is passing away, and the lust of it; but he who does the will of God abides forever.

Behold, now is the accepted time; behold, now is the day of salvation. ◊ Use this world as not misusing it. For the form of this world is passing away. ◊ Let us consider one another in order to stir up love and good works, not forsaking the assembling of ourselves together, as is the manner of some, but exhorting one another, and so much the more as you see the Day approaching.

PS 103:15-16.PS 90:12.MARK 8:36.IS 40:7-8.1 JOHN 2:17.2 COR 6:2.
1 COR 7:31.HEB 10:24-25

MORNING

What god is there in heaven or on earth who can do anything like Your works and Your mighty deeds?

Who in the heavens can be compared to the Lord? Who among the sons of the mighty can be likened to the Lord? . . . O Lord God of hosts, who is mighty like You, O Lord? Your faithfulness also surrounds You. ◇ Among the gods there is none like You, O Lord; nor are there any works like Your works. ◇ For Your word's sake, and according to Your own heart, You have done all these great things, to make Your servant know them. Therefore You are great, O Lord God. For there is none like You, nor is there any God besides You, according to all that we have heard with our ears.

Eye has not seen, nor ear heard, nor have entered into the heart of man the things which God has prepared for those who love Him. But God has revealed them to us through His Spirit. ◇ The secret things belong to the Lord our God, but those things which are revealed belong to us and to our children.

DEUT 3:24.PS 89:6,8.PS 86:8.2 SAM 7:21-22.1 COR 2:9-10.DEUT 29:29

EVENING

He who glories, let him glory in the Lord.

Let not the wise man glory in his wisdom, let not the mighty man glory in his might, nor let the rich man glory in his riches; but let him who glories glory in this, that he understands and knows Me, that I am the Lord.

I also count all things loss for the excellence of the knowledge of Christ Jesus my Lord, for whom I have suffered the loss of all things, and count them as rubbish, that I may gain Christ. ◇ I am not ashamed of the gospel of Christ, for it is the power of God to salvation for everyone who believes. ◇ I have reason to glory in Christ Jesus in the things which pertain to God.

Whom have I in heaven but You? And there is none upon earth that I desire besides You. ◇ My heart rejoices in the Lord; . . . I rejoice in Your salvation.

Not unto us, O Lord, not unto us, but to Your name give glory, because of Your mercy, and because of Your truth.

1 COR 1:31.JER 9:23-24.PHIL 3:8.ROM 1:16.ROM 15:17.PS 73:25.1 SAM
2:1.PS 115:1

AUGUST 19

**As He who called you is holy, you also be holy in all
your conduct.**

You know how we exhorted . . . and charged every one of you, . . . that you would have a walk worthy of God who calls you into His own kingdom and glory. ◊ You may proclaim the praises of Him who called you out of darkness into His marvelous light.

You were once darkness, but now you are light in the Lord. Walk as children of light (for the fruit of the Spirit is in all goodness, righteousness, and truth), proving what is acceptable to the Lord. And have no fellowship with the unfruitful works of darkness, but rather expose them. ◊ Being filled with the fruits of righteousness which are by Jesus Christ, to the glory and praise of God.

Let your light so shine before men, that they may see your good works and glorify your Father in heaven. ◊ Therefore, whether you eat or drink, or whatever you do, do all to the glory of God.

1 PET 1:15.1 THESS 2:11-12.1 PET 2:9.EPH 5:8-11.PHIL 1:11.MATT 5:16.1 COR 10:31

EVENING

**Ask Me of things to come concerning My sons; and
concerning the work of My hands, you command Me.**

I will give you a new heart and put a new spirit within you; I will take the heart of stone out of your flesh and give you a heart of flesh. I will put My Spirit within you and cause you to walk in My statutes. . . . Thus says the Lord God: "I will also let the house of Israel inquire of Me to do this for them."

If two of you agree on earth concerning anything that they ask, it will be done for them by My Father in heaven. For where two or three are gathered together in My name, I am there in the midst of them.

Have faith in God. For assuredly, I say to you, whoever says to this mountain, "Be removed and be cast into the sea," and does not doubt in his heart, but believes that those things he says will come to pass, he will have whatever he says.

IS 45:11.EZEK 36:26-27,37.MATT 18:19-20.MARK 11:22-23

MORNING

God is not a man, that He should lie, nor a son of man, that He should repent.

The Father of lights, with whom there is no variation or shadow of turning. ◊ Jesus Christ is the same yesterday, today, and forever.

His truth shall be your shield and buckler.

God, determining to show more abundantly to the heirs of promise the immutability of His counsel, confirmed it by an oath, that by two immutable things, in which it is impossible for God to lie, we might have strong consolation, who have fled for refuge to lay hold of the hope set before us.

The faithful God . . . keeps covenant and mercy for a thousand generations with those who love Him and keep His commandments. ◊ All the paths of the Lord are mercy and truth, to such as keep His covenant and His testimonies. ◊ Happy is he who has the God of Jacob for his help, whose hope is in the Lord his God, . . . who keeps truth forever.

NUM 23:19.JAMES 1:17.HEB 13:8.PS 91:4.HEB 6:17-18.DEUT 7:9.PS 25:10.PS 146:5-6

EVENING

If you faint in the day of adversity, your strength is small.

He gives power to the weak, and to those who have no might He increases strength. ◊ My grace is sufficient for you, for My strength is made perfect in weakness. ◊ He shall call upon Me, and I will answer him; I will be with him in trouble; I will deliver him. ◊ The eternal God is your refuge, and underneath are the everlasting arms; He will thrust out the enemy from before you.

I looked for someone to take pity, but there was none; and for comforters, but I found none.

For every priest taken from among men is appointed for men in things pertaining to God. . . . He can have compassion on those who are ignorant and going astray. . . . So also Christ, . . . though He was a Son, yet He learned obedience by the things which He suffered. And having been perfected, He became the author of eternal salvation to all who obey Him. ◊ Surely He has borne our griefs and carried our sorrows.

PROV 24:10.IS 40:29.2 COR 12:9.PS 91:15.DEUT 33:27.PS 69:20.HEB 5:1-2,5,8-9.IS 53:4

AUGUST 21

MORNING

You are my portion, O Lord.

All things are yours. . . . And you are Christ's, and Christ is God's. ◊ Our . . . Savior Jesus Christ . . . gave Himself for us. ◊ He . . . gave Him to be head over all things to the church. ◊ Christ . . . loved the church and gave Himself for it, . . . that He might present it to Himself a glorious church, not having spot or wrinkle or any such thing, but that it should be holy and without blemish.

My soul shall make its boast in the Lord. ◊ I will greatly rejoice in the Lord, my soul shall be joyful in my God; for He has clothed me with the garments of salvation, He has covered me with the robe of righteousness.

Whom have I in heaven but You? And there is none upon earth that I desire besides You. My flesh and my heart fail; but God is the strength of my heart and my portion forever. ◊ O my soul, you have said to the Lord, "You are my Lord." . . . You, O Lord, are the portion of my inheritance and my cup; You maintain my lot. The lines have fallen to me in pleasant places; yes, I have a good inheritance.

PS 119:57.1 COR 3:21,23.TITUS 2:13-14.EPH 1:22.EPH 5:25,27.PS 34:2.IS 61:10.PS 73:25-26.PS 16:2,5-6

EVENING

There is a way which seems right to a man, but its end is the way of death.

He who trusts in his own heart is a fool.

Your word is a lamp to my feet and a light to my path. ◊ Concerning the works of men, by the word of Your lips, I have kept myself from the paths of the destroyer.

If there arises among you a prophet or a dreamer of dreams, . . . saying, "Let us go after other gods which you have not known, and let us serve them," you shall not listen to the words of that prophet, . . . for the Lord your God is testing you to know whether you love the Lord your God with all your heart and with all your soul. You shall walk after the Lord your God and fear Him, and keep His commandments and obey His voice, and you shall serve Him and hold fast to Him.

I will instruct you and teach you in the way you should go; I will guide you with My eye.

PROV 14:12.PROV 28:26.PS 119:105.PS 17:4.DEUT 13:1-4.PS 32:8

MORNING

None of us lives to himself, and no one
dies to himself.

If we live, we live to the Lord; and if we die, we die to the Lord. Therefore, whether we live or die, we are the Lord's. ◊ Let no one seek his own, but each one the other's well-being. ◊ You were bought at a price; therefore glorify God in your body and in your spirit, which are God's.

Christ will be magnified in my body, whether by life or by death. For to me, to live is Christ, and to die is gain. But if I live on in the flesh, this will mean fruit from my labor; yet what I shall choose I cannot tell. For I am hard pressed between the two, having a desire to depart and be with Christ, which is far better.

I through the law died to the law that I might live to God. I have been crucified with Christ; it is no longer I who live, but Christ lives in me; and the life which I now live in the flesh I live by faith in the Son of God, who loved me and gave Himself for me.

ROM 14:7.ROM 14:8.1 COR 10:24.1 COR 6:20.PHIL 1:20-23.GAL 2:19-20

EVENING

God gave Solomon . . . largeness of heart like the
sand on the seashore.

Indeed a greater than Solomon is here. ◊ The . . . Prince of Peace.

Scarcely for a righteous man will one die; yet perhaps for a good man someone would even dare to die. But God demonstrates His own love toward us, in that while we were still sinners, Christ died for us. ◊ Who, being in the form of God, did not consider it robbery to be equal with God, but made Himself of no reputation, taking the form of a servant, and coming in the likeness of men. And being found in appearance as a man, He humbled Himself and became obedient to the point of death, even the death of the cross. ◊ The love of Christ . . . passes knowledge.

Christ the power of God and the wisdom of God. ◊ In whom are hidden all the treasures of wisdom and knowledge. ◊ The unsearchable riches of Christ. ◊ Of Him you are in Christ Jesus, who became for us wisdom from God—and righteousness and sanctification and redemption.

1 KIN 4:29.MATT 12:42.IS 9:6.ROM 5:7-8.PHIL 2:6-8.EPH 3:19.1 COR
1:24.COL 2:3.EPH 3:8.1 COR 1:30

AUGUST 23

**I have loved you with an everlasting love; therefore
with lovingkindness I have drawn you.**

We are bound to give thanks to God always for you, brethren beloved
by the Lord, because God from the beginning chose you for salvation
through sanctification by the Spirit and belief in the truth, to which He
called you by our gospel, for the obtaining of the glory of our Lord Jesus
Christ. ◊ [God] has saved us and called us with a holy calling, not
according to our works, but according to His own purpose and grace
which was given to us in Christ Jesus before time began. ◊ Your eyes
saw my substance, being yet unformed. And in Your book they all were
written, the days fashioned for me, when as yet there were none of them.

God so loved the world that He gave His only begotten Son, that
whoever believes in Him should not perish but have everlasting life.

In this is love, not that we loved God, but that He loved us and sent His
Son to be the propitiation for our sins.

JER 31:3.2 THESS 2:13-14.2 TIM 1:9.PS 139:16.JOHN 3:16.1 JOHN 4:10

EVENING

I have made, and I will bear.

Thus says the Lord, who created you, O Jacob, and He who formed
you, O Israel: "Fear not, for I have redeemed you; I have called you by
your name; you are Mine. When you pass through the waters, I will be
with you; and through the rivers, they shall not overflow you." ◊ Even
to your old age, I am He, and even to gray hairs I will carry you!

As an eagle stirs up its nest, hovers over its young, spreading out its
wings, taking them up, carrying them on its wings, so the Lord alone led
him. ◊ He bore them and carried them all the days of old.

Jesus Christ is the same yesterday, today, and forever. ◊ For I am
persuaded that neither . . . height nor depth, nor any other created thing,
shall be able to separate us from the love of God which is in Christ Jesus
our Lord.

Can a woman forget her nursing child, and not have compassion on
the son of her womb? Surely they may forget, yet I will not forget you.

IS 46:4.IS 43:1-2.IS 46:4.DEUT 32:11-12.IS 63:9.HEB 13:8.ROM 8:38-39.IS
49:15

MORNING

I know their sorrows.

A man of sorrows and acquainted with grief. ◊ Sympathize with our weaknesses.

Himself took our infirmities and bore our sicknesses. ◊ Jesus . . . being wearied from His journey, sat thus by the well.

When Jesus saw her weeping, and the Jews who came with her weeping, He groaned in the spirit and was troubled. . . . Jesus wept. ◊ For in that He Himself has suffered, being tempted, He is able to aid those who are tempted.

He looked down from the height of His sanctuary; from heaven the Lord viewed the earth, to hear the groaning of the prisoner, to loose those appointed to death. ◊ He knows the way that I take; when He has tested me, I shall come forth as gold. ◊ When my spirit was overwhelmed within me, then You knew my path.

He who touches you touches the apple of His eye. ◊ In all their affliction He was afflicted, and the Angel of His Presence saved them.

EX 3:7.IS 53:3.HEB 4:15.MATT 8:17.JOHN 4:6.JOHN 11:33,35.HEB 2:18.PS 102:19-20.JOB 23:10.PS 142:3.ZECH 2:8.IS 63:9

EVENING

I must work the works of Him who sent Me while it is day.

The soul of a sluggard desires, and has nothing; but the soul of the diligent shall be made rich. ◊ He who waters will also be watered.

My food is to do the will of Him who sent Me, and to finish His work. Do you not say, "There are still four months and then comes the harvest?" Behold, I say to you, lift up your eyes and look at the fields, for they are already white for harvest! And he who reaps receives wages, and gathers fruit for eternal life, that both he who sows and he who reaps may rejoice together. ◊ The kingdom of heaven is like a landowner who went out early in the morning to hire laborers for his vineyard. Now when he had agreed with the laborers for a denarius a day, he sent them into his vineyard.

Preach the word! Be ready in season and out of season. Do business till I come.

I labored more abundantly than they all, yet not I, but the grace of God which was with me.

JOHN 9:4.PROV 13:4.PROV 11:25.JOHN 4:34-36.MATT 20:1-2.2 TIM 4:2.LUKE 19:13.1 COR 15:10

AUGUST 25

MORNING

Look to the rock from which you were hewn, and to the hole of the pit from which you were dug.

Behold, I was brought forth in iniquity. ◊ No eye pitied you, . . . but you were thrown out into the open field, when you yourself were loathed on the day you were born. And when I passed by you and saw you struggling in your own blood, I said to you . . . , "Live!"

He also brought me up out of a horrible pit, out of the miry clay, and set my feet upon a rock, and established my steps. He has put a new song in my mouth—praise to our God.

When we were still without strength, in due time Christ died for the ungodly. For scarcely for a righteous man will one die; yet perhaps for a good man someone would even dare to die. But God demonstrates His own love toward us, in that while we were still sinners, Christ died for us. ◊ God, who is rich in mercy, because of His great love with which He loved us, even when we were dead in trespasses, made us alive together with Christ.

IS 51:1.PS 51:5.EZEK 16:5-6.PS 40:2-3.ROM 5:6-8.EPH 2:4-5

EVENING

I will greatly rejoice in the Lord, my soul shall be joyful in my God.

I will bless the Lord at all times; His praise shall continually be in my mouth. My soul shall make its boast in the Lord; the humble shall hear of it and be glad. Oh, magnify the Lord with me, and let us exalt His name together. ◊ The Lord will give grace and glory; no good thing will He withhold from those who walk uprightly. O Lord of hosts, blessed is the man who trusts in You! ◊ Bless the Lord, O my soul; and all that is within me, bless His holy name!

Is anyone cheerful? Let him sing psalms. ◊ Be filled with the Spirit, speaking to one another in psalms and hymns and spiritual songs, singing and making melody in your heart to the Lord, giving thanks always for all things. ◊ Singing with grace in your hearts to the Lord.

At midnight Paul and Silas were praying and singing hymns to God, and the prisoners were listening to them. ◊ Rejoice in the Lord always. Again I will say, rejoice!

IS 61:10.PS 34:1-3.PS 84:11-12.PS 103:1.JAMES 5:13.EPH 5:18-20.COL 3:16.ACTS 16:25.PHIL 4:4

MORNING

You shall also make a plate of pure gold and engrave on it, like the engraving of a signet: HOLINESS TO THE LORD.

Pursue . . . holiness, without which no one will see the Lord. ◊ God is Spirit, and those who worship Him must worship in spirit and truth. ◊ But we are all like an unclean thing, and all our righteousnesses are like filthy rags. ◊ By those who come near Me I must be regarded as holy; and before all the people I must be glorified.

This is the law of the temple: The whole area surrounding the mountaintop shall be most holy. ◊ Holiness adorns Your house, O Lord, forever.

For their sakes I sanctify Myself, that they also may be sanctified by the truth. ◊ Seeing . . . that we have a great High Priest who has passed through the heavens, Jesus the Son of God, let us . . . come boldly to the throne of grace, that we may obtain mercy and find grace to help in time of need.

EX 28:36.HEB 12:14.JOHN 4:24.IS 64:6.LEV 10:3.EZEK 43:12.PS
93:5.JOHN 17:19.HEB 4:14,16

EVENING

My cup runs over.

Oh, taste and see that the Lord is good; blessed is the man who trusts in Him! Oh, fear the Lord, you His saints! There is no want to those who fear Him. The young lions lack and suffer hunger; but those who seek the Lord shall not lack any good thing. ◊ His compassions fail not. They are new every morning; great is Your faithfulness.

You, O Lord, are the portion of my inheritance and my cup; You maintain my lot. The lines have fallen to me in pleasant places; yes, I have a good inheritance. ◊ Whether . . . the world or life or death, or things present or things to come all are yours. ◊ Blessed be the God and Father of our Lord Jesus Christ, who has blessed us with every spiritual blessing in the heavenly places in Christ.

I have learned in whatever state I am, to be content. ◊ Godliness with contentment is great gain. ◊ My God shall supply all your need according to His riches in glory by Christ Jesus.

PS 23:5.PS 34:8-10.LAM 3:22-23.PS 16:5-6.1 COR 3:22.EPH 1:3.PHIL
4:11.1 TIM 6:6.PHIL 4:19

AUGUST 27

MORNING

Your word is a lamp to my feet and a light to my path.

By the word of Your lips, I have kept myself from the paths of the destroyer. Uphold my steps in Your paths, that my footsteps may not slip. ◊ When you roam, they will lead you; when you sleep, they will keep you; and when you awake, they will speak with you. For the commandment is a lamp, and the law is light. ◊ Your ears shall hear a word behind you, saying, "This is the way, walk in it," whenever you turn to the right hand or whenever you turn to the left.

I am the light of the world. He who follows Me shall not walk in darkness, but have the light of life. ◊ We also have the prophetic word made more sure, which you do well to heed as a light that shines in a dark place. ◊ Now we see in a mirror, dimly, but then face to face. Now I know in part, but then I shall know just as I also am known. ◊ They need no lamp nor light of the sun, for the Lord God gives them light. And they shall reign forever and ever.

PS 119:105.PS 17:4-5.PROV 6:22-23.IS 30:21.JOHN 8:12.2 PET 1:19.
1 COR 13:12.REV 22:5

EVENING

What do you mean, sleeper? Arise.

This is not your rest; . . . it is defiled, it shall destroy you. ◊ Set your mind on things above, not on things on the earth. ◊ If riches increase, do not set your heart on them. ◊ Set your heart and your soul to seek the Lord your God. Therefore arise.

Why do you sleep? Rise and pray, lest you enter into temptation. ◊ Take heed to yourselves, lest your hearts be weighed down with carousing, drunkenness, and cares of this life, and that Day come on you unexpectedly.

While the bridegroom was delayed, they all slumbered and slept. ◊ Yet a little while, and He who is coming will come and will not tarry. ◊ Now it is high time to awake out of sleep; for now our salvation is nearer than when we first believed. ◊ Watch therefore, for you do not know when the master of the house is coming in the evening, at midnight, at the crowing of the rooster, or in the morning—lest, coming suddenly, he find you sleeping.

JON 1:6.MIC 2:10.COL 3:2.PS 62:10.1 CHR 22:19.LUKE 22:46.LUKE
21:34.MATT 25:5.HEB 10:37.ROM 13:11.MARK 13:35-36

MORNING

**The accuser of our brethren, who accused them before
our God day and night, has been cast down.**

They overcame him by the blood of the Lamb and by the word of their testimony. ◊ Who shall bring a charge against God's elect? It is God who justifies. Who is he who condemns? It is Christ who died, and furthermore is also risen, who is even at the right hand of God, who also makes intercession for us.

Having disarmed principalities and powers, He made a public spectacle of them. ◊ That through death He might destroy him who had the power of death, that is, the devil, and release those who through fear of death were all their lifetime subject to bondage. ◊ In all these things we are more than conquerors through Him who loved us. ◊ Put on the whole armor of God, that you may be able to stand against the wiles of the devil. . . . And take . . . the sword of the Spirit, which is the word of God. ◊ Thanks be to God, who gives us the victory through our Lord Jesus Christ.

REV 12:10.REV 12:11.ROM 8:33-34.COL 2:15.HEB 2:14-15.ROM
8:37.EPH 6:11,17.1 COR 15:57

EVENING

The tree of life.

God has given us eternal life, and this life is in His Son. ◊ He gave His only begotten Son, that whoever believes in Him should not perish but have everlasting life. ◊ As the Father raises the dead and gives life to them, even so the Son gives life to whom He will. . . . For as the Father has life in Himself, so He has granted the Son to have life in Himself.

To him who overcomes I will give to eat from the tree of life, which is in the midst of the Paradise of God. ◊ In the middle of its street, and on either side of the river, was the tree of life, which bore twelve fruits, each tree yielding its fruit every month. And the leaves of the tree were for the healing of the nations.

Happy is the man who finds wisdom. . . . Length of days is in her right hand. . . . She is a tree of life to those who take hold of her, and happy are all who retain her. ◊ Christ Jesus, . . . became for us wisdom.

GEN 2:9.1 JOHN 5:11.JOHN 3:16.JOHN 5:21,26.REV 2:7.REV
22:2.PROV 3:13,16,18.1 COR 1:30

AUGUST 29

MORNING

Whoever trusts in the Lord, happy is he.

[Abraham] did not waver at the promise of God through unbelief, but was strengthened in faith, giving glory to God, and being fully convinced that what He had promised He was also able to perform. ◊ The children of Judah prevailed, because they relied on the Lord God of their fathers.

God is our refuge and strength, a very present help in trouble. Therefore we will not fear, though the earth be removed, and though the mountains be carried into the midst of the sea. ◊ It is better to trust in the Lord than to put confidence in man. It is better to trust in the Lord than to put confidence in princes. ◊ The steps of a good man are ordered by the Lord, and He delights in his way. Though he fall, he shall not be utterly cast down; for the Lord upholds him with His hand.

Oh, taste and see that the Lord is good; blessed is the man who trusts in Him! Oh, fear the Lord, you His saints! There is no want to those who fear Him.

PROV 16:20.ROM 4:20-21.2 CHR 13:18.PS 46:1-2.PS 118:8-9.PS 37:23-24.PS 34:8-9

EVENING

I will both lie down in peace, and sleep; for You alone, O Lord, make me dwell in safety.

You shall not be afraid of the terror by night. ◊ He shall cover you with His feathers, and under His wings you shall take refuge. ◊ As a hen gathers her chicks under her wings. ◊ He will not allow your foot to be moved; He who keeps you will not slumber. Behold, He who keeps Israel shall neither slumber nor sleep. The Lord is your keeper; the Lord is your shade at your right hand.

I will abide in Your tabernacle forever; I will trust in the shelter of Your wings. ◊ The darkness shall not hide from You, but the night shines as the day; the darkness and the light are both alike to You.

He who did not spare His own Son, but delivered Him up for us all, how shall He not with Him also freely give us all things? ◊ You are Christ's, and Christ is God's. ◊ I will trust and not be afraid.

PS 4:8.PS 91:5.PS 91:4.MATT 23:37.PS 121:3-5.PS 61:4.PS 139:12.ROM 8:32.1 COR 3:23.IS 12:2

MORNING

**The king held out . . . the golden scepter. . . . Then
Esther went near and touched the top of the scepter.**

And it will be that when he cries to Me, I will hear, for I am gracious.

We have known and believed the love that God has for us. God is love, and he who abides in love abides in God, and God in him. Love has been perfected among us in this: that we may have boldness in the day of judgment; because as He is, so are we in this world. There is no fear in love; but perfect love casts out fear, because fear involves torment. But he who fears has not been made perfect in love. We love Him because He first loved us.

Let us draw near with a true heart in full assurance of faith, having our hearts sprinkled from an evil conscience and our bodies washed with pure water. ◊ For through Him we both have access by one Spirit to the Father. ◊ We have boldness and access with confidence through faith in Him. ◊ Let us therefore come boldly to the throne of grace, that we may obtain mercy and find grace to help in time of need.

ESTH 5:2.EX 22:27.1 JOHN 4:16-19.HEB 10:22.EPH 2:18.EPH 3:12.HEB 4:16

EVENING

**"What is it?" . . . Moses said to them, "This is the
bread which the Lord has given you to eat."**

Without controversy great is the mystery of godliness: God was manifested in the flesh. ◊ The bread of God is He who comes down from heaven and gives life to the world.

Your fathers ate the manna in the wilderness, and are dead. ◊ If anyone eats of this bread, he will live forever; and the bread that I shall give is My flesh, which I shall give for the life of the world. . . . For My flesh is food indeed, and My blood is drink indeed.

The children of Israel . . . gathered, some more, some less. . . . He who gathered much had nothing over, and he who gathered little had no lack. . . . They gathered it every morning, every man according to his need.

Therefore do not worry, saying, "What shall we eat?" or "What shall we drink?" . . . Your heavenly Father knows that you need all these things. But seek first the kingdom of God and His righteousness, and all these things shall be added to you.

EX 16:15.1 TIM 3:16.JOHN 6:33.JOHN 6:49.JOHN 6:51,55.EX 16:17-18, 21.MATT 6:31-33

AUGUST 31

MORNING

The free gift which came from many offenses resulted in justification.

Though your sins are like scarlet, they shall be as white as snow; though they are red like crimson, they shall be as wool. ◊ I, even I, am He who blots out your transgressions for My own sake; and I will not remember your sins. Put Me in remembrance; let us contend together; state your case, that you may be acquitted. ◊ I have blotted out, like a thick cloud, your transgressions, and like a cloud, your sins. Return to Me, for I have redeemed you.

God so loved the world that He gave His only begotten Son, that whoever believes in Him should not perish but have everlasting life. ◊ But the free gift is not like the offense. For if by the one man's offense many died, much more the grace of God and the gift by the grace of the one Man, Jesus Christ, abounded to many. ◊ And such were some of you. But you were washed, but you were sanctified, but you were justified in the name of the Lord Jesus and by the Spirit of our God.

ROM 5:16.IS 1:18.IS 43:25-26.IS 44:22.JOHN 3:16.ROM 5:15.1 COR 6:11

EVENING

Do business till I come.

It is like a man going to a far country, who left his house and gave authority to his servants, and to each his work, and commanded the doorkeeper to watch. ◊ To one he gave five talents, to another two, and to another one, to each according to his own ability; and immediately he went on a journey.

I must work the works of Him who sent Me while it is day; the night is coming when no one can work. ◊ Did you not know that I must be about My Father's business? ◊ Christ also suffered for us, leaving us an example, that you should follow His steps.

Preach the word! Be ready in season and out of season. Convince, rebuke, exhort, with all longsuffering and teaching. ◊ Each one's work will become manifest; for the Day will declare it. ◊ Therefore, my beloved brethren, be steadfast, immovable, always abounding in the work of the Lord, knowing that your labor is not in vain in the Lord.

LUKE 19:13.MARK 13:34.MATT 25:15.JOHN 9:4.LUKE 2:49.1 PET 2:21.
2 TIM 4:2.1 COR 3:13.1 COR 15:58

MORNING

The fruit of the Spirit is . . . kindness.

The humble . . . shall increase their joy in the Lord, and the poor among men shall rejoice in the Holy One of Israel. ◊ Unless you are converted and become as little children, you will by no means enter the kingdom of heaven. Therefore whoever humbles himself as this little child is the greatest in the kingdom of heaven. ◊ The incorruptible ornament of a gentle and quiet spirit . . . is very precious in the sight of God. ◊ Love does not parade itself, is not puffed up.

Pursue . . . gentleness. ◊ Take My yoke upon you and learn from Me, for I am gentle and lowly in heart. ◊ He was oppressed and He was afflicted, yet He opened not His mouth; He was led as a lamb to the slaughter, and as a sheep before its shearers is silent, so He opened not his mouth. ◊ Christ also suffered for us, leaving us an example, that you should follow His steps: "Who committed no sin, nor was guile found in His mouth"; who, when He was reviled, did not revile in return; . . . but committed Himself to Him who judges righteously.

GAL 5:22.IS 29:19.MATT 18:3-4.1 PET 3:4.1 COR 13:4.1 TIM 6:11.MATT 11:29.IS 53:7.1 PET 2:21-23

EVENING

If anyone desires to come after Me, let him deny himself, and take up his cross daily, and follow Me.

By honor and dishonor, by evil report and good report. ◊ All who desire to live godly in Christ Jesus will suffer persecution. ◊ The offense of the cross.

If I still pleased men, I would not be a servant of Christ.

If you are reproached for the name of Christ, blessed are you. . . . But let none of you suffer as a murderer, a thief, an evildoer, or as a busybody in other people's matters. Yet if anyone suffers as a Christian, let him not be ashamed, but let him glorify God in this matter.

To you it has been granted on behalf of Christ, not only to believe in Him, but also to suffer for His sake. ◊ If One died for all, then all died; and He died for all, that those who live should live no longer for themselves, but for Him who died for them and rose again. ◊ If we endure, we shall also reign with Him.

LUKE 9:23.2 COR 6:8.2 TIM 3:12.GAL 5:11.GAL 1:10.1 PET 4:14-16.PHIL 1:29.2 COR 5:14-15.2 TIM 2:12

SEPTEMBER 2

MORNING

Wait on the Lord; be of good courage, and He shall strengthen your heart.

Have you not known? Have you not heard? The everlasting God, the Lord, the Creator of the ends of the earth, neither faints nor is weary. He gives power to the weak, and to those who have no might He increases strength. ◊ Fear not, for I am with you; be not dismayed, for I am your God. I will strengthen you, yes, I will help you, I will uphold you with My righteous right hand. ◊ You have been a strength to the poor, a strength to the needy in his distress, a refuge from the storm, a shade from the heat; for the blast of the terrible ones is as a storm against the wall.

The testing of your faith produces patience. But let patience have its perfect work, that you may be perfect and complete, lacking nothing. ◊ Do not cast away your confidence, which has great reward. For you have need of endurance, so that after you have done the will of God, you may receive the promise.

PS 27:14.IS 40:28-29.IS 41:10.IS 25:4.JAMES 1:3-4.HEB 10:35-36

EVENING

He makes me to lie down in green pastures.

The wicked are like the troubled sea, when it cannot rest. . . . "There is no peace," says my God, "for the wicked."

Come to Me, all you who labor and are heavy laden, and I will give you rest. ◊ Rest in the Lord. . . . He who has entered His rest has himself also ceased from his works.

Do not be carried about with various and strange doctrines. For it is good that the heart be established by grace. ◊ We should no longer be children, tossed to and fro and carried about with every wind of doctrine, by the trickery of men, in the cunning craftiness by which they lie in wait to deceive, but, speaking the truth in love, may grow up in all things into Him who is the head—Christ.

I sat down in his shade with great delight, and his fruit was sweet to my taste. He brought me to the banqueting house, and his banner over me was love.

PS 23:2.IS 57:20-21.MATT 11:28.PS 37:7.HEB 4:10.HEB 13:9.EPH 4:14-15.SONG 2:3-4

MORNING

Nor shall leaven be seen among you in all your quarters.

The fear of the Lord is to hate evil. ◊ Abhor what is evil. ◊ Abstain from every form of evil. ◊ [Look] diligently lest anyone fall short of the grace of God; lest any root of bitterness springing up cause trouble, and by this many become defiled.

If I regard iniquity in my heart, the Lord will not hear.

Do you not know that a little leaven leavens the whole lump? Therefore purge out the old leaven, that you may be a new lump, since you truly are unleavened. For indeed Christ, our Passover, was sacrificed for us. Therefore let us keep the feast, not with old leaven, nor with the leaven of malice and wickedness, but with the unleavened bread of sincerity and truth. ◊ Let a man examine himself, and so let him eat of that bread and drink of that cup.

Let everyone who names the name of Christ depart from iniquity. ◊ Such a High Priest was fitting for us, who is holy, harmless, undefiled, separate from sinners. ◊ In Him there is no sin.

EX 13:7.PROV 8:13.ROM 12:9.1 THESS 5:22.HEB 12:15.PS 66:18.1 COR 5:6-8.1 COR 11:28.2 TIM 2:19.HEB 7:26.1 JOHN 3:5

EVENING

The serpent said to the woman, "You will not surely die. Your eyes will be opened, and you will be like God, knowing good and evil."

I fear, lest somehow, as the serpent deceived Eve by his craftiness, so your minds may be corrupted from the simplicity that is in Christ.

My brethren, be strong in the Lord and in the power of His might. Put on the whole armor of God, that you may be able to stand against the wiles of the devil. . . . Take up the whole armor of God, that you may be able to withstand in the evil day, and having done all, to stand. Stand therefore, having girded your waist with truth, having put on the breastplate of righteousness, and having shod your feet with the preparation of the gospel of peace; above all, taking the shield of faith with which you will be able to quench all the fiery darts of the wicked one. And take the helmet of salvation, and the sword of the Spirit, which is the word of God. ◊ Lest Satan should take advantage of us; for we are not ignorant of his devices.

GEN 3:4-5.2 COR 11:3.EPH 6:10-11,13-17.2 COR 2:11

SEPTEMBER 4

MORNING

Sit still, my daughter.

Take heed, and be quiet; do not fear or be fainthearted. ◇ Be still, and know that I am God. ◇ Did I not say to you that if you would believe you would see the glory of God? ◇ The loftiness of man shall be bowed down, and the haughtiness of men shall be brought low; the Lord alone will be exalted in that day.

Mary . . . sat at Jesus' feet and heard His word. ◇ Mary has chosen that good part, which will not be taken away from her. ◇ In returning and rest you shall be saved; in quietness and confidence shall be your strength. ◇ Meditate within your heart on your bed, and be still.

Rest in the Lord, and wait patiently for Him; do not fret because of him who prospers in his way, because of the man who brings wicked schemes to pass.

He will not be afraid of evil tidings; his heart is steadfast, trusting in the Lord. His heart is established.

Whoever believes will not act hastily.

RUTH 3:18.IS 7:4.PS 46:10.JOHN 11:40.IS 2:17.LUKE 10:39.LUKE 10:42.IS 30:15.PS 4:4.PS 37:7.PS 112:7-8.IS 28:16

EVENING

What I am doing you do not understand now, but you will know after this.

You shall remember that the Lord your God led you all the way these forty years in the wilderness, to humble you and test you, to know what was in your heart, whether you would keep His commandments or not.

"When I passed by you again and looked upon you, indeed your time was the time of love; . . . yes, I swore an oath to you and entered into a covenant with you, and you became Mine," says the Lord God. ◇ Whom the Lord loves He chastens.

Beloved, do not think it strange concerning the fiery trial which is to try you, as though some strange thing happened to you; but rejoice to the extent that you partake of Christ's sufferings, that when His glory is revealed, you may also be glad with exceeding joy. ◇ Our light affliction, which is but for a moment, is working for us a far more exceeding and eternal weight of glory, while we do not look at the things which are seen, but at the things which are not seen.

JOHN 13:7.DEUT 8:2.EZEK 16:8.HEB 12:6.1 PET 4:12-13.2 COR 4:17-18

MORNING

As the body is one and has many members, . . . so also is Christ.

He is the head of the body, the church. ◊ He . . . gave Him to be head over all things to the church, which is His body, the fullness of Him who fills all in all. ◊ We are members of His body, of His flesh and of His bones.

A body You have prepared for Me. ◊ Your eyes saw my substance, being yet unformed. And in Your book they all were written, the days fashioned for me, when as yet there were none of them.

They were Yours, You gave them to Me. ◊ He chose us in Him before the foundation of the world. ◊ Whom He foreknew, He also predestined to be conformed to the image of His Son.

Grow up in all things into Him who is the head—Christ—from whom the whole body, joined and knit together by what every joint supplies, . . . causes growth of the body for the edifying of itself in love.

1 COR 12:12. COL 1:18. EPH 1:22-23. EPH 5:30. HEB 10:5. PS 139:16. JOHN 17:6. EPH 1:4. ROM 8:29. EPH 4:15-16

EVENING

The fountain of living waters.

How precious is Your lovingkindness, O God! Therefore the children of men put their trust under the shadow of Your wings. They are abundantly satisfied with the fullness of Your house, and You give them drink from the river of Your pleasures. For with You is the fountain of life.

Thus says the Lord God: "Behold, My servants shall eat, but you shall be hungry; behold, My servants shall drink, but you shall be thirsty. ◊ Whoever drinks of the water that I shall give him will never thirst. But the water that I shall give him will become in him a fountain of water springing up into everlasting life." ◊ This He spoke concerning the Spirit, whom those believing in Him would receive.

Ho! Everyone who thirsts, come to the waters. ◊ The Spirit and the bride say, "Come!" And let him who hears say, "Come!" And let him who thirsts come. And whoever desires, let him take the water of life freely.

JER 2:13. PS 36:7-9. IS 65:13. JOHN 4:14. JOHN 7:39. IS 55:1. REV 22:17

SEPTEMBER 6

MORNING

Let us lift our hearts and hands to God in heaven.

Who is like the Lord our God, who dwells on high, who humbles Himself to behold the things that are in the heavens and in the earth? ◊ To You, O Lord, I lift up my soul. ◊ I spread out my hands to You; my soul longs for You like a thirsty land. Do not hide Your face from me, lest I be like those who go down into the pit. Cause me to hear Your lovingkindness in the morning, for in You do I trust; cause me to know the way in which I should walk, for I lift up my soul to You.

Because Your lovingkindness is better than life, my lips shall praise You. Thus I will bless You while I live; I will lift up my hands in Your name. ◊ Rejoice the soul of Your servant, for to You, O Lord, I lift up my soul. For You, Lord, are good, and ready to forgive, and abundant in mercy to all those who call upon You.

Whatever you ask in My name, that I will do.

LAM 3:41. PS 113:5-6. PS 25:1. PS 143:6-8. PS 63:3-4. PS 86:4-5. JOHN 14:13

EVENING

Watchman, what of the night?

It is high time to awake out of sleep; for now our salvation is nearer than when we first believed. The night is far spent, the day is at hand. Therefore let us cast off the works of darkness, and let us put on the armor of light.

Learn this parable from the fig tree: When its branch has already become tender and puts forth leaves, you know that summer is near. So you also, when you see all these things, know that it is near, at the very doors. . . . Heaven and earth will pass away, but My words will by no means pass away.

I wait for the Lord, my soul waits, and in His word I do hope. My soul waits for the Lord more than those who watch for the morning I say, more than those who watch for the morning.

He who testifies to these things says, "Surely I am coming quickly." Amen. Even so, come, Lord Jesus!

Watch . . . for you know neither the day nor the hour in which the Son of Man is coming.

IS 21:11. ROM 13:11-12. MATT 24:32-33,35. PS 130:5-6. REV 22:20. MATT 25:13

MORNING

Rejoicing in hope.

Hope . . . is laid up for you in heaven. ◊ If in this life only we have hope in Christ, we are of all men the most pitiable. ◊ We must through many tribulations enter the kingdom of God. ◊ Whoever does not bear his cross and come after Me cannot be My disciple. ◊ No one should be shaken by these afflictions; for you yourselves know that we are appointed to this.

Rejoice in the Lord always. Again I will say, rejoice! ◊ The God of hope fill you with all joy and peace in believing, that you may abound in hope by the power of the Holy Spirit. ◊ Blessed be the God and Father of our Lord Jesus Christ, who according to His abundant mercy has begotten us again to a living hope through the resurrection of Jesus Christ from the dead. ◊ Whom having not seen you love. Though now you do not see Him, yet believing, you rejoice with joy inexpressible and full of glory. ◊ Through [Him] also we have access by faith into this grace in which we stand, and rejoice in hope of the glory of God.

ROM 12:12.COL 1:5.1 COR 15:19.ACTS 14:22.LUKE 14:27.1 THESS 3:3.PHIL 4:4.ROM 15:13.1 PET 1:3.1 PET 1:8.ROM 5:2

EVENING

I am poor and needy; yet the Lord thinks upon me.

"I know the thoughts that I think toward you," says the Lord, "thoughts of peace and not of evil." ◊ "For My thoughts are not your thoughts, nor are your ways My ways," says the Lord. "For as the heavens are higher than the earth, so are My ways higher than your ways, and My thoughts than your thoughts."

How precious also are Your thoughts to me, O God! How great is the sum of them! If I should count them, they would be more in number than the sand; when I awake, I am still with You. ◊ O Lord, how great are Your works! Your thoughts are very deep. ◊ Many, O Lord my God, are Your wonderful works which You have done; and Your thoughts which are toward us.

Not many mighty, not many noble, are called. ◊ Has God not chosen the poor of this world to be rich in faith and heirs of the kingdom? ◊ Having nothing, and yet possessing all things. ◊ This grace was given that I should preach . . . the unsearchable riches of Christ.

PS 40:17.JER 29:11.IS 55:8-9.PS 139:17-18.PS 92:5.PS 40:5.1 COR 1:26.JAMES 2:5.2 COR 6:10.EPH 3:8

SEPTEMBER 8

MORNING

You have been weighed in the balances, and found wanting.

The Lord is the God of knowledge; and by Him actions are weighed. ◊ What is highly esteemed among men is an abomination in the sight of God. ◊ The Lord does not see as man sees; for man looks at the outward appearance, but the Lord looks at the heart. ◊ Do not be deceived, God is not mocked; for whatever a man sows, that he will also reap. For he who sows to his flesh will of the flesh reap corruption, but he who sows to the Spirit will of the Spirit reap everlasting life.

What is a man profited if he gains the whole world, and loses his own soul? Or what will a man give in exchange for his soul? ◊ What things were gain to me, these I have counted loss for Christ.

Behold, You desire truth in the inward parts. ◊ You have tested my heart; You have visited me in the night; You have tried me and have found nothing.

DAN 5:27.1 SAM 2:3.LUKE 16:15.1 SAM 16:7.GAL 6:7-8.MATT
16:26.PHIL 3:7.PS 51:6.PS 17:3

EVENING

Christ the firstfruits.

Unless a grain of wheat falls into the ground and dies, it remains alone; but if it dies, it produces much grain. ◊ If the firstfruit is holy, the lump is also holy; and if the root is holy, so are the branches. ◊ Now Christ is risen from the dead, and has become the firstfruits of those who have fallen asleep. ◊ If we have been united together in the likeness of His death, certainly we also shall be in the likeness of His resurrection. ◊ The Lord Jesus Christ, . . . will transform our lowly body that it may be conformed to His glorious body, according to the working by which He is able even to subdue all things to Himself.

He is . . . the firstborn from the dead. ◊ If the Spirit of Him who raised Jesus from the dead dwells in you, He who raised Christ from the dead will also give life to your mortal bodies through His Spirit who dwells in you.

I am the resurrection and the life. He who believes in Me, though he may die, he shall live.

1 COR 15:23.JOHN 12:24.ROM 11:16.1 COR 15:20.ROM 6:5.PHIL
3:20-21.COL 1:18.ROM 8:11.JOHN 11:25

MORNING

He has filled the hungry with good things, and the rich He has sent away empty.

You say, "I am rich, have become wealthy, and have need of nothing"—and do not know that you are wretched, miserable, poor, blind, and naked—I counsel you to buy from Me gold refined in the fire, that you may be rich. . . . As many as I love, I rebuke and chasten. Therefore be zealous and repent.

Blessed are those who hunger and thirst for righteousness, for they shall be filled. ◊ When the poor and needy seek water, and there is none, and their tongues fail for thirst, I, the Lord, will hear them; I, the God of Israel, will not forsake them. ◊ I am the Lord your God, . . . open your mouth wide, and I will fill it.

Why do you spend money for what is not bread, and your wages for what does not satisfy? Listen diligently to Me, and eat what is good, and let your soul delight itself in abundance. ◊ I am the bread of life. He who comes to Me shall never hunger, and he who believes in Me shall never thirst.

LUKE 1:53.REV 3:17-19.MATT 5:6.IS 41:17.PS 81:10.IS 55:2.JOHN 6:35

EVENING

My feet had almost stumbled; my steps had nearly slipped.

If I say, "My foot slips," Your mercy, O Lord, will hold me up.

The Lord said, "Simon, Simon! Indeed, Satan has asked for you, that he may sift you as wheat. But I have prayed for you, that your faith should not fail."

A righteous man may fall seven times and rise again. ◊ Though he fall, he shall not be utterly cast down; for the Lord upholds him with His hand.

Do not rejoice over me, my enemy; when I fall, I will arise; when I sit in darkness, the Lord will be a light to me. ◊ He shall deliver you in six troubles, yes, in seven no evil shall touch you.

If anyone sins, we have an Advocate with the Father, Jesus Christ the righteous. ◊ Therefore He is also able to save to the uttermost those who come to God through Him, since He ever lives to make intercession for them.

PS 73:2.PS 94:18.LUKE 22:31-32.PROV 24:16.PS 37:24.MIC 7:8.JOB 5:19.1 JOHN 2:1.HEB 7:25

SEPTEMBER 10

MORNING

I will give them one heart and one way, that they may fear Me forever, for the good of them and their children after them.

I will give you a new heart and put a new spirit within you. ◊ Good and upright is the Lord; therefore He teaches sinners in the way. The humble He guides in justice, and the humble He teaches His way. All the paths of the Lord are mercy and truth, to such as keep His covenant and His testimonies.

That they all may be one, as You, Father, are in Me, and I in You; that they also may be one in Us, that the world may believe that You sent Me.

I . . . beseech you to have a walk worthy of the calling with which you were called, with all lowliness and gentleness, . . . endeavoring to keep the unity of the Spirit in the bond of peace. There is one body and one Spirit, just as you were called in one hope of your calling; one Lord, one faith, one baptism; one God and Father of all, who is above all, and through all, and in you all.

JER 32:39. EZEK 36:26. PS 25:8-10. JOHN 17:21. EPH 4:1-6

EVENING

Those who wait on the Lord shall renew their strength.

When I am weak, then I am strong. ◊ My God shall be My strength. ◊ Most gladly I will rather boast in my infirmities, that the power of Christ may rest upon me. ◊ Let him take hold of My strength.

Cast your burden on the Lord, and He shall sustain you. ◊ The arms of his hands were made strong by the hands of the Mighty God of Jacob.

I will not let You go unless You bless me!

You come to me with a sword, with a spear, and with a javelin. But I come to you in the name of the Lord of hosts, the God of the armies of Israel, whom you have defied. ◊ Plead my cause, O Lord, with those who strive with me; fight against those who fight against me. Take hold of shield and buckler, and stand up for my help.

IS 40:31. 2 COR 12:10. IS 49:5. 2 COR 12:9. IS 27:5. PS 55:22. GEN 49:24. GEN 32:26. 1 SAM 17:45. PS 35:1-2

MORNING

Do not be conformed to this world, but be transformed by the renewing of your mind.

You shall not follow a crowd to do evil.

Do you not know that friendship with the world is enmity with God? Whoever therefore wants to be a friend of the world makes himself an enemy of God.

What fellowship has righteousness with lawlessness? And what communion has light with darkness? And what accord has Christ with Belial? Or what part has a believer with an unbeliever? And what agreement has the temple of God with idols? ◊ Do not love the world or the things in the world. If anyone loves the world, the love of the Father is not in him. . . . The world is passing away, and the lust of it; but he who does the will of God abides forever.

You once walked according to the course of this world, according to the prince of the power of the air, the spirit who now works in the sons of disobedience. ◊ You have not so learned Christ, if indeed you have heard Him, . . . as the truth is in Jesus.

ROM 12:2.EX 23:2.JAMES 4:4.2 COR 6:14-16.1 JOHN 2:15,17.EPH 2:2.EPH 4:20-21

EVENING

Man goes out to his work and to his labor until the evening.

In the sweat of your face you shall eat bread till you return to the ground. ◊ We commanded you this: If anyone will not work, neither shall he eat. ◊ Aspire to lead a quiet life, to mind your own business, and to work with your own hands.

Whatever your hand finds to do, do it with your might; for there is no work or device or knowledge or wisdom in the grave where you are going. ◊ The night is coming when no one can work.

Let us not grow weary while doing good, for in due season we shall reap if we do not lose heart. ◊ Always [abound] in the work of the Lord, knowing that your labor is not in vain in the Lord.

There remains . . . a rest for the people of God. ◊ To us who have borne the burden and the heat of the day. ◊ This is the rest with which you may cause the weary to rest, and this is the refreshing.

PS 104:23.GEN 3:19.2 THESS 3:10.1 THESS 4:11.ECCL 9:10.JOHN 9:4.GAL 6:9.1 COR 15:58.HEB 4:9.MATT 20:12.IS 28:12

SEPTEMBER 12

MORNING

I have seen his ways, and will heal him.

I am the Lord who heals you.

O Lord, You have searched me and known me. You know my sitting down and my rising up; You understand my thought afar off. You comprehend my path and my lying down, and are acquainted with all my ways. ◊ You have set our iniquities before You, our secret sins in the light of Your countenance. ◊ All things are naked and open to the eyes of Him to whom we must give account.

"Come now, and let us reason together," says the Lord, "though your sins are like scarlet, they shall be as white as snow; though they are red like crimson, they shall be as wool." ◊ He is gracious to him, and says, "Deliver him from going down to the Pit; I have found a ransom." ◊ He was wounded for our transgressions, He was bruised for our iniquities; the chastisement for our peace was upon Him, and by His stripes we are healed. ◊ He has sent Me to heal the brokenhearted. ◊ Your faith has made you well. Go in peace, and be healed of your affliction.

IS 57:18.EX 15:26.PS 139:1-3.PS 90:8.HEB 4:13.IS 1:18.JOB 33:24.IS 53:5.IS 61:1.MARK 5:34

EVENING

The Lord is for me.

May the Lord answer you in the day of trouble; may the name of the God of Jacob defend you; may He send you help from the sanctuary, and strengthen you out of Zion. . . . We will rejoice in your salvation, and in the name of our God we will set up our banners! . . . Some trust in chariots, and some in horses; but we will remember the name of the Lord our God. They have bowed down and fallen; but we have risen and stand upright.

When the enemy comes in like a flood, the Spirit of the Lord will lift up a standard against him. ◊ No temptation has overtaken you except such as is common to man; but God is faithful, who will not allow you to be tempted beyond what you are able, but with the temptation will also make the way of escape, that you may be able to bear it.

If God is for us, who can be against us? ◊ The Lord is on my side; I will not fear.

Our God whom we serve is able to deliver us . . . and He will deliver us.

PS 118:7.PS 20:1-2,5,7-8.IS 59:19.1 COR 10:13.ROM 8:31.PS 118:6.DAN 3:17

MORNING

If anyone thirsts, let him come to Me and drink.

My soul longs, yes, even faints for the courts of the Lord; my heart and my flesh cry out for the living God. ◊ O God, You are my God; early will I seek You; my soul thirsts for You; my flesh longs for You in a dry and thirsty land where there is no water. So I have looked for You in the sanctuary, to see Your power and Your glory.

Ho! Everyone who thirsts, come to the waters; and you who have no money, come, buy and eat. Yes, come, buy wine and milk without money and without price. ◊ The Spirit and the bride say, "Come!" And let him who hears say, "Come!" And let him who thirsts come. And whoever desires, let him take the water of life freely. ◊ Whoever drinks of the water that I shall give him will never thirst. But the water that I shall give him will become in him a fountain of water springing up into everlasting life. ◊ My blood is drink indeed.

Eat, O friends! Drink, yes, drink deeply, O beloved ones!

JOHN 7:37.PS 84:2.PS 63:1-2.IS 55:1.REV 22:17.JOHN 4:14.JOHN 6:55.SONG 5:1

EVENING

You are the salt of the earth.

The incorruptible ornament. ◊ Having been born again, not of corruptible seed but incorruptible, through the word of God which lives and abides forever. ◊ He who believes in Me, though he may die, he shall live. ◊ Sons of God, being sons of the resurrection. ◊ The incorruptible God.

If anyone does not have the Spirit of Christ, he is not His. And if Christ is in you, the body is dead because of sin, but the Spirit is life because of righteousness. But if the Spirit of Him who raised Jesus from the dead dwells in you, He who raised Christ from the dead will also give life to your mortal bodies through His Spirit who dwells in you. ◊ The body is sown in corruption, it is raised in incorruption.

Have salt in yourselves, and have peace with one another. ◊ Let no corrupt communication proceed out of your mouth, but what is good for necessary edification, that it may impart grace to the hearers.

MATT 5:13.1 PET 3:4.1 PET 1:23.JOHN 11:25.LUKE 20:36.ROM 1:23.ROM 8:9-11.1 COR 15:42.MARK 9:50.EPH 4:29

MORNING

I, even I, am He who comforts you.

Blessed be the God and Father of our Lord Jesus Christ, the Father of mercies and God of all comfort, who comforts us in all our tribulation, that we may be able to comfort those who are in any trouble, with the comfort with which we ourselves are comforted by God. ◊ As a father pities his children, so the Lord pities those who fear Him. For He knows our frame; He remembers that we are dust. ◊ As one whom his mother comforts, so I will comfort you. ◊ [Cast] all your care upon Him, for He cares for you.

You, O Lord, are a God full of compassion, and gracious, longsuffering and abundant in mercy and truth.

He will give you another Helper, . . . even the Spirit of truth. ◊ The Spirit . . . helps in our weaknesses.

God will wipe away every tear from their eyes; there shall be no more death, nor sorrow, nor crying; and there shall be no more pain, for the former things have passed away.

IS 51:12.2 COR 1:3-4.PS 103:13-14.IS 66:13.1 PET 5:7.PS 86:15.JOHN 14:16-17.ROM 8:26.REV 21:4

EVENING

You were called into the fellowship of His Son.

He received from God the Father honor and glory when such a voice came to Him from the Excellent Glory: "This is My beloved Son, in whom I am well pleased." ◊ Behold what manner of love the Father has bestowed on us, that we should be called children of God!

Be followers of God as dear children. ◊ If children, then heirs—heirs of God and joint heirs with Christ.

The brightness of His glory and the express image of His person. ◊ Let your light so shine before men, that they may see your good works and glorify your Father in heaven.

Jesus, the author and finisher of our faith, who for the joy that was set before Him endured the cross, despising the shame. ◊ These things I speak in the world, that they may have My joy fulfilled in themselves. ◊ As the sufferings of Christ abound in us, so our consolation also abounds through Christ.

1 COR 1:9.2 PET 1:17.1 JOHN 3:1.EPH 5:1.ROM 8:17.HEB 1:3.MATT 5:16.HEB 12:2.JOHN 17:13.2 COR 1:5

MORNING

Sin shall not have dominion over you, for you are not under law but under grace.

What then? Shall we sin because we are not under law but under grace? Certainly not! ◊ My brethren, you . . . have become dead to the law through the body of Christ, that you may be married to another, even to Him who was raised from the dead, that we should bear fruit to God. ◊ Being without law toward God, but under law toward Christ. ◊ The sting of death is sin, and the strength of sin is the law. But thanks be to God, who gives us the victory through our Lord Jesus Christ.

The law of the Spirit of life in Christ Jesus has made me free from the law of sin and death. ◊ Whoever commits sin is a slave of sin. ◊ If the Son makes you free, you shall be free indeed.

Stand fast therefore in the liberty by which Christ has made us free, and do not be entangled again with a yoke of bondage.

ROM 6:14.ROM 6:15.ROM 7:4.1 COR 9:21.1 COR 15:56-57.ROM 8:2.JOHN 8:34.JOHN 8:36.GAL 5:1

EVENING

A double-minded man, unstable in all his ways.

No one, having put his hand to the plow, and looking back, is fit for the kingdom of God.

He who comes to God must believe that He is, and that He is a rewarder of those who diligently seek Him. ◊ Let him ask in faith, with no doubting, for he who doubts is like a wave of the sea driven and tossed by the wind. For let not that man suppose that he will receive anything from the Lord. ◊ Whatever things you ask when you pray, believe that you receive them, and you will have them.

No longer be children, tossed to and fro and carried about with every wind of doctrine, by the trickery of men, in the cunning craftiness by which they lie in wait to deceive, but, speaking the truth in love, . . . grow up in all things into Him who is the head—Christ.

Abide in Me. ◊ Be steadfast, immovable, always abounding in the work of the Lord, knowing that your labor is not in vain in the Lord.

JAMES 1:8.LUKE 9:62.HEB 11:6.JAMES 1:6-7.MARK 11:24.EPH 4:14-15.JOHN 15:4.1 COR 15:58

SEPTEMBER 16

MORNING

The Lord weighs the hearts.

The Lord knows the way of the righteous, but the way of the ungodly shall perish. ◊ The Lord will show who is His and who is holy. ◊ Your Father who sees in secret will Himself reward you openly.

Search me, O God, and know my heart; try me, and know my anxieties; and see if there is any wicked way in me, and lead me in the way everlasting. ◊ There is no fear in love; but perfect love casts out fear.

Lord, all my desire is before You; and my sighing is not hidden from You. ◊ When my spirit was overwhelmed within me, then You knew my path. ◊ He who searches the hearts knows what the mind of the Spirit is, because He makes intercession for the saints according to the will of God.

The solid foundation of God stands, having this seal: "The Lord knows those who are His," and, "Let everyone who names the name of Christ depart from iniquity."

PROV 21:2.PS 1:6.NUM 16:5.MATT 6:4.PS 139:23-24.1 JOHN 4:18.PS 38:9.PS 142:3.ROM 8:27.2 TIM 2:19

EVENING

Weeping may endure for a night, but joy comes in the morning.

No one should be shaken by these afflictions; for you yourselves know that we are appointed to this. For, in fact, we told you before when we were with you that we would suffer tribulation. ◊ In Me you . . . have peace. In the world you will have tribulation; but be of good cheer, I have overcome the world.

I shall be satisfied when I awake in Your likeness. ◊ The night is far spent, the day is at hand. ◊ He shall be like the light of the morning when the sun rises, a morning without clouds, like the tender grass springing out of the earth, by clear shining after rain.

He will swallow up death forever, and the Lord God will wipe away tears from all faces. ◊ There shall be no more death, nor sorrow, nor crying; and there shall be no more pain, for the former things have passed away. ◊ We who are alive and remain shall be caught up together with them in the clouds to meet the Lord in the air. Therefore comfort one another with these words.

PS 30:5.1 THESS 3:3-4.JOHN 16:33.PS 17:15.ROM 13:12.2 SAM 23:4.IS 25:8.REV 21:4.1 THESS 4:17-18

MORNING

A bruised reed He will not break.

The sacrifices of God are a broken spirit, a broken and a contrite heart—these, O God, You will not despise. ◊ He heals the broken-hearted and binds up their wounds. ◊ Thus says the High and Lofty One who inhabits eternity, whose name is Holy: "I dwell in the high and holy place, with him who has a contrite and humble spirit, to revive the spirit of the humble, and to revive the heart of the contrite ones. For I will not contend forever, nor will I always be angry; for the spirit would fail before Me, and the souls which I have made."

I will seek what was lost and bring back what was driven away, bind up the broken and strengthen what was sick. ◊ Therefore strengthen the hands which hang down, and the feeble knees, and make straight paths for your feet, so that what is lame may not be dislocated, but rather be healed. ◊ Behold, your God . . . will come and save you.

MATT 12:20.PS 51:17.PS 147:3.IS 57:15-16.EZEK 34:16.HEB 12:12-13.IS
35:4

EVENING

**Oh, taste and see that the Lord is good; blessed is the
man who trusts in Him!**

When the master of the feast had tasted the water that was made wine, and did not know where it came from, . . . he said . . . , "Every man at the beginning sets out the good wine, and when the guests have well drunk, then that which is inferior; but you have kept the good wine until now."

The ear tests words as the palate tastes food. ◊ I believed and therefore I spoke. ◊ I know whom I have believed. ◊ I sat down in his shade with great delight, and his fruit was sweet to my taste.

The goodness of God. ◊ He who did not spare His own Son, but delivered Him up for us all, how shall He not with Him also freely give us all things?

As newborn babes, desire the pure milk of the word, that you may grow thereby, if indeed you have tasted that the Lord is gracious.

Let all those rejoice who put their trust in You; let them ever shout for joy.

PS 34:8.JOHN 2:9-10.JOB 34:3.2 COR 4:13.2 TIM 1:12.SONG 2:3.ROM
2:4.ROM 8:32.1 PET 2:2-3.PS 5:11

SEPTEMBER 18

MORNING

Open my eyes, that I may see wondrous things from Your law.

He opened their understanding, that they might comprehend the Scriptures. ◊ It has been given to you to know the mysteries of the kingdom of heaven, but to them it has not been given. ◊ I thank You, Father, Lord of heaven and earth, because You have hidden these things from the wise and prudent and have revealed them to babes. Even so, Father, for so it seemed good in Your sight. ◊ We have received, not the spirit of the world, but the Spirit who is from God, that we might know the things that have been freely given to us by God. ◊ How precious also are Your thoughts to me, O God! How great is the sum of them! If I should count them, they would be more in number than the sand. ◊ Oh, the depth of the riches both of the wisdom and knowledge of God! How unsearchable are His judgments and His ways past finding out! For who has known the mind of the Lord? Or who has become His counselor? . . . For of Him and through Him and to Him are all things, to whom be glory forever. Amen.

PS 119:18.LUKE 24:45.MATT 13:11.MATT 11:25-26.1 COR 2:12.PS 139:17-18.ROM 11:33-34,36

EVENING

He called its name En Hakkore [Spring of the Caller].

If you knew the gift of God, and who it is who says to you, "Give Me a drink," you would have asked Him, and He would have given you living water. ◊ If anyone thirsts, let him come to Me and drink. This He spoke concerning the Spirit, whom those believing in Him would receive.

"Prove Me now in this," says the Lord of hosts, "if I will not open for you the windows of heaven and pour out for you such blessing that there will not be room enough to receive it." ◊ If you . . . being evil, know how to give good gifts to your children, how much more will your heavenly Father give the Holy Spirit to those who ask Him! ◊ Ask, and it will be given to you; seek, and you will find.

Because you are sons, God has sent forth the Spirit of His Son into your hearts, crying out, "Abba, Father!" ◊ You did not receive the spirit of bondage again to fear, but you received the Spirit of adoption by whom we cry out, "Abba, Father."

JUDG 15:19.JOHN 4:10.JOHN 7:37,39.MAL 3:10.LUKE 11:13.LUKE 11:9.GAL 4:6.ROM 8:15

MORNING

The God of all grace.

I will proclaim the name of the Lord before you. I will be gracious to whom I will be gracious. ◊ He is gracious to him, and says, "Deliver him from going down to the Pit; I have found a ransom." ◊ Being justified freely by His grace through the redemption that is in Christ Jesus, whom God set forth to be a propitiation by His blood, through faith, to demonstrate His righteousness, because in His forbearance God had passed over the sins that were previously committed. ◊ Grace and truth came through Jesus Christ.

By grace you have been saved through faith, and that not of yourselves; it is the gift of God. ◊ Grace, mercy, and peace from God our Father and Jesus Christ our Lord. ◊ To each one of us grace was given according to the measure of Christ's gift. ◊ As each one has received a gift, minister it to one another, as good stewards of the manifold grace of God. ◊ He gives more grace.

Grow in the grace and knowledge of our Lord and Savior Jesus Christ. To Him be the glory both now and forever.

1 PET 5:10.EX 33:19.JOB 33:24.ROM 3:24-25.JOHN 1:17.EPH 2:8.1 TIM 1:2.EPH 4:7.1 PET 4:10.JAMES 4:6.2 PET 3:18

EVENING

I will lift up my eyes to the hills from whence comes my help? My help comes from the Lord.

As the mountains surround Jerusalem, so the Lord surrounds His people from this time forth and forever.

Unto You I lift up my eyes, O You who dwell in the heavens. Behold, as the eyes of servants look to the hand of their masters, as the eyes of a maid to the hand of her mistress, so our eyes look to the Lord our God, until He has mercy on us. ◊ Because You have been my help, therefore in the shadow of Your wings I will rejoice.

O our God, will You not judge them? For we have no power against this great multitude that is coming against us; nor do we know what to do, but our eyes are upon You. ◊ My eyes are ever toward the Lord, for He shall pluck my feet out of the net. ◊ Our help is in the name of the Lord, who made heaven and earth.

PS 121:1-2.PS 125:2.PS 123:1-2.PS 63:7.2 CHR 20:12.PS 25:15.PS 124:8

SEPTEMBER 20

MORNING

Happy is the man who finds wisdom, and the man who gains understanding.

Whoever finds me finds life, and obtains favor from the Lord.

Thus says the Lord: "Let not the wise man glory in his wisdom, let not the mighty man glory in his might, . . . but let him who glories glory in this, that he understands and knows Me, that I am the Lord." ◊ The fear of the Lord is the beginning of wisdom.

What things were gain to me, these I have counted loss for Christ. But indeed I also count all things loss for the excellence of the knowledge of Christ Jesus my Lord, for whom I have suffered the loss of all things, and count them as rubbish, that I may gain Christ. ◊ In [Him] are hidden all the treasures of wisdom and knowledge. ◊ Counsel is mine, and sound wisdom; I am understanding, I have strength.

Christ Jesus . . . became for us wisdom . . . and righteousness and sanctification and redemption.

He who wins souls is wise.

PROV 3:13.PROV 8:35.JER 9:23-24.PROV 9:10.PHIL 3:7-8.COL 2:3.PROV 8:14.1 COR 1:30.PROV 11:30

EVENING

Poor, yet making many rich.

You know the grace of our Lord Jesus Christ, that though He was rich, yet for your sakes He became poor, that you through His poverty might become rich. ◊ Of His fullness we have all received, and grace for grace. ◊ My God shall supply all your need according to His riches in glory by Christ Jesus. ◊ God is able to make all grace abound toward you, that you, always having all sufficiency in all things, have an abundance for every good work.

Has God not chosen the poor of this world to be rich in faith and heirs of the kingdom which He promised to those who love Him? ◊ Not many wise according to the flesh, not many mighty, not many noble, are called. But God has chosen the foolish things of the world to put to shame the wise, and God has chosen the weak things of the world to put to shame the things which are mighty.

We have this treasure in earthen vessels, that the excellence of the power may be of God and not of us.

2 COR 6:10.2 COR 8:9.JOHN 1:16.PHIL 4:19.2 COR 9:8.JAMES 2:5. 1 COR 1:26-27.2 COR 4:7

MORNING

We know that all things work together for good to those who love God.

Surely the wrath of man shall praise You; with the remainder of wrath You shall gird Yourself. ◊ You meant evil against me; but God meant it for good.

All things are yours: whether . . . the world or life or death, or things present or things to come all are yours. And you are Christ's, and Christ is God's. ◊ All things are for your sakes, that grace, having spread through the many, may cause thanksgiving to abound to the glory of God. Therefore we do not lose heart. Even though our outward man is perishing, yet the inward man is being renewed day by day. For our light affliction, which is but for a moment, is working for us a far more exceeding and eternal weight of glory.

My brethren, count it all joy when you fall into various trials, knowing that the testing of your faith produces patience. But let patience have its perfect work, that you may be perfect and complete, lacking nothing.

ROM 8:28.PS 76:10.GEN 50:20.1 COR 3:21-23.2 COR 4:15-17.JAMES
1:2-4

EVENING

The communion of the Holy Spirit be with you all.

I will pray the Father, and He will give you another Helper, that He may abide with you forever, even the Spirit of truth, whom the world cannot receive, because it neither sees Him nor knows Him; but you know Him, for He dwells with you and will be in you. ◊ He will not speak on His own authority, . . . He will glorify Me, for He will take of what is Mine and declare it to you.

The love of God has been poured out in our hearts by the Holy Spirit who was given to us.

He who is joined to the Lord is one spirit. . . . Do you not know that your body is the temple of the Holy Spirit who is in you, whom you have from God, and you are not your own?

Do not grieve the Holy Spirit of God, by whom you were sealed for the day of redemption. ◊ The Spirit also helps in our weaknesses. For we do not know what we should pray for as we ought, but the Spirit Himself makes intercession for us with groanings which cannot be uttered.

2 COR 13:14.JOHN 14:16-17.JOHN 16:13-14.ROM 5:5.1 COR 6:17,
19.EPH 4:30.ROM 8:26

SEPTEMBER 22

MORNING

May my meditation be sweet to Him; I will be glad in the Lord.

Like an apple tree among the trees of the woods, so is my beloved among the sons. I sat down in his shade with great delight, and his fruit was sweet to my taste. ◊ For who in the heavens can be compared to the Lord? Who among the sons of the mighty can be likened to the Lord?

My beloved is white and ruddy, chief among ten thousand. ◊ One pearl of great price. ◊ The ruler over the kings of the earth.

His head is like the finest gold; his locks are wavy, and black as a raven. ◊ Head over all things. ◊ He is the head of the body, the church.

His cheeks are like a bed of spices, like banks of scented herbs. ◊ He could not be hidden.

His lips are lilies, dripping liquid myrrh. ◊ No man ever spoke like this Man!

His countenance is like Lebanon, excellent as the cedars. ◊ Make Your face shine upon Your servant. ◊ Lord, lift up the light of Your countenance upon us.

PS 104:34.SONG 2:3.PS 89:6.SONG 5:10.MATT 13:46.REV 1:5.SONG 5:11.EPH 1:22.COL 1:18.SONG 5:13.MARK 7:24.SONG 5:13.JOHN 7:46.SONG 5:15.PS 31:16.PS 4:6

EVENING

O My Father, if it is possible, let this cup pass from Me; nevertheless, not as I will, but as You will.

Now My soul is troubled, and what shall I say? "Father, save Me from this hour"? But for this purpose I came to this hour.

I have come down from heaven, not to do My own will, but the will of Him who sent Me. ◊ He . . . became obedient to the point of death. ◊ In the days of His flesh, when He had offered up prayers and supplications, with vehement cries and tears to Him who was able to save Him from death, and was heard because of His godly fear, though He was a Son, yet He learned obedience by the things which He suffered.

Do you think that I cannot now pray to My Father, and He will provide Me with more than twelve legions of angels? ◊ Thus it is written, and thus it was necessary for the Christ to suffer and to rise from the dead the third day, and that repentance and remission of sins should be preached in His name to all nations, beginning at Jerusalem.

MATT 26:39.JOHN 12:27.JOHN 6:38.PHIL 2:8.HEB 5:7-8.MATT 26:53.LUKE 24:46-47

MORNING

Our God did not forsake us.

Beloved, do not think it strange concerning the fiery trial which is to try you, as though some strange thing happened to you. ◊ If you endure chastening, God deals with you as with sons; for what son is there whom a father does not chasten? But if you are without chastening, of which all have become partakers, then you are illegitimate and not sons.

The Lord your God is testing you to know whether you love the Lord your God with all your heart and with all your soul.

The Lord will not forsake His people, for His great name's sake, because it has pleased the Lord to make you His people. ◊ Can a woman forget her nursing child, and not have compassion on the son of her womb? Surely they may forget, yet I will not forget you. ◊ Happy is he who has the God of Jacob for his help, whose hope is in the Lord his God.

Shall God not avenge His own elect who cry out day and night to Him, though He bears long with them? I tell you that He will avenge them speedily.

EZRA 9:9.1 PET 4:12.HEB 12:7-8.DEUT 13:3.1 SAM 12:22.IS 49:15.PS 146:5.LUKE 18:7-8

EVENING

He who overcomes shall inherit all things.

If in this life only we have hope in Christ, we are of all men the most pitiable. ◊ Now they desire a better, that is, a heavenly country. Therefore God is not ashamed to be called their God, for He has prepared a city for them. ◊ An inheritance incorruptible and undefiled and that does not fade away, reserved in heaven for you.

All things are yours: Whether. . . the world or life or death, or things present or things to come all are yours. ◊ Eye has not seen, nor ear heard, nor have entered into the heart of man the things which God has prepared for those who love Him. But God has revealed them to us through His Spirit.

Look to yourselves, that we do not lose those things we worked for, but that we may receive a full reward. ◊ Let us lay aside every weight, and the sin which so easily ensnares us, and let us run with endurance the race that is set before us.

REV 21:7.1 COR 15:19.HEB 11:16.1 PET 1:4.1 COR 3:21-22.1 COR 2:9-10.2 JOHN 1:8.HEB 12:1

SEPTEMBER 24

MORNING

It is good for me to draw near to God.

Lord, I have loved the habitation of Your house, and the place where Your glory dwells. ◊ A day in Your courts is better than a thousand. I would rather be a doorkeeper in the house of my God than dwell in the tents of wickedness. ◊ Blessed is the man whom You choose, and cause to approach You, that he may dwell in Your courts. We shall be satisfied with the goodness of Your house, of Your holy temple.

The Lord is good to those who wait for Him, to the soul who seeks Him. ◊ Therefore the Lord will wait, that He may be gracious to you; and therefore He will be exalted, that He may have mercy on you. For the Lord is a God of justice; blessed are all those who wait for Him.

Therefore, brethren, having boldness to enter the Holiest by the blood of Jesus, by a new and living way which He consecrated for us, . . . let us draw near with a true heart in full assurance of faith, having our hearts sprinkled from an evil conscience.

PS 73:28.PS 26:8.PS 84:10.PS 65:4.LAM 3:25.IS 30:18.HEB 10:19-20,22

EVENING

You know the grace of our Lord Jesus Christ.

The Word became flesh and dwelt among us, and we beheld His glory, the glory as of the only begotten of the Father, full of grace and truth. ◊ You are fairer than the sons of men; grace is poured upon Your lips. ◊ All bore witness to Him, and marveled at the gracious words which proceeded out of His mouth.

You have tasted that the Lord is gracious. ◊ He who believes in the Son of God has the witness in himself. ◊ We speak what We know and testify what We have seen.

Oh, taste and see that the Lord is good; blessed is the man who trusts in Him! ◊ I sat down in his shade with great delight, and his fruit was sweet to my taste.

He said to me, "My grace is sufficient for you, for My strength is made perfect in weakness." ◊ To each one of us grace was given according to the measure of Christ's gift. ◊ As each one has received a gift, minister it to one another, as good stewards of the manifold grace of God.

2 COR 8:9.JOHN 1:14.PS 45:2.LUKE 4:22.1 PET 2:3.1 JOHN 5:10.JOHN 3:11.PS 34:8.SONG 2:3.2 COR 12:9.EPH 4:7.1 PET 4:10

MORNING

**Let patience have its perfect work, that you may be
perfect and complete, lacking nothing.**

Now for a little while, if need be, you have been grieved by various trials, that the genuineness of your faith, being much more precious than gold that perishes, though it is tested by fire, may be found to praise, honor, and glory at the revelation of Jesus Christ. ◊ We also glory in tribulations, knowing that tribulation produces perseverance; and perseverance, character; and character, hope.

It is good that one should hope and wait quietly for the salvation of the Lord. ◊ You have a better and an enduring possession for yourselves in heaven. Do not cast away your confidence, which has great reward. For you have need of endurance, so that after you have done the will of God, you may receive the promise. ◊ Our Lord Jesus Christ Himself, and our God and Father, who has loved us and given us everlasting consolation and good hope by grace, comfort your hearts.

JAMES 1:4.1 PET 1:6-7.ROM 5:3-4.LAM 3:26.HEB 10:34-36.2 THESS
2:16-17

EVENING

God will judge the secrets of men by Jesus Christ.

Judge nothing before the time, until the Lord comes, who will both bring to light the hidden things of darkness and reveal the counsels of the hearts; and then each one's praise will come from God. ◊ The Father judges no one, but has committed all judgment to the Son . . . because He is the Son of Man. ◊ The Son of God . . . has eyes like a flame of fire.

They say, "How does God know? And is there knowledge in the Most High?" ◊ These things you have done, and I kept silent; you thought that I was altogether like you; but I will reprove you, and set them in order before your eyes. ◊ There is nothing covered that will not be revealed, nor hidden that will not be known.

Lord, all my desire is before You; and my sighing is not hidden from You. ◊ Examine me, O Lord, and prove me; try my mind and my heart.

ROM 2:16.1 COR 4:5.JOHN 5:22,27.REV 2:18.PS 73:11.PS 50:21.LUKE
12:2.PS 38:9.PS 26:2

MORNING

A God of truth and without injustice; righteous and upright is He.

Him who judges righteously. ◊ We must all appear before the judgment seat of Christ, that each one may receive the things done in the body, according to what he has done, whether good or bad. ◊ Each of us shall give account of himself to God. ◊ The soul who sins shall die.

"Awake, O sword, against My Shepherd, against the Man who is My Companion," says the Lord of hosts. "Strike the Shepherd." ◊ The Lord has laid on Him the iniquity of us all. ◊ Mercy and truth have met together; righteousness and peace have kissed each other. ◊ Mercy triumphs over judgment.

The wages of sin is death, but the gift of God is eternal life in Christ Jesus our Lord.

A just God and a Savior; there is none besides Me. ◊ Just and the justifier of the one who has faith in Jesus. ◊ Justified freely by His grace through the redemption that is in Christ Jesus.

DEUT 32:4.1 PET 2:23.2 COR 5:10.ROM 14:12.EZEK 18:4.ZECH 13:7.IS 53:6.PS 85:10.JAMES 2:13.ROM 6:23.IS 45:21.ROM 3:26.ROM 3:24

EVENING

Death is swallowed up in victory.

Thanks be to God, who gives us the victory through our Lord Jesus Christ.

Inasmuch . . . as the children have partaken of flesh and blood, He Himself likewise shared in the same, that through death He might destroy him who had the power of death, that is, the devil, and release those who through fear of death were all their lifetime subject to bondage.

If we died with Christ, we believe that we shall also live with Him, knowing that Christ, having been raised from the dead, dies no more. Death no longer has dominion over Him. For the death that He died, He died to sin once for all; but the life that He lives, He lives to God.

Likewise you also, reckon yourselves to be dead indeed to sin, but alive to God in Christ Jesus our Lord.

Yet in all these things we are more than conquerors through Him who loved us.

1 COR 15:54.1 COR 15:57.HEB 2:14-15.ROM 6:8-11.ROM 8:37

MORNING

Humble yourselves under the mighty hand of God, that He may exalt you in due time.

Everyone who is proud in heart is an abomination to the Lord; though they join forces, none will go unpunished.

O Lord, You are our Father; we are the clay, and You our potter; and all we are the work of Your hand. Do not be furious, O Lord, nor remember iniquity forever; indeed, please look—we all are Your people! ◊ You have chastised me, and I was chastised, like an untrained bull; restore me, and I will return, for You are the Lord my God. Surely, after my turning, I repented; and after I was instructed, I struck myself on the thigh; I was ashamed, yes, even humiliated, because I bore the reproach of my youth. ◊ It is good for a man to bear the yoke in his youth.

Affliction does not come from the dust, nor does trouble spring from the ground; yet man is born to trouble, as the sparks fly upward.

1 PET 5:6.PROV 16:5.IS 64:8-9.JER 31:18-19.LAM 3:27.JOB 5:6-7

EVENING

Has God indeed said. . . ?

When the tempter came to Him, he said, "If You are the Son of God. . . ." He answered and said, "It is written. . . . It is written. . . . It is written. . . ." Then the devil left Him.

"I cannot return with you. . . . For I have been told by the word of the Lord, 'You shall not eat bread nor drink water there.' " . . . He said to him, "I too am a prophet as you are, and an angel spoke to me by the word of the Lord, saying, 'Bring him back with you to your house, that he may eat bread and drink water.' " But he lied to him. So he went back with him. . . . The man of God . . . was disobedient to the word of the Lord. Therefore the Lord has delivered him to the lion, which has torn him and killed him, according to the word of the Lord. ◊ If we, or an angel from heaven, preach any other gospel to you than what we have preached to you, let him be accursed. ◊ Your word I have hidden in my heart, that I might not sin against You.

GEN 3:1.MATT 4:3-4,7,10-11.1 KIN 13:16-19,26.GAL 1:8.PS 119:11

SEPTEMBER 28

MORNING

They shall put My name on the children of Israel, and I will bless them.

O Lord our God, other masters besides You have had dominion over us; but by You only we make mention of Your name. ◊ We have become like those of old, over whom You never ruled, those who were never called by Your name.

All peoples of the earth shall see that you are called by the name of the Lord, and they shall be afraid of you. ◊ The Lord will not forsake His people, for His great name's sake, because it has pleased the Lord to make you His people.

O Lord, hear! O Lord, forgive! O Lord, listen and act! Do not delay for Your own sake, my God, for Your city and Your people are called by Your name. ◊ Help us, O God of our salvation, for the glory of Your name; and deliver us, and provide atonement for our sins, for Your name's sake! Why should the nations say, "Where is their God?" ◊ The name of the Lord is a strong tower; the righteous run to it and are safe.

NUM 6:27.IS 26:13.IS 63:19.DEUT 28:10.1 SAM 12:22.DAN 9:19.PS 79:9-10.PROV 18:10

EVENING

The heavens declare the glory of God; and the firmament shows His handiwork.

Since the creation of the world His invisible attributes are clearly seen, being understood by the things that are made, even His eternal power and Godhead. ◊ He did not leave Himself without witness. ◊ Day unto day utters speech, and night unto night reveals knowledge. ◊ There is no speech nor language where their voice is not heard.

When I consider Your heavens, the work of Your fingers, the moon and the stars, which You have ordained, what is man that You are mindful of him, and the son of man that You visit him?

There is one glory of the sun, another glory of the moon, and another glory of the stars; for one star differs from another star in glory. So also is the resurrection of the dead. ◊ Those who are wise shall shine like the brightness of the firmament, and those who turn many to righteousness like the stars forever and ever.

PS 19:1.ROM 1:20.ACTS 14:17.PS 19:2-3.PS 8:3-4.1 COR 15:41-42.DAN 12:3

MORNING

**By this we know love, because He laid down His life
for us.**

The love of Christ . . . passes knowledge. ◊ Greater love has no one than this, than to lay down one's life for his friends. ◊ You know the grace of our Lord Jesus Christ, that though He was rich, yet for your sakes He became poor, that you through His poverty might become rich. ◊ Beloved, if God so loved us, we also ought to love one another. ◊ Be kind to one another, tenderhearted, forgiving one another, just as God in Christ also forgave you. ◊ [Bear] with one another, and [forgive] one another, if anyone has a complaint against another; even as Christ forgave you. ◊ For even the Son of Man did not come to be served, but to serve, and to give His life a ransom for many. ◊ Christ . . . suffered for us, leaving us an example, that you should follow His steps.

You also ought to wash one another's feet. For I have given you an example, that you should do as I have done to you. ◊ We also ought to lay down our lives for the brethren.

1 JOHN 3:16.EPH 3:19.JOHN 15:13.2 COR 8:9.1 JOHN 4:11.EPH
4:32.COL 3:13.MARK 10:45.1 PET 2:21.JOHN 13:14-15.1 JOHN 3:16

EVENING

**The Son can do nothing of Himself, but what He sees
the Father do; for whatever He does, the Son also does
in like manner.**

The Lord gives wisdom; from His mouth come knowledge and understanding. ◊ I will give you a mouth and wisdom which all your adversaries will not be able to contradict or resist.

Wait on the Lord; be of good courage, and He shall strengthen your heart. ◊ My grace is sufficient for you, for My strength is made perfect in weakness.

Those who are called, sanctified by God the Father. ◊ Both He who sanctifies and those who are being sanctified are all of one, for which reason He is not ashamed to call them brethren.

"Do I not fill heaven and earth?" says the Lord. ◊ "I, even I, am the Lord, and besides Me there is no savior." ◊ This is indeed the Christ, the Savior of the world.

Grace, mercy, and peace from God the Father and the Lord Jesus Christ our Savior.

JOHN 5:19.PROV 2:6.LUKE 21:15.PS 27:14.2 COR 12:9.JUDE 1:1.HEB
2:11.JER 23:24.IS 43:11.JOHN 4:42.TITUS 1:4

SEPTEMBER 30

MORNING

He knows the way that I take; when He has tested me, I shall come forth as gold.

He knows our frame. ◇ He does not afflict willingly, nor grieve the children of men.

The solid foundation of God stands, having this seal: "The Lord knows those who are His," and, "Let everyone who names the name of Christ depart from iniquity." But in a great house there are not only vessels of gold and silver, but also of wood and clay, some for honor and some for dishonor. Therefore if anyone cleanses himself from the latter, he will be a vessel for honor, sanctified and useful for the Master, prepared for every good work.

He will sit as a refiner and a purifier of silver; He will purify the sons of Levi, and purge them as gold and silver, that they may offer to the Lord an offering in righteousness. ◇ I . . . will refine them as silver is refined. . . . They will call on My name, and I will answer them. I will say, "This is My people"; and each one will say, "The Lord is my God."

JOB 23:10.PS 103:14.LAM 3:33.2 TIM 2:19-21.MAL 3:3.ZECH 13:9

EVENING

Show me Your ways, O Lord; teach me Your paths.

Moses said to the Lord, " . . . I pray, if I have found grace in Your sight, show me now Your way, that I may know You." . . . And He said, "My Presence will go with you, and I will give you rest." ◇ He made known His ways to Moses, His acts to the children of Israel.

The humble He guides in justice, and the humble He teaches His way. . . . Who is the man that fears the Lord? Him shall He teach in the way He chooses. ◇ Trust in the Lord with all your heart, and lean not on your own understanding; in all your ways acknowledge Him, and He shall direct your paths.

You will show me the path of life; in Your presence is fullness of joy; at Your right hand are pleasures forevermore. ◇ I will instruct you and teach you in the way you should go; I will guide you with My eye. ◇ The path of the just is like the shining sun, that shines ever brighter unto the perfect day.

PS 25:4.EX 33:12-14.PS 103:7.PS 25:9,12.PROV 3:5-6.PS 16:11.PS 32:8.PROV 4:18

MORNING

The fruit of the Spirit is . . . self-control.

Everyone who competes for the prize is temperate in all things. Now they do it to obtain a perishable crown, but we for an imperishable crown. Therefore I run thus: not with uncertainty. Thus I fight: not as one who beats the air. But I discipline my body and bring it into subjection, lest, when I have preached to others, I myself should become disqualified.

Do not be drunk with wine, in which is dissipation; but be filled with the Spirit.

If anyone desires to come after Me, let him deny himself, and take up his cross, and follow Me.

Let us not sleep, as others do, but let us watch and be sober. For those who sleep, sleep at night, and those who get drunk are drunk at night. But let us who are of the day be sober. ◊ Denying ungodliness and worldly lusts, we should live soberly, righteously, and godly in the present age, looking for the blessed hope and glorious appearing of our great God and Savior Jesus Christ.

GAL 5:22-23.1 COR 9:25-27.EPH 5:18.MATT 16:24.1 THESS 5:6-8.TITUS 2:12-13

EVENING

Grow up in all things into Him who is the head—Christ.

First the blade, then the head, after that the full grain in the head. ◊ Till we all come to the unity of the faith and the knowledge of the Son of God, to a perfect man, to the measure of the stature of the fullness of Christ.

They, measuring themselves by themselves, and comparing themselves among themselves, are not wise. . . . But He who glories, let him glory in the Lord. For not he who commends himself is approved, but whom the Lord commends.

The substance is of Christ. Let no one defraud you of your reward, taking delight in false humility and worship of angels, intruding into those things which he has not seen, vainly puffed up by his fleshly mind, and not holding fast to the Head, from whom all the body, nourished and knit together by joints and ligaments, grows with the increase which is from God.

Grow in the grace and knowledge of our Lord and Savior Jesus Christ.

EPH 4:15.MARK 4:28.EPH 4:13.2 COR 10:12,17-18.COL 2:17-19.2 PET 3:18

OCTOBER 2

MORNING

The goat shall bear on itself all their iniquities to an uninhabited land; and he shall release the goat in the wilderness.

As far as the east is from the west, so far has He removed our transgressions from us. ◊ "In those days and in that time," says the Lord, "the iniquity of Israel shall be sought, but there shall be none; and the sins of Judah, but they shall not be found; for I will pardon those whom I preserve." ◊ You will cast all our sins into the depths of the sea. ◊ Who is a God like You, pardoning iniquity?

All we like sheep have gone astray; we have turned, every one, to his own way; and the Lord has laid on Him the iniquity of us all. ◊ He shall bear their iniquities. Therefore I will divide Him a portion with the great, and He shall divide the spoil with the strong, because He poured out His soul unto death, and He was numbered with the transgressors, and He bore the sin of many, and made intercession for the transgressors. ◊ The Lamb of God who takes away the sin of the world!

LEV 16:22.PS 103:12.JER 50:20.MIC 7:19.MIC 7:18.IS 53:6.IS 53:11-12.JOHN 1:29

EVENING

Who makes you differ from another? And what do you have that you did not receive?

By the grace of God I am what I am. ◊ Of His own will He brought us forth by the word of truth. ◊ It is not of him who wills, nor of him who runs, but of God who shows mercy. ◊ Where is boasting then? It is excluded. ◊ Christ Jesus . . . became for us wisdom from God and righteousness and sanctification and redemption. . . . He who glories, let him glory in the Lord.

You He made alive, who were dead in trespasses and sins, in which you once walked according to the course of this world, according to the prince of the power of the air, the spirit who now works in the sons of disobedience, among whom also we all once conducted ourselves in the lusts of our flesh, fulfilling the desires of the flesh and of the mind, and were by nature children of wrath, just as the others. ◊ You were washed, . . . you were sanctified, . . . you were justified in the name of the Lord Jesus and by the Spirit of our God. ◊ Reckon yourselves to be dead indeed to sin, but alive to God in Christ Jesus our Lord.

1 COR 4:7.1 COR 15:10.JAMES 1:18.ROM 9:16.ROM 3:27.1 COR 1:30-31.EPH 2:1-3.1 COR 6:11.ROM 6:11

MORNING

**To Him who loved us and washed us from our sins in
His own blood.**

Many waters cannot quench love, nor can the floods drown it. . . . Love is as strong as death. ◊ Greater love has no one than this, than to lay down one's life for his friends.

[He] Himself bore our sins in His own body on the tree, that we, having died to sins, might live for righteousness by whose stripes you were healed. ◊ In Him we have redemption through His blood, the forgiveness of sins, according to the riches of His grace. ◊ You were washed, . . . you were sanctified, . . . you were justified in the name of the Lord Jesus and by the Spirit of our God. ◊ You are a chosen generation, a royal priesthood, a holy nation, His own special people, that you may proclaim the praises of Him who called you out of darkness into His marvelous light. ◊ I beseech you . . . brethren, by the mercies of God, that you present your bodies a living sacrifice, holy, acceptable to God, which is your reasonable service.

REV 1:5.SONG 8:7,6.JOHN 15:13.1 PET 2:24.EPH 1:7.1 COR 6:11.1 PET
2:9.ROM 12:1

EVENING

There are differences of ministries, but the same Lord.

Azmaveth the son of Adiel was over the king's treasuries; and Jehonathan . . . was over the storehouses. . . . Ezri . . . was over those who did the work of the field for tilling the ground. Shimei . . . was over the vineyards. . . . All these were the officials over King David's property.

God has appointed these in the church: first apostles, second prophets, third teachers, after that miracles, then gifts of healings, helps, administrations, varieties of tongues. ◊ One and the same Spirit works all these things, distributing to each one individually as He wills.

As each one has received a gift, minister it to one another, as good stewards of the manifold grace of God. If anyone speaks, let him speak as the oracles of God. If anyone ministers, let him do it as with the ability which God supplies, that in all things God may be glorified through Jesus Christ, to whom belong the glory and the dominion forever and ever.

1 COR 12:5.1 CHR 27:25-27,31.1 COR 12:28.1 COR 12:11.1 PET 4:10-11

OCTOBER 4

**Moses did not know that the skin of his face shone
while he talked with Him.**

Not unto us, O Lord, not unto us, but to Your name give glory. ◊
Lord, when did we see You hungry and feed You, or thirsty and give You
drink? ◊ In lowliness of mind let each esteem others better than himself.
. . . Be clothed with humility.

[Jesus] was transfigured before them. His face shone like the sun, and
His clothes became as white as the light. ◊ All who sat in the council,
looking steadfastly at [Stephen], saw his . . . face as the face of an angel.
◊ The glory which You gave Me I have given them. ◊ We all, with
unveiled face, beholding as in a mirror the glory of the Lord, are being
transformed into the same image from glory to glory, just as by the Spirit
of the Lord.

You are the light of the world. A city that is set on a hill cannot be
hidden. Nor do they light a lamp and put it under a basket, but on a
lampstand, and it gives light to all who are in the house.

EX 34:29.PS 115:1.MATT 25:37.PHIL 2:3.1 PET 5:5.MATT 17:2.ACTS
6:15.JOHN 17:22.2 COR 3:18.MATT 5:14-15

**There are diversities of activities, but it is the same
God who works all in all.**

Some from Manasseh defected to David. . . . And they helped David
against the bands of raiders, for they were all mighty men of valor. ◊ The
manifestation of the Spirit is given to each one for the profit of all.

The children of Issachar . . . had understanding of the times, to know
what Israel ought to do. ◊ To one is given the word of wisdom through
the Spirit, to another the word of knowledge through the same Spirit.

Of Zebulun there were fifty thousand who went out to battle, expert in
war with all weapons of war, stouthearted men who could keep ranks. ◊
A double-minded man, unstable in all his ways.

There should be no schism in the body, but . . . the members should
have the same care for one another. And if one member suffers, all the
members suffer with it; or if one member is honored, all the members
rejoice with it.

One Lord, one faith, one baptism.

1 COR 12:6.1 CHR 12:19,21.1 COR 12:7.1 CHR 12:32.1 COR 12:8.1 CHR
12:33.JAMES 1:8.1 COR 12:25-26.EPH 4:5

MORNING

**Call upon Me in the day of trouble; I will deliver you,
and you shall glorify Me.**

Why are you cast down, O my soul? And why are you disquieted within me? Hope in God; for I shall yet praise Him, the help of my countenance and my God. ◊ Lord, You have heard the desire of the humble; You will prepare their heart; You will cause Your ear to hear. ◊ For You, Lord, are good, and ready to forgive, and abundant in mercy to all those who call upon You.

Jacob said to his household, . . . "Let us arise and go up to Bethel; and I will make an altar there to God, who answered me in the day of my distress and has been with me in the way which I have gone. ◊ Bless the Lord, O my soul, and forget not all His benefits.

I love the Lord, because He has heard My voice and my supplications. Because He has inclined His ear to me, therefore I will call upon Him as long as I live. The pains of death encompassed me, and the pangs of Sheol laid hold of me; I found trouble and sorrow. Then I called upon the name of the Lord.

PS 50:15.PS 42:11.PS 10:17.PS 86:5.GEN 35:2-3.PS 103:2.PS 116:1-4

EVENING

**Yet a little while, and He who is coming will come
and will not tarry.**

Write the vision and make it plain on tablets, that he may run who reads it. The vision is yet for an appointed time; but at the end it will speak, and it will not lie. Though it tarries, wait for it; because it will surely come, it will not tarry.

Beloved, do not forget this one thing, that with the Lord one day is as a thousand years, and a thousand years as one day. The Lord is not slack concerning His promise, as some count slackness, but is longsuffering toward us, not willing that any should perish but that all should come to repentance. ◊ You, O Lord, are a God full of compassion, and gracious, longsuffering and abundant in mercy and truth. ◊ Oh, that You would rend the heavens! That You would come down! . . . For since the beginning of the world men have not heard nor perceived by the ear, nor has the eye seen any God besides You, who acts for the one who waits for Him.

HEB 10:37.HAB 2:2-3.2 PET 3:8-9.PS 86:15.IS 64:1,4

OCTOBER 6

MORNING_____

The Lord God Omnipotent reigns!

I know that You can do everything. ◊ The things which are impossible with men are possible with God. ◊ He does according to His will in the army of heaven and among the inhabitants of the earth. No one can restrain His hand or say to Him, "What have You done?" ◊ There is no one who can deliver out of My hand; I work, and who will reverse it? ◊ Abba, Father, all things are possible for You.

"Do you believe that I am able to do this?" They said to Him, "Yes, Lord." Then He touched their eyes, saying, "According to your faith let it be to you." ◊ "Lord, if You are willing, You can make me clean." Then Jesus put out His hand and touched him, saying, "I am willing; be cleansed." ◊ Mighty God. ◊ All authority has been given to Me in heaven and on earth.

Some trust in chariots, and some in horses; but we will remember the name of the Lord our God. ◊ Be strong and courageous; do not be afraid nor dismayed, . . . for there are more with us than with him.

REV 19:6.JOB 42:2.LUKE 18:27.DAN 4:35.IS 43:13.MARK 14:36.MATT 9:28-29.MATT 8:2-3.IS 9:6.MATT 28:18.PS 20:7.2 CHR 32:7

EVENING_____

What is the thing that the Lord has said to you?

He has shown you, O man, what is good; and what does the Lord require of you but to do justly, to love mercy, and to walk humbly with your God? ◊ And to keep the commandments of the Lord and His statutes which I command you today for your good?

As many as are of the works of the law are under the curse; for it is written, "Cursed is everyone who does not continue in all things which are written in the book of the law, to do them." But that no one is justified by the law in the sight of God is evident, for "The just shall live by faith." . . . What purpose then does the law serve? It was added because of transgressions, till the Seed should come to whom the promise was made.

God, who at various times and in different ways spoke in time past to the fathers by the prophets, has in these last days spoken to us by His Son.

Speak, Lord, for Your servant hears.

1 SAM 3:17.MIC 6:8.DEUT 10:13.GAL 3:10-11,19.HEB 1:1-2.1 SAM 3:9

MORNING

The humble He teaches His way.

Blessed are the meek.

I returned and saw under the sun that the race is not to the swift, nor the battle to the strong, nor bread to the wise, nor riches to men of understanding, nor favor to men of skill. ◊ A man's heart plans his way, but the Lord directs his steps.

Unto You I lift up my eyes, O You who dwell in the heavens. Behold, as the eyes of servants look to the hand of their masters, as the eyes of a maid to the hand of her mistress, so our eyes look to the Lord our God. ◊ Cause me to know the way in which I should walk, for I lift up my soul to You.

O our God, will You not judge them? For we have no power against this great multitude that is coming against us; nor do we know what to do, but our eyes are upon You.

If any of you lacks wisdom, let him ask of God, who gives to all liberally and without reproach, and it will be given to him.

When He, the Spirit of truth, has come, He will guide you into all truth.

PS 25:9.MATT 5:5.ECCL 9:11.PROV 16:9.PS 123:1-2.PS 143:8.2 CHR 20:12.JAMES 1:5.JOHN 16:13

EVENING

O Lord God, . . . with Your blessing let the house of Your servant be blessed forever.

You have blessed it, O Lord, and it shall be blessed forever. ◊ The blessing of the Lord makes one rich, and He adds no sorrow with it.

Remember the words of the Lord Jesus, that He said, "It is more blessed to give than to receive." ◊ When you give a feast, invite the poor, the maimed, the lame, the blind. And you will be blessed, because they cannot repay you; for you shall be repaid at the resurrection of the just. ◊ Come, you blessed of My Father, inherit the kingdom prepared for you from the foundation of the world: for I was hungry and you gave Me food; I was thirsty and you gave Me drink; I was a stranger and you took Me in; I was naked and you clothed Me; I was sick and you visited Me; I was in prison and you came to Me.

Blessed is he who considers the poor; the Lord will deliver him in time of trouble.

The Lord God is a sun and shield.

2 SAM 7:29.1 CHR 17:27.PROV 10:22.ACTS 20:35.LUKE 14:13-14.MATT 25:34-36.PS 41:1.PS 84:11

OCTOBER 8

MORNING

I will not fear. What can man do to me?

Who shall separate us from the love of Christ? Shall tribulation, or distress, or persecution, or famine, or nakedness, or peril, or sword? . . . Yet in all these things we are more than conquerors through Him who loved us.

My friends, do not be afraid of those who kill the body, and after that have no more that they can do. But I will show you whom you should fear: Fear Him who, after He has killed, has power to cast into hell; yes, I say to you, fear Him!

Blessed are those who are persecuted for righteousness' sake, for theirs is the kingdom of heaven. Blessed are you when they revile and persecute you, and say all kinds of evil against you falsely for My sake. Rejoice and be exceedingly glad, for great is your reward in heaven. ◊ None of these things move me; nor do I count my life dear to myself, so that I may finish my race with joy. ◊ I will speak of Your testimonies . . . before kings, and will not be ashamed.

HEB 13:6.ROM 8:35,37.LUKE 12:4-5.MATT 5:10-12.ACTS 20:24.PS 119:46

EVENING

He . . . set my feet upon a rock.

That Rock was Christ. ◊ Simon Peter . . . said, "You are the Christ, the Son of the living God." Jesus answered, . . . "On this rock I will build My church, and the gates of Hades shall not prevail against it." ◊ Nor is there salvation in any other, for there is no other name under heaven given among men by which we must be saved.

Full assurance of faith. . . . Hope without wavering. ◊ Faith, with no doubting. ◊ He who doubts is like a wave of the sea driven and tossed by the wind.

Who shall separate us from the love of Christ? Shall tribulation, or distress, or persecution, or famine, or nakedness, or peril, or sword? . . . Yet in all these things we are more than conquerors through Him who loved us. For I am persuaded that neither death nor life, nor angels nor principalities nor powers, nor things present nor things to come, nor height nor depth, nor any other created thing, shall be able to separate us from the love of God which is in Christ Jesus our Lord.

PS 40:2.1 COR 10:4.MATT 16:16,18.ACTS 4:12.HEB 10:22-23.JAMES 1:6.ROM 8:35,37-39

MORNING

You are God, ready to pardon, gracious and merciful.

The Lord is not slack concerning His promise, as some count slackness, but is longsuffering toward us, not willing that any should perish but that all should come to repentance. ◇ The longsuffering of our Lord is salvation.

For this reason I obtained mercy, that in me first Jesus Christ might show all longsuffering, as a pattern to those who are going to believe on Him for everlasting life. ◇ Whatever things were written before were written for our learning, that we through the patience and comfort of the Scriptures might have hope.

Do you despise the riches of His goodness, forbearance, and longsuffering, not knowing that the goodness of God leads you to repentance? ◇ Rend your heart, and not your garments; return to the Lord your God, for He is gracious and merciful, slow to anger, and of great kindness; and He relents from doing harm.

NEH 9:17.2 PET 3:9.2 PET 3:15.1 TIM 1:16.ROM 15:4.ROM 2:4.JOEL 2:13

EVENING

The words of the Lord are pure words.

Your word is very pure; therefore Your servant loves it. ◇ The statutes of the Lord are right, rejoicing the heart; the commandment of the Lord is pure, enlightening the eyes. ◇ Every word of God is pure; He is a shield to those who put their trust in Him. Do not add to His words, lest He reprove you, and you be found a liar.

Your word I have hidden in my heart, that I might not sin against You. . . . I will meditate on Your precepts, and contemplate Your ways. ◇ Brethren, whatever things are true, whatever things are noble, whatever things are just, whatever things are pure, whatever things are lovely, whatever things are of good report, if there is any virtue and if there is anything praiseworthy meditate on these things. ◇ As newborn babes, desire the pure milk of the word, that you may grow thereby.

We are not, as so many, peddling the word of God; but as of sincerity, but as from God, we speak in the sight of God in Christ. ◇ Nor handling the word of God deceitfully.

PS 12:6.PS 119:140.PS 19:8.PROV 30:5-6.PS 119:11,15.PHIL 4:8.1 PET 2:2.2 COR 2:17.2 COR 4:2

MORNING

The whole family in heaven and earth.

One God and Father of all, who is above all, and through all, and in you all. ◇ You are all sons of God through faith in Christ Jesus. ◇ That in the dispensation of the fullness of the times He might gather together in one all things in Christ, both which are in heaven and which are on earth in Him.

He is not ashamed to call them brethren. ◇ Here are My mother and My brothers! For whoever does the will of My Father in heaven is My brother and sister and mother. ◇ Go to My brethren and say to them, "I am ascending to My Father and your Father."

I saw under the altar the souls of those who had been slain for the word of God and for the testimony which they held. . . . And a white robe was given to each of them; and it was said to them that they should rest a little while longer, until both the number of their fellow servants and their brethren, who would be killed as they were, was completed. ◇ That they should not be made perfect apart from us.

EPH 3:15.EPH 4:6.GAL 3:26.EPH 1:10.HEB 2:11.MATT 12:49-50.JOHN
20:17.REV 6:9,11.HEB 11:40

EVENING

In this manner, . . . pray: Our Father in heaven, hallowed be Your name.

Jesus . . . lifted up His eyes to heaven, and said: "Father." ◇ My Father and your Father.

You are all sons of God through faith in Christ Jesus. ◇ You did not receive the spirit of bondage again to fear, but you received the Spirit of adoption by whom we cry out, "Abba, Father." The Spirit Himself bears witness with our spirit that we are children of God.

Because you are sons, God has sent forth the Spirit of His Son into your hearts, crying out, "Abba, Father!" Therefore you are no longer a slave but a son.

Most assuredly, I say to you, whatever you ask the Father in My name He will give you. Until now you have asked nothing in My name. Ask, and you will receive, that your joy may be full.

I will receive you. I will be a Father to you, and you shall be My sons and daughters, says the Lord Almighty.

MATT 6:9.JOHN 17:1.JOHN 20:17.GAL 3:26.ROM 8:15-16.GAL 4:6-
7.JOHN 16:23-24.2 COR 6:17-18

MORNING

Be not far from Me, for trouble is near.

How long, O Lord? Will You forget me forever? How long will You hide Your face from me? How long shall I take counsel in my soul, having sorrow in my heart daily? ◊ Do not hide Your face from me; do not turn Your servant away in anger; You have been my help; do not leave me nor forsake me, O God of my salvation.

He shall call upon Me, and I will answer him; I will be with him in trouble; I will deliver him and honor him. ◊ The Lord is near to all who call upon Him, to all who call upon Him in truth. He will fulfill the desire of those who fear Him; He also will hear their cry and save them.

I will not leave you orphans; I will come to you. ◊ Lo, I am with you always, even to the end of the age.

God is our refuge and strength, a very present help in trouble. ◊ Truly my soul silently waits for God; from Him comes my salvation. . . . My soul, wait silently for God alone, for my expectation is from Him.

PS 22:11.PS 13:1-2.PS 27:9.PS 91:15.PS 145:18-19.JOHN 14:18.MATT 28:20.PS 46:1.PS 62:1,5

EVENING

Hallowed be Your name.

For you shall worship no other god, for the Lord, whose name is Jealous, is a jealous God.

Who is like You, O Lord, among the gods? Who is like You, glorious in holiness, fearful in praises, doing wonders? ◊ Holy, holy, holy, Lord God Almighty.

Worship the Lord in the beauty of holiness! ◊ I saw the Lord sitting on a throne, high and lifted up, and the train of His robe filled the temple. Above it stood seraphim; . . . and one cried to another and said: "Holy, holy, holy is the Lord of hosts; the whole earth is full of His glory!" . . . Then I said: "Woe is me, for I am undone!" ◊ I have heard of You by the hearing of the ear, but now my eye sees You. Therefore I abhor myself.

The blood of Jesus Christ His Son cleanses us from all sin. ◊ That we may be partakers of His holiness. ◊ Therefore, brethren, having boldness to enter the Holiest by the blood of Jesus, . . . let us draw near with a true heart.

MATT 6:9.EX 34:14.EX 15:11.REV 4:8.1 CHR 16:29.IS 6:1-3,5.JOB 42:5-6. 1 JOHN 1:7.HEB 12:10.HEB 10:19,22

MORNING————————————————————————————

God was in Christ reconciling the world to Himself, not imputing their trespasses to them.

It pleased the Father that in Him all the fullness should dwell, and by Him to reconcile all things to Himself, . . . having made peace through the blood of His cross. ◊ Mercy and truth have met together; righteousness and peace have kissed each other.

I know the thoughts that I think toward you, says the Lord, thoughts of peace and not of evil. ◊ "Come now, and let us reason together," says the Lord, "though your sins are like scarlet, they shall be as white as snow; though they are red like crimson, they shall be as wool."

Who is a God like You, pardoning iniquity?

Now acquaint yourself with Him, and be at peace. ◊ Work out your own salvation with fear and trembling; for it is God who works in you both to will and to do for His good pleasure. ◊ Lord, You will establish peace for us, for You have also done all our works in us.

2 COR 5:19.COL 1:19-20.PS 85:10.JER 29:11.IS 1:18.MIC 7:18.JOB 22:21.PHIL 2:12-13.IS 26:12

EVENING————————————————————————————

Your kingdom come.

In the days of these kings the God of heaven will set up a kingdom which shall never be destroyed; and the kingdom shall not be left to other people; it shall break in pieces and consume all these kingdoms, and it shall stand forever. ◊ A stone . . . cut out without hands. ◊ "Not by might nor by power, but by My Spirit," says the Lord of hosts. ◊ The kingdom of God does not come with observation; nor will they say, "See here!" or "See there!" For indeed, the kingdom of God is within you.

To you it has been given to know the mystery of the kingdom of God. ◊ The kingdom of God is as if a man should scatter seed on the ground, and should sleep by night and rise by day, and the seed should sprout and grow, he himself does not know how. . . . But when the grain ripens, immediately he puts in the sickle, because the harvest has come.

Therefore you also be ready, for the Son of Man is coming at an hour when you do not expect Him.

The Spirit and the bride say, "Come!" And let him who hears say, "Come!"

MATT 6:10.DAN 2:44.DAN 2:34.ZECH 4:6.LUKE 17:20-21.MARK 4:11.MARK 4:26-27,29.MATT 24:44.REV 22:17

MORNING

From the first day that you set your heart to understand, and to humble yourself before your God, your words were heard.

Thus says the High and Lofty One who inhabits eternity, whose name is Holy: "I dwell in the high and holy place, with him who has a contrite and humble spirit, to revive the spirit of the humble, and to revive the heart of the contrite ones." ◊ The sacrifices of God are a broken spirit, a broken and a contrite heart—these, O God, You will not despise. ◊ Though the Lord is on high, yet He regards the lowly; but the proud He knows from afar. ◊ Humble yourselves under the mighty hand of God, that He may exalt you in due time. ◊ God resists the proud, but gives grace to the humble. Therefore submit to God.

You, Lord, are good, and ready to forgive, and abundant in mercy to all those who call upon You. Give ear, O Lord, to my prayer; and attend to the voice of my supplications. In the day of my trouble I will call upon You, for You will answer me.

DAN 10:12.IS 57:15.PS 51:17.PS 138:6.1 PET 5:6.JAMES 4:6-7.PS 86:5-7

EVENING

Your will be done on earth as it is in heaven.

Understand what the will of the Lord is.

It is not the will of your Father who is in heaven that one of these little ones should perish.

This is the will of God, your sanctification. ◊ That he no longer should live the rest of his time in the flesh for the lusts of men, but for the will of God. ◊ Of His own will He brought us forth by the word of truth. . . . Therefore lay aside all filthiness.

Be holy, for I am holy. ◊ [Jesus] said, . . . "For whoever does the will of God is My brother and My sister and mother." ◊ Therefore whoever hears these sayings of Mine, and does them, I will liken him to a wise man who built his house on the rock: and the rain descended, the floods came, and the winds blew and beat on that house; and it did not fall, for it was founded on the rock. ◊ The world is passing away, and the lust of it; but he who does the will of God abides forever.

MATT 6:10.EPH 5:17.MATT 18:14.1 THESS 4:3.1 PET 4:2.JAMES 1:18,21.1 PET 1:16.MARK 3:34-35.MATT 7:24-25.1 JOHN 2:17

OCTOBER 14

MORNING

Christ died and rose and lived again, that He might be Lord of both the dead and the living.

It pleased the Lord to bruise Him; He has put Him to grief. When You make His soul an offering for sin, He shall see His seed, He shall prolong His days, and the pleasure of the Lord shall prosper in His hand. He shall see the travail of His soul, and be satisfied. By His knowledge My righteous Servant shall justify many, for He shall bear their iniquities. ◊ Ought not the Christ to have suffered these things and to enter into His glory? ◊ We judge thus: that if One died for all, then all died; and He died for all, that those who live should live no longer for themselves, but for Him who died for them and rose again.

Let all the house of Israel know assuredly that God has made this Jesus, whom you crucified, both Lord and Christ. ◊ He indeed was foreordained before the foundation of the world, but was manifest in these last times for you who through Him believe in God.

ROM 14:9.IS 53:10-11.LUKE 24:26.2 COR 5:14-15.ACTS 2:36.1 PET 1:20-21

EVENING

Give us this day our daily bread.

I have been young, and now am old; yet I have not seen the righteous forsaken, nor his descendants begging bread. ◊ His . . . bread will be given him, his water will be sure. ◊ The ravens brought him bread and meat in the morning, and bread and meat in the evening; and he drank from the brook.

My God shall supply all your need according to His riches in glory by Christ Jesus. ◊ Be content with such things as you have. For He Himself has said, "I will never leave you nor forsake you."

He humbled you, allowed you to hunger, and fed you with manna . . . that He might make you know that man shall not live by bread alone; but man lives by every word that proceeds from the mouth of the Lord. ◊ Jesus said to them, "Most assuredly, I say to you, Moses did not give you the bread from heaven, but My Father gives you the true bread from heaven. For the bread of God is He who comes down from heaven and gives life to the world." Then they said to Him, "Lord, give us this bread always."

MATT 6:11.PS 37:25.IS 33:16.1 KIN 17:6.PHIL 4:19.HEB 13:5.DEUT 8:3.JOHN 6:32-34

MORNING

God is my defense.

The Lord is my rock, my fortress and my deliverer; the God of my strength, in Him I will trust, my shield and the horn of my salvation, my stronghold and my refuge; my Savior. ◊ The Lord is my strength and my shield; my heart trusted in Him, and I am helped; therefore my heart greatly rejoices, and with my song I will praise Him.

When the enemy comes in like a flood, the Spirit of the Lord will lift up a standard against him. ◊ We may boldly say: "The Lord is my helper; I will not fear. What can man do to me?"

The Lord is my light and my salvation; whom shall I fear? The Lord is the strength of my life; of whom shall I be afraid?

As the mountains surround Jerusalem, so the Lord surrounds His people from this time forth and forever. ◊ Because You have been my help, therefore in the shadow of Your wings I will rejoice.

For Your name's sake, lead me and guide me.

PS 59:9.2 SAM 22:2-3.PS 28:7.IS 59:19.HEB 13:6.PS 27:1.PS 125:2.PS 63:7.PS 31:3

EVENING

Forgive us our debts, as we forgive our debtors.

"Lord, how often shall my brother sin against me, and I forgive him? Up to seven times?" Jesus said to him, "I do not say to you, up to seven times, but up to seventy times seven." ◊ "You wicked servant! I forgave you all that debt because you begged me. Should you not also have had compassion on your fellow servant, just as I had pity on you?" And his master was angry, and delivered him to the torturers until he should pay all that was due to him. So My heavenly Father also will do to you if each of you, from his heart, does not forgive his brother his trespasses. ◊ Be kind to one another, tenderhearted, forgiving one another, just as God in Christ also forgave you. ◊ You . . . He has made alive, . . . having forgiven you all trespasses, having wiped out the handwriting of requirements that was against us. . . . He has taken it out of the way, having nailed it to the cross. ◊ Even as Christ forgave you, so you also must do.

MATT 6:12.MATT 18:21-22.MATT 18:32-35.EPH 4:32.COL 2:13-14.COL 3:13

MORNING

Not lagging in diligence, fervent in spirit, serving the Lord.

Whatever your hand finds to do, do it with your might; for there is no work or device or knowledge or wisdom in the grave where you are going. ◇ Whatever you do, do it heartily, as to the Lord and not to men, knowing that from the Lord you will receive the reward of the inheritance; for you serve the Lord Christ. ◇ Whatever good anyone does, he will receive the same from the Lord.

I must work the works of Him who sent Me while it is day; the night is coming when no one can work. ◇ Did you not know that I must be about My Father's business? ◇ Zeal for Your house has eaten Me up.

Brethren, be even more diligent to make your calling and election sure, for if you do these things you will never stumble. ◇ We desire that each one of you show the same diligence to the full assurance of hope until the end, that you do not become sluggish, but imitate those who through faith and patience inherit the promises. ◇ Run in such a way that you may obtain it.

ROM 12:11.ECCL 9:10.COL 3:23-24.EPH 6:8.JOHN 9:4.LUKE
2:49.JOHN 2:17.2 PET 1:10.HEB 6:11-12.1 COR 9:24

EVENING

Do not lead us into temptation, but deliver us from the evil one.

He who trusts in his own heart is a fool, but whoever walks wisely will be delivered.

Let no one say when he is tempted, "I am tempted by God"; for God cannot be tempted by evil, nor does He Himself tempt anyone. But each one is tempted when he is drawn away by his own desires and enticed. ◇ Therefore "Come out from among them and be separate," says the Lord. Do not touch what is unclean, and I will receive you.

Lot lifted his eyes and saw all the plain of Jordan, that it was well watered everywhere . . . like the garden of the Lord. . . . Then Lot chose for himself all the plain of Jordan. . . . But the men of Sodom were exceedingly wicked and sinful against the Lord. ◇ [The Lord] delivered righteous Lot, who was oppressed with the filthy conduct of the wicked. . . . The Lord knows how to deliver the godly out of temptations. ◇ Indeed, he will be made to stand, for God is able to make him stand.

MATT 6:13.PROV 28:26.JAMES 1:13-14.2 COR 6:17.GEN 13:10-11,13.
2 PET 2:7,9.ROM 14:4

MORNING

In Your name they rejoice all day long, and in Your righteousness they are exalted.

In the Lord I have righteousness and strength. To Him men shall come, and all shall be ashamed who are incensed against Him. In the Lord all the descendants of Israel shall be justified, and shall glory. ◊ Be glad in the Lord and rejoice, you righteous; and shout for joy, all you upright in heart!

The righteousness of God apart from the law is revealed, being witnessed by the Law and the Prophets, even the righteousness of God which is through faith in Jesus Christ to all and on all who believe. . . . to demonstrate at the present time His righteousness, that He might be just and the justifier of the one who has faith in Jesus.

Rejoice in the Lord always. Again I will say, rejoice! ◊ Jesus Christ, whom having not seen you love. Though now you do not see Him, yet believing, you rejoice with joy inexpressible and full of glory.

PS 89:16.IS 45:24-25.PS 32:11.ROM 3:21-22,26.PHIL 4:4.1 PET 1:7-8

EVENING

Yours is the kingdom and the power and the glory forever.

The Lord reigns, He is clothed with majesty. . . . Your throne is established from of old; You are from everlasting.

The Lord is . . . great in power. ◊ If God is for us, who can be against us? ◊ Our God whom we serve is able to deliver us. ◊ My Father, who has given them to Me, is greater than all; and no one is able to snatch them out of My Father's hand. ◊ He who is in you is greater than he who is in the world.

Not unto us, O Lord, not unto us, but to Your name give glory. ◊ Yours, O Lord, is the greatness, the power and the glory, the victory and the majesty; for all that is in heaven and in earth is Yours; Yours is the kingdom, O Lord, and You are exalted as head over all. . . . Now therefore, our God, we thank You and praise Your glorious name. But who am I, and who are my people, that we should be able to offer so willingly as this? For all things come from You, and of Your own we have given You.

MATT 6:13.PS 93:1-2.NAH 1:3.ROM 8:31.DAN 3:17.JOHN 10:29.
1 JOHN 4:4.PS 115:1.1 CHR 29:11,13-14

OCTOBER 18

MORNING

One of the soldiers pierced His side with a spear, and immediately blood and water came out.

Behold, the blood of the covenant which the Lord has made with you. ◊ The life of the flesh is in the blood, and I have given it to you upon the altar to make atonement for your souls. ◊ It is not possible that the blood of bulls and goats could take away sins.

"This is My blood of the new covenant, which is shed for many." ◊ With His own blood He entered the Most Holy Place . . . having obtained eternal redemption. ◊ Peace through the blood of His cross.

You were not redeemed with corruptible things, like silver or gold, . . . but with the precious blood of Christ, as of a lamb without blemish and without spot. He indeed was foreordained . . . , but was manifest in these last times for you.

Then I will sprinkle clean water on you, and you shall be clean; I will cleanse you . . . from all your idols. ◊ Let us draw near with a true heart in full assurance of faith, having our hearts sprinkled from an evil conscience.

JOHN 19:34.EX 24:8.LEV 17:11.HEB 10:4.MARK 14:24.HEB 9:12.COL 1:20.1 PET 1:18-20.EZEK 36:25.HEB 10:22

EVENING

Amen.

Amen! May the Lord God . . . say so too. ◊ He who blesses himself in the earth shall bless himself in the God of truth; and he who swears in the earth shall swear by the God of truth.

When God made a promise to Abraham, because He could swear by no one greater, He swore by Himself. . . . For men indeed swear by the greater, and an oath for confirmation is for them an end of all dispute. Thus God, determining to show more abundantly to the heirs of promise the immutability of His counsel, confirmed it by an oath, that by two immutable things, in which it is impossible for God to lie, we might have strong consolation, who have fled for refuge to lay hold of the hope set before us.

These things says the Amen, the Faithful and True Witness. ◊ For all the promises of God in Him are Yes, and in Him Amen, to the glory of God through us. ◊ Blessed be the Lord God, the God of Israel, who only does wondrous things! And blessed be His glorious name forever! . . . Amen and Amen.

MATT 6:13.1 KIN 1:36.IS 65:16.HEB 6:13,16-18.REV 3:14.2 COR 1:20.PS 72:18-19

MORNING

The Lord will be your confidence, and will keep your foot from being caught.

Surely the wrath of man shall praise You; with the remainder of wrath You shall gird Yourself. ◊ The king's heart is in the hand of the Lord, like the rivers of water; He turns it wherever He wishes. ◊ When a man's ways please the Lord, he makes even his enemies to be at peace with him.

I wait for the Lord, my soul waits, and in His word I do hope. My soul waits for the Lord more than those who watch for the morning I say, more than those who watch for the morning. ◊ I sought the Lord, and He heard me, and delivered me from all my fears.

The eternal God is your refuge, and underneath are the everlasting arms; He will thrust out the enemy from before you, and will say, "Destroy!" ◊ Blessed is the man who trusts in the Lord, and whose hope is the Lord.

What then shall we say to these things? If God is for us, who can be against us?

PROV 3:26.PS 76:10.PROV 21:1.PROV 16:7.PS 130:5-6.PS 34:4.DEUT 33:27.JER 17:7.ROM 8:31

EVENING

Consolation in Christ, . . . comfort of love, . . . fellowship of the Spirit.

Man who is born of woman is of few days and full of trouble. He comes forth like a flower and fades away; he flees like a shadow and does not continue. ◊ My flesh and my heart fail; but God is the strength of my heart and my portion forever.

The Father, . . . will give you another Helper, that He may abide with you forever. . . . the Holy Spirit, whom the Father will send in My name. ◊ Blessed be the God and Father of our Lord Jesus Christ, the Father of mercies and God of all comfort, who comforts us in all our tribulation, that we may be able to comfort those who are in any trouble, with the comfort with which we ourselves are comforted by God.

If we believe that Jesus died and rose again, even so God will bring with Him those who sleep in Jesus. . . . And thus we shall always be with the Lord. Therefore comfort one another with these words.

PHIL 2:1.JOB 14:1-2.PS 73:26.JOHN 14:16,26.2 COR 1:3-4.1 THESS 4:14,17-18

OCTOBER 20

MORNING

I delight in the law of God according to the inward man.

Oh, how I love Your law! It is my meditation all the day. ◊ Your words were found, and I ate them, and Your word was to me the joy and rejoicing of my heart. ◊ I sat down in his shade with great delight, and his fruit was sweet to my taste. ◊ I have treasured the words of His mouth more than my necessary food.

I delight to do Your will, O my God, and Your law is within my heart. ◊ My food is to do the will of Him who sent Me, and to finish His work.

The statutes of the Lord are right, rejoicing the heart; the commandment of the Lord is pure, enlightening the eyes. . . . More to be desired are they than gold, yea, than much fine gold; sweeter also than honey and the honeycomb. ◊ Be doers of the word, and not hearers only, deceiving yourselves. For if anyone is a hearer of the word and not a doer, he is like a man observing his natural face in a mirror.

ROM 7:22.PS 119:97.JER 15:16.SONG 2:3.JOB 23:12.PS 40:8.JOHN 4:34.PS 19:8,10.JAMES 1:22-23

EVENING

May the Lord your God accept you.

With what shall I come before the Lord, and bow myself before the High God? Shall I come before Him with burnt offerings, with calves a year old? Will the Lord be pleased with thousands of rams or ten thousand rivers of oil? Shall I give my firstborn for my transgression, the fruit of my body for the sin of my soul? He has shown you, O man, what is good; and what does the Lord require of you but to do justly, to love mercy, and to walk humbly with your God?

We are all like an unclean thing, and all our righteousnesses are like filthy rags. ◊ There is none righteous, no, not one. . . . for all have sinned and fall short of the glory of God, being justified freely by His grace through the redemption that is in Christ Jesus, whom God set forth to be a propitiation by His blood, through faith, to demonstrate His righteousness, . . . that He might be just and the justifier of the one who has faith in Jesus.

Accepted in the Beloved. ◊ You are complete in Him.

2 SAM 24:23.MIC 6:6-8.IS 64:6.ROM 3:10,23-26.EPH 1:6.COL 2:10

MORNING

**Of His fullness we have all received, and grace
for grace.**

This is My beloved Son, in whom I am well pleased. ◊ Behold what manner of love the Father has bestowed on us, that we should be called children of God!

His Son, whom He has appointed heir of all things. ◊ If children, then heirs heirs of God and joint heirs with Christ, if indeed we suffer with Him, that we may also be glorified together.

I and My Father are one. ◊ The Father is in Me, and I in Him. ◊ My Father and your Father, and . . . My God and your God. ◊ I in them, and You in Me; that they may be made perfect in one.

The church, which is His body, the fullness of Him who fills all in all.

Having these promises, beloved, let us cleanse ourselves from all filthiness of the flesh and spirit, perfecting holiness in the fear of God.

JOHN 1:16.MATT 17:5.1 JOHN 3:1.HEB 1:2.ROM 8:17.JOHN
10:30.JOHN 10:38.JOHN 20:17.JOHN 17:23.EPH 1:22-23.2 COR 7:1

EVENING

**A servant is not greater than his master; nor is he who
is sent greater than he who sent him. If you know
these things, happy are you if you do them.**

There was . . . rivalry among them, as to which of them should be considered the greatest. And He said to them, "The kings of the Gentiles exercise lordship over them, and those who exercise authority over them are called 'benefactors.' But not so among you; on the contrary, he who is greatest among you, let him be as the younger, and he who governs as he who serves. For who is greater, he who sits at the table, or he who serves? Is it not he who sits at the table? Yet I am among you as the One who serves." ◊ The Son of Man did not come to be served, but to serve, and to give His life a ransom for many.

Jesus . . . rose from supper and laid aside His garments, took a towel and girded Himself. After that, He poured water into a basin and began to wash the disciples' feet, and to wipe them with the towel with which He was girded.

JOHN 13:16-17.LUKE 22:24-27.MATT 20:28.JOHN 13:3-5.

MORNING

O God, my heart is steadfast.

The Lord is my light and my salvation; whom shall I fear? The Lord is the strength of my life; of whom shall I be afraid?

You will keep him in perfect peace, whose mind is stayed on You, because he trusts in You. ◊ He will not be afraid of evil tidings; his heart is steadfast, trusting in the Lord. His heart is established; he will not be afraid, until he sees his desire upon his enemies.

Whenever I am afraid, I will trust in You. ◊ In the time of trouble He shall hide me in His pavilion; in the secret place of His tabernacle He shall hide me; He shall set me high upon a rock. And now my head shall be lifted up above my enemies all around me; therefore I will offer sacrifices of joy in His tabernacle; I will sing, yes, I will sing praises to the Lord.

May the God of all grace, who called us to His eternal glory by Christ Jesus, after you have suffered a while, perfect, establish, strengthen, and settle you. To Him be the glory and the dominion forever and ever.

PS 108:1.PS 27:1.IS 26:3.PS 112:7-8.PS 56:3.PS 27:5-6.1 PET 5:10-11

EVENING

The Lord has established His throne in heaven, and His kingdom rules over all.

The lot is cast into the lap, but its every decision is from the Lord. ◊ If there is calamity in a city, will not the Lord have done it?

I am the Lord, and there is no other; there is no God besides Me. I will gird you, though you have not known Me, that they may know from the rising of the sun to its setting that there is none besides Me. I am the Lord, and there is no other; I form the light and create darkness, I make peace and create calamity; I, the Lord, do all these things.

He does according to His will in the army of heaven and among the inhabitants of the earth. No one can restrain His hand or say to Him, "What have You done?" ◊ If God is for us, who can be against us?

He must reign till He has put all enemies under His feet. ◊ Do not fear, little flock, for it is your Father's good pleasure to give you the kingdom.

PS 103:19.PROV 16:33.AMOS 3:6.IS 45:5-7.DAN 4:35.ROM 8:31.1 COR 15:25.LUKE 12:32

MORNING

One's life does not consist in the abundance of the things he possesses.

A little that a righteous man has is better than the riches of many wicked. ◇ Better is a little with the fear of the Lord, than great treasure with trouble. ◇ Godliness with contentment is great gain. . . . Having food and clothing, with these we shall be content.

Give me neither poverty nor riches—feed me with the food You prescribe for me; lest I be full and deny You, and say, "Who is the Lord?" Or lest I be poor and steal, and profane the name of my God. ◇ Give us this day our daily bread.

Do not worry about your life, what you will eat or what you will drink; nor about your body, what you will put on. Is not life more than food and the body more than clothing? ◇ "When I sent you without money bag, sack, and sandals, did you lack anything?" So they said, "Nothing." ◇ Let your conduct be without covetousness, and be content with such things as you have. For He Himself has said, "I will never leave you nor forsake you."

LUKE 12:15.PS 37:16.PROV 15:16.1 TIM 6:6,8.PROV 30:8-9.MATT
6:11.MATT 6:25.LUKE 22:35.HEB 13:5

EVENING

It is the Spirit who gives life.

The first man Adam became a living being. The last Adam became a life-giving spirit. ◇ That which is born of the flesh is flesh, and that which is born of the Spirit is spirit. ◇ Not by works of righteousness which we have done, but according to His mercy He saved us, through the washing of regeneration and renewing of the Holy Spirit.

If anyone does not have the Spirit of Christ, he is not His. And if Christ is in you, the body is dead because of sin, but the Spirit is life because of righteousness. But if the Spirit of Him who raised Jesus from the dead dwells in you, He who raised Christ from the dead will also give life to your mortal bodies through His Spirit who dwells in you.

It is no longer I who live, but Christ lives in me; and the life which I now live in the flesh I live by faith in the Son of God. ◇ Reckon yourselves to be dead indeed to sin, but alive to God in Christ Jesus our Lord.

JOHN 6:63.1 COR 15:45.JOHN 3:6.TITUS 3:5.ROM 8:9-11.GAL
2:20.ROM 6:11

OCTOBER 24

MORNING

**I have been cast out of Your sight; yet I will look
again toward Your holy temple.**

Zion said, "The Lord has forsaken me, and my Lord has forgotten
me." Can a woman forget her nursing child, and not have compassion on
the son of her womb? Surely they may forget, yet I will not forget you.

I have forgotten prosperity. And I said, "My strength and my hope
have perished from the Lord." ◊ Awake! Why do You sleep, O Lord?
Arise! Do not cast us off forever. ◊ Why do you say, O Jacob, and speak,
O Israel: "My way is hidden from the Lord, and my just claim is passed
over by my God?" ◊ "With a little wrath I hid My face from you for a
moment; but with everlasting kindness I will have mercy on you," says
the Lord, your Redeemer.

Why are you cast down, O my soul? And why are you disquieted
within me? Hope in God; for I shall yet praise Him, the help of my
countenance. ◊ We are hard pressed on every side, yet not crushed; we
are perplexed, but not in despair; persecuted, but not forsaken; struck
down, but not destroyed.

JON 2:4.IS 49:14-15.LAM 3:17-18.PS 44:23.IS 40:27.IS 54:8.PS 43:5.2 COR
4:8-9

EVENING

**When the poor and needy seek water, and there is
none, and their tongues fail for thirst, I, the Lord, will
hear them.**

There are many who say, "Who will show us any good?" ◊ What has
man for all his labor, and for the striving of his heart with which he has
toiled under the sun? For all his days are sorrowful, and his work
grievous; even in the night his heart takes no rest. ◊ All is vanity and
grasping for the wind. ◊ They have forsaken Me, the fountain of living
waters, and hewn themselves cisterns—broken cisterns that can hold no
water.

The one who comes to Me I will by no means cast out. ◊ I will pour
water on him who is thirsty. ◊ Blessed are those who hunger and thirst
for righteousness, for they shall be filled.

O God, You are my God; early will I seek You; my soul thirsts for You;
my flesh longs for you in a dry and thirsty land where there is no water.

IS 41:17.PS 4:6.ECCL 2:22-23.ECCL 2:17.JER 2:13.JOHN 6:37.IS
44:3.MATT 5:6.PS 63:1

MORNING

Lo, I am with you always, even to the end of the age.

I say to you that if two of you agree on earth concerning anything that they ask, it will be done for them by My Father in heaven. "For where two or three are gathered together in My name, I am there in the midst of them." ◊ He who has My commandments and keeps them, it is he who loves Me. And he who loves Me will be loved by My Father, and I will love him and manifest Myself to him.

"Lord, how is it that You will manifest Yourself to us, and not to the world?" . . . "If anyone loves Me, he will keep My word; and My Father will love him, and We will come to him and make Our home with him."

Now to Him who is able to keep you from stumbling, and to present you faultless before the presence of His glory with exceeding joy, to God our Savior, who alone is wise, be glory and majesty, dominion and power, both now and forever. Amen.

MATT 28:20.MATT 18:19-20.JOHN 14:21.JOHN 14:22-23.JUDE 1:24-25

EVENING

The end of all things is at hand.

I saw a great white throne and Him who sat on it, from whose face the earth and the heaven fled away. ◊ The heavens and the earth which now exist are kept in store . . . reserved for fire until the day of judgment

God is our refuge and strength, a very present help in trouble. Therefore we will not fear, though the earth be removed, and though the mountains be carried into the midst of the sea; though its waters roar and be troubled, though the mountains shake with its swelling. ◊ You will hear of wars and rumors of wars. See that you are not troubled.

We have a building from God, a house not made with hands, eternal in the heavens. ◊ We . . . look for new heavens and a new earth in which righteousness dwells. Therefore, beloved, looking forward to these things, be diligent to be found by Him in peace, without spot and blameless.

1 PET 4:7.REV 20:11.2 PET 3:7.PS 46:1-3.MATT 24:6.2 COR 5:1.2 PET 3:13-14

MORNING

The Lord reigns.

"Do you not fear Me?" says the Lord. "Will you not tremble at My presence, who have placed the sand as the bound of the sea, by a perpetual decree, that it cannot pass beyond it? And though its waves toss to and fro, yet they cannot prevail; though they roar, yet they cannot pass over it." ◊ Exaltation comes neither from the east nor from the west nor from the south. But God is the Judge: He puts down one, and exalts another.

He changes the times and the seasons; He removes kings and raises up kings; He gives wisdom to the wise and knowledge to those who have understanding. ◊ You will hear of wars and rumors of wars. See that you are not troubled.

If God is for us, who can be against us? ◊ Are not two sparrows sold for a copper coin? And not one of them falls to the ground apart from your Father's will. The very hairs of your head are all numbered. Do not fear therefore; you are of more value than many sparrows.

PS 99:1.JER 5:22.PS 75:6-7.DAN 2:21.MATT 24:6.ROM 8:31.MATT 10:29-31

EVENING

Take heed to your spirit.

"Master, we saw someone casting out demons in Your name, and we forbade him because he does not follow with us." . . . But Jesus said to him, "Do not forbid him, for he who is not against us is for us." ◊ "Lord, do You want us to command fire to come down from heaven and consume them, just as Elijah did?" But He . . . rebuked them, and said, "You do not know what manner of spirit you are of."

"Eldad and Medad are prophesying in the camp." So Joshua the son of Nun . . . answered and said, "Moses my lord, forbid them!" Then Moses said to him, "Are you zealous for my sake? Oh, that all the Lord's people were prophets and that the Lord would put His Spirit upon them!"

The fruit of the Spirit is love, joy, peace, longsuffering, kindness, goodness, faithfulness, gentleness, self-control. And those who are Christ's have crucified the flesh with its passions and desires. If we live in the Spirit, let us also walk in the Spirit. Let us not become conceited, provoking one another, envying one another.

MAL 2:15.LUKE 9:49-50.LUKE 9:54-55.NUM 11:27-29.GAL 5:22-26

MORNING

He Himself took our infirmities and bore our sicknesses.

Then the priest shall command to take for him who is to be cleansed two living and clean birds, cedar wood, scarlet, and hyssop. And the priest shall command that one of the birds be killed in an earthen vessel over running water. As for the living bird, he shall take it, the cedar wood and the scarlet and the hyssop, and dip them and the living bird in the blood of the bird that was killed over the running water. And he shall sprinkle it seven times on him who is to be cleansed from the leprosy, and shall pronounce him clean, and shall let the living bird loose in the open field.

Behold, a man who was full of leprosy saw Jesus; and he fell on his face and implored Him, saying, "Lord, if You are willing, You can make me clean." ◊ And Jesus, moved with compassion, put out His hand and touched him, and said to him, "I am willing; be cleansed." As soon as He had spoken, immediately the leprosy left him, and he was cleansed.

MATT 8:17.LEV 14:4-7.LUKE 5:12.MARK 1:41-42

EVENING

· He whom you bless is blessed.

Blessed are the poor in spirit, for theirs is the kingdom of heaven. Blessed are those who mourn, for they shall be comforted. Blessed are the meek, for they shall inherit the earth. Blessed are those who hunger and thirst for righteousness, for they shall be filled. Blessed are the merciful, for they shall obtain mercy. Blessed are the pure in heart, for they shall see God. Blessed are the peacemakers, for they shall be called sons of God. Blessed are those who are persecuted for righteousness' sake, for theirs is the kingdom of heaven. Blessed are you when they revile and persecute you, and say all kinds of evil against you falsely for My sake. Rejoice and be exceedingly glad, for great is your reward in heaven. ◊ Blessed are those who hear the word of God and keep it!

Blessed are those who do His commandments, that they may have the right to the tree of life, and may enter through the gates into the city.

NUM 22:6.MATT 5:3-12.LUKE 11:28.REV 22:14

OCTOBER 28

MORNING

He saw that there was no man, and wondered that there was no intercessor; therefore His own arm brought salvation for Him.

Sacrifice and offering You did not desire; my ears You have opened; burnt offering and sin offering You did not require. Then I said, "Behold, I come; in the scroll of the Book it is written of me. I delight to do Your will, O my God, and Your law is within my heart." ◊ I lay down My life that I may take it again. No one takes it from Me, but I lay it down of Myself. I have power to lay it down, and I have power to take it again.

There is no other God besides Me, a just God and a Savior; there is none besides Me. Look to Me, and be saved, all you ends of the earth! For I am God, and there is no other. ◊ There is no other name under heaven given among men by which we must be saved.

You know the grace of our Lord Jesus Christ, that though He was rich, yet for your sakes He became poor, that you through His poverty might become rich.

IS 59:16.PS 40:6-8.JOHN 10:17-18.IS 45:21-22.ACTS 4:12.2 COR 8:9

EVENING

The enemy.

Be sober, be vigilant; because your adversary the devil walks about like a roaring lion, seeking whom he may devour. ◊ Resist the devil and he will flee from you.

Put on the whole armor of God, that you may be able to stand against the wiles of the devil. For we do not wrestle against flesh and blood, but against principalities, against powers, against the rulers of the darkness of this age, against spiritual hosts of wickedness in the heavenly places. Therefore take up the whole armor of God, that you may be able to withstand in the evil day, and having done all, to stand. Stand therefore, having girded your waist with truth, having put on the breastplate of righteousness, and having shod your feet with the preparation of the gospel of peace; above all, taking the shield of faith with which you will be able to quench all the fiery darts of the wicked one.

Do not rejoice over me, my enemy; when I fall, I will arise; when I sit in darkness, the Lord will be a light to me.

LUKE 10:19.1 PET 5:8.JAMES 4:7.EPH 6:11-16.MIC 7:8

MORNING

He is altogether lovely.

May my meditation be sweet to Him. ◊ My beloved is . . . chief among ten thousand. ◊ A chief cornerstone, elect, precious, and he who believes on Him will by no means be put to shame. ◊ You are fairer than the sons of men; grace is poured upon Your lips. ◊ God . . . has highly exalted Him and given Him the name which is above every name. ◊ It pleased the Father that in Him all the fullness should dwell.

Whom having not seen you love. Though now you do not see Him, yet believing, you rejoice with joy inexpressible and full of glory.

I also count all things loss for the excellence of the knowledge of Christ Jesus my Lord, for whom I have suffered the loss of all things, and count them as rubbish, that I may gain Christ and be found in Him, not having my own righteousness, which is from the law, but that which is through faith in Christ, the righteousness which is from God by faith.

SONG 5:16.PS 104:34.SONG 5:10.1 PET 2:6.PS 45:2.PHIL 2:9.COL 1:19.
1 PET 1:8.PHIL 3:8-9

EVENING

David strengthened himself in the Lord his God.

Lord, to whom shall we go? You have the words of eternal life. ◊ I know whom I have believed and am persuaded that He is able to keep what I have committed to Him until that Day.

In my distress I called upon the Lord, and cried out to my God; He heard my voice from His temple, and my cry came before Him, even to His ears. . . . They confronted me in the day of my calamity, but the Lord was my support. He also brought me out into a broad place; He delivered me because He delighted in me.

I will bless the Lord at all times; His praise shall continually be in my mouth. My soul shall make its boast in the Lord; the humble shall hear of it and be glad. Oh, magnify the Lord with me, and let us exalt His name together. I sought the Lord, and He heard me, and delivered me from all my fears. ◊ Oh, taste and see that the Lord is good; blessed is the man who trusts in Him!

1 SAM 30:6.JOHN 6:68.2 TIM 1:12.PS 18:6,18-19.PS 34:1-4.PS 34:8

MORNING

It is good that one should hope and wait quietly for the salvation of the Lord.

Has God forgotten to be gracious? Has He in anger shut up His tender mercies? ◊ I said in my haste, "I am cut off from before Your eyes"; nevertheless You heard the voice of my supplications when I cried out to You.

Shall God not avenge His own elect who cry out day and night to Him, though He bears long with them? I tell you that He will avenge them speedily. ◊ Wait for the Lord, and He will save you. ◊ Rest in the Lord, and wait patiently for Him; do not fret because of him who prospers in his way, because of the man who brings wicked schemes to pass.

You will not need to fight in this battle. Position yourselves, stand still and see the salvation of the Lord.

Let us not grow weary while doing good, for in due season we shall reap if we do not lose heart. ◊ See how the farmer waits for the precious fruit of the earth, waiting patiently for it until it receives the early and latter rain.

LAM 3:26.PS 77:9.PS 31:22.LUKE 18:7-8.PROV 20:22.PS 37:7.2 CHR
20:17.GAL 6:9.JAMES 5:7

EVENING

Catch us the foxes, the little foxes that spoil the vines, for our vines have tender grapes.

Who can understand his errors? Cleanse me from secret faults. ◊ [Look] diligently lest anyone fall short of the grace of God; lest any root of bitterness springing up cause trouble, and by this many become defiled. ◊ You ran well. Who hindered you from obeying the truth?

He who has begun a good work in you will complete it until the day of Jesus Christ. . . . Only let your conduct be worthy of the gospel of Christ. ◊ The tongue is a little member and boasts great things. See how great a forest a little fire kindles! And the tongue is a fire, a world of iniquity. The tongue is so set among our members that it defiles the whole body, and sets on fire the course of nature; and it is set on fire by hell. . . . No man can tame the tongue. It is an unruly evil, full of deadly poison. ◊ Let your speech always be with grace, seasoned with salt.

SONG 2:15.PS 19:12.HEB 12:15.GAL 5:7.PHIL 1:6,27.JAMES 3:5-6,8.
COL 4:6

MORNING

"Not by might nor by power, but by My Spirit," says the Lord of hosts.

Who has directed the Spirit of the Lord, or as His counselor has taught Him?

God has chosen the foolish things of the world to put to shame the wise, and God has chosen the weak things of the world to put to shame the things which are mighty; and the base things of the world and the things which are despised God has chosen, and the things which are not, to bring to nothing the things that are, that no flesh should glory in His presence.

The wind blows where it wishes, and you hear the sound of it, but cannot tell where it comes from and where it goes. So is everyone who is born of the Spirit. ◊ Born, not of blood, nor of the will of the flesh, nor of the will of man, but of God.

My Spirit remains among you; do not fear! ◊ The battle is not yours, but God's. ◊ The Lord does not save with sword and spear; for the battle is the Lord's.

ZECH 4:6.IS 40:13.1 COR 1:27-29.JOHN 3:8.JOHN 1:13.HAG 2:5.2 CHR 20:15.1 SAM 17:47

EVENING

Do as You have said.

Establish Your word to Your servant, who is devoted to fearing You. . . . So shall I have an answer for him who reproaches me, for I trust in Your word. . . . Remember the word to Your servant, upon which You have caused me to hope. . . . Your statutes have been my songs in the house of my pilgrimage. . . . The law of Your mouth is better to me than thousands of shekels of gold and silver. . . . Forever, O Lord, Your word is settled in heaven. Your faithfulness endures to all generations.

God, determining to show more abundantly to the heirs of promise the immutability of His counsel, confirmed it by an oath, that by two immutable things, in which it is impossible for God to lie, we might have strong consolation, who have fled for refuge to lay hold of the hope set before us. This hope we have as an anchor of the soul, both sure and steadfast, and which enters the Presence behind the veil, where the forerunner has entered for us, even Jesus. ◊ Exceedingly great and precious promises.

2 SAM 7:25.PS 119:38,42,49,54,72,89-90.HEB 6:17-20.2 PET 1:4

NOVEMBER 1

MORNING

Blessed is the man who listens to me, watching daily at my gates, waiting at the posts of my doors.

Behold, as the eyes of servants look to the hand of their masters, as the eyes of a maid to the hand of her mistress, so our eyes look to the Lord our God, until He has mercy on us.

This shall be a continual burnt offering throughout your generations at the door of the tabernacle of meeting before the Lord, where I will meet you to speak with you. ◊ In every place where I record My name I will come to you, and I will bless you.

Where two or three are gathered together in My name, I am there in the midst of them.

The hour is coming, and now is, when the true worshipers will worship the Father in spirit and truth; for the Father is seeking such to worship Him. God is Spirit, and those who worship Him must worship in spirit and truth.

Praying always with all prayer and supplication in the Spirit. ◊ Pray without ceasing.

PROV 8:34.PS 123:2.EX 29:42.EX 20:24.MATT 18:20.JOHN 4:23-24.EPH 6:18.1 THESS 5:17

EVENING

His name will be called . . . Counselor.

The Spirit of the Lord shall rest upon Him, the Spirit of wisdom and understanding, the Spirit of counsel and might, the Spirit of knowledge and of the fear of the Lord. His delight is in the fear of the Lord.

Does not wisdom cry out, and understanding lift up her voice? . . . "To you, O men, I call, and my voice is to the sons of men. O you simple ones, understand prudence, and you fools, be of an understanding heart. Listen, for I will speak of excellent things, and from the opening of my lips will come right things. . . . Counsel is mine, and sound wisdom; I am understanding, I have strength."

The Lord of hosts. . . . is wonderful in counsel and excellent in guidance. ◊ If any of you lacks wisdom, let him ask of God, who gives to all liberally and without reproach, and it will be given to him. ◊ Trust in the Lord with all your heart, and lean not on your own understanding; in all your ways acknowledge Him, and He shall direct your paths.

IS 9:6.IS 11:2-3.PROV 8:1,4-6,14.IS 28:29.JAMES 1:5.PROV 3:5-6

MORNING

Always pursue what is good.

For to this you were called, because Christ also suffered for us, leaving us an example, that you should follow His steps: who committed no sin, nor was guile found in His mouth; who, when He was reviled, did not revile in return; . . . but committed Himself to Him who judges righteously. ◊ Consider Him who endured such hostility from sinners against Himself, lest you become weary and discouraged in your souls.

Let us lay aside every weight, and the sin which so easily ensnares us, and let us run with endurance the race that is set before us, looking unto Jesus, the author and finisher of our faith, who for the joy that was set before Him endured the cross, despising the shame, and has sat down at the right hand of the throne of God.

Finally, brethren, whatever things are true, whatever things are noble, whatever things are just, whatever things are pure, whatever things are lovely, whatever things are of good report, if there is any virtue and if there is anything praiseworthy meditate on these things.

1 THESS 5:15.1 PET 2:21-23.HEB 12:3.HEB 12:1-2.PHIL 4:8

EVENING

The . . . Mighty God.

You are fairer than the sons of men; grace is poured upon Your lips; therefore God has blessed You forever. Gird Your sword upon Your thigh, O Mighty One, with Your glory and Your majesty. And in Your majesty ride prosperously. . . . Your throne, O God, is forever and ever; a scepter of righteousness is the scepter of Your kingdom. ◊ Then You spoke in a vision to Your holy one, and said: "I have given help to one who is mighty." ◊ "The Man . . . is My Companion," says the Lord of hosts.

Behold, God is my salvation, I will trust and not be afraid; for YAH, the Lord, is my strength and my song; He also has become my salvation. ◊ Thanks be to God who always leads us in triumph in Christ.

Now to Him who is able to keep you from stumbling, and to present you faultless before the presence of His glory with exceeding joy, to God our Savior, who alone is wise, be glory and majesty, dominion and power, both now and forever.

IS 9:6.PS 45:2-4,6.PS 89:19.ZECH 13:7.IS 12:2.2 COR 2:14.JUDE 1:24-25

NOVEMBER 3

MORNING

The ways of the Lord are right; the righteous walk in them, but transgressors stumble in them.

To you who believe, He is precious; but to those who are disobedient, . . . a stone of stumbling and a rock of offense. ◊ The way of the Lord is strength for the upright, but destruction will come to the workers of iniquity.

He who has ears to hear, let him hear! ◊ Whoever is wise will observe these things, and they will understand the lovingkindness of the Lord. ◊ The lamp of the body is the eye. If therefore your eye is good, your whole body will be full of light. ◊ If anyone wants to do His will, he shall know concerning the doctrine, whether it is from God.

Whoever has, to him more will be given, and he will have abundance.

He who is of God hears God's words; therefore you do not hear, because you are not of God. ◊ You are not willing to come to Me that you may have life. ◊ My sheep hear My voice, and I know them, and they follow Me.

HOS 14:9.1 PET 2:7-8.PROV 10:29.MATT 11:15.PS 107:43.MATT 6:22.JOHN 7:17.MATT 13:12.JOHN 8:47.JOHN 5:40.JOHN 10:27

EVENING

The . . . Everlasting Father.

Hear, O Israel: The Lord our God, the Lord is one!

I and My Father are one. . . . The Father is in Me, and I in Him. ◊ If you had known Me, you would have known My Father also. ◊ Philip said to Him, "Lord, show us the Father, and it is sufficient for us." Jesus said to him, "Have I been with you so long, and yet you have not known Me, Philip? He who has seen Me has seen the Father." ◊ Here am I and the children whom God has given Me. ◊ He shall see the travail of His soul, and be satisfied. ◊ "I am the Alpha and the Omega, the Beginning and the End," says the Lord, "who is and who was and who is to come, the Almighty." ◊ "Before Abraham was, I AM." ◊ God said to Moses, "I AM WHO I AM." And He said, "Thus you shall say to the children of Israel, 'I AM has sent me to you.' "

To the Son He says: "Your throne, O God, is forever and ever." ◊ He is before all things, and in Him all things consist. ◊ In Him dwells all the fullness of the Godhead bodily.

IS 9:6.DEUT 6:4.JOHN 10:30,38.JOHN 8:19.JOHN 14:8-9.HEB 2:13.IS 53:11.REV 1:8.JOHN 8:58.EX 3:14.HEB 1:8.COL 1:17.COL 2:9

MORNING

Now for a little while, if need be, you have been grieved by various trials.

Beloved, do not think it strange concerning the fiery trial which is to try you, as though some strange thing happened to you; but rejoice to the extent that you partake of Christ's sufferings, that when His glory is revealed, you may also be glad with exceeding joy. ◊ The exhortation . . . speaks to you as to sons: "My son, do not despise the chastening of the Lord, nor be discouraged when you are rebuked by Him." ◊ Now no chastening seems to be joyful for the present, but grievous; nevertheless, afterward it yields the peaceable fruit of righteousness to those who have been trained by it.

We do not have a High Priest who cannot sympathize with our weaknesses, but was in all points tempted as we are, yet without sin. ◊ For in that He Himself has suffered, being tempted, He is able to aid those who are tempted. ◊ God is faithful, who will not allow you to be tempted beyond what you are able.

1 PET 1:6.1 PET 4:12-13.HEB 12:5.HEB 12:11.HEB 4:15.HEB 2:18.1 COR 10:13

EVENING

The . . . Prince of Peace.

He will judge Your people with righteousness, and Your poor with justice. The mountains will bring peace to the people, and the little hills, by righteousness. . . . He shall come down like rain upon the mown grass, like showers that water the earth. In His days the righteous shall flourish, and abundance of peace, until the moon is no more. ◊ "Glory to God . . . , and on earth peace, good will toward men!"

Through the tender mercy of our God, . . . the Dayspring from on high has visited us; to give light to those who sit in darkness and the shadow of death, to guide our feet into the way of peace. ◊ Peace through Jesus Christ—He is Lord of all.

These things I have spoken to you, that in Me you may have peace. In the world you will have tribulation; but be of good cheer, I have overcome the world. ◊ Peace I leave with you, My peace I give to you; not as the world gives do I give to you. ◊ The peace of God, which surpasses all understanding, will guard your hearts and minds through Christ Jesus.

IS 9:6.PS 72:2-3,6-7.LUKE 2:14.LUKE 1:78-79.ACTS 10:36.JOHN 16:33.JOHN 14:27.PHIL 4:7

NOVEMBER 5

MORNING_____

Take for yourself quality spices . . . and . . . you shall make from these a holy anointing oil.

It shall not be poured on man's flesh; nor shall you make any other like it, according to its composition. It is holy, and it shall be holy to you. ◊ One Spirit. ◊ Diversities of gifts, but the same Spirit.

Your God, has anointed You with the oil of gladness more than Your companions. ◊ God anointed Jesus of Nazareth with the Holy Spirit and with power. ◊ God does not give the Spirit by measure.

Of His fullness we have all received. ◊ As the same anointing teaches you concerning all things, and is true, and is not a lie, and just as it has taught you, you will abide in Him. ◊ He who . . . has anointed us is God, who also has sealed us and given us the Spirit in our hearts as a deposit.

The fruit of the Spirit is love, joy, peace, longsuffering, kindness, goodness, faithfulness, gentleness, self-control. Against such there is no law.

EX 30:23-25.EX 30:32.EPH 4:4.1 COR 12:4.PS 45:7.ACTS 10:38.JOHN 3:34.JOHN 1:16.1 JOHN 2:27.2 COR 1:21-22.GAL 5:22-23

EVENING_____

The form of this world is passing away.

All the days of Methuselah were nine hundred and sixty-nine years; and he died.

Let the lowly brother glory in his exaltation, but the rich in his humiliation, because as a flower of the field he will pass away. For no sooner has the sun risen with a burning heat than it withers the grass; its flower falls, and its beautiful appearance perishes. So the rich man also will fade away in his pursuits.

For what is your life? It is even a vapor that appears for a little time and then vanishes away. ◊ The world is passing away, and the lust of it; but he who does the will of God abides forever.

Lord, make me to know my end, and what is the measure of my days, that I may know how frail I am. ◊ When they say, "Peace and safety!" then sudden destruction comes upon them, as labor pains upon a pregnant woman. And they shall not escape. But you, brethren, are not in darkness, so that this Day should overtake you as a thief.

1 COR 7:31.GEN 5:27.JAMES 1:9-11.JAMES 4:14.1 JOHN 2:17.PS 39:4.
1 THESS 5:3-4

MORNING

When Christ who is our life appears, then you also will appear with Him in glory.

I am the resurrection and the life. He who believes in Me, though he may die, he shall live. ◊ God has given us eternal life, and this life is in His Son. He who has the Son has life; he who does not have the Son of God does not have life.

For the Lord Himself will descend from heaven with a shout, with the voice of an archangel, and with the trumpet of God. And the dead in Christ will rise first. Then we who are alive and remain shall be caught up together with them in the clouds to meet the Lord in the air. And thus we shall always be with the Lord. Therefore comfort one another with these words. ◊ When He is revealed, we shall be like Him, for we shall see Him as He is. ◊ It is sown in dishonor, it is raised in glory. It is sown in weakness, it is raised in power.

If I go and prepare a place for you, I will come again and receive you to Myself; that where I am, there you may be also.

COL 3:4.JOHN 11:25.1 JOHN 5:11-12.1 THESS 4:16-18.1 JOHN 3:2.
1 COR 15:43.JOHN 14:3

EVENING

Lead me in Your truth and teach me.

When . . . the Spirit of truth, has come, He will guide you into all truth. ◊ You have an anointing from the Holy One, and you know all things.

To the law and to the testimony! If they do not speak according to this word, it is because there is no light in them. ◊ All Scripture is given by inspiration of God, and is profitable for doctrine, for reproof, for correction, for instruction in righteousness, that the man of God may be complete, thoroughly equipped for every good work. ◊ The Holy Scriptures . . . are able to make you wise for salvation through faith which is in Christ Jesus.

I will instruct you and teach you in the way you should go; I will guide you with My eye. ◊ The lamp of the body is the eye. If therefore your eye is good, your whole body will be full of light. ◊ If anyone wants to do His will, he shall know concerning the doctrine, whether it is from God. ◊ Whoever walks the road, although a fool, shall not go astray.

PS 25:5.JOHN 16:13.1 JOHN 2:20.IS 8:20.2 TIM 3:16-17.2 TIM 3:15.PS
32:8.MATT 6:22.JOHN 7:17.IS 35:8

MORNING

Oh, that men would give thanks to the Lord for His goodness, and for His wonderful works to the children of men!

Oh, taste and see that the Lord is good; blessed is the man who trusts in Him! ◊ How great is Your goodness, which You have laid up for those who fear You.

This people I have formed for Myself; they shall declare My praise. ◊ Having predestined us to adoption as sons by Jesus Christ to Himself, according to the good pleasure of His will, to the praise of the glory of His grace, by which He has made us accepted in the Beloved. . . . that we who first trusted in Christ should be to the praise of His glory.

How great is their goodness and how great their beauty! ◊ The Lord is good to all, and His tender mercies are over all His works. All Your works shall praise You, O Lord, and Your saints shall bless You. They shall speak of the glory of Your kingdom, and talk of Your power, to make known to the sons of men His mighty acts, and the glorious majesty of His kingdom.

PS 107:8.PS 34:8.PS 31:19.IS 43:21.EPH 1:5-6,12.ZECH 9:17.PS 145:9-12

EVENING

Indeed we count them blessed who endure.

We . . . glory in tribulations, knowing that tribulation produces perseverance; and perseverance, character; and character, hope. Now hope does not disappoint, because the love of God has been poured out in our hearts by the Holy Spirit who was given to us. ◊ Now no chastening seems to be joyful for the present, but grievous; nevertheless, afterward it yields the peaceable fruit of righteousness to those who have been trained by it. ◊ My brethren, count it all joy when you fall into various trials, knowing that the testing of your faith produces patience. But let patience have its perfect work, that you may be perfect and complete, lacking nothing. ◊ Blessed is the man who endures temptation; for when he has been proved, he will receive the crown of life which the Lord has promised to those who love Him. ◊ Most gladly I will rather boast in my infirmities, that the power of Christ may rest upon me. For when I am weak, then I am strong.

JAMES 5:11.ROM 5:3-5.HEB 12:11.JAMES 1:2-4.JAMES 1:12.2 COR 12:9-10

MORNING

Let us who are of the day be sober, putting on the breastplate of faith and love, and as a helmet the hope of salvation.

Gird up the loins of your mind, be sober, and rest your hope fully upon the grace that is to be brought to you at the revelation of Jesus Christ. ◊ Stand therefore, having girded your waist with truth, having put on the breastplate of righteousness, . . . above all, taking the shield of faith with which you will be able to quench all the fiery darts of the wicked one. And take the helmet of salvation, and the sword of the Spirit, which is the word of God.

He will swallow up death forever, and the Lord God will wipe away tears from all faces; the rebuke of His people He will take away from all the earth; for the Lord has spoken. And it will be said in that day: "Behold, this is our God; we have waited for Him, and He will save us. This is the Lord; . . . we will be glad and rejoice in His salvation."

Faith is the substance of things hoped for, the evidence of things not seen.

1 THESS 5:8.1 PET 1:13.EPH 6:14.EPH 6:16-17.IS 25:8-9.HEB 11:1

EVENING

The children of Israel encamped before them like two little flocks of goats, while the Syrians filled the countryside.

Thus says the Lord: "Because the Syrians have said, 'The Lord is God of the hills, but He is not God of the valleys,' therefore I will deliver all this great multitude into your hand, and you shall know that I am the Lord." And they encamped opposite each other for seven days. So it was that on the seventh day the battle was joined; and the children of Israel killed one hundred thousand foot soldiers of the Syrians in one day. ◊ You are of God, little children, and have overcome them, because He who is in you is greater than he who is in the world.

Fear not, for I am with you; be not dismayed, for I am your God. I will strengthen you, yes, I will help you, I will uphold you with My righteous right hand.

They will fight against you, but they shall not prevail against you. "For I am with you," says the Lord, "to deliver you."

1 KIN 20:27.1 KIN 20:28-29.1 JOHN 4:4.IS 41:10.JER 1:19

NOVEMBER 9

MORNING

I have given help to one who is mighty; I have exalted one chosen from the people.

I, even I, am the Lord, and besides Me there is no savior. ◇ There is one God and one Mediator between God and men, the Man Christ Jesus. ◇ There is no other name under heaven given among men by which we must be saved.

The . . . Mighty God. ◇ Made Himself of no reputation, taking the form of a servant, and coming in the likeness of men. And being found in appearance as a man, He humbled Himself and became obedient to the point of death, even the death of the cross. Therefore God also has highly exalted Him and given Him the name which is above every name. ◇ We see Jesus, who was made a little lower than the angels, for the suffering of death crowned with glory and honor, that He, by the grace of God, might taste death for everyone. ◇ Inasmuch . . . as the children have partaken of flesh and blood, He Himself likewise shared in the same.

PS 89:19.IS 43:11.1 TIM 2:5.ACTS 4:12.IS 9:6.PHIL 2:7-9.HEB 2:9.HEB 2:14

EVENING

Gather My saints together to Me, those who have made a covenant with Me by sacrifice.

Christ was offered once to bear the sins of many. To those who eagerly wait for Him He will appear a second time, apart from sin, for salvation. ◇ He is the Mediator of the new covenant, by means of death, . . . that those who are called may receive the promise of the eternal inheritance.

Father, I desire that they also whom You gave Me may be with Me where I am. ◇ Then He will send His angels, and gather together His elect from the four winds, from the farthest part of earth to the farthest part of heaven. ◇ If any of you are driven out to the farthest parts under heaven, from there the Lord your God will gather you, and from there He will bring you.

The dead in Christ will rise first. Then we who are alive and remain shall be caught up together with them in the clouds to meet the Lord in the air. And thus we shall always be with the Lord.

PS 50:5.HEB 9:28.HEB 9:15.JOHN 17:24.MARK 13:27.DEUT 30:4. 1 THESS 4:16-17

MORNING

Fruitful in every good work and increasing in the knowledge of God.

I beseech you . . . brethren, by the mercies of God, that you present your bodies a living sacrifice, holy, acceptable to God, which is your reasonable service. And do not be conformed to this world, but be transformed by the renewing of your mind, that you may prove what is that good and acceptable and perfect will of God. ◊ Just as you presented your members as slaves of uncleanness, and of lawlessness leading to more lawlessness, so now present your members as slaves of righteousness for holiness. ◊ In Christ Jesus neither circumcision nor uncircumcision avails anything, but a new creation. And as many as walk according to this rule, peace and mercy be upon them.

By this My Father is glorified, that you bear much fruit; so you will be My disciples. ◊ I chose you and appointed you that you should go and bear fruit, and that your fruit should remain, that whatever you ask the Father in My name He may give you.

COL 1:10.ROM 12:1-2.ROM 6:19.GAL 6:15-16.JOHN 15:8.JOHN 15:16

EVENING

I sought him, but I did not find him.

Return to the Lord your God, for you have stumbled because of your iniquity; take words with you, and return to the Lord. Say to Him, "Take away all iniquity; receive us graciously."

Let no one say when he is tempted, "I am tempted by God." . . . But each one is tempted when he is drawn away by his own desires and enticed. . . . Do not be deceived, my beloved brethren. Every good gift and every perfect gift is from above, and comes down from the Father of lights, with whom there is no variation or shadow of turning.

Wait on the Lord; be of good courage, and He shall strengthen your heart; wait, I say, on the Lord! ◊ It is good that one should hope and wait quietly for the salvation of the Lord. ◊ Shall God not avenge His own elect who cry out day and night to Him, though He bears long with them?

Truly my soul silently waits for God; from Him comes my salvation. . . . My soul, wait silently for God alone, for my expectation is from Him.

SONG 3:1.HOS 14:1-2.JAMES 1:13-14,16-17.PS 27:14.LAM 3:26.LUKE 18:7.PS 62:1,5

NOVEMBER 11

MORNING

He led them on safely.

I traverse the way of righteousness, in the midst of the paths of justice.

Behold, I send an Angel before you to keep you in the way and to bring you into the place which I have prepared. ◊ In all their affliction He was afflicted, and the Angel of His Presence saved them; in His love and in His pity He redeemed them; and He bore them and carried them all the days of old.

They did not gain possession of the land by their own sword, nor did their own arm save them; but it was Your right hand, Your arm, and the light of Your countenance, because You favored them. ◊ So You lead Your people, to make Yourself a glorious name.

Lead me, O Lord, in Your righteousness because of my enemies; make Your way straight before my face. ◊ Oh, send out Your light and Your truth! Let them lead me; let them bring me to Your holy hill and to Your tabernacle. Then I will go to the altar of God, to God my exceeding joy; and on the harp I will praise You, O God, my God.

PS 78:53.PROV 8:20.EX 23:20.IS 63:9.PS 44:3.IS 63:14.PS 5:8.PS 43:3-4

EVENING

You were washed, . . . you were sanctified, . . . you were justified.

The blood of Jesus Christ His Son cleanses us from all sin. ◊ The chastisement for our peace was upon Him, and by His stripes we are healed.

Christ . . . loved the church and gave Himself for it, that He might sanctify and cleanse it with the washing of water by the word, that He might present it to Himself a glorious church, not having spot or wrinkle or any such thing, but that it should be holy and without blemish. ◊ To her it was granted to be arrayed in fine linen, clean and bright, for the fine linen is the righteous acts of the saints. ◊ Let us draw near with a true heart in full assurance of faith, having our hearts sprinkled from an evil conscience and our bodies washed with pure water.

Who shall bring a charge against God's elect? It is God who justifies. ◊ Blessed is he whose transgression is forgiven, whose sin is covered. Blessed is the man to whom the Lord does not impute iniquity, and in whose spirit there is no guile.

1 COR 6:11.1 JOHN 1:7.IS 53:5.EPH 5:25-27.REV 19:8.HEB 10:22.ROM 8:33.PS 32:1-2

MORNING

Godly sorrow produces repentance to salvation, not to be regretted.

Peter remembered the word of Jesus who had said to him, "Before the rooster crows, you will deny Me three times." Then he went out and wept bitterly. ◇ If we confess our sins, He is faithful and just to forgive us our sins and to cleanse us from all unrighteousness. ◇ The blood of Jesus Christ His Son cleanses us from all sin.

My iniquities have overtaken me, so that I am not able to look up; they are more than the hairs of my head; therefore my heart fails me. Be pleased, O Lord, to deliver me; O Lord, make haste to help me!

So you, by the help of your God, return; observe mercy and justice, and wait on your God continually.

The sacrifices of God are a broken spirit, a broken and a contrite heart—these, O God, You will not despise. ◇ He heals the broken-hearted and binds up their wounds. ◇ He has shown you, O man, what is good; and what does the Lord require of you but to do justly, to love mercy, and to walk humbly with your God?

2 COR 7:10.MATT 26:75.1 JOHN 1:9.1 JOHN 1:7.PS 40:12-13.HOS 12:6.PS 51:17.PS 147:3.MIC 6:8

EVENING

"Is it well with you?" . . . And she answered, "It is well."

We have the same spirit of faith.

As chastened, and yet not killed; as sorrowful, yet always rejoicing; as poor, yet making many rich; as having nothing, and yet possessing all things.

We are hard pressed on every side, yet not crushed; we are perplexed, but not in despair; persecuted, but not forsaken; struck down, but not destroyed—always carrying about in the body the dying of the Lord Jesus, that the life of Jesus also may be manifested in our body. . . . Therefore we do not lose heart. Even though our outward man is perishing, yet the inward man is being renewed day by day. For our light affliction, which is but for a moment, is working for us a far more exceeding and eternal weight of glory, while we do not look at the things which are seen, but at the things which are not seen.

Beloved, I pray that you may prosper in all things and be in health, just as your soul prospers.

2 KIN 4:26.2 COR 4:13.2 COR 6:9-10.2 COR 4:8-10,16-18.3 JOHN 1:2

NOVEMBER 13

MORNING

**Christ . . . loved the church and gave Himself for it,
. . . that He might sanctify and cleanse it with the
washing of water by the word.**

Walk in love, as Christ also has loved us and given Himself for us, an offering and a sacrifice to God for a sweet-smelling aroma. ◊ Love one another fervently with a pure heart, having been born again, not of corruptible seed but incorruptible, through the word of God which lives and abides forever.

Sanctify them by Your truth. Your word is truth. ◊ Unless one is born of water and the Spirit, he cannot enter the kingdom of God. ◊ Not by works of righteousness which we have done, but according to His mercy He saved us, through the washing of regeneration and renewing of the Holy Spirit. ◊ Your word has given me life.

The law of the Lord is perfect, converting the soul; the testimony of the Lord is sure, making wise the simple; the statutes of the Lord are right, rejoicing the heart; the commandment of the Lord is pure, enlightening the eyes.

EPH 5:25-26. EPH 5:2. 1 PET 1:22-23. JOHN 17:17. JOHN 3:5. TITUS 3:5. PS 119:50. PS 19:7-8

EVENING

**Through Him we both have access by one Spirit
to the Father.**

I in them, and You in Me; that they may be made perfect in one.

Whatever you ask in My name, that I will do, that the Father may be glorified in the Son. If you ask anything in My name, I will do it. And I will pray the Father, and He will give you another Helper, that He may abide with you forever, even the Spirit of truth, whom the world cannot receive, because it neither sees Him nor knows Him; but you know Him, for He dwells with you and will be in you. ◊ There is one body and one Spirit, just as you were called in one hope of your calling; one Lord, one faith, one baptism; one God and Father of all, who is above all, and through all, and in you all. ◊ When you pray, say: Our Father in heaven.

Brethren, having boldness to enter the Holiest by the blood of Jesus, by a new and living way . . . , let us draw near.

EPH 2:18. JOHN 17:23. JOHN 14:13-14,16-17. EPH 4:4-6. LUKE 11:2. HEB 10:19-20,22

MORNING

**You are my help and my deliverer; do not delay,
O my God.**

The steps of a good man are ordered by the Lord, and He delights in his way. Though he fall, he shall not be utterly cast down; for the Lord upholds him with His hand. ◊ In the fear of the Lord there is strong confidence, and His children will have a place of refuge. ◊ Who are you that you should be afraid of a man who will die, and of the son of a man who will be made like grass? And you forget the Lord your Maker.

I am with you to deliver you. ◊ Be strong and of good courage, do not fear nor be afraid of them; for the Lord your God, He is the One who goes with you. He will not leave you nor forsake you.

I will sing of Your power; yes, I will sing aloud of Your mercy in the morning; for You have been my defense and refuge in the day of my trouble. ◊ You are my hiding place; You shall preserve me from trouble; You shall surround me with songs of deliverance.

PS 40:17.PS 37:23-24.PROV 14:26.IS 51:12-13.JER 1:8.DEUT 31:6.PS 59:16.PS 32:7

EVENING

How will you do in the flooding of the Jordan?

For the Jordan overflows all its banks during the whole time of harvest.

The priests who bore the ark of the covenant of the Lord stood firm on dry ground in the midst of the Jordan; and all Israel crossed over on dry ground, until all the people had crossed completely over the Jordan.

We see Jesus, who was made a little lower than the angels, for the suffering of death crowned with glory and honor, that He, by the grace of God, might taste death for everyone.

Though I walk through the valley of the shadow of death, I will fear no evil; for You are with me; Your rod and Your staff, they comfort me. ◊ When you pass through the waters, I will be with you; and through the rivers, they shall not overflow you.

Do not be afraid; I am the First and the Last. I am He who lives, and was dead, and behold, I am alive forevermore. Amen. And I have the keys of Hades and of Death.

JER 12:5.JOSH 3:15.JOSH 3:17.HEB 2:9.PS 23:4.IS 43:2.REV 1:17-18

MORNING

God is faithful, by whom you were called into the fellowship of His Son, Jesus Christ our Lord.

Let us hold fast the confession of our hope without wavering, for He who promised is faithful. ◊ God has said: "I will dwell in them and walk among them. I will be their God, and they shall be My people." ◊ Truly our fellowship is with the Father and with His Son Jesus Christ. ◊ Rejoice to the extent that you partake of Christ's sufferings, that when His glory is revealed, you may also be glad with exceeding joy.

That you, being rooted and grounded in love, may be able to comprehend with all the saints what is the width and length and depth and height—to know the love of Christ which passes knowledge; that you may be filled with all the fullness of God.

Whoever confesses that Jesus is the Son of God, God abides in him, and he in God. ◊ He who keeps His commandments abides in Him, and He in him.

1 COR 1:9.HEB 10:23.2 COR 6:16.1 JOHN 1:3.1 PET 4:13.EPH 3:17-19.
1 JOHN 4:15.1 JOHN 3:24

EVENING

We are His workmanship.

The king commanded them to quarry large stones, costly stones, and hewn stones, to lay the foundation of the temple. ◊ The temple, when it was being built, was built with stone finished at the quarry, so that no hammer or chisel or any iron tool was heard in the temple while it was being built.

You also, as living stones, are being built up a spiritual house. ◊ Built on the foundation of the apostles and prophets, Jesus Christ Himself being the chief cornerstone, in whom the whole building, being joined together, grows into a holy temple in the Lord, in whom you also are being built together for a habitation of God in the Spirit. ◊ Who once were not a people but are now the people of God.

You are God's building. ◊ Therefore, if anyone is in Christ, he is a new creation; old things have passed away; behold, all things have become new. ◊ Now He who has prepared us for this very thing is God, who also has given us the Spirit as a guarantee.

EPH 2:10.1 KIN 5:17.1 KIN 6:7.1 PET 2:5.EPH 2:20-22.1 PET 2:10.1 COR
3:9.2 COR 5:17.2 COR 5:5

MORNING

Sanctify them by Your truth. Your word is truth.

You are already clean because of the word which I have spoken to you. ◊ Let the word of Christ dwell in you richly in all wisdom.

How can a young man cleanse his way? By taking heed according to Your word. With my whole heart I have sought You; oh, let me not wander from Your commandments!

When wisdom enters your heart, and knowledge is pleasant to your soul, discretion will preserve you; understanding will keep you.

My foot has held fast to His steps; I have kept His way and not turned aside. I have not departed from the commandment of His lips; I have treasured the words of His mouth more than my necessary food. ◊ I have more understanding than all my teachers, for Your testimonies are my meditation. ◊ If you abide in My word, you are My disciples indeed. And you shall know the truth, and the truth shall make you free.

JOHN 17:17.JOHN 15:3.COL 3:16.PS 119:9-10.PROV 2:10-11.JOB 23:11-12.PS 119:99.JOHN 8:31-32

EVENING

Fellow citizens with the saints.

You have come to Mount Zion and to the city of the living God, the heavenly Jerusalem, to an innumerable company of angels, to the general assembly and church of the firstborn who are registered in heaven, to God the Judge of all, to the spirits of just men made perfect.

These all died in faith, not having received the promises, but having seen them afar off were assured of them, embraced them, and confessed that they were strangers and pilgrims on the earth. ◊ For our citizenship is in heaven, from which we also eagerly wait for the Savior, the Lord Jesus Christ, who will transform our lowly body that it may be conformed to His glorious body, according to the working by which He is able even to subdue all things to Himself. ◊ The Father . . . has delivered us from the power of darkness and translated us into the kingdom of the Son of His love.

As sojourners and pilgrims, abstain from fleshly lusts which war against the soul.

EPH 2:19.HEB 12:22-23.HEB 11:13.PHIL 3:20-21.COL 1:12-13.1 PET 2:11

NOVEMBER 17

MORNING

Your thoughts are very deep.

We . . . do not cease to pray for you, and to ask that you may be filled with the knowledge of His will in all wisdom and spiritual understanding. ◊ That you, being rooted and grounded in love, may be able to comprehend with all the saints what is the width and length and depth and height—to know the love of Christ which passes knowledge; that you may be filled with all the fullness of God.

Oh, the depth of the riches both of the wisdom and knowledge of God! How unsearchable are His judgments and His ways past finding out! ◊ "My thoughts are not your thoughts, nor are your ways My ways," says the Lord. "For as the heavens are higher than the earth, so are My ways higher than your ways, and My thoughts than your thoughts." ◊ Many, O Lord my God, are Your wonderful works which You have done; and Your thoughts which are toward us cannot be recounted to You in order; if I would declare and speak of them, they are more than can be numbered.

PS 92:5.COL 1:9.EPH 3:17-19.ROM 11:33.IS 55:8-9.PS 40:5

EVENING

Whatever a man sows, that he will also reap.

Those who plow iniquity and sow trouble reap the same. ◊ They sow the wind, and reap the whirlwind. ◊ He who sows to his flesh will of the flesh reap corruption.

To him who sows righteousness will be a sure reward. ◊ He who sows to the Spirit will of the Spirit reap everlasting life. Let us not grow weary while doing good, for in due season we shall reap if we do not lose heart. As we have opportunity, let us do good to all, especially to those who are of the household of faith.

There is one who scatters, yet increases more; and there is one who withholds more than is right, but it leads to poverty. The generous soul will be made rich, and he who waters will also be watered himself. ◊ He who sows sparingly will also reap sparingly, and he who sows bountifully will also reap bountifully.

GAL 6:7.JOB 4:8.HOS 8:7.GAL 6:8.PROV 11:18.GAL 6:8-10.PROV
11:24-25.2 COR 9:6

MORNING

He removes it by His rough wind in the day of the east wind.

Let us fall into the hand of the Lord, for His mercies are great. ◊ "I am with you," says the Lord, "to save you; . . . I will correct you in justice, and will not let you go altogether unpunished." ◊ He will not always strive with us, nor will He keep His anger forever. He has not dealt with us according to our sins, nor punished us according to our iniquities. . . . For He knows our frame; He remembers that we are dust. ◊ I will spare them as a man spares his own son who serves him.

God is faithful, who will not allow you to be tempted beyond what you are able, but with the temptation will also make the way of escape, that you may be able to bear it. ◊ Satan has asked for you, that he may sift you as wheat. But I have prayed for you, that your faith should not fail.

You have been a strength to the poor, a strength to the needy in his distress, a refuge from the storm, a shade from the heat; for the blast of the terrible ones is as a storm against the wall.

IS 27:8.2 SAM 24:14.JER 30:11.PS 103:9-10,14.MAL 3:17.1 COR 10:13.LUKE 22:31-32.IS 25:4

EVENING

I did not believe the words until I came and saw it with my own eyes; and indeed the half was not told me.

The queen of the South will rise up in the judgment with this generation and condemn it, for she came from the ends of the earth to hear the wisdom of Solomon; and indeed a greater than Solomon is here. ◊ We beheld His glory, the glory as of the only begotten of the Father, full of grace and truth.

My speech and my preaching were . . . in demonstration of the Spirit and of power, that your faith should not be in the wisdom of men but in the power of God. . . . But as it is written: "Eye has not seen, nor ear heard, nor have entered into the heart of man the things which God has prepared for those who love Him." But God has revealed them to us through His Spirit. For the Spirit searches all things, yes, the deep things of God.

Your eyes will see the King in His beauty. ◊ We shall see Him as He is. ◊ In my flesh I shall see God. ◊ I shall be satisfied.

1 KIN 10:7.MATT 12:42.JOHN 1:14.1 COR 2:4-5,9-10.IS 33:17.1 JOHN 3:2.JOB 19:26.PS 17:15

NOVEMBER 19

MORNING

By their fruits you will know them.

Little children, let no one deceive you. He who practices righteousness is righteous, just as He is righteous. ◊ Does a spring send forth fresh water and bitter from the same opening? Can a fig tree, my brethren, bear olives, or a grapevine bear figs? Thus no spring can yield both salt water and fresh. Who is wise and understanding among you? Let him show by good conduct that his works are done in the meekness of wisdom. ◊ Having your conduct honorable among the Gentiles, that when they speak against you as evildoers, they may, by your good works which they observe, glorify God in the day of visitation.

Either make the tree good and its fruit good, or else make the tree bad and its fruit bad; for a tree is known by its fruit. ◊ A good man out of the good treasure of his heart brings forth good things, and an evil man out of the evil treasure brings forth evil things.

What more could have been done to My vineyard that I have not done in it?

MATT 7:20.1 JOHN 3:7.JAMES 3:11-13.1 PET 2:12.MATT 12:33.MATT 12:35.IS 5:4

EVENING

I will make the place of My feet glorious.

Thus says the Lord: "Heaven is My throne, and earth is My footstool."

But will God indeed dwell with men on the earth? Behold, heaven and the heaven of heavens cannot contain You; how much less this temple which I have built!

Thus says the Lord of hosts: "Once more (it is a little while) I will shake heaven and earth, the sea and dry land; and I will shake all nations, and they shall come to the Desire of All Nations, and I will fill this temple with glory," says the Lord of hosts. . . . "The glory of this latter temple shall be greater than the former," says the Lord of hosts.

I saw a new heaven and a new earth, for the first heaven and the first earth had passed away. Also there was no more sea. . . . And I heard a loud voice from heaven saying, "Behold, the tabernacle of God is with men, and He will dwell with them, and they shall be His people, and God Himself will be with them and be their God."

IS 60:13.IS 66:1.2 CHR 6:18.HAG 2:6-7,9.REV 21:1,3

MORNING

When I sit in darkness, the Lord will be a light to me.

When you pass through the waters, I will be with you; and through the rivers, they shall not overflow you. When you walk through the fire, you shall not be burned, nor shall the flame scorch you. For I am the Lord your God, the Holy One of Israel, your Savior. ◇ I will bring the blind by a way they did not know; I will lead them in paths they have not known. I will make darkness light before them, and crooked places straight. These things I will do for them, and not forsake them.

Yea, though I walk through the valley of the shadow of death, I will fear no evil; for You are with me; Your rod and Your staff, they comfort me. ◇ Whenever I am afraid, I will trust in You. In God (I will praise His word), in God I have put my trust; I will not fear. What can flesh do to me? ◇ The Lord is my light and my salvation; whom shall I fear? The Lord is the strength of my life; of whom shall I be afraid?

MIC 7:8.IS 43:2-3.IS 42:16.PS 23:4.PS 56:3-4.PS 27:1

EVENING

One God and one Mediator between God and men, the Man Christ Jesus.

Hear, O Israel: The Lord our God, the Lord is one! ◇ A mediator does not mediate for one only, but God is one.

We have sinned with our fathers, we have committed iniquity, we have done wickedly. Our fathers in Egypt did not understand Your wonders; they did not remember the multitude of Your mercies. . . . therefore He said that He would destroy them, had not Moses His chosen one stood before Him in the breach, to turn away His wrath, lest He destroy them.

Therefore, holy brethren, partakers of the heavenly calling, consider the Apostle and High Priest of our confession, Christ Jesus, who was faithful to Him who appointed Him, as Moses also was faithful in all His house.

He is also Mediator of a better covenant, which was established on better promises. . . . I will be merciful to their unrighteousness, and their sins and their lawless deeds I will remember no more.

1 TIM 2:5.DEUT 6:4.GAL 3:20.PS 106:6-7,23.HEB 3:1-2.HEB 8:6,12

NOVEMBER 21

MORNING

The one who comes to Me I will by no means cast out.

It will be that when he cries to Me, I will hear, for I am gracious. ◊ I will not cast them away, nor shall I abhor them, to utterly destroy them and break My covenant with them; for I am the Lord their God. ◊ I will remember My covenant with you in the days of your youth, and I will establish an everlasting covenant with you.

"Come now, and let us reason together," says the Lord, "though your sins are like scarlet, they shall be as white as snow; though they are red like crimson, they shall be as wool." ◊ Let the wicked forsake his way, and the unrighteous man his thoughts; let him return to the Lord, and He will have mercy on him; and to our God, for He will abundantly pardon. ◊ "Lord, remember me when You come into Your kingdom." And Jesus said to him, "Assuredly, I say to you, today you will be with Me in Paradise."

A bruised reed He will not break, and smoking flax He will not quench.

JOHN 6:37.EX 22:27.LEV 26:44.EZEK 16:60.IS 1:18.IS 55:7.LUKE 23:42-43.IS 42:3

EVENING

The Son of His love.

Suddenly a voice came from heaven, saying, "This is My beloved Son, in whom I am well pleased." ◊ Behold! My Servant whom I uphold, My Elect One in whom My soul delights! ◊ The only begotten Son, who is in the bosom of the Father.

In this the love of God was manifested toward us, that God has sent His only begotten Son into the world, that we might live through Him. In this is love, not that we loved God, but that He loved us and sent His Son to be the propitiation for our sins. . . . And we have known and believed the love that God has for us. God is love.

The glory which You gave Me I have given them, that they may be one just as We are one: I in them, and You in Me; that they may be made perfect in one, and that the world may know that You have sent Me, and have loved them as You have loved Me. ◊ Behold what manner of love the Father has bestowed on us, that we should be called children of God!

COL 1:13.MATT 3:17.IS 42:1.JOHN 1:18.1 JOHN 4:9-10,16.JOHN 17:22-23.1 JOHN 3:1

MORNING

Praying in the Holy Spirit.

God is Spirit, and those who worship Him must worship in spirit and truth. ◊ We . . . have access by one Spirit to the Father.

O My Father, if it is possible, let this cup pass from Me; nevertheless, not as I will, but as You will.

The Spirit . . . helps in our weaknesses. For we do not know what we should pray for as we ought, but the Spirit Himself makes intercession for us with groanings which cannot be uttered. Now He who searches the hearts knows what the mind of the Spirit is, because He makes intercession for the saints according to the will of God. ◊ This is the confidence that we have in Him, that if we ask anything according to His will, He hears us. ◊ When He, the Spirit of truth, has come, He will guide you into all truth.

Praying always with all prayer and supplication in the Spirit, being watchful to this end with all perseverance and supplication.

JUDE 1:20.JOHN 4:24.EPH 2:18.MATT 26:39.ROM 8:26-27.1 JOHN 5:14.JOHN 16:13.EPH 6:18

EVENING

There is hope for a tree, if it is cut down, that it will sprout again, and that its tender shoots will not cease.

A bruised reed He will not break.

He restores my soul. ◊ Godly sorrow produces repentance to salvation, not to be regretted; but the sorrow of the world produces death. ◊ No chastening seems to be joyful for the present, but grievous; nevertheless, afterward it yields the peaceable fruit of righteousness to those who have been trained by it.

Before I was afflicted I went astray, but now I keep Your word. ◊ And after all that has come upon us for our evil deeds and for our great guilt, since You our God have punished us less than our iniquities deserve, and have given us such deliverance as this.

Do not rejoice over me, my enemy; when I fall, I will arise; when I sit in darkness, the Lord will be a light to me. He will bring me forth to the light, and I will see His righteousness.

JOB 14:7.IS 42:3.PS 23:3.2 COR 7:10.HEB 12:11.PS 119:67.EZRA 9:13.MIC 7:8-9

NOVEMBER 23

MORNING

Whoever listens to me will dwell safely, and will be secure, without fear of evil.

Lord, You have been our dwelling place in all generations. ◊ He who dwells in the secret place of the Most High shall abide under the shadow of the Almighty. . . . His truth shall be your shield and buckler.

Your life is hidden with Christ in God. ◊ He who touches you touches the apple of His eye. ◊ Stand still, and see the salvation of the Lord. . . . The Lord will fight for you, and you shall hold your peace. ◊ God is our refuge and strength, a very present help in trouble. Therefore we will not fear.

Jesus spoke to them, saying, "Be of good cheer! It is I; do not be afraid." ◊ "Why are you troubled? And why do doubts arise in your hearts? Behold My hands and My feet, that it is I Myself. Handle Me and see, for a spirit does not have flesh and bones as you see I have." ◊ I know whom I have believed and am persuaded that He is able to keep what I have committed to Him until that Day.

PROV 1:33.PS 90:1.PS 91:1,4.COL 3:3.ZECH 2:8.EX 14:13-14.PS 46:1-2.MATT 14:27.LUKE 24:38-39.2 TIM 1:12

EVENING

My kingdom is not from here.

This Man, after He had offered one sacrifice for sins forever, sat down at the right hand of God, . . . from that time waiting till His enemies are made His footstool. ◊ Hereafter you will see the Son of Man sitting at the right hand of the Power, and coming on the clouds of heaven.

He must reign till He has put all enemies under His feet.

Thanks be to God, who gives us the victory through our Lord Jesus Christ. ◊ He raised Him from the dead and seated Him at His right hand in the heavenly places, far above all principality and power and might and dominion, and every name that is named, not only in this age but also in that which is to come. And He put all things under His feet, and gave Him to be head over all things to the church, which is His body, the fullness of Him who fills all in all. ◊ He who is the blessed and only Potentate, the King of kings and Lord of lords.

JOHN 18:36.HEB 10:12-13.MATT 26:64.1 COR 15:25.1 COR 15:57.EPH 1:20-23.1 TIM 6:15

MORNING

**My mother and My brothers are these who hear the
word of God and do it.**

Both He who sanctifies and those who are being sanctified are all of
one, for which reason He is not ashamed to call them brethren, saying, "I
will declare your name to My brethren; in the midst of the congregation I
will sing praise to You." ◊ In Christ Jesus neither circumcision nor
uncircumcision avails anything, but faith working through love. ◊ You
are My friends if you do whatever I command you. ◊ Blessed are those
who hear the word of God and keep it!

Not everyone who says to Me, "Lord, Lord," shall enter the kingdom
of heaven, but he who does the will of My Father in heaven. ◊ My food is
to do the will of Him who sent Me.

If we say that we have fellowship with Him, and walk in darkness, we
lie and do not practice the truth. ◊ Whoever keeps His word, truly the
love of God is perfected in him. By this we know that we are in Him.

LUKE 8:21.HEB 2:11-12.GAL 5:6.JOHN 15:14.LUKE 11:28.MATT
7:21.JOHN 4:34.1 JOHN 1:6.1 JOHN 2:5

EVENING

What are you doing here, Elijah?

He knows the way that I take. ◊ O Lord, You have searched me and
known me. You know my sitting down and my rising up; You
understand my thought afar off. You comprehend my path and my lying
down, and are acquainted with all my ways. . . . Where can I go from
Your Spirit? Or where can I flee from Your presence? . . . If I take the
wings of the morning, and dwell in the uttermost parts of the sea, even
there Your hand shall lead me, and Your right hand shall hold me.

Elijah was a man with a nature like ours. ◊ The fear of man brings a
snare, but whoever trusts in the Lord shall be safe. ◊ Though he fall, he
shall not be utterly cast down; for the Lord upholds him with His hand.
◊ A righteous man may fall seven times and rise again.

Let us not grow weary while doing good, for in due season we shall
reap if we do not lose heart. ◊ The spirit indeed is willing, but the flesh is
weak. ◊ As a father pities his children, so the Lord pities those who fear
Him.

1 KIN 19:9.JOB 23:10.PS 139:1-3,7,9-10.JAMES 5:17.PROV 29:25.PS
37:24.PROV 24:16.GAL 6:9.MATT 26:41.PS 103:13

MORNING_____

Having been set free from sin, you became slaves of righteousness.

You cannot serve God and mammon. ◊ When you were slaves of sin, you were free in regard to righteousness. What fruit did you have then in the things of which you are now ashamed? For the end of those things is death. But now having been set free from sin, and having become slaves of God, you have your fruit to holiness, and the end, everlasting life.

Christ is the end of the law for righteousness to everyone who believes.

If anyone serves Me, let him follow Me; and where I am, there My servant will be also. If anyone serves Me, him My Father will honor. ◊ Take My yoke upon you and learn from Me, for I am gentle and lowly in heart, and you will find rest for your souls. For My yoke is easy and My burden is light.

O Lord our God, other masters besides You have had dominion over us; but by You only we make mention of Your name. ◊ I will run in the way of Your commandments, for You shall enlarge my heart.

ROM 6:18.MATT 6:24.ROM 6:20-22.ROM 10:4.JOHN 12:26.MATT 11:29-30.IS 26:13.PS 119:32

EVENING_____

Whoever calls on the name of the Lord shall be saved.

Manasseh . . . did evil in the sight of the Lord, according to the abominations of the nations whom the Lord had cast out. . . . He raised up altars for Baal. . . . And he built altars for all the host of heaven in the two courts of the house of the Lord. Also he made his son pass through the fire, practiced soothsaying, used witchcraft, and consulted spiritists and mediums. He did much evil in the sight of the Lord, to provoke Him to anger. ◊ Now when he was in affliction, he implored the Lord his God, and humbled himself greatly before the God of his fathers, and prayed to Him; and He received his entreaty, heard his supplication.

"Come now, and let us reason together," says the Lord, "though your sins are like scarlet, they shall be as white as snow; though they are red like crimson, they shall be as wool." ◊ The Lord is . . . longsuffering toward us, not willing that any should perish.

ACTS 2:21.2 KIN 21:1-3,5-6.2 CHR 33:12-13.IS 1:18.2 PET 3:9

MORNING————————————————————

The Lord delights in you.

But now, thus says the Lord, who created you, O Jacob, and He who formed you, O Israel: "Fear not, for I have redeemed you; I have called you by your name; you are Mine." ◊ Can a woman forget her nursing child, and not have compassion on the son of her womb? Surely they may forget, yet I will not forget you. See, I have inscribed you on the palms of My hands; your walls are continually before Me.

The steps of a good man are ordered by the Lord, and He delights in his way. ◊ My delight was with the sons of men. ◊ The Lord takes pleasure in those who fear Him, in those who hope in His mercy. ◊ "They shall be Mine," says the Lord of hosts, "on the day that I make them My jewels. And I will spare them as a man spares his own son who serves him."

You, who once were alienated and enemies in your mind by wicked works, yet now He has reconciled in the body of His flesh through death, to present you holy, and blameless, and irreproachable in His sight.

IS 62:4.IS 43:1.IS 49:15-16.PS 37:23.PROV 8:31.PS 147:11.MAL 3:17.COL
1:21-22

EVENING————————————————————

The sorrow of the world produces death.

When Ahithophel saw that his counsel was not followed, he saddled his donkey, and arose and went home to his house, to his city. Then he put his household in order, and hanged himself, and died. ◊ Who can bear a broken spirit?

Is there no balm in Gilead, is there no physician there? Why then is there no recovery for the health of the daughter of my people? ◊ The Lord has anointed Me to preach good tidings to the poor; He has sent Me to heal the brokenhearted, . . . to comfort all who mourn, to console those who mourn in Zion, to give them beauty for ashes, the oil of joy for mourning, the garment of praise for the spirit of heaviness. ◊ Come to Me, all you who labor and are heavy laden, and I will give you rest. Take My yoke upon you and learn from Me, for I am gentle and lowly in heart, and you will find rest for your souls. For My yoke is easy and My burden is light.

Philip . . . preached Jesus to him. ◊ He heals the broken-hearted and binds up their wounds.

2 COR 7:10.2 SAM 17:23.PROV 18:14.JER 8:22.IS 61:1-3.MATT 11:28-
30.ACTS 8:35.PS 147:3

MORNING

The glory which You gave Me I have given them.

I saw the Lord sitting on a throne, high and lifted up, and the train of His robe filled the temple. Above it stood seraphim. . . . And one cried to another and said: "Holy, holy, holy is the Lord of hosts; the whole earth is full of His glory!" ◊ These things Isaiah said when he saw His glory and spoke of Him. ◊ On the likeness of the throne was a likeness . . . of a man high above it. . . . Like the appearance of a rainbow in a cloud on a rainy day, so was the appearance of the brightness all around it. This was the appearance of the likeness of the glory of the Lord.

"Please, show me Your glory." . . . But He said, "You cannot see My face; for no man shall see Me, and live." ◊ No one has seen God at any time. The only begotten Son, who is in the bosom of the Father, He has declared Him. ◊ God who commanded light to shine out of darkness who has shone in our hearts to give the light of the knowledge of the glory of God in the face of Jesus Christ.

JOHN 17:22.IS 6:1-3.JOHN 12:41.EZEK 1:26,28.EX 33:18,20.JOHN 1:18.
2 COR 4:6

EVENING

My son, if sinners entice you, do not consent.

She took of its fruit and ate. She also gave to her husband with her, and he ate. ◊ Did not Achan the son of Zerah commit a trespass in the accursed thing, and wrath fell on all the congregation of Israel? And that man did not perish alone in his iniquity.

You shall not follow a crowd to do evil.

Wide is the gate and broad is the way that leads to destruction, and there are many who go in by it.

None of us lives to himself. ◊ You, brethren, have been called to liberty; only do not use liberty as an opportunity for the flesh, but through love serve one another. ◊ Beware lest somehow this liberty of yours become a stumbling block to those who are weak. . . . When you thus sin against the brethren, and wound their weak conscience, you sin against Christ.

All we like sheep have gone astray; we have turned, every one, to his own way; and the Lord has laid on Him the iniquity of us all.

PROV 1:10.GEN 3:6.JOSH 22:20.EX 23:2.MATT 7:13.ROM 14:7.GAL
5:13.1 COR 8:9,12.IS 53:6

MORNING

**As the body without the spirit is dead, so faith
without works is dead also.**

Not everyone who says . . . , "Lord, Lord," shall enter the kingdom of
heaven, but he who does the will of My Father in heaven. ◊ Pursue . . .
holiness, without which no one will see the Lord. ◊ Add to your faith
virtue, to virtue knowledge, to knowledge self-control, to self-control
perseverance, to perseverance godliness, to godliness brotherly kindness, and to brotherly kindness love. For if these things are yours and
abound, you will be neither barren nor unfruitful in the knowledge of our
Lord Jesus Christ. For he who lacks these things is shortsighted, even to
blindness, and has forgotten that he was purged from his old sins.
Therefore, brethren, be even more diligent to make your calling and
election sure, for if you do these things you will never stumble.

By grace you have been saved through faith, and that not of
yourselves; it is the gift of God, not of works, lest anyone should boast.

JAMES 2:26.MATT 7:21.HEB 12:14.2 PET 1:5-10.EPH 2:8-9

EVENING

**As the children have partaken of flesh and blood, He
Himself likewise shared in the same, that . . . He
might . . . release those who through fear of death
were all their lifetime subject to bondage.**

O Death, where is your sting? O Hades, where is your victory? . . .
Thanks be to God, who gives us the victory through our Lord Jesus
Christ. ◊ Therefore we do not lose heart. Even though our outward man
is perishing, yet the inward man is being renewed day by day.

We know that if our earthly house, this tent, is destroyed, we have a
building from God, a house not made with hands, eternal in the heavens.
. . . Therefore we are always confident, knowing that while we are at
home in the body we are absent from the Lord. . . . We are . . . well
pleased rather to be absent from the body and to be present with the
Lord.

Let not your heart be troubled; you believe in God, believe also in Me.
In My Father's house are many mansions; if it were not so, I would have
told you. I go to prepare a place for you.

HEB 2:14-15.1 COR 15:55,57.2 COR 4:16.2 COR 5:1,6,8.JOHN 14:1-2

MORNING

We shall be satisfied with the goodness of Your house.

One thing I have desired of the Lord, that will I seek: that I may dwell in the house of the Lord all the days of my life, to behold the beauty of the Lord, and to inquire in His temple. . . .

Blessed are those who hunger and thirst for righteousness, for they shall be filled. ◊ He has filled the hungry with good things, and the rich He has sent away empty.

He satisfies the longing soul, and fills the hungry soul with goodness. ◊ I am the bread of life. He who comes to Me shall never hunger, and he who believes in Me shall never thirst.

How precious is Your lovingkindness, O God! Therefore the children of men put their trust under the shadow of Your wings. They are abundantly satisfied with the fullness of Your house, and You give them drink from the river of Your pleasures. For with You is the fountain of life; in Your light we see light.

PS 65:4.PS 27:4.MATT 5:6.LUKE 1:53.PS 107:9.JOHN 6:35.PS 36:7-9

EVENING

Do you now believe?

What does it profit, my brethren, if someone says he has faith but does not have works? Can faith save him? . . . Faith . . . , if it does not have works, is dead.

By faith Abraham, when he was tested, offered up Isaac, and he who had received the promises offered up his only begotten son, . . . accounting that God was able to raise him up, even from the dead. ◊ Was not Abraham our father justified by works when he offered Isaac his son on the altar? . . . You see then that a man is justified by works, and not by faith only.

He who looks into the perfect law of liberty and continues in it, and is not a forgetful hearer but a doer of the work, this one will be blessed in what he does.

By their fruits you will know them. Not everyone who says to Me, "Lord, Lord," shall enter the kingdom of heaven, but he who does the will of My Father in heaven. ◊ If you know these things, happy are you if you do them.

JOHN 16:31.JAMES 2:14,17.HEB 11:17,19.JAMES 2:21.JAMES
2:24.JAMES 1:25.MATT 7:20-21.JOHN 13:17

MORNING_____

The Lord of peace Himself give you peace always in every way. The Lord be with you all.

Peace from Him who is and who was and who is to come. ◊ The peace of God, which surpasses all understanding, will guard your hearts and minds through Christ Jesus.

Jesus Himself stood in the midst of them, and said to them, "Peace to you." ◊ Peace I leave with you, My peace I give to you; not as the world gives do I give to you. Let not your heart be troubled, neither let it be afraid.

The Helper . . . the Spirit of truth. ◊ The fruit of the Spirit is love, joy, peace. ◊ The Spirit Himself bears witness with our spirit that we are children of God.

My Presence will go with you, and I will give you rest. . . . Then he said to Him, "If Your Presence does not go with us, do not bring us up from here. For how then will it be known that Your people and I have found grace in Your sight, except You go with us?"

2 THESS 3:16.REV 1:4.PHIL 4:7.LUKE 24:36.JOHN 15:26.GAL 5:22.ROM 8:16.EX 33:14-16

EVENING_____

We . . . glory in tribulations.

If in this life only we have hope in Christ, we are of all men the most pitiable.

Beloved, do not think it strange concerning the fiery trial which is to try you, as though some strange thing happened to you; . . . but rejoice to the extent that you partake of Christ's sufferings, that when His glory is revealed, you may also be glad with exceeding joy. ◊ Sorrowful, yet always rejoicing.

Rejoice in the Lord always. Again I will say, rejoice! ◊ They departed from the presence of the council, rejoicing that they were counted worthy to suffer shame for His name. ◊ The God of hope fill you with all joy and peace in believing.

Though the fig tree may not blossom, nor fruit be on the vines; though the labor of the olive may fail, and the fields yield no food; though the flock be cut off from the fold, and there be no herd in the stalls—yet I will rejoice in the Lord, I will joy in the God of my salvation.

ROM 5:3.1 COR 15:19.1 PET 4:12-13.2 COR 6:10.PHIL 4:4.ACTS 5:41.ROM 15:13.HAB 3:17-18

DECEMBER 1

MORNING

A man will be as a hiding place from the wind, and a cover from the tempest.

Inasmuch . . . as the children have partaken of flesh and blood, He Himself likewise shared in the same. ◊ "The Man who is My Companion," says the Lord of hosts. ◊ I and My Father are one.

He who dwells in the secret place of the Most High shall abide under the shadow of the Almighty. ◊ There will be a tabernacle for shade in the daytime from the heat, for a place of refuge, and for a shelter from storm and rain. ◊ The Lord is your shade at your right hand. The sun shall not strike you by day, nor the moon by night.

When my heart is overwhelmed; lead me to the rock that is higher than I. ◊ You are my hiding place; You shall preserve me from trouble. ◊ You have been a strength to the poor, a strength to the needy in his distress, a refuge from the storm, a shade from the heat; for the blast of the terrible ones is as a storm against the wall.

IS 32:2.HEB 2:14.ZECH 13:7.JOHN 10:30.PS 91:1.IS 4:6.PS 121:5-6.PS 61:2.PS 32:7.IS 25:4

EVENING

Behold, I create new heavens and a new earth.

The new heavens and the new earth which I will make shall remain before Me. . . . So shall your descendants and your name remain.

We, according to His promise, look for new heavens and a new earth in which righteousness dwells.

I saw a new heaven and a new earth, for the first heaven and the first earth had passed away. Also there was no more sea. Then I, John, saw the holy city, New Jerusalem, coming down out of heaven from God, prepared as a bride adorned for her husband. And I heard a loud voice from heaven saying, "Behold, the tabernacle of God is with men, and He will dwell with them, and they shall be His people, and God Himself will be with them and be their God. And God will wipe away every tear from their eyes; there shall be no more death, nor sorrow, nor crying; and there shall be no more pain, for the former things have passed away. Then He who sat on the throne said, 'Behold, I make all things new.' "

IS 65:17.IS 66:22.2 PET 3:13.REV 21:1-5

MORNING

You have an anointing from the Holy One, and you know all things.

God anointed Jesus of Nazareth with the Holy Spirit and with power. ◊ It pleased the Father that in Him all the fullness should dwell. ◊ Of His fullness we have all received, and grace for grace.

You anoint my head with oil. ◊ The anointing which you have received from Him abides in you, and you do not need that anyone teach you; but as the same anointing teaches you concerning all things, and is true, and is not a lie, and just as it has taught you, you will abide in Him.

The Helper, the Holy Spirit, whom the Father will send in My name, He will teach you all things, and bring to your remembrance all things that I said to you.

The Spirit also helps in our weaknesses. For we do not know what we should pray for as we ought, but the Spirit Himself makes intercession for us with groanings which cannot be uttered.

1 JOHN 2:20.ACTS 10:38.COL 1:19.JOHN 1:16.PS 23:5.1 JOHN 2:27.JOHN 14:26.ROM 8:26

EVENING

Having our hearts sprinkled from an evil conscience.

If the blood of bulls and goats and the ashes of a heifer, sprinkling the unclean, sanctifies for the purifying of the flesh, how much more shall the blood of Christ, who through the eternal Spirit offered Himself without spot to God, purge your conscience from dead works to serve the living God? ◊ The blood of sprinkling . . . speaks better things than that of Abel.

We have redemption through His blood, the forgiveness of sins, according to the riches of His grace.

When Moses had spoken every precept to all the people according to the law, he took the blood of calves and goats, with water, scarlet wool, and hyssop, and sprinkled both the book itself and all the people. . . . Then likewise he sprinkled with blood both the tabernacle and all the vessels of the ministry. And according to the law almost all things are purged with blood, and without shedding of blood there is no remission.

HEB 10:22.HEB 9:13-14.HEB 12:24.EPH 1:7.HEB 9:19,21-22

DECEMBER 3

I would seek God, and to God I would commit my cause.

Is anything too hard for the Lord? ◊ Commit your way to the Lord, trust also in Him, and He shall bring it to pass. ◊ Be anxious for nothing, but in everything by prayer and supplication, with thanksgiving, let your requests be made known to God. ◊ [Cast] all your care upon Him, for He cares for you.

Hezekiah received the letter from the hand of the messengers, and read it; and Hezekiah went up to the house of the Lord, and spread it before the Lord. Then Hezekiah prayed to the Lord.

It shall come to pass that before they call, I will answer; and while they are still speaking, I will hear. ◊ The effective, fervent prayer of a righteous man avails much.

I love the Lord, because He has heard My voice and my supplications. Because He has inclined His ear to me, therefore I will call upon Him as long as I live.

JOB 5:8.GEN 18:14.PS 37:5.PHIL 4:6.1 PET 5:7.IS 37:14-15.IS 65:24.JAMES 5:16.PS 116:1-2

Our bodies washed with pure water.

You shall . . . make a laver of bronze. . . . You shall put it between the tabernacle of meeting and the altar. And you shall put water in it, for Aaron and his sons shall wash their hands and their feet in water from it. When they go into the tabernacle of meeting, . . . they shall wash with water, lest they die. They shall wash their hands and their feet, lest they die. ◊ Your body is the temple of the Holy Spirit who is in you. ◊ If anyone defiles the temple of God, God will destroy him. For the temple of God is holy, which temple you are.

In my flesh I shall see God, whom I shall see for myself, and my eyes shall behold, and not another. ◊ There shall by no means enter it anything that defiles. ◊ You are of purer eyes than to behold evil, and cannot look on wickedness. ◊ I beseech you therefore, brethren, by the mercies of God, that you present your bodies a living sacrifice, holy, acceptable to God, which is your reasonable service.

HEB 10:22.EX 30:18-21.1 COR 6:19.1 COR 3:17.JOB 19:26-27.REV 21:27.HAB 1:13.ROM 12:1

MORNING

Where can wisdom be found?

If any of you lacks wisdom, let him ask of God, who gives to all liberally and without reproach, and it will be given to him. But let him ask in faith, with no doubting. ◊ Trust in the Lord with all your heart, and lean not on your own understanding; in all your ways acknowledge Him, and He shall direct your paths. ◊ God . . . alone is wise. ◊ Do not be wise in your own eyes.

"Ah, Lord God! Behold, I cannot speak, for I am a youth." But the Lord said to me: "Do not say, 'I am a youth,' for you shall go to all to whom I send you, and whatever I command you, you shall speak. Do not be afraid of their faces, for I am with you to deliver you," says the Lord.

Whatever you ask the Father in My name He will give you. Until now you have asked nothing in My name. Ask, and you will receive, that your joy may be full. ◊ And all things, whatever you ask in prayer, believing, you will receive.

JOB 28:12.JAMES 1:5-6.PROV 3:5-6.1 TIM 1:17.PROV 3:7.JER 1:6-8.JOHN 16:23-24.MATT 21:22

EVENING

I would not live forever.

And I said, "Oh, that I had wings like a dove! For then I would fly away and be at rest. . . . I would hasten my escape from the windy storm and tempest."

In this we groan, earnestly desiring to be clothed with our habitation which is from heaven. . . . For we who are in this tent groan, being burdened, not because we want to be unclothed, but further clothed, that mortality may be swallowed up by life. ◊ Having a desire to depart and be with Christ, which is far better.

Let us run with endurance the race that is set before us, looking unto Jesus, the author and finisher of our faith, who for the joy that was set before Him endured the cross, despising the shame, and has sat down at the right hand of the throne of God. For consider Him who endured such hostility from sinners against Himself, lest you become weary and discouraged in your souls.

Let not your heart be troubled, neither let it be afraid.

JOB 7:16.PS 55:6,8.2 COR 5:2,4.PHIL 1:23.HEB 12:1-3.JOHN 14:27

DECEMBER 5

**It is good for me that I have been afflicted, that I may
learn Your statutes.**

Though He was a Son, yet He learned obedience by the things which
He suffered. ◊ We suffer with Him, that we may also be glorified
together. For I consider that the sufferings of this present time are not
worthy to be compared with the glory which shall be revealed in us.

He knows the way that I take; when He has tested me, I shall come
forth as gold. My foot has held fast to His steps; I have kept His way and
not turned aside.

You shall remember that the Lord your God led you all the way these
forty years in the wilderness, to humble you and test you, to know what
was in your heart, whether you would keep His commandments or not.
. . . So you should know in your heart that as a man chastens his son, so
the Lord your God chastens you. Therefore you shall keep the
commandments of the Lord your God, to walk in His ways and to fear
Him.

PS 119:71.HEB 5:8.ROM 8:17-18.JOB 23:10-11.DEUT 8:2,5-6

By strength no man shall prevail.

Then David said to the Philistine, "You come to me with a sword, with
a spear, and with a javelin. But I come to you in the name of the Lord of
hosts, the God of the armies of Israel, whom you have defied." . . . Then
David put his hand in his bag and took out a stone; and he slung it. . . . So
David prevailed over the Philistine with a sling and a stone.

No king is saved by the multitude of an army; a mighty man is not
delivered by great strength. . . . Behold, the eye of the Lord is on those
who fear Him, on those who hope in His mercy. ◊ Both riches and honor
come from You, and You reign over all. In Your hand is power and might;
in Your hand it is to make great and to give strength to all.

I will rather boast in my infirmities, that the power of Christ may rest
upon me. Therefore I take pleasure in infirmities, in reproaches, in
needs, in persecutions, in distresses, for Christ's sake. For when I am
weak, then I am strong.

1 SAM 2:9.1 SAM 17:45,49-50.PS 33:16,18.1 CHR 29:12.2 COR 12:9-10

MORNING

It is God who works in you.

Not that we are sufficient of ourselves to think of anything as being from ourselves, but our sufficiency is from God. ◊ A man can receive nothing unless it has been given to him from heaven. ◊ No one can come to Me unless the Father who sent Me draws him; and I will raise him up at the last day. ◊ I will give them one heart and one way, that they may fear Me forever.

Do not be deceived, my beloved brethren. Every good gift and every perfect gift is from above, and comes down from the Father of lights, with whom there is no variation or shadow of turning. Of His own will He brought us forth by the word of truth, that we might be a kind of firstfruits of His creatures.

For we are His workmanship, created in Christ Jesus for good works, which God prepared beforehand that we should walk in them.

Lord, You will establish peace for us, for You have also done all our works in us.

PHIL 2:13.2 COR 3:5.JOHN 3:27.JOHN 6:44.JER 32:39.JAMES 1:16-18.EPH 2:10.IS 26:12

EVENING

The spirit indeed is willing, but the flesh is weak.

In the way of Your judgments, O Lord, we have waited for You; the desire of our soul is for Your name and for the remembrance of You. With my soul I have desired You in the night, yes, by my spirit within me I will seek You early.

I know that in me (that is, in my flesh) nothing good dwells; for to will is present with me, but how to perform what is good I do not find. . . . For I delight in the law of God according to the inward man. But I see another law in my members, warring against the law of my mind, and bringing me into captivity to the law of sin which is in my members. ◊ The flesh lusts against the Spirit, and the Spirit against the flesh; and these are contrary to one another, so that you do not do the things that you wish.

I can do all things through Christ who strengthens me. ◊ Our sufficiency is from God. ◊ My grace is sufficient for you.

MATT 26:41.IS 26:8-9.ROM 7:18,22-23.GAL 5:17.PHIL 4:13.2 COR 3:5.
2 COR 12:9

DECEMBER 7

He made Him who knew no sin to be sin for us, that we might become the righteousness of God in Him.

The Lord has laid on Him the iniquity of us all. ◊ [He] Himself bore our sins in His own body on the tree, that we, having died to sins, might live for righteousness by whose stripes you were healed. ◊ As by one man's disobedience many were made sinners, so also by one Man's obedience many will be made righteous.

But when the kindness and the love of God our Savior toward man appeared, not by works of righteousness which we have done, but according to His mercy He saved us, through the washing of regeneration and renewing of the Holy Spirit, whom He poured out on us abundantly through Jesus Christ our Savior, that having been justified by His grace we should become heirs according to the hope of eternal life. ◊ There is therefore now no condemnation to those who are in Christ Jesus, who do not walk according to the flesh, but according to the Spirit. THE LORD OUR RIGHTEOUSNESS.

2 COR 5:21. IS 53:6. 1 PET 2:24. ROM 5:19. TITUS 3:4-7. ROM 8:1. JER 23:6

I will be like the dew to Israel.

The meekness and gentleness of Christ.

A bruised reed He will not break, and smoking flax He will not quench.

"The Spirit of the Lord is upon Me, because He has anointed Me to preach the gospel to the poor. He has sent Me to heal the brokenhearted, to preach deliverance to the captives and recovery of sight to the blind, to set at liberty those who are oppressed, to preach the acceptable year of the Lord." . . . And He began to say to them, "Today this Scripture is fulfilled in your hearing." So all bore witness to Him, and marveled at the gracious words which proceeded out of His mouth.

And the Lord turned and looked at Peter. And Peter remembered the word of the Lord, how He had said to him, "Before the rooster crows, you will deny Me three times." Then Peter went out and wept bitterly.

He will feed His flock like a shepherd; He will gather the lambs with His arm, and carry them in His bosom, and gently lead those who are with young.

HOS 14:5. 2 COR 10:1. IS 42:3. LUKE 4:18-19,21-22. LUKE 22:61-62. IS 40:11

MORNING

Through love serve one another.

Brethren, if a man is overtaken in any trespass, you who are spiritual restore such a one in a spirit of gentleness, considering yourself lest you also be tempted. Bear one another's burdens, and so fulfill the law of Christ.

Brethren, if anyone among you wanders from the truth, and someone turns him back, let him know that he who turns a sinner from the error of his way will save a soul from death and cover a multitude of sins. ◊ Since you have purified your souls in obeying the truth through the Spirit in sincere love of the brethren, love one another fervently with a pure heart. ◊ Owe no one anything except to love one another, for he who loves another has fulfilled the law. ◊ Be kindly affectionate to one another with brotherly love, in honor giving preference to one another. ◊ Yes, all of you be submissive to one another, and be clothed with humility, for "God resists the proud, but gives grace to the humble."

We then who are strong ought to bear with the scruples of the weak, and not to please ourselves.

GAL 5:13.GAL 6:1-2.JAMES 5:19-20.1 PET 1:22.ROM 13:8.ROM 12:10.
1 PET 5:5.ROM 15:1

EVENING

The dust will return to the earth as it was.

The body is sown in corruption. . . . It is sown in dishonor. . . . It is sown in weakness. . . . It is sown a natural body. ◊ The first man was of the earth, made of dust.

Dust you are, and to dust you shall return. ◊ One dies in his full strength, being wholly at ease and secure. . . . Another man dies in the bitterness of his soul, never having eaten with pleasure. They lie down alike in the dust, and worms cover them.

My flesh . . . will rest in hope. ◊ After my skin is destroyed, this I know, that in my flesh I shall see God. ◊ The Lord Jesus Christ. . . . will transform our lowly body that it may be conformed to His glorious body, according to the working by which He is able even to subdue all things to Himself.

Lord, make me to know my end, and what is the measure of my days, that I may know how frail I am. ◊ So teach us to number our days, that we may gain a heart of wisdom.

ECCL 12:7.1 COR 15:42-44.1 COR 15:47.GEN 3:19.JOB 21:23,25-26.PS
16:9.JOB 19:26.PHIL 3:20-21.PS 39:4.PS 90:12

DECEMBER 9

MORNING

To do righteousness and justice is more acceptable to the Lord than sacrifice.

He has shown you, O man, what is good; and what does the Lord require of you but to do justly, to love mercy, and to walk humbly with your God? ◇ Has the Lord as great delight in burnt offerings and sacrifices, as in obeying the voice of the Lord? Behold, to obey is better than sacrifice, and to heed than the fat of rams. ◇ To love Him with all the heart, with all the understanding, with all the soul, and with all the strength, and to love one's neighbor as oneself, is more than all the whole burnt offerings and sacrifices.

So you, by the help of your God, return; observe mercy and justice, and wait on your God continually. ◇ Mary . . . sat at Jesus' feet and heard His word. . . . One thing is needed, and Mary has chosen that good part, which will not be taken away from her.

It is God who works in you both to will and to do for His good pleasure.

PROV 21:3.MIC 6:8.1 SAM 15:22.MARK 12:33.HOS 12:6.LUKE 10:39, 42.PHIL 2:13

EVENING

The spirit will return to God who gave it.

The Lord God formed man of the dust of the ground, and breathed into his nostrils the breath of life; and man became a living being. ◇ There is a spirit in man, and the breath of the Almighty gives him understanding. ◇ The first man Adam became a living being. ◇ The spirit of the sons of men . . . goes upward.

While we are at home in the body we are absent from the Lord. . . . We are confident, yes, well pleased rather to be absent from the body and to be present with the Lord. ◇ With Christ, which is far better. ◇ I do not want you to be ignorant, brethren, concerning those who have fallen asleep, lest you sorrow as others who have no hope. For if we believe that Jesus died and rose again, even so God will bring with Him those who sleep in Jesus.

I go to prepare a place for you. And if I go and prepare a place for you, I will come again and receive you to Myself; that where I am, there you may be also.

ECCL 12:7.GEN 2:7.JOB 32:8.1 COR 15:45.ECCL 3:21.2 COR 5:6,8.PHIL 1:23.1 THESS 4:13-14.JOHN 14:2-3

MORNING

No one is able to snatch them out of My Father's hand.

I know whom I have believed and am persuaded that He is able to keep what I have committed to Him until that Day. ◊ The Lord will deliver me from every evil work and preserve me for His heavenly kingdom. ◊ We are more than conquerors through Him who loved us. For I am persuaded that neither death nor life, nor angels nor principalities nor powers, nor things present nor things to come, nor height nor depth, nor any other created thing, shall be able to separate us from the love of God which is in Christ Jesus our Lord. ◊ Your life is hidden with Christ in God.

Has God not chosen the poor of this world to be rich in faith and heirs of the kingdom which He promised to those who love Him?

Our Lord Jesus Christ Himself, and our God and Father, who has loved us and given us everlasting consolation and good hope by grace, comfort your hearts and establish you in every good word and work.

JOHN 10:29. 2 TIM 1:12. 2 TIM 4:18. ROM 8:37-39. COL 3:3. JAMES 2:5. 2 THESS 2:16-17

EVENING

The perfect law of liberty.

You shall know the truth, and the truth shall make you free. . . . Most assuredly, I say to you, whoever commits sin is a slave of sin. . . . Therefore if the Son makes you free, you shall be free indeed.

Stand fast therefore in the liberty by which Christ has made us free, and do not be entangled again with a yoke of bondage. . . . For you, brethren, have been called to liberty; only do not use liberty as an opportunity for the flesh, but through love serve one another. For all the law is fulfilled in one word, even in this: "You shall love your neighbor as yourself." ◊ Having been set free from sin, you became slaves of righteousness. ◊ For the woman who has a husband is bound by the law to her husband as long as he lives. But if the husband dies, she is released from the law of her husband.

The law of the Spirit of life in Christ Jesus has made me free from the law of sin and death. ◊ I will walk at liberty, for I seek Your precepts.

JAMES 1:25. JOHN 8:32,34,36. GAL 5:1,13-14. ROM 6:18. ROM 7:2. ROM 8:2. PS 119:45

DECEMBER 11

MORNING

Do not let your good be spoken of as evil.

Abstain from every form of evil. ◊ [Provide] honorable things, not only in the sight of the Lord, but also in the sight of men. ◊ For this is the will of God, that by doing good you may put to silence the ignorance of foolish men.

But let none of you suffer as a murderer, a thief, an evildoer, or as a busybody in other people's matters. Yet if anyone suffers as a Christian, let him not be ashamed, but let him glorify God in this matter.

For you, brethren, have been called to liberty; only do not use liberty as an opportunity for the flesh, but through love serve one another. ◊ Beware lest somehow this liberty of yours become a stumbling block to those who are weak. ◊ Whoever causes one of these little ones who believe in Me to sin, it would be better for him if a millstone were hung around his neck, and he were drowned in the depth of the sea. ◊ Inasmuch as you did it to one of the least of these My brethren, you did it to Me.

ROM 14:16.1 THESS 5:22.2 COR 8:21.1 PET 2:15.1 PET 4:15-16.GAL
5:13.1 COR 8:9.MATT 18:6.MATT 25:40

EVENING

**Awake, you who sleep, arise from the dead, and
Christ will give you light.**

It is high time to awake out of sleep; for now our salvation is nearer than when we first believed. ◊ Therefore let us not sleep, as others do, but let us watch and be sober. For those who sleep, sleep at night, and those who get drunk are drunk at night. But let us who are of the day be sober, putting on the breastplate of faith and love, and as a helmet the hope of salvation.

Arise, shine; for your light has come! And the glory of the Lord is risen upon you. For behold, the darkness shall cover the earth, and deep darkness the people; but the Lord will arise over you, and His glory will be seen upon you.

Therefore gird up the loins of your mind, be sober, and rest your hope fully upon the grace that is to be brought to you at the revelation of Jesus Christ. ◊ Let your waist be girded and your lamps burning; and you yourselves be like men who wait for their master.

EPH 5:14.ROM 13:11.1 THESS 5:6-8.IS 60:1-2.1 PET 1:13.LUKE 12:35-36

MORNING

The Lord is in your midst.

Fear not, for I am with you; be not dismayed, for I am your God. I will strengthen you, yes, I will help you, I will uphold you with My righteous right hand. ◊ Strengthen the weak hands, and make firm the feeble knees. Say to those who are fearful-hearted, "Be strong, do not fear! Behold, your God will come with vengeance, with the recompense of God; He will come and save you." ◊ The Lord your God in your midst, the Mighty One, will save; He will rejoice over you with gladness, He will quiet you in His love, He will rejoice over you with singing. ◊ Wait on the Lord; be of good courage, and He shall strengthen your heart.

I heard a loud voice from heaven saying, "Behold, the tabernacle of God is with men, and He will dwell with them, and they shall be His people, and God Himself will be with them and be their God." And God will wipe away every tear from their eyes; there shall be no more death, nor sorrow, nor crying; and there shall be no more pain.

ZEPH 3:15.IS 41:10.IS 35:3-4.ZEPH 3:17.PS 27:14.REV 21:3-4

EVENING

Why do you cry to Me? Tell the children of Israel to go forward.

Be of good courage, and let us be strong for our people and for the cities of our God. And may the Lord do what is good in His sight. ◊ We made our prayer to our God, and . . . set a watch against them day and night.

Not everyone who says to Me, "Lord, Lord," shall enter the kingdom of heaven, but he who does the will of My Father in heaven. ◊ If anyone wants to do His will, he shall know concerning the doctrine, whether it is from God. ◊ Let us know, let us pursue the knowledge of the Lord.

Watch and pray, lest you enter into temptation. ◊ Watch, stand fast in the faith, be brave, be strong. ◊ Not lagging in diligence, fervent in spirit, serving the Lord.

Strengthen the weak hands, and make firm the feeble knees. Say to those who are fearful-hearted, "Be strong, do not fear!"

EX 14:15.1 CHR 19:13.NEH 4:9.MATT 7:21.JOHN 7:17.HOS 6:3.MATT 26:41.1 COR 16:13.ROM 12:11.IS 35:3-4

DECEMBER 13

MORNING

Be strong in the grace that is in Christ Jesus.

[Be] strengthened with all might, according to His glorious power. ◊ As you have therefore received Christ Jesus the Lord, so walk in Him, rooted and built up in Him and established in the faith, as you have been taught, abounding in it with thanksgiving.

They may be called trees of righteousness, the planting of the Lord, that He may be glorified. ◊ You are . . . built on the foundation of the apostles and prophets, Jesus Christ Himself being the chief cornerstone, in whom the whole building, being joined together, grows into a holy temple in the Lord, in whom you also are being built together for a habitation of God in the Spirit.

I commend you to God and to the word of His grace, which is able to build you up and give you an inheritance among all those who are sanctified. ◊ [Be] filled with the fruits of righteousness which are by Jesus Christ, to the glory and praise of God.

Fight the good fight of faith. ◊ Not in any way terrified by your adversaries.

2 TIM 2:1.COL 1:11.COL 2:6-7.IS 61:3.EPH 2:19-22.ACTS 20:32.PHIL
1:11.1 TIM 6:12.PHIL 1:28

EVENING

You render to each one according to his work.

For no other foundation can anyone lay than that which is laid, which is Jesus Christ. . . . If anyone's work which he has built on it endures, he will receive a reward. If anyone's work is burned, he will suffer loss; but he himself will be saved, yet so as through fire. ◊ We must all appear before the judgment seat of Christ, that each one may receive the things done in the body, according to what he has done, whether good or bad.

When you do a charitable deed, do not let your left hand know what your right hand is doing, that your charitable deed may be in secret; and your Father who sees in secret will Himself reward you openly. ◊ After a long time the lord of those servants came and settled accounts with them.

Not that we are sufficient of ourselves to think of anything as being from ourselves, but our sufficiency is from God. ◊ Lord, You will establish peace for us, for You have also done all our works in us.

PS 62:12.1 COR 3:11,14-15.2 COR 5:10.MATT 6:3-4.MATT 25:19.2 COR
3:5.IS 26:12

MORNING

Make His praise glorious.

This people I have formed for Myself; they shall declare My praise. ◊ I will cleanse them from all their iniquity by which they have sinned against Me, and I will pardon all their iniquities by which they have sinned and by which they have transgressed against Me. Then it shall be to Me a name of joy, a praise, and an honor before all nations of the earth. ◊ Therefore by Him let us continually offer the sacrifice of praise to God, that is, the fruit of our lips, giving thanks to His name.

I will praise You, O Lord my God, with all my heart, and I will glorify Your name forevermore. For great is Your mercy toward me, and You have delivered my soul from the depths of Sheol. ◊ Who is like You, O Lord, . . . glorious in holiness, fearful in praises, doing wonders? ◊ I will praise the name of God with a song, and will magnify Him with thanksgiving. ◊ They sing the song of Moses, the servant of God, and the song of the Lamb, saying: "Great and marvelous are Your works, Lord God Almighty!"

PS 66:2. IS 43:21. JER 33:8-9. HEB 13:15. PS 86:12-13. EX 15:11. PS 69:30. REV 15:3

EVENING

By nature children of wrath, just as the others.

We ourselves were also once foolish, disobedient, deceived, serving various lusts and pleasures, living in malice and envy, hateful and hating one another. ◊ Do not marvel that I said to you, "You must be born again."

Job answered the Lord and said: . . . "Behold, I am vile; what shall I answer You? I lay my hand over my mouth." ◊ The Lord said to Satan, "Have you considered My servant Job, that there is none like him on the earth, a blameless and upright man, one who fears God and shuns evil?"

Behold, I was brought forth in iniquity, and in sin my mother conceived me. ◊ David . . . to whom also He gave testimony and said, "I have found David the son of Jesse, a man after My own heart, who will do all My will."

I was formerly a blasphemer, a persecutor, and an insolent man; but I obtained mercy.

That which is born of the flesh is flesh, and that which is born of the Spirit is spirit.

EPH 2:3. TITUS 3:3. JOHN 3:7. JOB 40:3-4. JOB 1:8. PS 51:5. ACTS 13:22. 1 TIM 1:13. JOHN 3:6

DECEMBER 15

MORNING

Bear one another's burdens, and so fulfill the law of Christ.

Let each of you look out not only for his own interests, but also for the interests of others. Let this mind be in you which was also in Christ Jesus, who . . . made Himself of no reputation, taking the form of a servant. ◊ Even the Son of Man did not come to be served, but to serve, and to give His life a ransom for many. ◊ He died for all, that those who live should live no longer for themselves, but for Him who died for them and rose again.

When Jesus saw her weeping, and the Jews who came with her weeping, He groaned in the spirit and was troubled. . . . Jesus wept. ◊ Rejoice with those who rejoice, and weep with those who weep.

All of you be of one mind, having compassion for one another; love as brothers, be tenderhearted, be courteous; not returning evil for evil or reviling for reviling, but on the contrary blessing, knowing that you were called to this, that you may inherit a blessing.

GAL 6:2.PHIL 2:4-7.MARK 10:45.2 COR 5:15.JOHN 11:33,35.ROM 12:15.1 PET 3:8-9

EVENING

Son, go, work today in my vineyard.

Therefore you are no longer a slave but a son, and if a son, then an heir of God through Christ.

You also, reckon yourselves to be dead indeed to sin, but alive to God in Christ Jesus our Lord. Therefore do not let sin reign in your mortal body, that you should obey it in its lusts. And do not present your members as instruments of unrighteousness to sin, but present yourselves to God as being alive from the dead, and your members as instruments of righteousness to God. ◊ As obedient children, not conforming yourselves to the former lusts, as in your ignorance; but as He who called you is holy, you also be holy in all your conduct, because it is written, "Be holy, for I am holy." ◊ If anyone cleanses himself from the latter, he will be . . . sanctified and useful for the Master, prepared for every good work.

Therefore, my beloved brethren, be steadfast, immovable, always abounding in the work of the Lord, knowing that your labor is not in vain in the Lord.

MATT 21:28.GAL 4:7.ROM 6:11-13.1 PET 1:14-16.2 TIM 2:21.1 COR 15:58

MORNING

Having loved His own who were in the world, He loved them to the end.

I pray for them. I do not pray for the world but for those whom You have given Me, for they are Yours. And all Mine are Yours, and Yours are Mine, and I am glorified in them. . . . I do not pray that You should take them out of the world, but that You should keep them from the evil one. They are not of the world, just as I am not of the world.

As the Father loved Me, I also have loved you; abide in My love. ◊ Greater love has no one than this, than to lay down one's life for his friends. You are My friends if you do whatever I command you. ◊ A new commandment I give to you, that you love one another; as I have loved you, that you also love one another.

He who has begun a good work in you will complete it until the day of Jesus Christ. ◊ Christ . . . loved the church and gave Himself for it, that He might sanctify and cleanse it with the washing of water by the word.

JOHN 13:1.JOHN 17:9-10,15-16.JOHN 15:9.JOHN 15:13-14.JOHN 13:34.PHIL 1:6.EPH 5:25-26

EVENING

The deep things of God.

No longer do I call you servants, for a servant does not know what his master is doing; but I have called you friends, for all things that I heard from My Father I have made known to you. ◊ It has been given to you to know the mysteries of the kingdom of heaven.

We have received, not the spirit of the world, but the Spirit who is from God, that we might know the things that have been freely given to us by God.

For this reason I bow my knees to the Father of our Lord Jesus Christ, from whom the whole family in heaven and earth is named, that He would grant you, according to the riches of His glory, to be strengthened with might through His Spirit in the inner man, . . . that you, being rooted and grounded in love, may be able to comprehend with all the saints what is the width and length and depth and height—to know the love of Christ which passes knowledge; that you may be filled with all the fullness of God.

1 COR 2:10.JOHN 15:15.MATT 13:11.1 COR 2:12.EPH 3:14-19

DECEMBER 17

MORNING

Revive us, and we will call upon Your name.

It is the Spirit who gives life. ◊ The Spirit also helps in our weaknesses. For we do not know what we should pray for as we ought, but the Spirit Himself makes intercession for us with groanings which cannot be uttered. Now He who searches the hearts knows what the mind of the Spirit is, because He makes intercession for the saints according to the will of God. ◊ [Pray] always with all prayer and supplication in the Spirit, being watchful to this end with all perseverance.

I will never forget Your precepts, for by them You have given me life. ◊ The words that I speak to you are spirit, and they are life. ◊ The letter kills, but the Spirit gives life. ◊ If you abide in Me, and My words abide in you, you will ask what you desire, and it shall be done for you. ◊ This is the confidence that we have in Him, that if we ask anything according to His will, He hears us.

No one can say that Jesus is Lord except by the Holy Spirit.

PS 80:18.JOHN 6:63.ROM 8:26-27.EPH 6:18.PS 119:93.JOHN 6:63.2 COR 3:6.JOHN 15:7.1 JOHN 5:14.1 COR 12:3

EVENING

Have no fellowship with the unfruitful works of darkness, but rather expose them.

Do not be deceived: Evil company corrupts good habits. ◊ Do you not know that a little leaven leavens the whole lump? Therefore, purge out the old leaven. . . . I wrote to you in my epistle not to keep company with sexually immoral people. Yet I certainly did not mean with the sexually immoral people of this world, or with the covetous, or extortioners, or idolaters, since then you would need to go out of the world. But now I have written to you not to keep company with anyone named a brother, who is a fornicator, or covetous, or an idolater, or a reviler, or a drunkard, or an extortioner not even to eat with such a person. ◊ Become blameless and harmless, children of God without fault in the midst of a crooked and perverse generation, among whom you shine as lights in the world.

In a great house there are not only vessels of gold and silver, but also of wood and clay, some for honor and some for dishonor.

EPH 5:11.1 COR 15:33.1 COR 5:6-7,9-11.PHIL 2:15.2 TIM 2:20

MORNING

**Let us therefore come boldly to the throne of grace,
that we may obtain mercy and find grace to help in
time of need.**

Be anxious for nothing, but in everything by prayer and supplication, with thanksgiving, let your requests be made known to God; and the peace of God, which surpasses all understanding, will guard your hearts and minds through Christ Jesus. ◊ You did not receive the spirit of bondage again to fear, but you received the Spirit of adoption by whom we cry out, "Abba, Father."

I did not say to the seed of Jacob, "Seek Me in vain." ◊ Therefore . . . having boldness to enter the Holiest by the blood of Jesus, by a new and living way which He consecrated for us, through the veil, that is, His flesh, and having a High Priest over the house of God, let us draw near with a true heart in full assurance of faith, having our hearts sprinkled from an evil conscience and our bodies washed with pure water. ◊ We may boldly say: "The Lord is my helper; I will not fear. What can man do to me?"

HEB 4:16.PHIL 4:6-7.ROM 8:15.IS 45:19.HEB 10:19-22.HEB 13:6

EVENING

**You shall know the truth, and the truth shall make
you free.**

Where the Spirit of the Lord is, there is liberty. ◊ The law of the Spirit of life in Christ Jesus has made me free from the law of sin and death. ◊ If the Son makes you free, you shall be free indeed.

Brethren, we are not children of the bondwoman but of the free. ◊ Knowing that a man is not justified by the works of the law but by faith in Jesus Christ, even we have believed in Christ Jesus, that we might be justified by faith in Christ and not by the works of the law; for by the works of the law no flesh shall be justified.

He who looks into the perfect law of liberty and continues in it, and is not a forgetful hearer but a doer of the work, this one will be blessed in what he does. ◊ Stand fast therefore in the liberty by which Christ has made us free, and do not be entangled again with a yoke of bondage.

JOHN 8:32.2 COR 3:17.ROM 8:2.JOHN 8:36.GAL 4:31.GAL 2:16.JAMES
1:25.GAL 5:1

DECEMBER 19

MORNING

Unto the upright there arises light in the darkness.

Who among you fears the Lord? Who obeys the voice of His Servant? Who walks in darkness and has no light? Let him trust in the name of the Lord and rely upon his God. ◊ Though he fall, he shall not be utterly cast down; for the Lord upholds him with His hand. ◊ The commandment is a lamp, and the law is light.

Do not rejoice over me, my enemy; when I fall, I will arise; when I sit in darkness, the Lord will be a light to me. I will bear the indignation of the Lord, because I have sinned against Him, until He pleads my case and executes justice for me; He will bring me forth to the light, and I will see His righteousness.

The lamp of the body is the eye. If therefore your eye is good, your whole body will be full of light. But if your eye is bad, your whole body will be full of darkness. If therefore the light that is in you is darkness, how great is that darkness!

PS 112:4.IS 50:10.PS 37:24.PROV 6:23.MIC 7:8-9.MATT 6:22-23

EVENING

He will feed His flock like a shepherd; He will gather the lambs with His arm, and carry them in His bosom, and gently lead those who are with young.

I have compassion on the multitude, because they have now continued with Me three days and have nothing to eat. I do not want to send them away hungry, lest they faint on the way. ◊ We do not have a High Priest who cannot sympathize with our weaknesses.

Then they brought young children to Him. . . . And He took them up in His arms, put His hands on them, and blessed them.

I have gone astray like a lost sheep; seek Your servant. ◊ The Son of Man has come to seek and to save that which was lost. ◊ You were like sheep going astray, but have now returned to the Shepherd and Overseer of your souls.

Do not fear, little flock, for it is your Father's good pleasure to give you the kingdom. ◊ "I will feed My flock, and I will make them lie down," says the Lord God.

IS 40:11.MATT 15:32.HEB 4:15.MARK 10:13,16.PS 119:176.LUKE 19:10.
1 PET 2:25.LUKE 12:32.EZEK 34:15

MORNING

He chose us in Him before the foundation
of the world.

That we should be holy and without blame before Him in love.

God from the beginning chose you for salvation through sanctification by the Spirit and belief in the truth, to which He called you . . . for the obtaining of the glory of our Lord Jesus Christ. ◊ Whom He foreknew, He also predestined to be conformed to the image of His Son, that He might be the firstborn among many brethren. Moreover whom He predestined, these He also called; whom He called, these He also justified; and whom He justified, these He also glorified. ◊ Elect according to the foreknowledge of God the Father, in sanctification of the Spirit, for obedience and sprinkling of the blood of Jesus Christ.

I will give you a new heart and put a new spirit within you; I will take the heart of stone out of your flesh and give you a heart of flesh. ◊ God did not call us to uncleanness, but in holiness.

EPH 1:4.EPH 1:4.2 THESS 2:13-14.ROM 8:29-30.1 PET 1:2.EZEK 36:26.
1 THESS 4:7

EVENING

If the Lord would make windows in heaven, could
this thing be?

Have faith in God. ◊ Without faith it is impossible to please Him. ◊ With God all things are possible.

Is My hand shortened at all that it cannot redeem? Or have I no power to deliver?

"For My thoughts are not your thoughts, nor are your ways My ways," says the Lord. "For as the heavens are higher than the earth, so are My ways higher than your ways, and My thoughts than your thoughts." ◊ "Prove Me now in this," says the Lord of hosts, "if I will not open for you the windows of heaven and pour out for you such blessing that there will not be room enough to receive it."

Behold, the Lord's hand is not shortened, that it cannot save; nor His ear heavy, that it cannot hear. ◊ Lord, it is nothing for You to help, whether with many or with those who have no power.

We should not trust in ourselves but in God who raises the dead.

2 KIN 7:2.MARK 11:22.HEB 11:6.MATT 19:26.IS 50:2.IS 55:8-9.MAL
3:10.IS 59:1.2 CHR 14:11.2 COR 1:9

DECEMBER 21

MORNING

The days of your mourning shall be ended.

In the world you will have tribulation. ◊ The whole creation groans and labors with birth pangs together until now. And not only they, but we also who have the firstfruits of the Spirit, even we ourselves groan within ourselves, eagerly waiting for the adoption, the redemption of our body. ◊ We who are in this tent groan, being burdened, not because we want to be unclothed, but further clothed, that mortality may be swallowed up by life.

These are the ones who come out of the great tribulation, and washed their robes and made them white in the blood of the Lamb. Therefore they are before the throne of God, and serve Him day and night in His temple. And He who sits on the throne will dwell among them. They shall neither hunger anymore nor thirst anymore; the sun shall not strike them, nor any heat; for the Lamb who is in the midst of the throne will shepherd them and lead them to living fountains of waters. And God will wipe away every tear from their eyes.

IS 60:20.JOHN 16:33.ROM 8:22-23.2 COR 5:4.REV 7:14-17

EVENING

Teacher, do You not care that we are perishing?

The Lord is good to all, and His tender mercies are over all His works.

Every moving thing that lives shall be food for you. I have given you all things, even as the green herbs. ◊ While the earth remains, seedtime and harvest, and cold and heat, and winter and summer, and day and night shall not cease.

The Lord is good, a stronghold in the day of trouble; and He knows those who trust in Him. ◊ God heard the voice of the lad. Then the angel of God called to Hagar out of heaven, and said to her, "What ails you, Hagar? Fear not, for God has heard the voice of the lad where he is." . . . And God opened her eyes, and she saw a well of water. Then she went and filled the skin with water, and gave the lad a drink.

Do not worry, saying,"What shall we eat?" or "What shall we drink?" . . . For your heavenly Father knows that you need all these things. ◊ Trust . . . in the living God, who gives us richly all things to enjoy.

MARK 4:38.PS 145:9.GEN 9:3.GEN 8:22.NAH 1:7.GEN 21:17,19.MATT 6:31-32.1 TIM 6:17

MORNING

Your work of faith.

This is the work of God, that you believe in Him whom He sent.

Faith . . . if it does not have works, is dead. ◊ Faith working through love. ◊ He who sows to his flesh will of the flesh reap corruption, but he who sows to the Spirit will of the Spirit reap everlasting life. ◊ We are His workmanship, created in Christ Jesus for good works, which God prepared beforehand that we should walk in them. ◊ [He] gave Himself for us, that He might redeem us from every lawless deed and purify for Himself His own special people, zealous for good works.

We are bound to thank God always for you, brethren, as it is fitting, because your faith grows exceedingly, and the love of every one of you all abounds toward each other. . . . Therefore we also pray always for you that our God would count you worthy of this calling, and fulfill all the good pleasure of His goodness and the work of faith with power. ◊ It is God who works in you both to will and to do for His good pleasure.

1 THESS 1:3.JOHN 6:29.JAMES 2:17.GAL 5:6.GAL 6:8.EPH 2:10.TITUS
2:14.2 THESS 1:3,11.PHIL 2:13

EVENING

Where is the promise of His coming?

Enoch, the seventh from Adam, prophesied about these men also, saying, "Behold, the Lord comes with ten thousands of His saints, to execute judgment on all." ◊ Behold, He is coming with clouds, and every eye will see Him, and they also who pierced Him. And all the tribes of the earth will mourn because of Him.

The Lord Himself will descend from heaven with a shout, with the voice of an archangel, and with the trumpet of God. And the dead in Christ will rise first. Then we who are alive and remain shall be caught up together with them in the clouds to meet the Lord in the air. And thus we shall always be with the Lord.

The grace of God that brings salvation has appeared to all men, teaching us that, denying ungodliness and worldly lusts, we should live soberly, righteously, and godly in the present age, looking for the blessed hope and glorious appearing of our great God and Savior Jesus Christ.

2 PET 3:4.JUDE 1:14-15.REV 1:7.1 THESS 4:16-17.TITUS 2:11-13

DECEMBER 23

MORNING

Let him take hold of My strength, that he may make peace with Me; and he shall make peace with Me.

I know the thoughts that I think toward you, says the Lord, thoughts of peace and not of evil. ◊ "There is no peace," says the Lord, "for the wicked."

In Christ Jesus you who once were far off have been made near by the blood of Christ. For He Himself is our peace.

It pleased the Father that in Him all the fullness should dwell, and by Him to reconcile all things to Himself, . . . having made peace through the blood of His cross. ◊ Christ Jesus, whom God set forth to be a propitiation by His blood, through faith, to demonstrate His righteousness . . . over the sins that were previously committed, . . . that He might be just and the justifier of the one who has faith in Jesus. ◊ If we confess our sins, He is faithful and just to forgive us our sins and to cleanse us from all unrighteousness.

Trust in the Lord forever, for in YAH, the Lord, is everlasting strength.

IS 27:5.JER 29:11.IS 48:22.EPH 2:13-14.COL 1:19-20.ROM 3:24-26.
1 JOHN 1:9.IS 26:4

EVENING

God has given us eternal life, and this life is in His Son.

As the Father has life in Himself, so He has granted the Son to have life in Himself. . . . As the Father raises the dead and gives life to them, even so the Son gives life to whom He will.

I am the resurrection and the life. He who believes in Me, though he may die, he shall live. And whoever lives and believes in Me shall never die. ◊ I am the good shepherd. The good shepherd gives His life for the sheep. . . . I lay down My life that I may take it again. No one takes it from Me, but I lay it down of Myself. I have power to lay it down, and I have power to take it again. This command I have received from My Father. ◊ No one comes to the Father except through Me. ◊ He who has the Son has life; he who does not have the Son of God does not have life. ◊ For you died, and your life is hidden with Christ in God. When Christ who is our life appears, then you also will appear with Him in glory.

1 JOHN 5:11.JOHN 5:26.JOHN 5:21.JOHN 11:25-26.JOHN 10:11,17-
18.JOHN 14:6.1 JOHN 5:12.COL 3:3-4

MORNING

If you live according to the flesh you will die; but if by the Spirit you put to death the deeds of the body, you will live.

Now the works of the flesh are evident, which are: adultery, fornication, . . . and the like; of which I tell you beforehand, just as I also told you in time past, that those who practice such things will not inherit the kingdom of God. But the fruit of the Spirit is love, joy, peace, longsuffering, kindness, goodness, faithfulness, gentleness, self-control. Against such there is no law. And those who are Christ's have crucified the flesh with its passions and desires. If we live in the Spirit, let us also walk in the Spirit.

The grace of God that brings salvation has appeared to all men, teaching us that, denying ungodliness and worldly lusts, we should live soberly, righteously, and godly in the present age, looking for the blessed hope and glorious appearing of our great God and Savior Jesus Christ, who gave Himself for us, that He might redeem us from every lawless deed.

ROM 8:13.GAL 5:19,21-25.TITUS 2:11-14

EVENING

Then the princes of the Philistines said, "What are these Hebrews doing here?"

If you are reproached for the name of Christ, blessed are you, for the Spirit of glory and of God rests upon you. On their part He is blasphemed, but on your part He is glorified. But let none of you suffer as a murderer, a thief, an evildoer, or as a busybody in other people's matters.

Do not let your good be spoken of as evil. ◊ [Have] your conduct honorable among the Gentiles.

Do not be unequally yoked together with unbelievers. For what fellowship has righteousness with lawlessness? And what communion has light with darkness? . . . You are the temple of the living God. . . . Therefore "Come out from among them and be separate," says the Lord. "Do not touch what is unclean."

You are a chosen generation, a royal priesthood, a holy nation, His own special people, that you may proclaim the praises of Him who called you out of darkness into His marvelous light.

1 SAM 29:3.1 PET 4:14-15.ROM 14:16.1 PET 2:12.2 COR 6:14,16-17.1 PET
2:9

DECEMBER 25

MORNING

The kindness and the love of God our Savior toward man appeared.

I have loved you with an everlasting love.

In this the love of God was manifested toward us, that God has sent His only begotten Son into the world, that we might live through Him. In this is love, not that we loved God, but that He loved us and sent His Son to be the propitiation for our sins.

When the fullness of the time had come, God sent forth His Son, born of a woman, born under the law, to redeem those who were under the law, that we might receive the adoption as sons. ◊ The Word became flesh and dwelt among us, and we beheld His glory, the glory as of the only begotten of the Father, full of grace and truth. ◊ Great is the mystery of godliness: God was manifested in the flesh.

As the children have partaken of flesh and blood, He Himself likewise shared in the same, that through death He might destroy him who had the power of death, that is, the devil.

TITUS 3:4.JER 31:3.1 JOHN 4:9-10.GAL 4:4-5.JOHN 1:14.1 TIM 3:16.HEB 2:14

EVENING

Thanks be to God for His indescribable gift!

Make a joyful shout to the Lord, all you lands! Serve the Lord with gladness; come before His presence with singing. . . . Enter into His gates with thanksgiving, and into His courts with praise. Be thankful to Him, and bless His name. ◊ For unto us a Child is born, unto us a Son is given; and the government will be upon His shoulder. And His name will be called Wonderful, Counselor, Mighty God, Everlasting Father, Prince of Peace.

He . . . did not spare His own Son, but delivered Him up for us all. ◊ Therefore still having one son, his beloved, he also sent him.

Oh, that men would give thanks to the Lord for His goodness, and for His wonderful works to the children of men! ◊ Bless the Lord, O my soul; and all that is within me, bless His holy name!

My soul magnifies the Lord, and my spirit has rejoiced in God my Savior.

2 COR 9:15.PS 100:1-2,4.IS 9:6.ROM 8:32.MARK 12:6.PS 107:21.PS 103:1.LUKE 1:46-47

MORNING

Be steadfast, immovable, always abounding in the work of the Lord.

Your labor is not in vain in the Lord. ◊ As you have . . . received Christ Jesus the Lord, so walk in Him, rooted and built up in Him and established in the faith, as you have been taught, abounding in it with thanksgiving. ◊ He who endures to the end shall be saved. ◊ The ones that fell on the good ground are those who, having heard the word with a noble and good heart, keep it and bear fruit with patience.

By faith you stand.

I must work the works of Him who sent Me while it is day; the night is coming when no one can work.

He who sows to his flesh will of the flesh reap corruption, but he who sows to the Spirit will of the Spirit reap everlasting life. And let us not grow weary while doing good, for in due season we shall reap if we do not lose heart. Therefore, as we have opportunity, let us do good to all, especially to those who are of the household of faith.

1 COR 15:58.1 COR 15:58.COL 2:6-7.MATT 24:13.LUKE 8:15.2 COR 1:24.JOHN 9:4.GAL 6:8-10

EVENING

He is also able to save to the uttermost those who come to God through Him.

I am the way, the truth, and the life. No one comes to the Father except through Me. ◊ Nor is there salvation in any other, for there is no other name under heaven given among men by which we must be saved.

My sheep hear My voice, and I know them, and they follow Me. And I give them eternal life, and they shall never perish; neither shall anyone snatch them out of My hand. ◊ He who has begun a good work in you will complete it until the day of Jesus Christ. ◊ Is anything too hard for the Lord?

Now to Him who is able to keep you from stumbling, and to present you faultless before the presence of His glory with exceeding joy, to God our Savior, who alone is wise, be glory and majesty, dominion and power, both now and forever. Amen.

HEB 7:25.JOHN 14:6.ACTS 4:12.JOHN 10:27-28.PHIL 1:6.GEN 18:14.JUDE 1:24-25

DECEMBER 27

We do not look at the things which are seen, but at the things which are not seen. For the things which are seen are temporary, but the things which are not seen are eternal.

Here we have no continuing city. ◊ You have a better and an enduring possession for yourselves in heaven. ◊ Do not fear, little flock, for it is your Father's good pleasure to give you the kingdom. ◊ Now for a little while, if need be, you have been grieved by various trials. ◊ There the wicked cease from troubling, and there the weary are at rest.

We who are in this tent groan, being burdened. ◊ God will wipe away every tear from their eyes; there shall be no more death, nor sorrow, nor crying; and there shall be no more pain, for the former things have passed away.

The sufferings of this present time are not worthy to be compared with the glory which shall be revealed in us. ◊ Our light affliction, which is but for a moment, is working for us a far more exceeding and eternal weight of glory.

2 COR 4:18. HEB 13:14. HEB 10:34. LUKE 12:32. 1 PET 1:6. JOB 3:17. 2 COR 5:4. REV 21:4. ROM 8:18. 2 COR 4:17

EVENING

He Himself is our peace.

God was in Christ reconciling the world to Himself, not imputing their trespasses to them. . . . For He made Him who knew no sin to be sin for us, that we might become the righteousness of God in Him. ◊ [He] made peace through the blood of His cross. And you, who once were alienated and enemies in your mind by wicked works, yet now He has reconciled in the body of His flesh through death, to present you holy, and blameless. ◊ And you . . . He has made alive . . . , having wiped out the handwriting of requirements that was against us, which was contrary to us. And He has taken it out of the way, having nailed it to the cross. ◊ He himself is our peace, . . . having abolished in His flesh the enmity, that is, the law of commandments contained in ordinances, so as to create in Himself one new man from the two, thus making peace.

Peace I leave with you, My peace I give to you; not as the world gives do I give to you. Let not your heart be troubled, neither let it be afraid.

EPH 2:14. 2 COR 5:19,21. COL 1:20-22. COL 2:13-14 EPH. 2:14-15. JOHN 14:27

MORNING

Your sins are forgiven you.

I will forgive their iniquity, and their sin I will remember no more. ◊ Who can forgive sins but God alone?

I, even I, am He who blots out your transgressions for My own sake; and I will not remember your sins. ◊ Blessed is he whose transgression is forgiven, whose sin is covered. Blessed is the man to whom the Lord does not impute iniquity. ◊ Who is a God like You, pardoning iniquity.

God in Christ . . . forgave you. ◊ The blood of Jesus Christ His Son cleanses us from all sin. If we say that we have no sin, we deceive ourselves, and the truth is not in us. If we confess our sins, He is faithful and just to forgive us our sins and to cleanse us from all unrighteousness.

As far as the east is from the west, so far has He removed our transgressions from us. ◊ Sin shall not have dominion over you, for you are not under law but under grace. . . . Having been set free from sin, you became slaves of righteousness.

MARK 2:5.JER 31:34.MARK 2:7.IS 43:25.PS 32:1-2.MIC 7:18.EPH 4:32.1
JOHN 1:7-9.PS 103:12.ROM 6:14,18

EVENING

We wish to see Jesus.

O Lord, we have waited for You; the desire of our soul is for Your name and for the remembrance of You.

The Lord is near to all who call upon Him, to all who call upon Him in truth.

For where two or three are gathered together in My name, I am there in the midst of them. ◊ I will not leave you orphans; I will come to you. ◊ Lo, I am with you always, even to the end of the age.

Let us run with endurance the race that is set before us, looking unto Jesus, the author and finisher of our faith.

Now we see in a mirror, dimly, but then face to face. ◊ Having a desire to depart and be with Christ, which is far better.

Beloved, now we are children of God; and it has not yet been revealed what we shall be, but we know that when He is revealed, we shall be like Him, for we shall see Him as He is. And everyone who has this hope in Him purifies himself, just as He is pure.

JOHN 12:21.IS 26:8.PS 145:18.MATT 18:20.JOHN 14:18.MATT
28:20.HEB 12:1-2.1 COR 13:12.PHIL 1:23.1 JOHN 3:2-3

DECEMBER 29

MORNING

Understand what the will of the Lord is.

This is the will of God, your sanctification. ◊ Now acquaint yourself with Him, and be at peace; thereby good will come to you. ◊ This is eternal life, that they may know You, the only true God, and Jesus Christ whom You have sent. ◊ We know that the Son of God has come and has given us an understanding, that we may know Him who is true; and we are in Him who is true, in His Son Jesus Christ. This is the true God and eternal life.

We . . . do not cease to pray for you, and to ask that you may be filled with the knowledge of His will in all wisdom and spiritual understanding. ◊ The God of our Lord Jesus Christ, the Father of glory, . . . give to you the spirit of wisdom and revelation in the knowledge of Him, the eyes of your understanding being enlightened; that you may know what is the hope of His calling, what are the riches of the glory of His inheritance in the saints, and what is the exceeding greatness of His power toward us who believe, according to the working of His mighty power.

EPH 5:17.1 THESS 4:3.JOB 22:21.JOHN 17:3.1 JOHN 5:20.COL 1:9.EPH 1:17-19

EVENING

Draw near to God and He will draw near to you.

Enoch walked with God. ◊ Can two walk together, unless they are agreed? ◊ It is good for me to draw near to God.

The Lord is with you while you are with Him. If you seek Him, He will be found by you; but if you forsake Him, He will forsake you. . . . When in their trouble [Israel] turned to the Lord God of Israel, and sought Him, He was found by them.

"For I know the thoughts that I think toward you," says the Lord, "thoughts of peace and not of evil, to give you a future and a hope. Then you will call upon Me and go and pray to Me, and I will listen to you. And you will seek Me and find Me, when you search for Me with all your heart."

Therefore, brethren, having boldness to enter the Holiest by the blood of Jesus, by a new and living way . . . and having a High Priest over the house of God, let us draw near with a true heart in full assurance of faith.

JAMES 4:8.GEN 5:24.AMOS 3:3.PS 73:28.2 CHR 15:2,4.JER 29:11-13.HEB 10:19-22

MORNING

Blameless in the day of our Lord Jesus Christ.

You, who once were alienated and enemies in your mind by wicked works, yet now He has reconciled in the body of His flesh through death, to present you holy, and blameless, and irreproachable in His sight—if indeed you continue in the faith, grounded and steadfast, and are not moved away from the hope of the gospel. ◊ That you may become blameless and harmless, children of God without fault in the midst of a crooked and perverse generation, among whom you shine as lights in the world.

Therefore, beloved, looking forward to these things, be diligent to be found by Him in peace, without spot and blameless. ◊ Be sincere and without offense till the day of Christ.

Now to Him who is able to keep you from stumbling, and to present you faultless before the presence of His glory with exceeding joy, to God our Savior, who alone is wise, be glory and majesty, dominion and power, both now and forever.

1 COR 1:8.COL 1:21-23.PHIL 2:15.2 PET 3:14.PHIL 1:10.JUDE 1:24-25

EVENING

He will guard the feet of His saints.

If we say that we have fellowship with Him, and walk in darkness, we lie and do not practice the truth. But if we walk in the light as He is in the light, we have fellowship with one another, and the blood of Jesus Christ His Son cleanses us from all sin. ◊ He who is bathed needs only to wash his feet, but is completely clean.

I have taught you in the way of wisdom; I have led you in right paths. When you walk, your steps will not be hindered, and when you run, you will not stumble. . . . Do not enter the path of the wicked, and do not walk in the way of evil. Avoid it, do not travel on it; turn away from it and pass on. . . . Let your eyes look straight ahead, and your eyelids look right before you. Ponder the path of your feet, and let all your ways be established. Do not turn to the right or the left; remove your foot from evil.

The Lord will deliver me from every evil work and preserve me for His heavenly kingdom. To Him be glory forever and ever. Amen!

1 SAM 2:9.1 JOHN 1:6-7.JOHN 13:10.PROV 4:11-12,14-15,25-27.2 TIM 4:18

DECEMBER 31

MORNING

The Lord your God carried you, as a man carries his son, in all the way that you went until you came to this place.

I bore you on eagles' wings and brought you to Myself. ◊ In His love and in His pity He redeemed them; and He bore them and carried them all the days of old. ◊ As an eagle stirs up its nest, hovers over its young, spreading out its wings, taking them up, carrying them on its wings, so the Lord alone led him.

Even to your old age, I am He, and even to gray hairs I will carry you! I have made, and I will bear; even I will carry, and will deliver you. ◊ This is God, our God forever and ever; He will be our guide even to death.

Cast your burden on the Lord, and He shall sustain you. ◊ Do not worry about your life, what you will eat or what you will drink; nor about your body, what you will put on. . . . For your heavenly Father knows that you need all these things.

Thus far the Lord has helped us.

DEUT 1:31.EX 19:4.IS 63:9.DEUT 32:11-12.IS 46:4.PS 48:14.PS 55:22.MATT 6:25,32.1 SAM 7:12

EVENING

There remains very much land yet to be possessed.

Not that I have already attained, or am already perfected; but I press on, that I may lay hold of that for which Christ Jesus has also laid hold of me.

Therefore you shall be perfect. ◊ Giving all diligence, add to your faith virtue, to virtue knowledge, to knowledge self-control, to self-control perseverance, to perseverance godliness, to godliness brotherly kindness, and to brotherly kindness love.

I pray, that your love may abound still more and more in knowledge and all discernment.

Eye has not seen, nor ear heard, nor have entered into the heart of man the things which God has prepared for those who love Him. But God has revealed them to us through His Spirit.

There remains . . . a rest for the people of God. ◊ Your eyes will see the King in His beauty; they will see the land that is very far off.

JOSH 13:1.PHIL 3:12.MATT 5:48.2 PET 1:5-7.PHIL 1:9.1 COR 2:9-10.HEB 4:9.IS 33:17

MORNING

**You crown the year with Your goodness,
and Your paths drip with abundance.**

The Lord is good to all, and His tender mercies are over all His works. ◊ He makes His sun rise on the evil and on the good, and sends rain on the just and on the unjust.

Oh, how great is Your goodness, which You have laid up for those who fear You, which You have prepared for those who trust in You in the presence of the sons of men! ◊ My people shall be satisfied with my goodness.

The Lord, the Lord God, merciful and gracious, long-suffering and abounding in goodness and truth. ◊ The goodness of God endures continually. ◊ Oh, give thanks to the Lord . . . Oh, give thanks to the God of gods . . . Oh, give thanks to the Lord of lords!

In everything give thanks; for this is the will of God in Christ Jesus for you. . . . He who calls you is faithful.

PS 65:11.PS 86:5.PS 145:9.MATT 5:45.PS 31:19.JER 31:14.EX 34:6.
PS 52:1.PS 136:1–3.1 THESS 5:18,24

EVENING

**Oh come, let us worship and bow down;
let us kneel before the Lord our Maker.**

Know that the Lord, He is God; it is He who has made us, and not we ourselves. ◊ And the Lord God formed man of the dust of the ground, and breathed into his nostrils the breath of life; and man became a living being. ◊ So God created man in His own image; in the image of God He created Him.

You are worthy, O Lord, to receive glory and honor and power; for You created all things, and by Your will they exist and were created.

Through one man sin entered the world, and death through sin. ◊ For as in Adam all die, even so in Christ shall all be made alive.

There is none righteous, no, not one. ◊ All our righteousnesses are like filthy rags. ◊ For He made Him who knew no sin to be sin for us, that we might become the righteousness of God in Him.

The wages of sin is death, but the gift of God is eternal life in Christ Jesus our Lord. ◊ Thanks be to God for His indescribable gift!

PS 95:6.PS 100:3.GEN 2:7.GEN 1:27.ROM 5:12.1 COR 15:22.ROM 3:10.IS 64:6.
2 COR 5:21.ROM 6:23.2 COR 9:15

THANKSGIVING

MORNING

Then they cried out to the Lord in their trouble, and He saved them out of their distresses.

Oh, that men would give thanks to the Lord for His goodness, and for His wonderful works to the children of men! ◊ Were there not ten cleansed? But where are the nine? ◊ Forget not all His benefits. ◊ God, who answered me in the day of my distress.

I sought the Lord, and He heard me, and delivered me from all my fears. ◊ I love the Lord, because He has heard my voice and my supplications. Because he has inclined His ear to me, therefore I will call upon Him as long as I live. ◊ My heart trusted in Him, and I am helped; therefore my heart greatly rejoices, and with my song I will praise Him.

Call upon Me in the day of trouble; I will deliver you. ◊ Whoever offers praise glorifies Me.

Giving thanks always for all things to God the Father in the name of our Lord Jesus Christ.

PS 107:19.PS 107:21.LUKE 17:17.PS 103:2.GEN 35:3.PS 34:4.PS 116:1–2.PS 28:7.
PS 50:15,23.EPH 5:20

EVENING

It is good to give thanks to the Lord.

Oh, give thanks to the Lord! Call upon His name; make known His deeds among the peoples. ◊ I will praise you, O Lord, among the peoples, and I will sing praises to You among the nations. ◊ I will sing to the Lord as long as I live; I will sing praise to my God while I have my being.

Come and hear, all you who fear God, and I will declare what He has done for my soul. ◊ Bless the Lord, O my soul; and all that is within me, bless His holy name! ◊ I will extol You, my God, O King; and I will bless your name forever and ever. Every day I will bless You and I will praise Your name forever and ever. ◊ Let everything that has breath praise the Lord.

Oh, give thanks to the Lord for He is good!

PS 92:1.PS 105:1.PS 108:3.PS 104:33.PS 66:16.PS 103:1.PS 145:1–2.PS 150:6.
PS 118:1

MORNING

Unless the Lord builds the house, they labor in vain who build it.

Beware, lest you forget the Lord. . . . You shall fear the Lord your God and serve Him. . . . You shall do what is right and good in the sight of the Lord, that it may be well with you. ◊ You shall have no other gods before me.

But seek first the kingdom of God and His righteousness. ◊ As for me and my house, we will serve the Lord. ◊ And as the bridegroom rejoices over the bride, so shall your God rejoice over you.

Marriage is honorable among all. ◊ The Lord God said, "It is not good that man should be alone; I will make him a helper comparable to him."

I will walk within my house with a perfect heart. ◊ But there shall by no means enter it anything that defiles or causes an abomination.

The Lord our God we will serve, and His voice we will obey.

PS 127:1.DEUT 6:12,13,18.EX 20:3.MATT 6:33.JOSH 24:15.IS 62:5.HEB 13:4.
GEN 2:18.PS 101:2.REV 21:27.JOSH 24:24

EVENING

A man shall leave his father and mother and be joined to his wife and they shall become one.

He who finds a wife finds a good thing and obtains favor from the Lord. ◊ A prudent wife is from the Lord. ◊ An excellent wife is the crown of her husband.

Husbands, love your wives, just as Christ also loved the church and gave Himself for it. ◊ Rejoice with the wife of your youth. . . . And always be enraptured with her love. ◊ [Give] honor to the wife, as to the weaker vessel, and as being heirs together of the grace of life, that your prayers may not be hindered.

Wives, submit to your own husbands, as to the Lord. ◊ Let the wife see that she respects her husband. ◊ Let your beauty be . . . a gentle and quiet spirit, which is very precious in the sight of God.

So then, they are no longer two but one flesh. Therefore what God has joined together, let not man separate.

GEN 2:24.PROV 18:22.PROV 19:14.PROV 12:4.1 PET 3:7.COL 3:19.PROV 5:18–19.
EPH 5:22.EPH 5:33.1 PET 3:3–4.MATT 19:6

MORNING

Be of one mind, having compassion for one another.

Be tenderhearted, be courteous; not returning evil for evil or reviling for reviling, but on the contrary blessing, knowing that you were called to this. ◊ Be kindly affectionate . . . , in honor giving preference to one another.

Love one another as I have loved you. ◊ Love suffers long and is kind; love does not envy; love does not parade itself, is not puffed up; does not behave rudely, does not seek its own, is not provoked, thinks no evil; does not rejoice in iniquity, but rejoices in the truth; bears all things, believes all things, hopes all things, endures all things.

If we love one another, God abides in us, and His love has been perfected in us. . . . And we have known and believed the love that God has for us. God is love, and he who abides in love abides in God, and God in him.

1 PET 3:8.1 PET 3:8.ROM 12:9.JOHN 15:2.1 COR 13:4–7.1 JOHN 4:12,16

EVENING

Children are a heritage from the Lord.

"Who are these with you?" "The children whom God has graciously given your servant." ◊ A woman, when she is in labor, has sorrow . . . but as soon as she hath given birth to the child, she no longer remembers the anguish, for joy that a human being has been born into the world.

Train up a child in the way he should go. ◊ Fathers, do not provoke your children to wrath, but bring them up in the training and admonition of the Lord.

Do not withhold correction from a child. ◊ The rod and reproof give wisdom, but a child left to himself brings shame to his mother.

Children's children are the crown of old men, and the glory of children is their father.

PS 127:3.GEN 33:5.JOHN 16:21.PROV 22:6.EPH 6:4.PROV 23:13.PROV 29:15.
PROV 17:6

MORNING

So teach us to number our days, that we may gain a heart of wisdom.

Are not my days few? ◊ Man who is born of woman is of few days. ◊ As for man, his days are like grass . . . but the mercy of the Lord is from everlasting to everlasting. ◊ Oh, satisfy us early with Your mercy, that we may rejoice and be glad all our days!

Behold, the fear of the Lord, that is wisdom. ◊ The wisdom that is from above is first pure, then peaceable, gentle, willing to yield, full of mercy and good fruits.

A wise man will hear. ◊ Whoever hears these sayings of Mine, and does them, I will liken him to a wise man who built his house on the rock. ◊ That Rock was Christ.

PS 90:12.JOB 10:20.JOB 14:1.PS 103:15,17.PS 90:14.JOB 28:28.JAMES 3:17.
PROV 1:5.MATT 7:24.1 COR 10:4

EVENING

Let the Lord be magnified who has pleasure in the prosperity of His servant.

Blessed is the man who walks not in the counsel of the ungodly, nor stands in the paths of sinners, nor sits in the seat of the scornful; but his delight is in the law of the Lord, and in His law he meditates day and night. He shall be like a tree planted by the rivers of water, that brings forth its fruit in its season, whose leaf also shall not wither; and what-soever he does shall prosper. ◊ The Lord was with him; he prospered wherever he went.

Honor the Lord with your possessions and with the firstfruits of all your increase; so your barns will be filled with plenty, and your vats will overflow with new wine.

This Book of the Law shall not depart from your mouth, but you shall meditate in it day and night, that you may observe to do according to all that is written in it. For then you will make your way prosperous.

My son, do not forget my law, but let your heart keep my commands; for length of days and long life and peace they will add to you.

PS 35:27.PS 1:1,3.2 KIN 18:7.PROV 3:9-10.JOSH 1:8.PROV 3:1-2

FOR A BIRTHDAY

MORNING

The Lord bless you and keep you.

The Lord who made heaven and earth bless you. ◊ Our God and Father. ◊ The living God, who gives us richly all things to enjoy.

For your heavenly Father knows that you need all these things. ◊ For the Father Himself loves you.

No good thing will He withhold from those who walk uprightly. ◊ He stores up sound wisdom for the upright; He is a shield to those who walk uprightly. ◊ Blessed are those who keep His testimonies, who seek Him with the whole heart!

He who keeps you will not slumber. Behold, He who keeps Israel shall neither slumber nor sleep. ◊ For the Lord will be your confidence, and will keep your foot from being caught. ◊ You will keep him in perfect peace, whose mind is stayed on you, because he trusts in you.

The Lord of peace Himself give you peace always in every way.

NUM 6:24.PS 134:3.2 THESS 2:16.1 TIM 6:17.MATT 6:32.JOHN 16:27.PS 84:11.
PROV 2:7.PS 119:2.PS 121:3–4.PROV. 3:26.IS 26:3.2 THESS 3:16

EVENING

Oh, send out Your light and Your truth!
Let them lead me.

Where is the way to the dwelling of light? ◊ The Lord will be to you an everlasting light. ◊ God is light and in Him is no darkness at all. If we walk in the light as He is in the light, we have fellowship with one another, and the blood of Jesus Christ His Son cleanses us from all sin.

Show me Your ways, O Lord. . . . Lead me in Your truth and teach me, for You are the God of my salvation; on You I wait all the day. ◊ Your word is a lamp to my feet and a light to my path. ◊ Your word is truth.

The Lord is my light and my salvation; whom shall I fear? ◊ He leads me in the paths of righteousness for His name's sake. Surely goodness and mercy shall follow me all the days of my life; and I will dwell in the house of the Lord forever.

PS 43:3.JOB 38:19.IS 60:19.1 JOHN 1:5,7.PS 25:4,5.PS 119:105.JOHN 17:17.
PS 27:1.PS 23:3,6

MORNING

Shall we indeed accept good from God, and shall we not accept adversity?

The sufferings of this present time are not to be compared with the glory which shall be revealed in us. ◇ Have mercy on me, O Lord, for I am weak; O Lord, heal me. ◇ The prayer of faith will heal the sick.

When my heart is overwhelmed; lead me to the rock that is higher than I. ◇ The Lord is the strength of my life. ◇ The eternal God is your refuge.

You are near, O Lord. ◇ You have heard my voice . . . You drew near on the day I called You, and said, "Do not fear!" ◇ A very present help in trouble.

Bless the Lord . . . who forgives all your iniquities, who heals all your diseases, who redeems your life from destruction.

Be anxious for nothing, but in everything by prayer and supplication, with thanksgiving, let your requests be made known to God; and the peace of God, which surpasses all understanding, will guard your hearts and minds through Christ Jesus.

JOB 2:10.ROM 8:18.PS 6:2.JAMES 5:15.PS 61:2.PS 27:1.DEUT 33:27.PS 119:151.
LAM 3:56–57.PS 46:1.PS 103:2–4.PHIL 4:6–7

EVENING

Be not far from me, for trouble is near; for there is none to help.

Fear not, I will help you. ◇ Do not be afraid. ◇ I will never leave you nor forsake you. ◇ I am with you always. ◇ Weeping may endure for a night but joy comes in the morning.

He has sent me to heal the brokenhearted. ◇ Cast your burdens on the Lord, and He shall sustain you. ◇ Underneath are the everlasting arms.

For You will light my lamp; the Lord my God will enlighten my darkness.

My strength and my redeemer. ◇ The everlasting God, the Lord, the Creator of the ends of the earth neither faints nor is weary.

He gives power to the weak, and to those who have no might He increases strength.

PS 22:11.IS 41:13.REV 1:17.HEB 13:5.MATT 28:20.PS 30:5.LUKE 4:18.PS 55:22.
DEUT 33:27.PS 18:28.PS 19:14.IS 40:28.IS 40:29

SICKNESS

Lord, behold, he whom You love is sick.

Surely He has borne our griefs and carried our sorrows. ◊ He Himself took our infirmities and bore our sicknesses. ◊ He, being full of compassion. ◊ As a father pities his children, so the Lord pities those who fear Him. For He knows our frame.

Who shall separate us from the love of Christ? Shall tribulation, or distress? ◊ Whom the Lord loves He chastens. ◊ Now no chastening seems to be joyful for the present, but grievous; nevertheless, afterward it yields the peaceable fruit of righteousness to those who have been trained by it. ◊ We know that all things work together for good to those who love God.

And He said to me, "My grace is sufficient for you, for My strength is made perfect in weakness." Therefore most gladly I will boast in my infirmities, that the power of Christ may rest upon me.

JOHN 11:3.IS 53:4.MATT 8:17.PS 78:38.PS 103:13,14.ROM 8:35.
HEB 12:6.HEB 12:11.ROM 8:28.2 COR 12:9

Save me, O God! For the waters have come up to my neck.

O My Father, if it is possible, let this cup pass from Me; nevertheless, not as I will, but as You will. ◊ Being in agony. ◊ Jesus wept.

Surely He has borne our griefs and carried our sorrows. ◊ We do not have a High Priest who cannot sympathize with our weaknesses, but was in all points tempted as we are, yet without sin. Let us therefore come boldly to the throne of grace, that we may . . . find grace to help in time of need.

He cares for you. ◊ I have called you by your name; you are Mine. When you pass through the waters, I will be with you, and through the rivers, they shall not overflow you. ◊ I will never leave you nor forsake you.

Though He slay me, yet will I trust Him. ◊ My flesh and my heart fail; but God is the strength of my heart and my portion forever.

PS 69:1.MATT 26:39.LUKE 22:44.JOHN 11:35.IS 53:4.HEB 4:15–16.1 PET 5:7.
IS 43:1–2.HEB 13:5.JOB 13:15.PS 73:26

MORNING

Father, I desire that they also whom You gave Me may be with Me where I am.

While we are at home in the body we are absent from the Lord. . . . We are confident, yes, well pleased rather to be absent from the body and to be present with the Lord. ◊ I am hard pressed between the two, having a desire to depart and be with Christ, which is far better. ◊ Whether we live or die, we are the Lord's.

You have a better and an enduring possession for yourselves in heaven. ◊ It has not yet been revealed what we shall be, but we know that when He is revealed, we shall be like Him, for we shall see Him as He is. ◊ Now we see in a mirror, dimly, but then face to face. ◊ I will see your face in righteousness; I shall be satisfied when I awake in Your likeness.

We shall always be with the Lord. Therefore comfort one another with these words.

JOHN 17:24.2 COR 5:6,8.PHIL 1:23.ROM 14:8.HEB 10:34.1 JOHN 3:2.
1 COR 13:12.PS 17:15.1 THESS 4:17–18

EVENING

Blessed are the dead who die in the Lord.

Precious in the sight of the Lord is the death of His saints. ◊ Let me die the death of the righteous. ◊ He shall enter into peace.

I will ransom them from the power of the grave; I will redeem them from death. O Death, I will be your plagues! O Grave, I will be your destruction! ◊ And the ransomed of the Lord shall return, and come to Zion with singing, with everlasting joy on their heads. They shall obtain joy and gladness, and sorrow and sighing shall flee away.

And this is the will of Him who sent Me, that everyone who sees the Son and believes in Him may have everlasting life; and I will raise him up at the last day. ◊ But I do not want you to be ignorant, brethren, concerning those who have fallen asleep, lest you sorrow as others who have no hope. For if we believe that Jesus died and rose again, even so God will bring with Him those who sleep in Jesus.

REV 14:13.PS 116:15.NUM 23:10.IS 57:2.HOS 13:14.IS 35:10.JOHN 6:40.
1 THESS 4:13–14

BEREAVEMENT

MORNING_____

As one whom his mother comforts, so I will comfort you.

I looked for . . . comforters, but I found none. ◊ His brethren came to comfort him. ◊ My soul refused to be comforted.

I will come. ◊ I will turn their mourning to joy, will comfort them. ◊ I, even I, am He who comforts you. ◊ Your comforts delight my soul.

You shall . . . comfort me on every side. ◊ Your rod and Your staff, they comfort me. ◊ You, Lord, have helped me and comforted me.

Blessed be the God and Father of our Lord Jesus Christ, the Father of mercies and God of all comfort, who comforts us in all our tribulation, that we may be able to comfort those who are in any trouble, with the comfort with which we ourselves are comforted by God.

IS 66:13.PS 69:20.1 CHR 7:22.PS 77:2.JOHN 14:18.JER 31:13.IS 51:12.PS 94:19.
PS 71:21.PS 23:4.PS 86:17.2 COR 1:3–4

EVENING_____

There shall be no more death.

The bitterness of death is past. ◊ Our Savior Jesus Christ . . . has abolished death. ◊ I am the resurrection and the life. He who believes in Me, though he may die, he shall live.

That He, by the grace of God, might taste death for everyone. ◊ That through death He might . . . release those who through fear of death were all their lifetime subject to bondage.

The last enemy that shall be destroyed is death. ◊ Then shall be brought to pass the saying that is written: Death is swallowed up in victory. O Death, where is your sting? O Hades, where is your victory? The sting of death is sin, and the strength of sin is the law. But thanks be to God, who gives us the victory through our Lord Jesus Christ. Therefore, my beloved brethren, be steadfast, immovable, always abounding in the work of the Lord, knowing that your labor is not in vain in the Lord.

REV 21:4.1 SAM 15:32.2 TIM 1:10.JOHN 11:25.HEB 2:9.HEB 2:14–15.
1 COR 15:26.1 COR 15:54–58